THE POLITICS AND CULTURE OF HONOUR
IN BRITAIN AND IRELAND, 1541–1641

Through an exploration of overlapping concepts of noble honour amongst English and Irish elites, this book provides a cultural analysis of 'British' high politics in the early modern period. Analysing English- and Irish-language sources, Brendan Kane argues that between the establishment of the Irish kingdom under the English crown in 1541 and the Irish rebellion of 1641, honour played a powerful role in determining the character of Anglo-Irish society, politics and cultural contact. In this age, before the rise of a more bureaucratic and participatory state, political power was intensely personal and largely the concern of elites. And those elites were preoccupied with honour. By exploring contemporary 'honour politics', this book brings a cultural perspective to our understanding of the character of English imperialism in Ireland and of the Irish responses to it. In so doing it highlights understudied aspects of the origins of the 'British' state.

BRENDAN KANE is an Assistant Professor of History at the University of Connecticut, Storrs.

CAMBRIDGE STUDIES IN EARLY MODERN BRITISH HISTORY

SERIES EDITORS

John Morrill *Professor of British and Irish History, University of Cambridge, and Fellow of Selwyn College*
Ethan Shagan *Associate Professor of History, University of California, Berkeley*
Alexandra Walsham *Professor of Reformation History, University of Exeter*

This is a series of monographs and studies covering many aspects of the history of the British Isles between the late fifteenth century and the early eighteenth century. It includes the work of established scholars and pioneering work by a new generation of scholars. It includes both reviews and revisions of major topics and books which open up new historical terrain or which reveal startling new perspectives on familiar subjects. All the volumes set detailed research into our broader perspectives, and the books are intended for the use of students as well as of their teachers.

For a list of the titles in the series, go to
www.cambridge.org/earlymodernbritishhistory

THE POLITICS AND CULTURE OF HONOUR IN BRITAIN AND IRELAND, 1541–1641

BRENDAN KANE

University of Connecticut

CAMBRIDGE UNIVERSITY PRESS
Cambridge, New York, Melbourne, Madrid, Cape Town, Singapore, São Paulo, Delhi

Cambridge University Press
The Edinburgh Building, Cambridge CB2 8RU, UK

Published in the United States of America by Cambridge University Press, New York

www.cambridge.org
Information on this title: www.cambridge.org/9780521898645

First published 2010

Printed in the United Kingdom at the University Press, Cambridge

A catalogue record for this publication is available from the British Library.

Library of Congress Cataloguing in Publication data
Kane, Brendan Michael, 1968–
The politics and culture of honour in Britain and Ireland, 1541–1641 / Brendan Kane.
p.   cm. – (Cambridge studies in early modern British history)
ISBN 978-0-521-89864-5 (hardback)
1. Great Britain – Foreign relations – Ireland.   2. Ireland – Foreign relations – Great Britain.
3. Honor – Political aspects – Great Britain – History.   4. Honor – Political
aspects – Ireland – History.   5. Monarchy – Great Britain – History – 16th century.
6. Monarchy – Great Britain – History – 17th century.   7. Great Britain – Politics and
government – 1485–1603.   8. Great Britain – Politics and government – 1603–1649.   9. Ireland –
Politics and government – 16th century.   10. Ireland – Politics and government – 17th century.
11. Great Britain – History – Tudors, 1485–1603.   12. Great Britain – History – Stuarts, 1603–1714.
I. Title. II. Series.
DA47.9.I73K36   2009
941.05–dc22
2009035492

ISBN: 978-0-521-89864-5 Hardback

For Sandy

Contents

Abbreviations	*page*	ix
List of illustrations		x
A note on names and the citation of Irish words		xi
Acknowledgements		xii

	Introduction: honour in Britain and Ireland	1
Chapter 1	The honour revolution of 1541	20
Chapter 2	Gaelic honour in Tudor Ireland	44
	Gaelic response in annals and poetry: introduction	46
	The Annals of Loch Cé	52
	Gaelic response in poetry	66
	The Maguire poembook	67
	The poems of Tadhg Dall Ó hUiginn	75
Chapter 3	'British' honour and the Nine Years' War	92
	Gaelic and Old English honour and the Nine Years' War	102
	Aristocratic versus monarchical honour in the Nine Years' War	112
	Honour politics and the war's conclusion	116
Chapter 4	Making the Irish European: Gaelic honour after the Nine Years' War	122
	Introduction	122
	Tadhg Ó Cianáin's grand tour of the earls	123
	Avant-garde traditionalism? *Beatha Aodha Ruaidh Uí Dhomhnaill* and the Europeanization of 'medieval' Gaelic honour	135
	Making the Irish European	144
Chapter 5	Gaelic and Old English honour in early Stuart 'Britain'	146
	Gaelic fears of social inversion	147
	Ethnicity, anglicization and ancient honour: Donough O'Brien, Earl of Thomond, and his pedigrees	158

Old English and English honour: the case of Richard Burke,
Earl of Clanricard and St Albans 181
The social dangers of precedence disputes 192

Chapter 6   A hierarchy transformed? Precedence disputes, the
defence of honour and 'British' high-politics,
1603–1632 194
British honour and the Irish Parliament of 1613–15 195
English precedence and politics and the threat from
the provinces 208

Chapter 7   Wentworth, the Irish Lord Deputyship and the
Caroline politics of honour 221
Wentworth and the honour politics of Stuart England 224
Wentworth as viceroy 230

Conclusion 268

Bibliography 279
Index 294

Abbreviations

AFM:	*The annals of the four masters*, vols I–VI, ed. and trans. John O'Donovan (Dublin, 1856)
Cal. Carew:	*Calendar of the Carew manuscripts preserved in the archiepiscopal library at Lambeth*, 6 vols (London, 1867–73)
CSPI:	*Calendar of state papers relating to Ireland*, 24 vols (London, 1860–1911)
IHS:	*Irish Historical Studies*
JBS:	*Journal of British Studies*
P&P:	*Past & Present*
SP:	National Archives State papers
SP Hen. VIII:	State papers published under the authority of his Majesty's commission Henry VIII, 11 vols (London, 1830–52)
Strafforde letters:	*The letters and dispatches of the Earl of Strafforde*, 2 vols, ed. W. Knowler (London, 1739)
WP:	*Wentworth papers 1597–1628*, ed. J. P. Cooper (London, 1973)

List of illustrations

5.1 Genealogical tree of the O'Brien Earls of Thomond. Lambeth
Palace Library, Carew MS 635 fol. 23   *page* 174

5.2 Fear Flatha Ó Gnímh's pedigree of Randal MacDonnell,
a Scotsman made Viscount Dunluce in the Irish peerage.
Lambeth Palace Library, Carew MS 635 fol. 139   175

5.3 Pictorial representation of the heads of noble lines descended
from Hiberus, third son of Milo. Image courtesy of the
National Library of Ireland, NLI G.O. MS 158   176

5.4 A more subdued illustrated pedigree of the immediate family
of the O'Brien Earls of Thomond taken from a collection of
Gaelic pedigrees produced from records in Thomond's
possession and completed in 1617. Lambeth Palace Library,
Carew MS 599 fol. 192   177

5.5 Pedigree showing the descendants of Owen O'Neill, a map of
Ulster, and the apparent end of the O'Neill claim to nobility
with the 2nd Earl of Tyrone's 'open actione' against the Queen.
Lambeth Palace Library, Carew MS 635 fol. 139a   178

5.6 Pictorial representation of the disgrace of the O'Donnell Earls
of Tyrconnell. This image appears in Donough O'Brien's 1614
genealogy of Gaelic families. Image courtesy of the National
Library of Ireland, NLI G.O. MS 158 fol. 148   179

5.7 The fall of the O'Neill Earls of Tyrone as depicted in Donough
O'Brien's 1614 genealogy of Gaelic families. Image courtesy of
the National Library of Ireland, NLI G.O. MS 158 fol. 158   180

A note on names and the citation of Irish words

What to call the various interest groups in late-medieval and early modern Ireland has sparked tremendous debate over the years. For this study, I have chosen to refer to the descendants in Ireland of the twelfth-century Anglo-Norman invasion as 'English-Irish' when discussing the period before roughly 1550, and as 'Old English' for later periods. Periodically, I use 'Gael' and 'Gall'.[1] These are traditional terms in Irish, the former meaning 'native', the latter 'foreigner'.

In referencing names of Gaelic actors, I follow the convention of the chosen source. At times this means I left them in their Gaelic original, and did not 'anglicize' them. This I deemed worthwhile for readers who may wish to consult the source in question, but who may not be prepared to move from English forms of names back to their Irish originals.

In referencing Irish-language words, I use the present-day dictionary form in the body of the text. Spelling and case variations in the original sources are then given in parentheses, quotations, or in a footnote. When citing the originals, I give them as they appear in the source rather than in their dictionary forms. Thus in the lexical section (Chapter 2) there are numerous instances in which the word in quotations looks different than the one purported to be under investigation. Nevertheless, I believed this would make tracking back to the original easier. Furthermore, quotations from contemporary sources have typically been left in the original. On occasion, however, I have silently expanded out abbreviations for the sake of readability.

---

[1] Here I follow suggestions found in Nicholas Canny, 'Revising the revisionist', *IHS* 118 (1996), pp. 242–54.

Acknowledgements

This study has been long in the making, and there are many people to thank. First among them is Peter Lake, who oversaw the dissertation out of which this book grew. I could not have asked for a better advisor and mentor. His encouragement, willingness to let me work on an Anglo–Irish subject, and general expertise in early modern English and European history were necessary for the project's completion. But more than any particular knowledge of the material, what he brought in his supervision of this project was a certain mode of thinking that is incredibly subtle, at times subversive, and which is never happy to settle for the sorts of simplistic dichotomies that are often served up in discussions of the early modern period. I can only hope that some of the power of his thinking has rubbed off on me and is detectable in the following study. For that, and for his great humanity and fellowship, I will always be grateful.

This subject itself is the direct result of a lecture given by Richard Cust as part of the British Studies series that Peter ran at Princeton. Richard's subject that day – honour and politics in the late sixteenth and early seventeenth centuries in England – was entirely new to me, and I found it to be fascinating. As the presentation unfolded, I found myself matching the material Richard drew upon – treatises, literary works, pedigrees, funerary monuments, and so on – to Irish equivalents. In particular, my mind drifted towards Irish Gaelic works, which, although they have been heavily mined for information on national consciousness and confessionalization, seemed, by my memory, to have plenty to say on the question of honour. Sitting there in Dickinson 211, I thought that if these sorts of sources and questions were meaningful in the English historiography, then they must have something worthwhile to say about the Irish situation as well. Moreover, I thought that if ideas of honour were in fact so important to early modern politics, then they probably held some clue to understanding the political interactions between the people of these two kingdoms in the period of the Tudor reconquest and subsequent colonization of Ireland. The following pages represent my attempts to work out that initial idea.

As this book developed out of my dissertation, I wish to thank the rest of the members of my examining committee. In addition to generously offering his time and encouragement (and the occasional library introduction letter), Anthony Grafton's peerless knowledge of early modern European intellectual history and its classical antecedents has made me think far more deeply about the abstract notions of honour and nobility about which I was at times talking in pure historical ignorance. Nigel Smith's presence has proven indispensable as I tried my hand at literary critique. Imagining myself to be a budding social historian when I came to graduate school, it was with serious trepidation that I waded into literary texts as historical sources. His expertise and encouragement have vastly improved the project and given me more confidence to approach these sources. Far more terrifying than English-language literary sources to me were Irish-language sources. For bravely agreeing to oversee my first attempts at using these sources, I wish to thank Mícheál Mac Craith of the National University of Ireland, Galway. His fine-toothed comb spared me from some rather shame-inducing gaffs.

There are many informal advisors to thank, too. Denver Brunsman, Eileen Kane and Thierry Rigogne served as something of a second committee. Without them the original thesis would never have been finished – or if it had, doing so would have been a much less enjoyable experience! Zur Shalev served as something of a fifth committee member. In addition to his general encouragement, advice and friendship, he also put me up (and put up with me) on my trips to Oxford. Tom Brophy did the same on my trips to Ireland, and has been a wonderfully supportive friend and confidant along the way. I have also been fortunate enough to experience what lordly hospitality in medieval Ireland must have looked like: Mike and Ness Kelly have generously hosted me and my family over the years, most crucially as I began the final editing changes.

The initial revisions of the manuscript were done during a fellowship year at the University of Notre Dame's Keough Institute for Irish Studies. One could hardly ask for a more congenial and intellectually stimulating environment. I wish to thank Chris Fox, Éamonn Ó Ciardha, Beth Bland, Peter McQuillen, Joseph McMinn, Sarah McKibben, Luke Gibbons and Angela Bourke for making my stay there both pleasant and productive. Especial thanks are due Breandán Ó Buachalla and Jim Smyth, model mentors who gave selflessly of their time and expertise. Final revisions were completed while at the University of Connecticut. I am very grateful to my colleagues for their support and for providing an ideal environment in which to work and write.

Along the way I have benefited from conversations with and comments of numerous scholars, colleagues and friends. Although by no means an exhaustive list (nor in any particular order), I owe thanks to John Murrin, Nicholas Canny, Roslyn Blynn LaDrew, Alastair Bellany, Richard Cust, John Hintermaier, Guy Geltner, Robert Cross, Alec Dun, David Como, Margaret Sena, Brian Cowan, Sara Brooks, Paul Muldoon, Karl Bottigheimer, Bernadette Cunningham, Peter Brown, Jenny Weber, Vincent Carey, Annie Gladden, Malcolm Smuts, Ciaran O'Scea, Janet Watson, Michael Dintenfass, Charles Lansing, Matt McKenzie, Melina Pappademos, Mark Overmyer-Velazquez, Mary Burke, Vera Keller and Lochlainn Ó Tuaraisg. At Princeton, Audrey Mainzer and Tina Erdos went well beyond the call of duty to keep me pointed in the right direction. I must thank the attendees at those forums at which I aired bits of this project: the Mid-Atlantic Conference on British Studies, the Grian Conference, the Columbia Irish Studies seminar, the Fund for Irish Studies at Princeton, the Harvard Celtic Colloquium, the British Studies series at Princeton, and the Renaissance Colloquium at Princeton. Special thanks go to the Graduate School and the Council on Regional Studies for providing vital summer support, and to the Princeton University Center for Human Values for allowing me the chance to spend an entire year dedicated exclusively to the dissertation. I am deeply appreciative of the support of the editors of Cambridge University Press' *Studies in Early Modern British History* Series, John Morrill, Alexandra Walsham and, particularly, Ethan Shagan, whose advice and mentoring have been invaluable over many years. Michael Watson, Helen Waterhouse and Jodie Barnes at Cambridge University Press have been wonderfully helpful (and patient!) during production; Mark McClellan's keen eyes on the text have greatly improved both accuracy and style. To them all I am deeply indebted.

Chapter 4 of this study appeared originally as an article and I thank the editors of *Renaissance Quarterly*, where it originally appeared, as well as the Syndics of Cambridge University Press, for permission to republish that material. Article and chapter have both benefited greatly from Erika Suffern's tremendous editorial skills.

In the course of researching the book I have also benefited from the generous assistance of the librarians, archivists and staffs of numerous libraries and archives. Among these I specifically wish to note Firestone Library, Princeton (particularly the staffs of the inter-library loan and microforms departments); the Bodleian Library, Oxford; Cambridge University Library; the National Library of Ireland; the Royal Irish Academy; the Library of Trinity College, Dublin; the British Library;

Lambeth Palace Library; and the Public Record Offices of Ireland, England, Essex and Kent. In particular I wish to thank the National Library of Ireland and Lambeth Palace Library for their kind permission to publish images from manuscripts in their collections. On a final research note, I am grateful to Brian Donovan and David Edwards for compiling *British sources for Irish history 1485–1641*. Without this wonderful resource, my very rewarding tour of English county archives may simply never have happened.

In finishing the book, a number of brave friends and colleagues have generously read through large chunks of the text. These include Bill Bulman, Thierry Rigogne, Valerie McGowan Doyle, Christopher Maginn, Gerald Power and Denver Brunsman. Two people in particular deserve my eternal gratitude for their incredibly close reads, and unstinting support and friendship: Ken Gouwens and Brían Ó Conchubhair.

In keeping with the terms explored in this project, the honour of any successes achieved by this book should redound upon all those named above. The shame of its faults, however, must lie with me alone.

And lastly my deepest thanks go to my family, without whose encouragement this project would never have been started (let alone completed). Sibyl, Adrian and Joshua have all lovingly helped to see me through. My sister Andrea has done more to get me to this point than she could ever imagine, or than I could every repay. My mother Alison's encouragement not only helped lead me onto this path but has continued unabated since I began. Particular thanks are due my sons Eoin and Gavin who have put up with my periodic disappearance to mysterious archives, and with the too-frequent appearance of my laptop at the kitchen table. My greatest thanks, however, are reserved for Sandy, without whom this would not have been possible. An insignificant gesture to be sure – given your work, patience and encouragement on my behalf – this text is nonetheless dedicated to you.

Introduction: honour in Britain and Ireland

By the time Henry VIII ascended to the English throne, Ireland had already been a thorn in the monarchical paw for centuries. In spite of the twelfth-century Anglo-Norman invasion and the subsequent establishment of Ireland as a lordship controlled by England's monarchs, the island and its peoples continued to cause headaches for their titular overlords. It was a perennial money sink, a drain on Crown coffers as frequent subventions were required to prop up the coastal and urban stongholds of the Anglo-Normans' descendants, or 'Englishry', against the creeping resurgence of Gaelic lords and culture. Periodically it served as a staging ground for challenges to the Crown, spectacularly so at the beginning of the Tudor period when Dublin championed the two Yorkist pretenders Perkin Warbeck and Lambert Simnel. With Henry's break from Rome, Ireland became the potential site for foreign invasion in defence of the old faith – or at least of anti-Crown agitation that could profitably claim religious intent. That terrifying possibility became manifest in 1538, with the conspiracy of the Geraldine League. Here, the two great Gaelic lords of Ulster – the chief of the O'Neills and the chief of the O'Donnells – put their traditional enmities aside and combined forces with the 'English-Irish' Fitzgeralds in an effort to slough off Henry's authority. Not only did this conspiracy transcend traditional intra-Gaelic and Gaelic–English rivalries, it also sought support from continental, Catholic sympathizers, chiefly Henry's great rival Charles V. During Henry's reign, Ireland was a greater threat to the English peace than ever before.

As early as 1520, Henry had attempted to address his Irish problem with force. In that year he charged the Earl of Surrey with reforming the lordship, by arms if necessary. Surrey took up his post as governor accompanied by a military force of several hundred.[1] But this amounted to little, in large part because it required too much money to be effective. Consequently, Henry

---

[1] S. J. Connolly, *Contested island: Ireland 1460–1630* (Oxford, 2007), p. 78.

and his council fell back on the traditional means by which the lordship (the English-controlled part of the island) was governed: the delegation of local executive authority to an aristocrat of Anglo-Norman descent, in this case the Earl of Kildare. The Earls of Kildare had enjoyed near continuous control of the island's governorship since the 1450s, but maintaining favour with the King was as difficult in Ireland as it was in England. In 1533, Henry summoned Kildare to court to answer charges that he was working against Crown interests. To demonstrate how necessary the Earl's presence was to Irish law and order, his son 'Silken' Thomas led a 'loyal' rebellion protesting his father's imprisonment. It was crushed, and with it the delegated authority enjoyed by the Kildares. In a new departure, the Crown placed an English-born, Crown-picked lord deputy in Dublin. At the appointment of Leonard Grey in 1536 came a return to the politics of force. He used a heavy hand to pacify Kildare's remaining supporters.[2] Still, Henry's Irish problem persisted. Indeed, it was the suppression of the Kildares and the introduction of an English chief governor that helped spark the anti-Henrician Geraldine League. Three decades into Henry's relationship with Ireland, force had proven ineffectual in rendering island and people (be they Gaelic or 'English-Irish') quiescent and loyal.

Flying in the face of his predecessors' policies, Deputy Anthony St Leger advanced the opinion in 1540 that perhaps honey would work in Ireland where vinegar had failed. Rather than repeat Surrey and Grey's failed efforts at strong-arming the Irish into obedience, St Leger suggested an effort to win their hearts and minds.[3] The means to effect this were ingeniously simple: change Ireland's constitutional relationship to England by recasting it from a lordship to a kingdom in its own right with the English monarch assuming the Irish crown. In one stroke the former 'Irish enemies' of the Crown would become subjects, subsumed under the laws and protection of the English king.[4] As St Leger and the Irish council put it to Henry, the Irish 'wolde more gladder obey Your Highnes by name of King of this your

[2] Ciaran Brady calls attention to overlooked conciliatory elements in Grey's governance. See Brady, *The chief governors: the rise and fall of reform government in Tudor Ireland, 1536–1588* (Cambridge, 1994), p. 29. This point has been challenged, however, in Gerald Power, 'The viceroy and his critics: Leonard Grey's journey through the west of Ireland, June–July 1538', *Journal of the Galway Archaeological and Historical Society* 60 (2008), pp. 78–87. I wish to thank Dr Power for providing me with a copy of this article, and for helpful discussion of this chapter's arguments.
[3] On the points of contact between St Leger's and Grey's policies, see Brady, *Chief governors*, chapter 1. For a recent opposing view see Gerald Power, ibid.
[4] On this change by which the Gaelic Irish could no longer be termed enemies of the Crown see Brendan Bradshaw, *The Irish constitutional revolution of the sixteenth century* (Cambridge, 1979), p. 266.

lande, then by the name of Lorde therof'.[5] And once 'bothe Englishe and Yrish' recognized him as king, peace, self-sufficiency and even profit would follow.[6] Lordship of the island was simply too amorphous; the rights and responsibilities linking the Crown and the Irish under it were too ambiguous, too inexact. Making the Irish subjects would clarify those relations for all parties and so promote stability.

Surely Henry VIII – that most imperial-minded of early modern English kings and self-fashioned Henry V figure – would leap at the chance to place another crown on his head, especially if doing so required no manoeuvres in the field. But he did not. Undoubtedly this approach would appeal to Henry's sense of himself as a reformer, a prince who could effect socio-political change through humanist-influenced statecraft rather than crude reliance on muscle. But it did not. Instead, Henry agonized over the new title, and grilled his councillors about 'whither it be either honor or wisdom for Us to [take] uppon Us that title of a King, and not to have revenues there, suffycyent to maynteyn the state of the same'. He further cautioned that it must also be 'wayed, what dishonor it maye be to Us' were he to give land of 'our oune inheritance to those which have unjustly intruded and usurped the same'.[7] Clever as St Leger's idea was, it ran up against the honour imperatives inherent in monarchical rule. Its success promised much, namely the end to the financial drag and cauldron of rebellion that was Ireland as a lordship; but its failure threatened more: the international shaming of a very prideful Henry VIII. Faced with the seeming intractability of his Irish problem, and the possibility of its exacerbation through intervention by his continental Catholic enemies, Henry accepted his deputy's proposal the following year: Ireland in 1541 was made a kingdom and he its king. From that moment forward, Henry's concerns about honour became political realities in Anglo-Irish relations. He was now, as Brendan Bradshaw has written, 'in honour bound to exercise the functions of king of Ireland'.[8]

The engagement of monarchical honour would transform Anglo-Irish relations. It lent a personal character to cross-border politics not seen before in the two polities' long relationship. With that came great possibilities for social stability, as St Leger envisioned, but equally great chances for instability. For, as Henry cautioned, with every engagement of honour came the opportunity for dishonour. A century after St Leger's 'revolution', Charles I's deputy in Ireland, Thomas Wentworth, would give eloquent expression to the fact that the pursuit of honour imperatives in the governance of

---

[5] SP Hen. VIII, III, p. 278. [6] Ibid., p. 341. [7] Ibid., p. 331.
[8] Bradshaw, *The Irish constitutional revolution*, p. 235.

Ireland remained both a monarchical priority and a potential source of instability. Faced with an insubordinate Irish Lord Chancellor (the English-born Adam Loftus, Viscount Ely), Wentworth wrote to his King that 'I do very much fear if the Honour and Justice of this State be not … vigorously borne forth against … Untruths and Incivilities, the Regal Authority will perchance be shortly as much invaded, as roughly dealt with in this Kingdom as in other Places'.[9] Written against the backdrop of the Bishops' Wars, Wentworth's allusions to invasion and rough dealing demonstrated the seriousness with which Crown and Castle, not to mention Irish officials and elites, took matters of honour a century after St Leger's experiment.

This book explores the culture and politics of honour in Britain and Ireland from 1541 to 1641, the years linking St Leger's initiation of an Anglo–Irish honour politics to the end of Wentworth's struggle with Lord Chancellor Loftus on the eve of the War of the Three Kingdoms. It is a study born out of the fact that while the connection between honour and politics in early modern Anglo–Irish relations was obvious to Henry VIII, Charles I, and the Lords Deputy St Leger and Wentworth, it has not been so readily apparent to later historians. This is surprising because over the last twenty years or so, scholars have been very attentive to the role of honour in society. Its study has greatly enriched the writing of early modern European history, primarily by offering a unit of analysis that falls in the interstices between individuals' feelings of worth and collective notions of propriety and status. This literature has greatly expanded our understanding of the dialectical relationship between cultural norms and expectations, on the one hand, and politics, power and authority on the other. Within this growing body of work, however, there has as yet been no systematic discussion of what honour looked like in Ireland in this period, nor any sustained study of how honour politics may have affected Anglo-Irish relations and the process of British state building.

There are four principal reasons that this has been the case, each related to limitations within the various sub-fields such a study would have to traverse. The most fundamental of these is the fact that scholars are still at odds over what honour in England itself looked like. With that domestic question open, there has been no effort to look at how English honour may have worked across borders. The importance of honour to early modern English politics received its first systematic exploration in Mervyn James' seminal article,

---

[9] *Strafforde letters* II, p. 387.

'English politics and the concept of honour, 1485–1642'.[10] James set out to explain why personal violence was endemic among the nobility in late medieval England, and why its frequency decreased so dramatically by the early seventeenth century. The answer, he found, lay in differences between the honour codes of late medieval and early modern noble culture. These were loosely defined complexes of behaviours and social expectations, yet each contained certain unique defining features. For the early period, this amounted to 'might makes right'. It was incumbent upon the man of noble honour to be aggressive in defence of his name or patrimony, and in pursuit of fame and power. James noted, however, that the make-up of the code shifted dramatically over the course of the sixteenth century. The forces of humanism, education, the Reformation and state centralization all combined to tame the nobility: the late fifteenth-century warrior nobility had become the Elizabethan service nobility. James' tale was one of modernization. Honourable though they may have been, his medieval lords were nonetheless archetypal pre-moderns: uneducated, hot-headed, violent, overmighty, only nominally Christian, and obsessed with fate. By contrast, his Elizabethan nobles had turned the civilizing corner. They had sublimated their personal ambitions to the interests of the state, pursued their disagreements in the courts, abandoned their great retinues, read the classics, and given themselves over to proper worship of a state-sanctioned faith. In the words of James, the honour affinity and the nation had become co-terminous. In a classic modernizing transition, violence had become the monopoly of the state.

James' study remains the starting point for anyone interested in the topic, but his thesis has come under increasing challenge. A number of scholars have contended that James greatly underplayed the role of royal service and virtue to notions of noble honour pre-1500, and that he had equally under-played the importance of military glory and lineage post-1600. In a word, his tale was too schematic.[11] Nor was James' thesis helped by developments

---

[10] Mervyn James, 'English politics and the concept of honour, 1485–1642', in James (ed.), *Society, politics and culture: studies in early modern England* (Cambridge, 1986), pp. 308–415.

[11] Richard Cust, 'Honour and politics in early Stuart England: the case of Beaumont v. Hastings', *P&P* 149 (1995), pp. 57–94; William Palmer, 'Scenes from provincial life: history, honor and meaning in the Tudor north', *Renaissance Quarterly* 53 (2000), pp. 425–48; Steven Ellis, *Tudor frontiers and noble power: the making of the British state* (Oxford, 1995); G. W. Bernard, 'The Tudor nobility in perspective', in Bernard (ed.), *The Tudor nobility* (New York, 1992), pp. 1–48. This criticism was in many ways reminiscent of J. P. Cooper's criticisms of earlier work on changing notions of nobility and aristocracy. Cooper believed scholars were too selective in their choice of evidence and that the cost of looking for change over time was an overly schematic argument. Cooper, 'Ideals of gentility in early modern England', in Cooper (ed.), *Land, men and beliefs: studies in early modern history* (London, 1983), pp. 43–77.

in the historiography of late medieval England. Important to his model was a notion of the Wars of the Roses as the highpoint of aristocratic anarchy and as a sign that medieval order was, if not non-existent, then at least inherently unstable. But as those 'Wars' come to look less like the natural phenomena of a society lacking order and more like the products of a breakdown in order, the harder it becomes to think of the 'medieval' exhausting itself in a final orgy of honour violence only to be supplanted by a restrained Christian, humanist 'modern'.[12] Moreover, recent work on English Catholics in the early modern period calls James' trajectory into question. Underlying his argument was an implicit understanding that England had become an ideologically and demographically Protestant polity by the mid-sixteenth century. The work of such diverse scholars as Eamon Duffy, Christopher Haigh, Richard Cust, Peter Lake, Michael Questier and Ethan Shagan has demonstrated that Catholics remained numerous and their religious style influential well past Henry VIII's break with Rome and that they held to their own peculiar strains of honour principles.[13] Linda Pollock has even been so bold as to take the very bedrock of violence out from under early modern English honour culture altogether, arguing instead that honour codes promoted stability. She poses a question of fundamental importance: how do we reconcile our understandings of the landed elite as both a group 'striving to create social harmony, and a violent, touchy warrior class'?[14] Her answer, in short, is to explore the workings of honour in everyday situations, not just moments of violent outburst, and show how it typically concerned peacekeeping and social harmony. As the history of honour in early modern England continues to be written, James' search for monolithic codes of honour seems quixotic; honour in England

---

[12] K. B. MacFarlane, *The nobility of later medieval England* (Oxford, 1973); J. R. Lander, 'The crown and the aristocracy in England, 1450–1509', *Albion* 8 (1976), pp. 203–18; Michael Hicks, *English political culture in the fifteenth century* (New York, 2002); John Watts, *Henry VI and the politics of kingship* (Cambridge, 1996).

[13] For example, see Eamon Duffy, *The stripping of the altars: traditional religion in England, c. 1400–c. 1580* (New Haven, 1992); Christopher Haigh, *English reformations: religion, politics, and society under the Tudors* (New York, 1993); Peter Lake and Michael Questier (eds.), *Conformity and orthodoxy in the English church, c. 1560–1660* (Rochester, NY, 2000); Michael Questier, *Catholicism and community in early modern England: politics, aristocratic patronage and religion, c. 1550–1640* (Cambridge, 2006); Ethan Shagan (ed.), *Catholics and the 'Protestant nation': religious politics and identity in early modern England* (Manchester, 2005); Cust, 'Honour and politics in early Stuart England'; and 'Catholicism, antiquarianism and gentry honour: the writings of Sir Thomas Shirley', *Midland History* 23 (1998), pp. 40–70.

[14] Linda Pollock, 'Honor, gender, and reconciliation in elite culture, 1570–1700', *JBS* 46 (2007), pp. 3–29, quote p. 4. See also Palmer, 'Scenes from provincial life', in which the author downplays northern magnates' resort to violence, and then goes farther to claim that those elites did not hold to codes of honour at all.

was multi-valent, not something onto which one could map the rise of modernity. As such, the study of honour in early modern England remains a rich field for research, one result of which being that there has been little effort to extend explorations of English honour culture beyond its national borders, or to see how a larger 'British' honour culture may have affected the home variety.

To broaden the pursuit of honour culture across the Irish Sea would immediately present an analogous problem: we have only a restricted sense of what honour looked like in Ireland. There is important scholarly treatment of the subject for the early modern period, but most of it is incidental to other inquiries.[15] Katherine Simms has written on the 'might makes right' aggressiveness of Irish aristocratic honour, noting that 'the qualities most admired in private patrons or kings were a lively sense of honour or "face" which felt any injury inflicted on a protégé to be a personal affront, a blush-making insult, and sufficient courage and martial ability to vindicate this honour by avenging all breaches of their protection'.[16] Joep Leerssen sees Gaelic honour as based primarily upon military valour, lineage and, increasingly over the course of the sixteenth century, an adherence to Gaelic culture and resistance to anglicization.[17] Marc Caball, too, stresses the place of cultural exclusivity, even a sense of national consciousness, in bardic definitions of honour and nobility by the 1590s.[18] The central place of hospitality to Irish elite honour has been highlighted by Catherine O'Sullivan.[19] What comes most clearly out of these studies is the court poets' central role in determining honour and dishonour. Later commentators typically refer to these men as bards, which can give the incorrect impression of them as simple rhymers or entertainers. Quite the contrary, they were powerful members of Ireland's aristocratic courts and vital players in its political life. That their poetic encomia brought honour, and satire

---

[15] This is not the case for the medieval period, however. See Philip O'Leary, '*Fír fer*: an internalized ethical concept in early Irish literature?', *Éigse* 22 (1987), pp. 1–14; 'Magnanimous conduct in Irish heroic literature', *Éigse* 25 (1991), pp. 28–44; 'Verbal deceit in the Ulster Cycle', *Éigse* 21 (1986), pp. 16–26.

[16] Katherine Simms, *From kings to warlords: the changing political structure of Gaelic Ireland in the later middle ages* (Dublin, 1987), p. 107.

[17] Joep Leerssen, *Mere Irish and Fíor-Ghael: studies in the idea of Irish nationality, its development and literary expression prior to the nineteenth century* (Dublin, 1990). David Edwards also stresses the importance of raiding and plundering to Gaelic notions of nobility. Edwards, 'The escalation of violence in sixteenth-century Ireland', in David Edwards, Pádraig Lenihan and Clodagh Tait (eds.), *Age of atrocity: violence and political conflict in early modern Ireland* (Dublin, 2007), pp. 34–78; see p. 41.

[18] Marc Caball, *Poets and politics: reaction and continuity in Irish poetry, 1558–1625* (Notre Dame, 1998), pp. 40–82.

[19] Catherine Marie O'Sullivan, *Hospitality in medieval Ireland, 900–1500* (Dublin, 2004); see particularly chapter 4.

dishonour, has long been acknowledged – Edmund Campion's 'Two bokes of the histories of Ireland' (1580) included the description of how 'Greedie of praise theie [the Irish] be, and fearfull of dishonour'.[20] But what the poets deemed honourable and dishonourable remains understudied. There is, for example, no sustained lexical study of Irish words connoting honour.[21] Consequently, we know much less about honour in Ireland than in England.

Even were one to produce workable descriptions of English and Irish honour cultures, there would be no models to follow in trying to link them together in a single study. Works on honour in early modern Europe cleave closely to national boundaries (even when those nations did not yet exist). While English historians write of English honour, Irish of Irish, they are not alone in studying honour cultures as nationally specific. The growing body of excellent work on French honour culture is consistently constrained by political boundaries.[22] Even the classic studies of the Italian 'point of honour' subsume inter-state differences under the blanket descriptor, 'Italian'.[23] In these national settings, honour exists as a set of uniquely defining cultural assumptions and behaviours that helps to create identity, structure social interactions, and feed politics in ways that mark off individual European polities from one another. Whereas scholars have crossed lines of class and gender in the study of honour, they have not transcended 'cultural' borders that are implicitly seen as coterminous with national ones.[24] Even the seeming exceptions prove this rule. Anna Bryson and Markku Peltonen have brilliantly explored the importation of Italianate notions of honour and courtesy into England in the seventeenth century.[25]

[20] A. F. Vossen (ed.), *Edmund Campion's two bokes of the histories of Ireland* (Assen, 1963), p. 19. For an enlightening study of the power of satire, see Roisin McLaughlin, 'A threat of satire by Tadhg (Mac Dáire) Mac Bruaideadha', *Ériu* 55 (2005), pp. 37–57.

[21] This has been brilliantly done for early modern English. See Charles Barber, *The theme of honour's tongue: a study of social attitudes in the English drama from Shakespeare to Dryden* (Göteborg, 1985); and Barber, *The idea of honour in the English drama, 1591–1700* (Göteborg, 1957).

[22] Ellery Schalk, *From valor to pedigree: ideas of nobility in France in the sixteenth and seventeenth centuries* (Princeton, 1986); William M. Reddy, *The invisible code: honor and sentiment in postrevolutionary France, 1814–1848* (Berkeley, 1997); Kristen Neuschel, *Word of honor: interpreting noble culture in sixteenth-century France* (Ithaca, 1989).

[23] Frederick R. Bryson, *The point of honor in sixteenth-century Italy: an aspect of the life of the gentleman* (New York, 1935); and Bryson, *The sixteenth-century Italian duel: a study in Renaissance social history* (Chicago, 1938).

[24] The literature on women's honour and on gendered concepts of honour continues to grow. An excellent example, made all the better for its rich bibliography of studies covering Britain and continental Europe, is Pollock, 'Honor, gender, and reconciliation'.

[25] Markku Peltonen, *The duel in early modern England: civility, politeness and honour* (Cambridge, 2003); Anna Bryson, *From courtesy to civility: changing codes of conduct in early modern England* (Oxford, 1998).

Both chart a one-way street of cultural influence: Italy does not seem to have been troubled with an influx of English nobles bearing strange honour codes, nor inundated with a printed literature describing competing English aristocratic norms. Nor do Bryson and Peltonen describe droves of Italian aristocrats crowding English elite society and forcing it to reckon with the cultural differences made manifest in their more aggressive, duel-obsessed notions of honour. Instead, they tell of English travellers and the print trade bringing foreign honour principles to England. As such, their studies detail the internal consumption and domestication of imported products: the raw materials may be Italianate, but the process of socio-cultural production is entirely English, and England the sole marketplace for its products. Just such a unilateral approach is demonstrated in studies of Irish honour; no scholar has considered whether there were English notions of honour operative in Ireland at the time and how they may have affected the development of Irish ones. The English presence may have spurred changes to what the bards deemed honourable, a point stressed by Leerssen and Caball, but what role alternative models of honour played in those changes remains unexplored.[26] Conversely, the few attempts to track the role of English ideas of honour in Anglo-Irish politics have been similarly unidirectional in focus: neither Nicholas Canny's attribution of 'English' honour to Richard Boyle, 1st Earl of Cork, nor Hiram Morgan's consideration of Elizabeth I's concern to protect monarchical honour in the prosecution of Tyrone's Rebellion, addresses potentially competing Irish notions of honour.[27] While it seems agreed that honour was important in European societies, it also seems agreed that it did not travel well, and that when it did so, it did not alter according to local conditions.

The one attempt to look at honour and politics in Anglo-Irish affairs – William Palmer's pioneering article, 'That "Insolent Liberty": honor, rites of power, and persuasion in sixteenth-century Ireland' – demonstrates the fourth and final problem facing the study of honour in Britain and Ireland: even if honour principles could in theory interact and operate across borders, was the cultural gap between England and Ireland too great for them in fact to do so?[28] If the study of honour and politics is one way to

---

[26] Leerssen, *Mere Irish*; Caball, *Poets and politics*.

[27] Nicholas Canny, *The upstart earl: a study of the social and mental world of Richard Boyle, first earl of Cork, 1566–1643* (Cambridge, 1982), p. 132; Hiram Morgan, *Tyrone's rebellion: the outbreak of the Nine Years War in Tudor Ireland* (Dublin, 1993), p. 220; Morgan, 'Tom Lee: the posing peacemaker', in Brendan Bradshaw, Andrew Hadfield and Willy Maley (eds.), *Representing Ireland: literature and the origins of conflict, 1534–1660* (Cambridge, 1993), pp. 132–65.

[28] William Palmer, 'That "Insolent Liberty": honor, rites of power, and persuasion in sixteenth-century Ireland', *Renaissance Quarterly* 46 (1993), pp. 308–27.

connect culture to matters of state, is there conceivably a situation in which cultural difference was simply too great for honour politics to work? Palmer's study suggests that colonial Ireland was just such a place. Although he acknowledges the importance of honour to both Irish and English, and establishes its function as a potential mediator between culture and politics in Tudor Ireland, the study ends up arguing that the respective honour codes were so different as to render them merely one more insuperable point of difference separating native and newcomer: the Irish were warlike and pagan and so honour to them equated to 'might makes right'; the English by contrast were lovers of virtue, central government and the law and so their sense of honour was based on service to the commonweal, the holding of civil office, and loyalty to a state-sanctioned religion. Honour was not merely useless in bridging a perceived civil–savage divide, it widened it.

As the above discussion aims to show, there was no more consensus among contemporaries as to what defined honour as there has been among historians. Honour, then, should not be seen as a static thing tied inseparably to 'national' cultures, but rather as comprising various discourses deployable before different audiences. Such inexactness might suggest its weakness as a tool for comprehending early modern society. This would be a mistake, for notions of honour played a vital social and political function in this period. In attempting to 'map the main contours of English cultural landscape in the period around 1600', Malcolm Smuts has identified four 'frames of reference within which contemporaries conceived of the operation of power': honour, the common law, religious providence, and humanist political language.[29] He goes on to claim that 'at the heart [of the early modern English] cultural system lay a concept of honour that structured both patterns of behaviour and a distinctive vision of society'.[30] Indeed, honour provided the social glue for early modern English and Irish societies, as it did for all of Europe. In a world with no police force, no standing army, and limited access to law courts, the willingness on the part of individuals to internalize standards of honour, and on the part of communities to enforce them, was often the best guarantee of keeping the peace. Honour's pull could be felt either horizontally, as the bonds that held social peers together as part of a particular honour group, or vertically, as ties of deference and responsibility inherent in a hierarchical social structure. To understand how such a fundamentally contested concept could carry such social and political weight, it may help to keep in mind the religious and

---

[29] Malcolm Smuts, *Culture and power in England, 1585–1685* (Cambridge, 1998), p. 7.   [30] Ibid., p. 9.

legal parallels suggested by Smuts. We take for granted the importance of these 'frames of reference' and yet when seeking to analyse them, we find ourselves in a morass of conflicting ideas, definitions and beliefs. Indeed, the study of the contours and functions of early modern religion and law forms academic industries. The inability to provide a concise definition of these terms does not, however, lead us to question their importance. The same should apply to ideas of honour. That discussions of honour were everywhere in England, Ireland and the rest of Europe attests to its social and political relevance; its multiplicity of definitions reveals it to be a contested concept, just like law and religion. It falls to the historian to tease out those different discourses of honour, identify their contexts and functions, and to chart change, or note continuity, across time.

If notions of honour were not static, but rather multivalent, contested, and less constitutive of national identity than the prevailing literature assumes, then perhaps we should be more open to seeing them in circulation across national borders. This seems an especially fruitful approach when studying the nobility. As Ronald Asch has written, 'It is hardly an exaggeration to say that the life of a nobleman … had one principal purpose: to prove their claim to honour and superiority, to prove that they belonged to the privileged elite.'[31] Indeed, the pursuit of honour and glory could trump 'dynastic and national loyalties'.[32] He goes on to add that while heterogeneity was the rule among European elites – which is to say that there were all sorts of distinguishing social and cultural traits unique to national nobilities, and thus no one pan-European aristocracy – different countries' nobles at least recognized each other as such. This does not mean that relative status was easily negotiated, but simply that such claims could be made.[33] Combining these two points opens the door for a transnational study of honour: if European nobilities were largely defined by their pursuit of honour, and they recognized one another as fellow elites, how did they navigate the honour codes that defined them?

This book seeks to address that question, using British and Irish elite culture and politics as the case study. In doing so, it attempts an integrative, or holistic, rather than comparative, approach.[34] It is not about honour in

---

[31] Ronald Asch, *Nobilities in transition 1550–1700: courtiers and rebels in Britain and Europe* (London, 2003), p. 10.

[32] Asch, *Nobilities in transition*, p. 1. For a similar sentiment regarding the Irish context, see Simms, *From kings to warlords*, p. 106.

[33] Asch gives the example of tension between German and French nobles over relative status. Asch, *Nobilities in transition*, pp. 6, 9, 20–1.

[34] 'Holistic' is the term used by John Morrill to discuss the method underlying the practice of what has come to be known as the 'new British history'. It accurately gets at the notion of ideas and patterns of

Ireland, nor is it about English honour as it manifested itself in Ireland.[35] Rather, it is about various discourses of honour operative in England and Ireland and the ways in which they structured politics in the singular situation of early modern Anglo-Irish relations, and how they were in turn reshaped by that very context. This decision is less one of choice than of necessity, for a comparative framework does not fit well. The nobility in the kingdom of Ireland was a provincial one, and thus the story here is in part one of elite formation. But unlike, say, the incorporation of northern English magnates under the Tudors, or Languedocian ones under the Bourbons, the incorporation of the Irish nobility retained something of an 'international' flavour by virtue of Ireland's being a separate realm.[36] With that said, the international comparative model used for studies of the nobility – say those of Asch or Jonathan Dewald – does not work either, for the English and Irish peerages were centred on the same monarchical fount of honour, and were filled by men born of both realms.[37] There is a curious domestic–international aspect to Anglo-Irish honour, therefore, that demands a holistic approach.

This explains the use of 'British' throughout the text.[38] A comparative study would necessitate detailing what honour looked like within each polity in order to compare them. That I am not concerned to do. Given the multivalent character of honour in any 'national' setting, it would require far more space than is available here. Moreover, it would miss the point that there is something unique and worth investigating about the honour culture of Britain and Ireland collectively. It is undoubtedly the case, to again invoke Malcolm Smuts' observation, that in England

behaviour across England and Ireland evolving in concert. Morrill, 'The British problem, *c.* 1534–1707', in Brendan Bradshaw and John Morrill (eds.), *The British problem, c. 1534–1707: state formation in the Atlantic archipelago* (New York, 1996), pp. 1–38.

[35] Moreover, it is most emphatically not about who was or was not truly honourable. That Hugh O'Neill and Thomas Wentworth, for example, have come down to us as models of dishonourable behaviour in no way discounts their acknowledgement of honour's importance and their attempts to couch their actions – however Machiavellian or hypocritical we may think them to have been – as honourable. Thus, I am not concerned with whether individual actors' actions were 'in fact' honourable, or if their behaviour matched their rhetoric, but rather with how they mobilized a discourse of honour to explain and justify their actions and behaviour.

[36] An example of such a study is William Beik, *Absolutism and society in seventeenth-century France: state power and provincial aristocracy in Languedoc* (Cambridge, 1985). See, however, Steven Ellis, who likens the medieval Irish lordship (here meaning the culturally English portion of Ireland) to the north of England. Ellis, *Tudor frontiers.*

[37] Jonathan Dewald, *The European nobility, 1400–1800* (Cambridge, 1996).

[38] I find particularly helpful Steven Ellis' comment that when studying the 150 years prior to 1603, the 'British' context is 'as useful as any other anachronism like autonomous nations'. Ellis and Christopher Maginn, *The making of the British Isles: the state of Britain and Ireland, 1450–1660* (New York, 2007), p. xiii.

honour 'structured both patterns of behaviour and a distinctive vision of society'.[39] But it must be borne in mind that that concept was grounded in the notion of the king as the fount of all honour – a fact that bears significant implications for any notion of the national character of honour. For once Ireland was made a kingdom, the Tudor monarchy became a multiple or composite one, and the honour bonds extending from the monarchical fount did not conform to any one realm but to all those over which the prince ruled. English honour and Irish honour were from that moment on redefined as subsets of the honour circle inscribed by the expanding dynastic state. As culturally distinctive as each may have been, there were equally distinctive characteristics to that new, larger honour circle comprehending both the English and Irish peerages, and a 'British' approach, with its focus on state building, not nation formation, seems to offer the best means to get at them.

The issue of cultural contact, our fourth problem, remains the greatest impediment to a cross-border study of honour culture and politics. For if the cultural gap separating English and Irish was too great, perhaps then English elites did not recognize Irish elites as such. There is certainly an ample literature to suggest that this was the case; that the Irish constituted England's savage 'other' and that the story of Anglo-Irish relations is one of colonial encounter not of European exchange.[40] It could also be argued that whatever the prevalence of aristocratic mutual recognition on the ground, Ireland (be it lordship, kingdom or colony) was simply too violent and chaotic a place for honour principles to have played any role in effecting social stability.[41] Neither of these positions invalidates the usefulness of honour to understanding the early modern Anglo-Irish world. Even were the cultural gap between native and newcomer so great as to make these two polities the exception to Asch's rule (that European elites recognized each other as such), and thus a colonial framework the best one for understanding their relations, there would still be a need to address questions of honour. There is a simple evidentiary reason for this: English- and Irish-language writers alike obsessed over honour in this period. Concerned as many scholars have been to chart the rise of faith and fatherland in Ireland, or to track the 'othering' gaze of a creepingly imperial Britain, it has gone largely unremarked that discussions of honour and status often dominated

---

[39] Smuts, *Culture and power in England*, p. 9.
[40] The literature on English colonial views of the Irish is now voluminous. Essential starting points are D. B. Quinn, *The Elizabethans and the Irish* (Ithaca, 1966), and Nicholas Canny, *The Elizabethan conquest of Ireland: a pattern established* (London, 1976).
[41] See the essays collected in Edwards, et al. (eds.), *Age of atrocity*.

the period's texts. It is worthwhile taking honour seriously precisely because contemporaries did.

A complementary structural reason necessitates the study of honour: in colonial settings, where political and legal institutions and precedents were thin on the ground, we should expect to see people making appeals to honour in their attempts to boost their status and get ahead. James Brooks has demonstrated exactly this point in his remarkable study of Spanish interactions with the indigenous peoples of what is now the American southwest. This was truly a situation of cultural encounter. And yet it was precisely codes of masculine honour that allowed colonizer and colonized to interact and build working community relations across vast cultural distance.[42] Even acknowledging that English planters and officials frequently interacted with the Crown's Gaelic subjects across significant cultural gaps, it is hard to accept that these gaps were as large as those separating conquistador and Indian. All the talk of honour in English and Irish sources from the latter half of the sixteenth century, when Ireland took on the qualities of an English colony, should therefore be understood not as merely decorative rhetoric, but instead as potentially revealing something important about Anglo-Irish politics and society. That Ireland was chaotic and violent – indeed spectacularly so – should no more discourage the exploration of honour than should its colonial status. Mervyn James, after all, saw in early modern honour codes the basis for elite violence, and there are many authors since who have agreed with him. So regardless of whether one chooses to see Ireland as part of a continuum of European hierarchical societies, a colonial setting characterized by cultural encounter, or a uniquely violent and chaotic European border society, close attention to the language of honour can facilitate our making sense of British politics in Anglo-Irish perspective.

During the period under discussion here, Ireland in fact satisfied the requirements for all three categories: kingdom, colony and borderland. In each setting, honour served as an aristocratic lingua franca that bridged cultural, social and political gaps. It could do so because, as noted above, honour is not a static, easily defined, 'thing'. Rather than a series of set codes, honour is better understood as a dynamic two-part 'claim-right'. This is how it will be used in the chapters that follow. On the one hand, it is

---

[42] James Brooks, *Captives & cousins: slavery, kinship, and community in the southwest borderlands* (Chapel Hill, 2002), particularly chapter 1. Examples of 'honourable' treatment of indigenous peoples can be found, of course, in the histories of every European power that operated in the Americas. Brooks, however, is the first to study honour's role in the long-term viability of mixed communities of natives and newcomers.

the claim by an individual to be treated a certain way by a certain group of people; on the other it is the right of that certain group's members to accept or reject the individual's claim. Adapted from anthropologist Frank Henderson Stewart's model, this definition accounts for both the individualistic/internal (virtue and worth) and the communal/external (reputation and status) aspects of honour.[43] Necessarily, then, this study must address two things when discussing honour culture in Britain and Ireland: first, the basis for, or foundation of, any particular claim made, with attention paid to its material, mental, behavioural and performative aspects; and, second, the negotiation of that claim, from the symbiotic perspectives of the individual making the claim, and of the group assessing its validity. It must also be reiterated that honour can manifest itself horizontally, as the bonds among social peers that connect them as part of a particular honour group (noble to noble, for instance), or vertically, as ties of deference and responsibility inherent in a hierarchical social structure (most obviously, king to subject). This study focuses chiefly on the vertical bonds between monarch and noble, and the horizontal ones linking the nobles themselves. It does so because while every person, no matter his or her station, held on to some sense of honour, contemporaries most often took honour to be the special preserve of the nobility. Moreover, this study's emphasis on high politics and the nature of the sources available for Gaelic Ireland necessarily restricts the investigation to aspects of noble honour.

The study of noble honour in early modern Britain and Ireland can offer insights into the cultural aspects of state building in the Tudor and Stuart multiple monarchies. Primarily, it can help flesh out the 'personal' aspects of power as operative in the realms. It is certainly the case that much of English-Irish relations in this period can be read in terms of the imposition of political forms and institutions on an unwilling populace. Nevertheless, power was both very personal and mediated through cultural forms; indeed, St Leger and Henry's experiment only made this more the case. The making of Ireland as both kingdom and site of plantation was as much the work of individuals and small groups as of the state, and there were many on the ground in Ireland quite willing to go along with, and at times guide or reshape, that process. The study of honour can help us address some of the connections and disconnections between collective and individual inputs into Anglo-Irish relations because, as Richard Cust has written, 'Honour can be said to mediate between the aspirations of the individual and the judgment of society. It therefore provides a means of exploring the values

---

[43] Frank Henderson Stewart, *Honor* (Chicago, 1994).

and norms of a society, and also the ways in which individuals compete to sustain or increase their status and power within that society.'[44] Exploring the personal character of British high politics also allows us to see how Irish elites were motivated by concerns over matters of status and standing (in addition to the more closely studied ones of faith and fatherland) and how the expansion of the Tudor/Stuart aristocratic honour circle threatened English nobles' privileges and sense of corporate identity. The focus on claims to honour also allows the study of personal politics to avoid becoming simply an ahistorical study of the politics of 'personality' or faction. It must be pointed out, however, that this book does not aim for, or pretend to, comprehensive coverage of all aspects of elite honour culture in Britain and Ireland.[45] Rather, it presents a number of chronological case studies detailing aspects of its importance in elite politics and identity formation. In doing so it proceeds from two assumptions: that Ireland did take on, at least in part, the character of a colony by the end of the sixteenth century; and that religion served as the primary dividing line between noble in-groups and out-groups. The focus here is upon how elites could, and did, use a language of honour to navigate the shifting shoals thrown up by centralization, colonization and confessionalization.

The book begins with the creation of Ireland as a kingdom under the English crown and considers the effects of that dramatic constitutional change on noble culture. Chapter 1 looks at the Crown's attempt to reform Ireland by integrating its native elites – Gaelic and 'English-Irish' alike – into a 'British' network of nobility. It asks the fundamental question of how St Leger could have seen in the Irish nobility potential allies in British state-building. To answer this, it explores the points of contact among three honour systems – Gaelic, 'English-Irish' and English/continental – and argues for a much narrower cultural distance between native and newcomer than that described by other commentators. Chapter 2 considers some of the ways in which Gaelic intellectuals – bardic poets and annalists – dealt with the subject of noble honour in light of these changes. There is an

---

[44] Cust, 'Honour and politics', p. 59.
[45] One vitally important aspect of early modern Irish conceptions of honour that is not covered here is the role played by notions of gender. On this subject see Sarah McKibben, 'Bardic poetry and the postcolonial politics of close reading', in *Proceedings of the Harvard Celtic Colloquium* 21–2 (2000–1), actual publication date: 2007; and John Ball, 'Popular violence in the Irish uprising of 1641: the 1641 depositions, Irish resistance to English colonialism, and its representation in English sources' (unpublished PhD dissertation, The Johns Hopkins University, 2006). Full discussion of this topic awaits the publication of McKibben's book manuscript, 'Endangered masculinities: gender, colonialism, and sexuality in early modern literature in Irish, 1540–1780'.

increasingly sophisticated literature on the mechanics and meanings of surrender and regrant;[46] this chapter is meant to complement that historiography by providing the first lexical study of Irish terms for honour and status from the period 1541–1600. It focuses on three sets of texts: *The Annals of Loch Cé*; the bardic poems of Tadhg Dall Ó hUiginn; and poems written to the chief of the Maguires in the late sixteenth century. In doing so it compares prose and poetry – genres typically dealt with in isolation – and shows the extent to which Gaelic intellectuals understood the honour principles invoked by the Crown and were able to synchronize them with Gaelic norms. By the end of the century, many of them rejected surrender and regrant and the new amalgamated Anglo-Irish aristocracy. This rejection was due, however, not to insuperable cultural misunderstandings between native and newcomer – the inevitable effect of colonial encounter – but instead to Gaelic intellectuals' belief that the English were acting in violation of shared notions of honour.

Chapter 3 considers the breakdown of the attempted integration of honour systems during the Nine Years' War. For all its promise, surrender and regrant failed as a social engineering project. Beginning in 1556, Ireland became the site of English plantation schemes. Changed too was the culture of honour that bound England and Ireland. For the war's Gaelic leaders, honour had changed from a tool of assimilation and cultural convergence into a basis for resistance theory. Moreover, the chapter shows how the honour politics of the conflict affected England. This I demonstrate through a focus on three aspects of the war: Elizabeth's concern for the defence of honour in the prosecution of the conflict; the fear of social dilution in England from the number of knights created in fighting the Irish rebels; and the different (indeed, disastrously so) understandings of honour expressed by Elizabeth and her lord lieutenant and general of the army, Robert Devereux, 2nd Earl of Essex. The politics of honour in Anglo-Irish relations, launched with such promise in 1541, were to destabilize both polities by 1603.

Defeat in the Nine Years' War is understood to have marked the end of the Gaelic order; but did it also mark the end of the politics of honour between the realms? Chapter 4 looks at how honour was constructed by

---

[46] See particularly Christopher Maginn's ongoing work on the programme in his *'Civilizing' Gaelic Leinster: the extension of Tudor rule in the O'Byrne and O'Toole lordships* (Dublin, 2005); ' "Surrender and regrant" in the historiography of sixteenth-century Ireland', *Sixteenth Century Journal* 38 (2007), pp. 956–61; and 'The limitations of Tudor reform: the policy of "surrender and regrant" and the O'Rourkes', *Breifne: Journal of Cumann Seanchais Bhréifne* xi (2007), pp. 429–60. I am grateful to Dr Maginn for sharing the above articles with me prior to their publication.

Gaelic intellectuals in the aftermath of the War and at how ideals of honour were altered to address the self-exile to the continent of Ulster's pre-eminent Gaelic lords in 1607 (the so-called Flight of the Earls). It addresses two prose works – Tadhg Ó Cianáin's *The Flight of the Earls* and Lughaidh Ó Cléirigh's *The Life of Red Hugh O'Donnell* – and demonstrates how their authors creatively modified Irish notions of honour and nobility so as to recast Gaelic and Old English elites as members of an emergent Catholic, European aristocracy.

Most Irish elites did not, however, leave Ireland for exile. Chapter 5 looks at honour at 'home' as viewed from three perspectives: that of the Gaelic intelligentsia, a Gaelic noble, and an Old English nobleman. The first brings to light Gaelic authors' fears about social inversion and the end of Gaelic noble honour. The second focuses on Donough O'Brien, 4th Earl of Thomond, and how he manipulated Gaelic and anglicized ideals of honour to cement his authority in early Stuart Ireland. The third case study is of Richard Burke, 4th Earl of Clanricard, the only Irish peer to also become a member of the English peerage (as the Earl of St Albans). The chapter closes with a discussion of a precedence dispute between Clanricard and the 5th Earl of Thomond. This was an unpleasant affair, fought out largely in England using English archives and expertise. The episode reminds us that the pursuit of honour was a serious business, and that it was not constrained by national borders.

Chapter 6 further explores precedence disputes across borders. It looks at how these disputes disrupted Parliamentary sessions, initially in Ireland, and then in England. The English case is particularly interesting in that the precedence contests discussed were not between individuals but instead pitted the English nobility against the 'foreign' nobility of Ireland and Scotland. Taken to impinge upon the honour of the monarch himself, these disputes provoked a growing sense that the honour of the Crown needed more muscular defence in Ireland to obviate social and political chaos in both polities.

Chapter 7 focuses on the appointment of Sir Thomas Wentworth (the eventual Earl of Strafford) as Lord Deputy, and thus as the 'point man' in Charles' efforts to protect the honour of the Crown and its representatives in Ireland. It begins by briefly reconstructing Wentworth's views on honour principles in the contexts of Jacobean and Caroline elite culture. In doing so it highlights his social and political advancement and culminates with his appointment to the deputyship. The chapter continues by arguing that Wentworth's, and Charles', pursuit of honour politics amounted to an effort to effect a reformation of manners in Ireland amongst the

Old English, and, more importantly, amongst the New English. Wentworth's clashes with Ireland's elites have garnered significant historiographical attention, generally being explained as personality clashes or as practical examples of an absolutist ('thorough', to use Wentworth's own term) political theory. The present study, by contrast, argues that they were also products of a broader Caroline concern to defend and manage honour across the Stuart realms. To demonstrate this point, it looks at two disputes between the Deputy and local Irish nobles and the different discourses of honour and modes of honourable behaviour Wentworth deployed in each. The first pitted him against Clanricard/St Albans. Here Wentworth – a mere viscount – deployed the honour of office to combat the power of a social superior. The second saw him lock horns with the English-born Lord Chancellor, Adam Loftus, and revolved around matters of family honour and proper masculine conduct.

This final chapter closes the circle of Anglo-Irish honour politics as begun by St Leger and Henry. In a way, the Wentworth deputyship mirrored that of St Leger in the 1540s. The latter had been sent by Henry VIII to effect reform of his western lordship and had received monarchical permission to do so through creation of a 'British' honour circle inclusive of English and Irish elites loyal to one prince. Wentworth had a similar mandate from Charles I, even if the nobility he sought to reform comprised New English officials and peers, not Gaelic and Gaelicized lords. Similar too was the outcome of these reforming projects: both failed. The conflict that engulfed the Wentworth deputyship, however, was of a different order of magnitude than any of the sixteenth century Irish rebellions. It would prove general to the British Isles.

CHAPTER I

The honour revolution of 1541

The historiography of early modern English-Irish relations stresses cultural difference. It is the unifying theme in otherwise widely divergent takes on the subject. Traditional nationalist accounts saw in this period the struggle between two emergent nations; sectarian accounts, two different confessional communities. Later authors, unconcerned to trace either national consciousness or religious identity, focused on the colonial nature of the relationship and on the unbridgeable cultural gulfs that allowed one neighbour to dehumanize and dispossess the other.[1] Recent work on atrocity and violence in sixteenth-century Ireland takes this as a given.[2] The one exception here may seem to be the recent work on Tudor reform efforts in Ireland.[3] But these studies also start from the assumption that English and Irish cultural systems were worlds apart; they simply diverge from other studies by positing that English efforts to bridge difference were characterized by negotiation and not force. Whatever the framework they use to investigate Anglo-Irish history, historians have seen their task primarily as one of explaining the origins and effects of English expansion into alien territory.[4]

---

[1] A brief sample includes Quinn, *Elizabethans and the Irish*; Canny, *Elizabethan conquest*; Ronald Takaki, 'The "Tempest" in the wilderness: the racialization of savagery', *Journal of American History* 79 (1992), pp. 892–912.

[2] See the collected essays in Edwards, Lenihan and Tait (eds.), *Age of atrocity*. This subject is the ongoing research of Vincent Carey; see his 'John Derricke's *Image of Irelande*, Sir Henry Sidney, and the massacre at Mullaghmast', *IHS* 31 (1999), pp. 305–27. See also Patricia Palmer, '"An headlesse ladie" and "a horses loade of heades": writing the beheading', *Renaissance Quarterly* 60 (2007), pp. 25–57.

[3] Examples include Bradshaw, *Irish constitutional revolution*; Brady, *Chief governors*; and Steven Ellis, *Ireland in the age of the Tudors: English expansion and the end of Gaelic Ireland* (New York, 1998).

[4] Steven Ellis is eloquent on this point: 'The consensus of historical opinion has been that geographical, cultural and social differences within the island and between Ireland and England created conditions that were so extraordinary by English standards as to constitute an intractable problem of government: Tudor government failed in Ireland because it failed to appreciate the need for extraordinary remedies for exceptional problems.' With Ellis, I believe that 'there is some truth in this argument, but also much Whiggery', and that the similarities demand investigation. *Ireland in the age of the Tudors*, p. 353.

While this emphasis on Anglo-Irish difference has yielded important findings, it perforce obscures the fact that the initial effort to bring the kingdom of Ireland under Tudor control was a peaceable one built upon perceived points of socio-cultural similarity. As a result, the process through which this was attempted, surrender and regrant, has gone understudied.[5] Irish historians – the only ones to deal with it in any depth – typically have interpreted it in one of two ways: (1) as little more than a treacherous bait-and-switch by an imperialistic and bigoted England; or (2) as a particularly enlightened example of the Tudor interest in reform.[6] Radically different as these interpretations are in assessing motivation, both proceed from the point that what needs to be explained is the English government's strategy for dealing with a strange people and their strange ways.

The present chapter attempts a different approach and argues that there were significant points of social and cultural contact between England and Gaelic and Gaelicized Ireland and that surrender and regrant was conceived and deployed as a means to capitalize on them. Historians have long acknowledged certain commonalities between English and Gaelic culture. In their analyses, however, they have tended to focus on the points of difference. Here I wish to highlight those commonalities so as to think anew about the intersection of culture and politics in early modern Anglo-Irish relations. The argument proceeds by exploring briefly the programme's development from conception, through initial implementation to established practice. The chapter aims first to answer the following basic question: if English and Gaelic cultural systems were as incompatible as scholars tend to assume, how could Henry VIII's Irish deputy St Leger have believed that Irish elites could be made into 'English' peers? The answer suggested here is that, in spite of very real social, cultural and political differences separating English from Irish, the Deputy saw Ireland's Gaelic and 'English-Irish' elites as simply variations on a recognized model of European nobilities. As such, the effort to incorporate them into a cross-realm, or British (for lack of a better term), ruling class was as politically promising as it was sensible. Second, the chapter explores from a Tudor state perspective some of the promises and potential pitfalls of this cultural/political experiment. For what surrender and regrant did was create an aristocratic honour culture, inclusive of England and Ireland and centred

---

[5] The results of Christopher Maginn's systematic study of the programme are eagerly awaited.

[6] In the words of Ciaran Brady, the policy was seen as 'utopian or Machiavellian' depending on ideological perspective. Brady, 'The O'Reillys of East Breifne and the problem of "surrender and regrant"', *Breifne: Journal of Cumann Seanchais Bhréifne* 6 (1985), p. 223. For a review of the literature, see Maginn, '"Surrender and regrant" in the historiography', pp. 956–61.

on the person of the king. The king was thus bound in honour to rule as justly in Ireland as in England; Irish nobles were bound in return to obey. Although this launching of an Anglo-Irish politics of honour held the potential to normalize relations between the two societies, it simultaneously threatened to destabilize them dramatically by offering previously unknown opportunities to bring dishonour to Crown and monarch.

The chapter's final section considers briefly the practical workings and development of surrender and regrant settlements. This is not an attempt to write the history of such arrangements across the latter half of the sixteenth century, but rather an argument based on brief case studies for seeing them, imperfect and problematic though they may have been, as having had the potential to effect St Leger's hopes for a unified elite caste spanning England and Ireland and linked through the person of the monarch. Even with surrender and regrant's end as a recognizable policy by mid century, and the emergence of plantation schemes and new forms of provincial governance at the centre of Crown policy towards Ireland, it survived as an ad hoc tool for use with individual Gaelic and 'English-Irish' lords. Whether Ireland was kingdom or colony, English and Irish actors saw honour culture and high politics within the realms as intimately intertwined, and as constituting a game at which all could play – whether for good or for ill, for assimilation or for resistance. In short, this chapter suggests an alternative approach to Anglo–Irish history in the sixteenth century: instead of trying to explain how the negotiation of cultural difference turned so violent and chaotic, it asks why a focus on cultural difference came to dominate when the points of contact seemed so strong.

I.

Undoubtedly much appeared alien as St Leger gazed out from Dublin Castle upon the Irish. Gaelic society looked nothing like the centralized monarchy of England. There was a history of an Irish highkingship, but not since Brian Boru in the eleventh century had someone laid effective claim to it. The ideal of the high-king (*ard-rí*) was kept alive by bards and brehons (practitioners of the native legal system, or brehon law), but the reality of Gaelic Ireland was a fractured polity of roughly one hundred semi-sovereign local lordships. Not all lordships were created equal, and reciprocal bonds of rights and duties linked lords of differing status. Thus, for instance, the powerful Ulster family of the Maguires held sway in Fermanagh, but their doing so was largely contingent upon their paying regular tribute and fealty to their more powerful neighbours, the O'Neills. Strange too must have been the fact that Irish elites did not practice primogeniture; each new chief of the name was chosen by representatives of an extended family network known as the *deirbhfine*. While the elective process by which Irish lords were created may seem refreshingly modern in a stiflingly static late-medieval world of father-to-son aristocratic inheritance, it was only too often the occasion for chaos as rival claimants fought over the lordship. Gaelic elite culture was in general a highly militarized environment. Nobilities across Europe were by origin a warrior caste, so this should not have surprised. But the incessant raiding of rival lords' territories to steal cattle, burn crops and take hostages for ransom was seen by English eyes as frighteningly primitive. So too were the extra-familial bonds the Irish formed through the fostering out of sons to other noble houses. English officials, concerned to bring law and order to the island, decried the fact that the network of Gaelic family loyalties was as divided as the island's political authority and often as incomprehensible as the local language. On top of it all was their outlandish clothes and appearance: the infamous mantle, a cloak worn by men and women alike, was believed to hide a variety of sins; the long-hanging fringe of hair, the glib, was thought to aid and abet shiftiness as one could rarely see their eyes behind it. Gaelic society, politics and culture – whether practised by ethnic Gaels or Gaelicized 'English-Irish' – could look quite alien to English observers.[7]

But it did not need to do so, and to St Leger it apparently did not. In the midst of all that was strange there was much recognizable. Gaelic lords were hereditary elites who sat atop a carefully stratified social hierarchy and who held court in their fortified great houses.[8] These were not courts to rival those of the English monarchy or peerage, but they nevertheless were sites of pageantry, feasting, hospitality, the public performance of learning, and the dispensing of justice. Staple figures at these courts included major ecclesiastics (bishops and archbishops) and the judges and scholars of the island's ancient legal system, Brehon law. Most prominent were the poets – masters of genealogy, history and panegyric – the greatest of whom was the so-called 'chief's poet'.[9] Typically from a long-standing bardic family, this man would have gone through years of intensive training in the memorization and composition of court encomia. He was the arbiter of honour; his verse

---

[7] The Statutes of Kilkenny (1366) provide a brief primer on prevailing prejudices. Edmund Curtis and R. B. McDowell (eds.), *Irish historical documents, 1172–1922* (London, 1943), pp. 52–9.

[8] James Lyttleton and Tadhg O'Keeffe (eds.), *The manor in medieval and early modern Ireland* (Dublin, 2004).

[9] Generally, see Pádraig Breatnach, 'The chief's poet', *Proceedings of the Royal Irish Academy* 83c (1983), pp. 37–79.

praise, performed live to music at the court, helped establish and maintain a lord's legitimacy. No man could be a lord, the chief of the name, without patronizing a poet. Whereas the former controlled the purse, and rewarded the successful poet with gifts of land and privileges of access during feasting, the latter helped bestow legitimacy on the lord and, when aggrieved, composed satire as a means to strike back at an errant or offending patron.[10] To be sure, the particulars of Irish court culture differed in important ways from those obtaining among the English nobility, but their structure and many of their dynamics might well have struck St Leger as variations on a well-known theme.[11]

The similarities between English and Irish elite culture went well beyond the simple fact that both practised some variety of European-style court culture. Granted, the designation of Gaelic noble status looked markedly different from English custom: rather than attaching a title that signified relative status and that carried territorial reference (the Earl of Essex, for instance), Gaelic lords simply bore the family name (the O'Neill, or the O'Donnell). With that said, however, the Gaelic nobility understood and at times embraced heraldic practice common within Anglo-continental aristocratic culture; the O'Neills reportedly having been the first to do so in the early fourteenth century.[12] Trade and travel kept them abreast of continental trends in elite taste: feasts featured Spanish and French wines;[13] houses, religious sites and burial monuments reflected continental architectural standards and forms; chivalric tales were popular in translation, and chivalric themes were worked into the strict metres of traditional bardic panegyric.[14] The classics too were kept alive in Ireland. The teachings of Aristotle

---

[10] See McLaughlin, 'A threat of satire'.

[11] David Edwards urges extreme caution in comparing noble power in England and Ireland; Ken Nicholls warns against seeing English and Irish society as equivalent. David Edwards, *The Ormond lordship in County Kilkenny, 1515–1642: the rise and fall of Butler feudal power* (Dublin, 2003), ix; Nicholls, 'Worlds apart? The Ellis two-nation theory on late medieval Ireland', *History Ireland* (Summer, 1999), pp. 22–6. I do not mean to disagree; the aim here is not to say the courts were the same, but merely to argue that they were different by degree not kind.

[12] John Barry, 'Guide to records of the genealogical office, Dublin, with a commentary on heraldry in Ireland and on the history of the office', *Analecta Hibernica* 26 (1970), pp. 3–43; see p. 20. See also Freya Verstraten, 'Images of Gaelic lordship in Ireland, c. 1200–1400', in Linda Doran and James Lyttleton (eds.), *Lordship in medieval Ireland: image and reality* (Dublin, 2007), pp. 47–74, and Nicholas Williams, *Armas: sracfhéacaint ar araltas na hÉireann* (Dublin, 2001), pp. 4–15.

[13] This is not to say that wine was easy to procure. See Katherine Simms, 'Guesting and feasting in Gaelic Ireland', *Journal of the Royal Society of Antiquaries of Ireland* 108 (1978), pp. 87–8.

[14] The literature on Irish connections with the continent continues to burgeon. Starting points include Rachel Moss, Colmán Ó Clabaigh and Salvador Ryan (eds.), *Art and devotion in late medieval Ireland* (Dublin, 2006); Clodagh Tait, *Death, burial and commemoration in Ireland, 1550–1650* (Basingstoke and New York, 2002); Mary Ann Lyons, *Franco-Irish relations, 1500–1610: politics migration and trade*

and other luminaries of pagan learning were both copied out in Latin and translated into Irish; Gaelic eulogists often compared their subjects to Caesar or Alexander.[15] They also demonstrated awareness of international politics, and of the reality of more powerful crowned kings in the states about them: medieval Irish chroniclers may have called local lords *rí* (king), but they reserved the term 'crowned king' for the rulers of Europe's established kingdoms.[16] Their periodic swearing of allegiance to English monarchs makes clear their understanding of the relations of lord and patron, liege and master, and their willingness to take part in such relations when necessary or advantageous. Numerous sixteenth-century Gaelic lords saw the Crown as a potential ally against local rivals. As such, there appears to have been a periodic Irish 'pull' towards greater intervention by London in Irish affairs that complemented the Tudors' expansionist 'push'.[17] The flirting by the leaders of the Geraldine League with fealty to Charles V shows the continental, pan-European breadth of that understanding.[18] The Irish – lay and religious – were also participants in the international world of late medieval Latin Christendom; they had a particularly strong attachment to the orders, and Gaelic and Old English nobles went periodically on pilgrimage to Rome. The O'Donnells ruled over one of the most physically

(Woodbridge, 2003); Darren Mac Eiteagáin, 'The Renaissance and the late medieval lordship of Tír Chonaill 1461–1555', in William Nolan, Liam Ronayne and Mairead Dunlevy (eds.), *Donegal history and society: interdisciplinary essays on the history of an Irish county* (Dublin, 1995), pp. 203–28. For an example of popular chivalry tales in late medieval Irish, see R. A. Stewart Macalister (ed. and trans.), *The story of the crop-eared dog and the story of eagle-boy: two Arthurian legends* (Dublin, 1908).

[15] See Mícheál Mac Craith, 'Gaelic Ireland and the Renaissance', in Glanmor Williams and Robert O. Jones, *The Celts and the Renaissance* (Cardiff, 1990), pp. 57–89; Mac Craith, 'Literature in Irish, *c.* 1550–1690: from the Elizabethan settlement to the Battle of the Boyne', in Margaret Kelleher and Philip O'Leary (eds.), *The Cambridge history of Irish literature*, 2 vols (Cambridge, 2006), I, pp. 191–231; Breandán Ó Buachalla, '*Annala Ríoghachta Éireann* is *Foras Feasa ar Éireann*: an comhthéacs comhaimseartha', *Studia Hibernica*, 22–3 (1985), pp. 59–105. However, the extent to which the discussion of classical authors and figures was a matter of 'Renaissance' recovery, or simply continuity with medieval practice, needs further investigation. I thank Kenneth Gouwens for discussion on this point.

[16] Simms, *Kings to warlords*, p. 38; Verstraten, 'Images of Gaelic lordship', p. 51. Generally, see Breandán Ó Buachalla, *Aisling ghéar: na Stíobhartaigh agus an taos léinn, 1603–1788* (Dublin, 1996), chapter 1; and *The crown of Ireland* (Galway, 2006).

[17] Numerous Ulster lords sought London's help in fending off the predations of the O'Neills. On the Maguires, see Brendan Bradshaw, 'Cromwellian reform and the origins of the Kildare Rebellion, 1533–34', *Transactions of the Royal Historical Society* 27 (1977), pp. 69–93, see p. 83; on the O'Rourkes, see Brady, 'The O'Reillys of East Breifne', p. 239, and Bernadette Cunningham, 'The anglicisation of East Breifne: The O'Reillys and the emergence of County Cavan', in Raymond Gillespie (ed.), *Cavan: essays on the history of an Irish county* (Irish Academic Press, 1995), pp. 51–72, see p. 56. Leinster lords, too, sought connections with the state; see Maginn, *Civilizing Gaelic Leinster*, p. 185.

[18] Declan M. Downey, 'Irish-European integration: the legacy of Charles V', in Judith Devlin and Howard B. Clarke (eds.), *European encounters: essays in memory of Albert Lovett* (Dublin, 2003), pp. 97–117.

remote Gaelic lordships during Henry's reign (present-day Donegal). They seemingly would have been perfect candidates for the alien wild Irish brought squinting into the fresh light of St Leger's new kingdom of Ireland. But it was hardly the action of a savage to go on pilgrimage to Rome and stop at London on his way home – as did Hugh Duff O'Donnell in 1511 – or to pen a hagiography of the family's patron saint (Colum Cille) – as did Manus O'Donnell in 1532. From Manus O'Donnell – whom Brendan Bradshaw has gone so far as to label a 'Renaissance prince'[19] – to Barnaby Fitzpatrick, whipping boy turned favoured companion of Edward VI, the Gaelic Irish nobility could look quite familiar to English eyes.

Gaelic familiarity with Anglo-continental honour culture was in part a product of Anglo-Norman influence. The self-styled 'English of Ireland' dominated Dublin politics and urbanized Ireland more generally; the three great earldoms of Kildare, Ormond and Desmond covered a vast territorial swathe from outside Dublin down to Kerry. There has been considerable debate about the extent to which this 'Englishry' adopted Gaelic social and cultural forms.[20] Unfortunately, this focus on so-called 'Gaelicization' has obscured the ways in which Ireland's Gaelic population was, if not anglicized, at least affected by and receptive to English cultural and social forms pre-1541. Native Irish interaction at the elite level with Anglo-Norman culture, and with the 'English-Irish' themselves, was profound and longstanding. Often, of course, it was violently competitive; the enclosure of 'the English Pale' in 1495 bears witness to the Crown's and Dublin's desire to hold Gaelic Ireland at bay. And yet legislation aimed at arresting the influence of Gaelic culture amongst the Englishry suggests the strength of cultural intermingling, not simply Gaelic threat. For all their 'colonial' bluster, the Statutes of Kilkenny and the anti-nativist acts of the Parliament that oversaw the creation of the Pale were simply legislative interventions intended to erect a cultural wall between native and newcomer where one barely existed in practice. Distinctly Gaelic and English cultural forms were certainly recognized and recognizable, but the reality was frequently a richly syncretic mix of the two, particularly along the border of the English-controlled lordship.[21] In

---

[19] Brendan Bradshaw, 'Manus "the Magnificent": O'Donnell as Renaissance prince', in Art Cosgrove and D. McCartney (eds.), *Studies in Irish history, presented to R. Dudley Edwards* (Dublin, 1986), pp. 15–36.

[20] An excellent, brief primer on this question is provided by the *History Ireland* debate between Steven Ellis and Kenneth Nicholls: Ellis, 'More Irish than the Irish themselves? The "Anglo-Irish" in Tudor Ireland', *History Ireland* (Spring, 1999), pp. 22–6; Nicholls, 'Worlds apart?'.

[21] See, generally, Kenneth Nicholls, *Gaelic and gaelicized Ireland in the middle ages* (Dublin, 1972), and Patrick J. Duffy, David Edwards and Liz FitzPatrick (eds.), *Gaelic Ireland c. 1250–c. 1650* (Dublin, 2001).

S. J. Connolly's elegant phrase, 'cultural frontiers were clearly defined but constantly crossed'.[22] The frequent intermarriage among Gaelic and Old English houses blurred the genealogies – ethnic as well as cultural – of progressive generations of nobles.[23] For every 'English-Irish' lord who took to speaking Irish, or even composed poetry in it as did Gearóid Íarla, the 3rd Earl of Desmond (1358–98), so there was a Gaelic lord who adopted the trappings of heraldic display or a bardic poet willing to adapt to the cultural peculiarities of an 'English-Irish' court in his search for patronage.[24]

Looking on Irish elite society, then, St Leger evidently did not see an alien other. Ireland was not a colonial theatre, and the English presence in Henrician Ireland was not some form of encounter akin to the English presence in the Americas (where, of course, the English had barely set foot).[25] Instead, St Leger looked on the Gaelic nobility as a co-optable one. Should the loyalties of its constituents be won, those of their inferiors would follow. England's Irish problem would be solved by making Ireland a kingdom and binding its inhabitants with the ties of vertical honour natural to the relationship between prince and subject; its nobility would be formally linked to England's through horizontal 'class' bonds.

II.

St Leger's belief in the co-optability of the Irish aristocracy took form in the programme that has subsequently come to be known as surrender and regrant.[26] Anxious though he was to ensure Ireland's religious conformity and loyalty to the Crown following Henry's break with Rome, the Lord Deputy did not suggest that the new kingdom should be governed through the mass appointment of English-born loyalists to the new Henrician church. Rather, he hoped to extend Crown influence by incorporating existing local Irish elites into something of a feudal

---

[22] Connolly, *Contested island*, p. 9.

[23] To take one example – the intermarriage of the Gaelic O'Rourkes with Pale elites such as the Nugents – see Cunningham, 'The anglicisation of East Breifne'.

[24] Simms, 'Guesting and feasting', and 'Bards and barons: the Anglo-Irish aristocracy and the native culture', in Robert Bartlett and Angus MacKay (eds.), *Medieval frontier societies* (Oxford, 1989), pp. 177–97.

[25] Christopher Maginn comes to a similar conclusion regarding St Leger's lord, Henry VIII: 'Much like Richard II, Henry viewed the Gaelic population more as rebels in defiance of the original conquest of Ireland than as an alien people who somehow lay outside royal control'. Maginn, *Civilizing Gaelic Leinster*, p. 74. For the provocative argument that later sixteenth century commentators on Gaelic society likened it not to New World savagery, but rather to late-medieval English aristocracy, see Debora Shuger, 'Irishmen, aristocrats, and other white barbarians', *Renaissance Quarterly* 50 (1997), pp. 494–525.

[26] On the history of the term, see Maginn, ' "Surrender and regrant" in the historiography'.

network.[27] Through surrender and regrant, Gaelic and Gaelicized lords would renounce their traditional titles and territorial claims and make a formal submission of loyalty to the king. In return, the monarch would grant them English-style titles, and they would receive their lands back by royal grant.[28] In theory, then, Ireland would be governed much in the same way as, say, the north of England or Wales were. The Crown would bolster its authority on the backs of established local elites, who in turn would see their own prestige and power rise in the localities through their association with the Crown. Law and order would be assured as Ireland's natural leaders would become invested in maintaining good relations with the Crown and, thus, in keeping the king's peace. As Michael Braddick has written, 'British state formation was a process of elite incorporation'; surrender and regrant was the programme through which this was attempted in Ireland.[29]

As novel as the constitutional change was, so too were its implications for honour. Henry well understood that making the Irish his subjects committed him to them in a way no previous English monarch had been. When Ireland was a lordship, the vertical honour bonds connecting the monarch and the Gaelic Irish were tenuous at best. In certain situations, such as in the fealty oaths taken by Gaelic lords before the persons of Henry II and Richard II, those ties were strong and explicit. But typically the Gaelic Irish lived their lives in ignorance of the king and his wishes. In return, the king was not bound to protect them as he was his English subjects, and rebellions and other civil disturbances in Ireland were less a blemish on his reputation than were domestic ones, in as much as those in revolt were not acting against their sovereign. In short, there was still an element of the 'external' to the relationship between Crown and Ireland – a distance that allowed only a limited investment of the king's personal and monarchical honour in the island's governance. This is borne out by two contemporary terms for the island's ethnic groups: the 'Englishry' and 'the king's Irish enemies'. Were Ireland made a kingdom, Henry VIII would be honour-bound to rule as justly in Ireland as he was in England.

---

[27] Feudal is of course an intensely complex term whose applicability to England in this period, let alone Ireland, is highly debatable. Nevertheless, I use it here to denote the changed relationship between king and Irish subject as one in which fealty was owed a rightful and acknowledged sovereign. On the pitfalls of the term's use, see E. A. R. Brown, 'The tyranny of a construct: feudalism and historians of medieval Europe', in L. K. Little and B. H. Rosenwein, *Debating the Middle Ages: issues and readings* (Oxford, 1998), pp. 148–69. I wish to thank Sherri Olson for this reference.
[28] On surrender and regrant generally, see Bradshaw, *Irish constitutional revolution*; Brady, *Chief governors*; Colm Lennon, *Sixteenth-century Ireland: the incomplete conquest* (New York, 1995), pp. 155–9; and Ellis, *Ireland in the age of the Tudors*.
[29] Michael Braddick, *State formation in early modern England, c. 1550–1700* (Cambridge, 2000), p. 337.

This was no small consideration, for Henry was obsessed with honour. The obsession marked the culture of his court. Surrounded by a coterie of neo-chivalric hawks, the young King famously preferred the pleasures of hunting and tilting to the minutiae of governance. The careers of Charles Brandon and Thomas Wolsey well illustrate the King's style: the martial, boon companion Brandon would be made a duke; the bookish, butcher's son Wolsey would be allowed to rise to tremendous power on account of being left largely alone in the day-to-day running of the realm. It was also an obsession that affected his relations with his nobility. Unlike his father, Henry VIII was not fearful of his nobles.[30] He did not see them as dangerous rivals who needed to be tethered to the prince's will through bonds and recognizances, and it was no coincidence that one of the young King's first moves was to allow the arrest and execution for treason of the Council Learned in the Law's pair of hard men, Richard Empson and Edmund Dudley. The distinction between royal and aristocratic blood was, of course, jealously guarded; those who crossed that line and *did* appear as rivals in Henry's eyes were brutally and swiftly crushed, most notably Edward Stafford, 3rd Duke of Buckingham, in 1521. But these were aberrant cases, and generally with Henry we see a paradigmatic example of late-medieval political theory: a strong state was one with a strong king *and* a strong nobility.[31] Crucial for the Anglo-Irish case, Henry's honour obsession played into his imperial visions. The foolhardiness of his French adventures has been attributed to his quest for chivalric honour in imitation of Henry V.[32] But if the effort to restore the French crown to an English monarch's head required feats of arms against a worthy and ancient foe, adding an Irish crown – which first had to be created – required little more than paperwork and the approval of compliant parliaments. At stake was not military glory and continental power and prestige, but rather the decidedly less alluring guardianship of a marginal island and its backwards peoples. This was work for the Wolseys of the world, not the Brandons, and the King was not very enthusiastic about it.

[30] Helen Miller, *Henry VIII and the English nobility* (New York, 1986). Henry's restoration of families reduced by his father may perhaps have served as a model for the similar elevation/restoration of his Irish 'enemies'. I thank Peter Lake for his comments on this possibility.
[31] Lander, 'The crown and the aristocracy'; Bernard (ed.), *The Tudor nobility*; Miller, *Henry VIII and the English nobility*; Christine Carpenter, *The Wars of the Roses: politics and the constitution in England, c. 1437–1509* (Cambridge, 1997); Watts, *Henry VI and the politics of kingship*.
[32] Thomas Mayer, 'On the road to 1534: the occupation of Tournai and Henry VIII's theory of sovereignty', in Dale Hoak (ed.), *Tudor political culture* (Cambridge, 1995), p. 7. See, too, Hiram Morgan, 'British policies before the British state', in Bradshaw and Morrill (eds.), *The British problem*, p. 70.

St Leger had foreseen Henry's concerns about honour and dishonour and attempted to address them pre-emptively when arguing for surrender and regrant. On the matter of establishing Irish land titles, for instance, he admitted to Henry that while it was probably bureaucratically easiest simply to confirm nobles in the lands they currently claimed, it would be more honourable first to secure a formal submission.[33] To this the King readily acceded. Thus, to take one example, Henry made it clear that before the chief of the O'Briens (whose lordship spanned much of present-day counties Clare and Limerick) could take the momentous step of attending Parliament, he was first to repair to court to receive 'some estate and honor at our hand, mete to be placed in our Parlyament; for it can neither stand with our honor, nor with state of our Parliament, to have any man placed there as a Pere, but he have, in dede, thestate of a Pere, by the right cours and order of our lawes'.[34] Henry did, however, have periodic misgivings about granting lands to the Gaelic Irish at all. Sensitive to the fact that as king all Irish land was ultimately his, he insisted to St Leger that it be 'wayed, what dishonor it maye be to Us' should he grant out land of 'our oune inheritance to those which have unjustly intruded and usurped the same'. To this he reiterated his perennial fiscal concerns, insisting that the Irish council should enter into no 'pacte or indenture with any Yrisheman of name and estimacion' before they know what rents or subsidies that subject was willing and able to pay.[35] Extending the monarchical honour circle to include a newly created nobility thus bore something of the quality of maintaining an affinity: the honour of the one at the top was very much affected by the status, means and honour of those below. Thus, Henry's monarchical honour was dependent not only upon the size of his 'retinue' but upon the honour of its individual members too.

Using Henry's own language, St Leger and the Irish council assured the King that they had indeed 'wayed' his honour in determining which leases to approve.[36] Moreover, the Deputy argued from a logical standpoint that, once made subjects, the Irish would respond loyally toward the Crown simply because they would now be integrated into the vertical honour bonds connecting prince and subject; they would, he wrote, 'do ther dewtoes for the honour of your Highness'.[37] St Leger would go one step further and inject a little martial glamour into the otherwise custodial dullness of the kingship of Ireland. He baldly flattered his honour-obsessed

---

[33] SP Hen. VIII, III, p. 267.   [34] Ibid., p. 368.   [35] Ibid., pp. 331–2.   [36] Ibid., pp. 406–7.
[37] Ibid., p. 285. On the political value of Henry's change of title, see Ellis, *Ireland in the age of the Tudors*, p. 151.

prince by declaring that not even Richard II, who had travelled to Ireland in person accompanied by 20,000 men 'in wages, to his exceding charges', had had more 'notable Yrishemen … summytt themselves to hym, then, to Hys Graces greate honour and perpetuall renomme, shall, with moche lesse diffycultie and charges, resorte to his Highnes into England, to summytt themselffes, yf yt so may stande with his high pleasure to have them so to doo, and to be entertayned accordingly'.[38] Having already convinced the King of the benefit of making Ireland a kingdom, the Lord Deputy here sealed the case for surrender and regrant by audaciously attending to what he perceived to be his master's chief concerns about this radical shift in Irish policy: financial gain, ease of execution, promotion of Irish loyalty and the promise of personal/monarchical glory.

The programme realized immediate, and some rather spectacular, successes. The first ennobled was Brian MacGillapatrick, created baron of Upper Ossory;[39] the greatest was Conn Bacach O'Neill, chief of the mighty O'Neills, who made his submission in London in 1542 and returned to Ulster as the Earl of Tyrone. The O'Neill case was a fraught one, however, and reveals the King's personal investment in the process. This most powerful of Gaelic lords only conceded to submission following a difficult military campaign. Once he had done so he then angered Henry by requesting to be styled Earl of Ulster. Unlike the newly created heraldic titles granted other Irish nobles – to take an example, the earldom of Thomond bestowed on the O'Brien lords – the earldom of Ulster was an extant, historical title to which Henry laid claim.[40] The initial willingness of St Leger and his council to entertain granting O'Neill this title roused Henry to remind them to 'hensforth the more depely waye our honor' in making arrangements with Irish lords. Once provoked by O'Neill's seemingly inappropriate demands, Henry carried on to warn that should the Irish push too hard 'at their submissions, our honor maye not susteyn it, but shal enforce Us to loke upon them in such sort, as shalbe to the exemple of all others'.[41] In other words, the Irish should start acting as loyal, submissive subjects from the outset of negotiations or risk being the victims of exemplary royal

---

[38] SP Hen. VIII, III, p. 417. A later example of this occurred in 1549. Discussing the efforts to effect the submission of O'Connor of Offaly, St Leger and the Irish council wrote how the 'simple submission of O'Connor cannot but tend to the king's honour'. *CSPI*, 1, p. 99.

[39] Not all surrender and regrant arrangements brought a peerage title. The Leinsterman Turlough O'Toole was in fact the first to enter into such an agreement, but was not ennobled. For a detailed description of O'Toole's experience with the policy, see Maginn, *Civilizing Gaelic Leinster*, pp. 65–76.

[40] Connolly, *Contested island*, p. 43.   [41] SP Hen. VIII, III, pp. 366, 368.

punishment.[42] Tough talk from the monarch aside, the programme continued to attract the cream of Gaelic society. 'English-Irish' nobles also availed themselves of its provisions: whereas the Earl of Desmond took the occasion to renew his dynasty's long links to the Crown, the head of the Galway Burkes travelled to London to be created Earl of Clanricard.

There are a number of factors for the programme's effectiveness. Undoubtedly many made the simple Machiavellian calculation that resisting it would bring trouble with an aggrandizing state, whereas going along would most likely not alter life too greatly since the ability of the Crown to oversee local affairs was minimal. As Bernadette Cunningham has written, the ceremonial aspects of surrender were intended to appeal to 'the concept of honour within Gaelic society'.[43] With the pageantry complete, so David Edwards has argued, a newly ennobled Gaelic lord could carry on as before while adopting only the most superficial of appearances of anglicization.[44] But we should not discount voluntary interest. Those who made their submissions tended not to slink away to rule as before in the fastnesses of remote lordships. Gaelic attendance at successive parliaments, for example, demonstrated that these men believed themselves worthy of inclusion in this novel intra-realm honour circle. The programme was also structurally well suited for incorporating members of a kinship-based social structure. This was, of course, an experiment in social engineering that sought fundamental changes to Gaelic and Gaelicized society and culture.[45] But many of the programme's innovations were likely not overly shocking because they mapped so closely onto traditional patterns and practices of this lineage society.[46] The education of Irish elites traditionally involved spending a period during adolescence in the homes of other noble families. After this period of fosterage, these young men returned home both wiser in the arts of governance and better connected politically. State efforts to see

[42] Helen Miller's comments on the English context would also stand for the Irish: 'In the eyes of Henry VIII a grant of nobility was as much a call to further effort as a reward for past services.' Miller, *Henry VIII and the English nobility*, p. 34.
[43] Cunningham, 'The anglicisation of East Breifne', p. 60.
[44] David Edwards, 'Collaboration without anglicisation: the MacGiollapadraig lordship and Tudor reform', in Duffy, et al. (eds.), *Gaelic Ireland*, pp. 77–96.
[45] Brady writes that St Leger was interested in creating a 'king's party' and that his popularity in Ireland was 'founded in the first place not on some vague aspirations towards long-term cultural transformation, but on widespread fraud and a conspiracy of remunerative silence'. Regardless of the tactics used to establish a new Irish peerage, surrender and regrant logically involved the emergence of a novel British elite culture. Brady, *Chief governors*, p. 40.
[46] On the compatibility of kinship networks and notions of kin bonds across cultures, see Brooks, *Captives and cousins*, chapter 1.

these youths schooled in the Pale or England, and proposals to have them marry into English families, may have been culturally radical, but they mimicked the rites of fosterage: in both cases the young men were taken out of their localities, given practical tutelage in living as nobility, and then were returned home bearing new loyalties owed their fostering family or the family into which they had been fitted. Just as fosterage tended to create multi-generational bonds between families, so too did removal to elite households in England or the Pale. The classic example is provided by Hugh O'Neill, the 2nd Earl of Tyrone, with his connections to the New English Hovendons (with whom he lived during adolescence) and to the house of Essex (who was an early patron), and his 'diplomatic' marriage to Mabel Bagenal, daughter of his bête noir Henry Bagenal, marshal of the queen's army. Surrender and regrant was not, therefore, an unequivocally modern-looking, reformist attempt at cultural construction; it was also very much a state-driven integration of two societies sharing profound cultural, social and structural similarities. They also knew great differences, of course, but it was St Leger's genius to try to overcome those by playing to the commonalities.

Those Irish lords who did successfully avail themselves of the pro-gramme of surrender and regrant became partners in a web of honour at whose centre was the monarch (the fount of all honour) and which connected the nobilities of England and Ireland. With that came an abrupt change in the exercise of law-and-order. A certain amount of unruliness was acceptable in a lordship; in a kingdom it was not, especially if those behind the disturbances were among the recently ennobled. Violence instigated by Irish nobles was thus recast from marcher chaos – frustrating but not surprising or necessarily worrisome to London – to insurrection and a direct affront to the sovereign who had overseen the agitators' social elevation. As the fall of the Duke of Buckingham in 1521 or the fate of the Pilgrimage of Grace's leaders in 1536 made clear, anti-monarchical demonstrations by Henry's subjects were not to be countenanced. After 1541, physical-force diplomacy, which had been so long the normative behaviour amongst Gaelic and Gaelicized elites, would come to attract the unwanted attention of a government which saw it as rebellion, pure and simple. Reflecting on the submissions of O'Neill, O'Brien, Burke and the others who were now attending Parliament, the King declared his gladness to favour them and, assuming their continued obedience, his hope to increase that favour. But should they 'attempt the contrary, and abuse our clemencye nowe showed unto them, We shalbe enforced to considre them, as to our honor apperteyneth'.[47] If the King was now bound in honour to protect his Irish subjects, the defence of honour also opened the door for him to punish them for conduct previously deemed unremarkable in Irish elite society. Thus, the establishment of surrender and regrant carried with it equally great possibilities for stability and instability in Anglo-Irish relations.

III.

In attempting to assess the programme's effects, we must look at England as well as Ireland. The making of Ireland as a kingdom in 1541 and the creation of an Irish peerage have been typically discussed in terms of their effects on Ireland alone. But the constitutional change of 1541 brought significant change to England too. It made it part of a true multiple monarchy (the Henrician fantasy of the French crown being exactly that, a fantasy), and nearly doubled the territory under direct control of the Crown.[48] As for surrender and regrant, it was part of a larger Crown effort to restructure the aristocracies in both realms. In 1536, Henry VIII oversaw the passage of an 'Act of Absentees' by which Englishmen were forced to abandon lands and titles in Ireland, and Irishmen to do the same with any English holdings.[49] In the opinion of a later, if anonymous, English commentator, it was the Kildare Revolt of 1534 that spurred the act. Stung by the revolt, so the analysis went, Henry lashed out at those English nobles who retained Irish lands but did not reside there, arguing that in the absence of honourable men at the top of the social hierarchy, Ireland was left to be overrun by the wild Irish.[50] The same argument could hardly work in reverse, and so depriving those in the Irish peerage of their English holdings was, in Richard Hadsor's 1604 'Discourse', chalked up to previous attainders and to the vague catch-all, 'other means'.[51] Chief among the policy's victims were the 'English-Irish' Earls of Ormond, forced to surrender their claim to

[47] SP Hen. VIII, III, p. 418.

[48] Steven Ellis prefers the term 'multinational state' for this period, arguing that it was not a 'multiple monarchy'. Ellis, *Ireland in the age of the Tudors*, ix; and 'Civilizing Northumberland: representations of Englishness in the Tudor state', *Journal of Historical Sociology* 12 (1999), p. 104.

[49] David B. Quinn, 'The bills and statutes of the Irish Parliaments of Henry VII and Henry VIII', *Analecta Hibernica* 10 (1941), p. 154.

[50] Lincoln's Inn, Hale MS 83, fol. 296r.

[51] Joseph McLaughlin, 'New light on Richard Hadsor, II: select documents XLVII: Richard Hadsor's "Discourse" on the Irish state, 1604', *Irish Historical Studies* xxx (1997), p. 349.

the earldom of Wiltshire,[52] and the English Earls of Shrewsbury, who had to relinquish the title of Earls of Waterford.[53] This reordering of the nobility along strictly national lines was driven in part by reformist intentions, the aim being to establish a resident, loyal ruling caste to help forestall a repeat of the Kildare ascendancy. But it also provided Henry with significant new lands and titles to be bestowed at his favour. While not the windfall that the dissolution of the monasteries was, this decision nevertheless strengthened significantly the arsenal of the King's largesse.[54]

Whatever the disappointments of men like Ormond and Shrewsbury, the real losers in this transition were those Gaelic Irish who saw, at least in theory, their claims to local lordship permanently quashed by the adoption of primogeniture. Gaelic succession was always problematic in that the successful candidate could come from that wide network of claimants collectively known as the *deirbfhine*. Struggles between rival claimants were a perpetual destabilizing force in Gaelic society.[55] The shift to primo-geniture greatly reduced the number of potential claimants to lordship, and thus simplified the chain of succession. Simultaneously, however, it reduced a great number of Gaelic and Gaelicized elites – second- and bastard-sons, members of collateral branches, and so on – to permanent second-rank status. Thus, in solving one set of problems, surrender and regrant created a host of new ones. On the one hand, those now excluded from the paths to local power were always a threat to press their claims in opposition to the preferences of the Crown and its newly minted Anglo-Gaelic aristocrats. On the other hand, even when those men acquiesced in the power transferral, they could create problems for the newly entitled elites by attempting to reach their own accommodations directly with the Crown. Fearing they would be reduced to mere vassals of overmighty Irish earls, whose authority would not be checked by the competition for succession from the *deir-bfhine*, many of these lesser elites sought to bypass the newly enhanced authority of their traditional clan chief and arrange for holding properties

---

[52] This is discussed in Trinity College Dublin (TCD) MS 842: Rothe's biography of Ormond. See, too, Edwards, *Ormond lordship*, p. 143.

[53] Hale Ms 83 deals with the controversy pitting Shrewsbury and Lumley over the right to bear the name Waterford in their list of titles. There it is noted that the present Earl of Shrewsbury could not lay claim to the earldom of Waterford since his immediate predecessor had not done so, 'it being conceived that the said honour was taken away by the said statute of 28 Henry 8'. p. 296v.

[54] A possibility that would be exploited not by a monarch but by a royal favourite, Buckingham, in the early seventeenth century. This will be discussed in Chapter 6, below.

[55] It should be noted, however, that Katherine Simms argues that the problem (i.e., the cause of violence) was not the succession system itself and its flaws, but rather the fact that land-tenure was by overlordship and not ownership, and thus had to be defended, for if taken it was lost. Simms, *From kings to warlords*, p. 59.

directly from the Crown. Where this was successful it essentially undercut the authority invested in those recently entitled through surrender and regrant and left them feeling aggrieved. As Steven Ellis points out, St Leger saw primogeniture as a weakness for the programme's adoption, and could only hold out hope that by the third generation a pattern would have been firmly established.[56]

The politics of the O'Neill lordship over the course of the sixteenth century offer a good case study in the promises and problems of surrender and regrant for Gaelic Ireland. Nicholas Canny has written that Conn O'Neill's agreement with the Crown in 1542 was a 'direct onslaught on both the Gaelic laws of property and succession'.[57] The implications of this fiddling with tradition would play out dramatically in the struggle between his sons, Matthew and Shane, for the title. Matthew had received the state's backing to inherit the earldom upon Conn's death and, moreover, sought to secure the title in perpetuity for his heirs. Thus, cut from the line of succession, Shane murdered Matthew in 1558 and had himself declared the O'Neill by election of the freeholders. In spite of its efforts to bring him to heel,[58] the Crown eventually accepted his submission in 1562, thereby legitimating his claim to the O'Neillship, albeit still withholding the earldom which he greatly desired. Nevertheless, Shane attempted to benefit from the chaos brought to Ulster politics by the Tudor constitutional revolution and aggressively sought to increase his authority at the expense of his family and of neighbouring lordships. Although his rapacity served to disrupt greatly the region's politics, he was more respectful of Gaelic tradition than his brother Matthew, in that Shane never sought to have his sons installed in the lordship after him. Nevertheless, to quote Canny once more, 'the cancer that Matthew had introduced was eating into the very heart of the body politic'.[59] This, combined with the sort of expansionist aggression exemplified by Shane O'Neill, ensured that by the 1580s, relations between the various septs of Tyrone were in complete disarray. Eventually, the instability of the O'Neill lordship, occasioned by these succession struggles which were supposed to have been short-circuited

---

[56] Ellis, *Ireland in the age of the Tudors*, p. 155.
[57] Nicholas Canny, 'Hugh O'Neill, earl of Tyrone, and the changing face of Gaelic Ulster', *Studia Hibernica* 10 (1970), p. 19. See also Canny, 'Taking sides in early modern Ireland: the case of Hugh O'Neill, earl of Tyrone', in Vincent Carey and Uta Lotz-Huemann (eds.), *Taking sides? Colonial and confessional mentalités in early modern Ireland* (Dublin, 2003), pp. 94–105; and Morgan, *Tyrone's rebellion*.
[58] Lord Deputy Sussex oversaw two unsuccessful and costly offensives against Shane in 1560 and 1561. He would try once again after Shane's surrender, but with similar results.
[59] Canny, 'Hugh O'Neill', p. 23.

by surrender and regrant, allowed an outside candidate, Hugh O'Neill, to claim the earldom in 1587. Once made earl, Hugh, using Matthew's precedent, attempted to move Ulster more into line with English tradition by favouring his close family and direct descendants. But in so doing, he rankled the collaterals and sublords to such an extent that even at the height of his power he could barely control them. Surrender and regrant was supposed to have brought stability and peace to an endemically violent Gaelic society. Instead, it so disturbed the traditional socio-political fabric of Ulster that eventually only force could hold the lordship together. Violence would thus remain a 'constitutional' necessity in the 'reformed' Ireland.

Sticking with the politics in the vicinity of the O'Neill territories, the case of the Maguires of Fermanagh, particularly the early career of Cú Chonnacht Maguire, may serve as an example of the strained relations between the O'Neill lords, their erstwhile subordinates, and the Crown. While his elder brother Seaán Maguire held the lordship of Fermanagh, Cú Chonnacht attached himself to Shane O'Neill, whose death in 1567 left him somewhat at the mercy of Toirdhealbhach Luineach, the successful claimant to the O'Neill lordship. Maguire complained to Dublin of Toirdhealbhach Luineach's conduct towards him, arguing that it contravened an order of the Lord Deputy Sir Henry Sidney meant to maintain the peace between them. The Dublin authorities were willing to overlook Cú Chonnacht's recent attachment to the hated Shane O'Neill in their interest in seeing that neither chaos nor the O'Neills would engulf the important border territory of Fermanagh. Thus, Lord Deputy Sir Henry Sidney wrote in December 1575 that 'O'Donnell … and McGuire, Lord of Fermanagh, who wrote humbly unto me, live wealthfully and deny not to pay rent and service to her Majestie so as they may be discharged from the exactions of others'.[60] Not only did Cú Chonnacht complain often of O'Neill's advances, he also begged that his letters be kept secret for fear that Toirdhealbhach Luineach would destroy him were he to find out about them.[61] In the Maguire lordship, as in the O'Neill lordship to which it was traditionally beholden, surrender and regrant had proven more destabilizing than otherwise.

But by no means was the situation similarly bleak in all provincial lordships. The cases of the O'Brien Earls of Thomond and the Burke Earls of Clanricard are ones of greater long-term success. Each faced significant

---

[60] Quoted in Greene (ed. and trans.), *Duanaire Mhéig Uidhir: the poembook of Cú Chonnacht Mág Uidhir, Lord of Fermanagh 1566–1589* (Dublin, 1991), p. vii.
[61] Ibid. On earlier Maguire appeals to Henry VIII for support against the O'Neills, see Bradshaw, 'Cromwellian reform', p. 83.

difficulties in making the crossover to inclusion in a 'British' peerage. The case of Thomond is particularly instructive of the sort of negotiation that could come under the heading of surrender and regrant. Although the grant of the earldom was to one Murrough O'Brien, the Crown accepted the claim of the tanist (heir apparent) Donough, Murrough's nephew, to the earldom. When Donough sought to end any future such negotiations by making an agreement with Edward VI that the land and title would pass to his descendants in perpetuity, he found himself at war with his brothers. Though he was killed within a year of ascending to the peerage, his son, Connor, would successfully take up the earldom. Doing so, however, would require the assistance of English troops at the behest of the Lord Deputy, the Earl of Sussex, in 1558. From that point on, however, the Thomond earldom existed as a model of cultural convergence. The 4th Earl, Donough, Connor's eldest son, was raised Protestant in England as a ward of the court. He would distinguish himself by anglicizing his territory and vigorously working to put down the revolt of the Ulster lords O'Neill and O'Donnell at the end of Elizabeth's reign. The Burke situation was slightly more fraught. The 2nd Earl – known as Richard Sassanach (Englishman) – was a willing anglicizer who encroached in the name of the state on his neighbours' patrimonies. Although he held the earldom for nearly forty years, his sons fought bitterly over the inheritance to the great dismay of Castle and Crown. Matters would stabilize with the succession of his eldest son Ulicke. In turn, his son Richard would, like Donough O'Brien, complete his rise in British noble circles through his role in defeating O'Neill and O'Donnell. Early seventeenth-century Irish society and politics would be largely dominated by the Earls of Thomond and Clanricard, both of whom would also purchase estates in England.[62]

Nor were the problems that plagued the O'Neill and Maguire lordships in the mid- to late-sixteenth century of Irish origin alone. The government too was partly responsible since it proved incapable of producing a consistent policy for dealing with its new Irish subjects or the region more generally. To take but one example, Shane O'Neill's attempts to make accommodations with the Crown were frequently scuttled by factional interests at court. As Ciaran Brady has argued, '[A]t the back of the conflict between Sussex and Shane there lay … no crude confrontation between the English conquistador and the native chief, but a question of how the O'Neill was to be fitted into the reformed and anglicized Ulster envisaged

---

[62] The best study of these important lordships remains Bernadette Cunningham's MA thesis: 'Political and social change in the lordships of Clanricard and Thomond, 1569–1641' (unpublished MA thesis, U.C.G., 1979).

in the process of surrender and regrant'.[63] Thus, the problem with integrating the Irish into some sort of anglicized polity loyal to the English crown lay as much with the inability of the Crown and its representatives to play by their own rules of reform as it did with the socio-cultural dissonance that those rules created amongst assorted *deirbfhine*. In short, trying to work out in practice the changes that surrender and regrant brought to Anglo-Irish culture, society and politics was a difficult one for all parties. Tragically, of course, the effects of that difficulty would fall almost exclusively on the Irish. But it was not their cultural otherness or unwillingness to adapt to new modes of civility that lay exclusively behind it.

IV.

Surrender and regrant was not an unqualified success, but it seemed to offer a way in which some sort of cultural convergence on an elite level could be effected that would, in turn, usher in a version of political and social reform in line with the centralizing schemes of the Crown and amenable to the self-interests of the principal lines of Ireland's noble families. It continued to do so over the course of the sixteenth century, and the politics of honour that undergirded it would remain vital to Anglo-Irish relations. This claim might seem to fly in the face of not only historiographical convention, but also historical reality. Historians from the seventeenth century on have assured us that the hardening of socio-cultural, even ethnic or proto-racial, difference was the defining feature of sixteenth-century relations between the realms. Certainly with the Crown's gradual move away from assimilative to coercive measures, Ireland went from brave new feudal world to local site of the 'darker side of the Renaissance'.[64] Following Elizabeth's excommunication in 1570, socio-cultural tension was exacerbated by the addition of confessional difference. And yet, surrender and regrant lived on. In spite of the increasingly common language of inherent Irish treachery and savagery that English officials used to justify innovations in local government and the plantations, and the fact that it ceased to be a recognizable 'policy' after St Leger's deputyship, surrender and regrant remained in the government's arsenal as an ad hoc negotiating tool to be used with individual lords. Nearly every deputy, over the remainder of the sixteenth century, made such

---

[63] Ciaran Brady, *Shane O'Neill* (Dundalk, 1996), p. 42.

[64] The phrase is Walter Mignolo's, coined to describe European destruction of new world cultural systems. Mignolo, *The darker side of the Renaissance: literacy, territoriality, and colonization* (Ann Arbor, 1995). On English linguistic imperialism and culture war in Ireland see Patricia Palmer, *Language and conquest in early modern Ireland* (Cambridge, 2001).

arrangements and accepted Irish elites from all four provinces into the peerage. One of the major alterations in state strategy was to focus on the lesser lords and use new settlements to scale back the perceived overly generous grants made during St Leger's tenure; if the 1540s saw the creation of Irish earls, the 1560s forward witnessed the making of viscounts and barons.[65] By century's end, all the Gaelic overlords (excepting the O'Donnells) and numerous lesser ones had entered into such agreements.

Surrender and regrant's continued viability, and thus the goal of an inter-realm governing elite, was allowed in part because it was no more a 'policy' over the latter half of the sixteenth century than was plantation. Both might be better considered as recurring features of policy, deployable according to local circumstances, and closely linked ones at that.[66] These were not diametrically opposed approaches – the one favouring reform, the latter coercion – for it was typically transgression of the former that triggered the latter. The first concerted colonization effort in Leix-Offaly was made possible by the raiding activities of two midland septs, the O'Mores and the O'Connors, against the Pale and the lands of their traditional enemies, the Butler Earls of Ormond. Such activity in the new kingdom of Ireland was no longer border violence but rebellion. As in England, rebellion led to governmental confiscation of rebels' lands. The seizure of the septs' territories, and the eventual construction of the fortified plantation towns of Maryborough and Philipstown, was not the realization of long-planned efforts to root out savages[67] but very much an attempt to punish those whose rebellion had violated the honour of the monarch.[68] And while the experiment was carried out in a time when some governmental figures were expressing an interest in applying classical imperial models to Ireland, its chief overseer, the Lord Deputy Sir James Croft, did not advocate the project as the vanguard of a general plan for Ireland. Indeed, Gaelic Irish proprietors were amongst those who received plots

---

[65] Brady, *Chief governors*, p. 73; Canny, *Elizabethan conquest*, pp. 50, 105. Maginn cautions that Sidney's rash of agreements should not be seen as mirror copies of the arrangements made in the early 1540s. Maginn, '"Surrender and regrant" in the historiography', p. 965.

[66] See Canny's comment that both paths to civility were being pursued in Ireland: by force in Ulster and by persuasion elsewhere. Canny, *Elizabethan conquest*, p. 64. See, too, Brady who notes Sussex's urging Mary in 1557 for both a return to surrender and regrant and expanded plantation. Brady, *Chief governors*, p. 72.

[67] Government claims of these families' 'barbarism' look little more than rhetorical anyway once we remember that the O'Connors sent a representative to the French court seeking aid in reclaiming their authority. Connolly, *Contested island*, p. 116.

[68] This appears to follow many of the classic features of Crown crackdown on an honour revolt. See Mervyn James, 'The concept of order and the Northern Rising of 1569', *P&P* 60 (1973), pp. 49–83.

in the plantation.[69] The greatest Tudor plantation, that in Munster, also resulted from dispossession following noble revolt. But if the Leix-Offaly project dispossessed lesser Gaelic nobility, that in Munster ousted one of the great Old English grandees, the Earl of Desmond. Desmond's rebellion has gone down in history as the first burst of the new, revolutionary ideologies of faith and fatherland. At its inception, however, the earl's frustrations were owed to status and privilege having been denied; at its explosive conclusion they were expanded to include matters of religious and political self-determination. At no time did he bear the torch of socio-cultural defence against English 'civility'; his demands on the Crown may have been enraging, but they were always comprehensible.[70] As Nicholas Canny has written, the English could not conceive of power without nobility, and thus Crown efforts across the sixteenth century were aimed at curbing, not destroying, native aristocratic power. Local reaction against that 'curbing' took the form of 'feudal' rebellion, not colonial 'total' war.[71]

Nor did Irish elites spurn surrender and regrant arrangements, or the honour culture they sought to construct, in the wake of the Leix-Offaly plantation. There emerged, of course, a Gaelic equivalent to the discourse of civility that informed the colonial schemes of Lord Deputy Croft. Bardic poets began mid-century to decry the settler's new ways and to equate noble honour with adherence to strict Gaelic cultural forms. The two best-known instances of this are the anonymous 'Fúbún fúibh, a shluagh Gaoidheal', which encouraged rejection of the new Irish peerage and a more general pan-Gaelic resistance to English expansion, and Laoiseach Mac an Bháird's 'A fhir ghlacas a ghalldacht', which lampooned the aping of English ways by a member of the Gaelic gentry.[72] These poems are something like native versions of the Statutes of Kilkenny in their demonization of an alien other and their calls for the defence of cultural purity. But as with the framers of the Statutes of Kilkenny, and Croft too, their authors protest too much: what seems to have terrified all of them was not the presence of

---

[69] As Braddick writes, 'In general rebellion in sixteenth-century Ireland was less a rejection of alien rule than an expression of magnate politics akin to the rebellions of Tudor England. It was supported by personal followings and informed by ideals of honour emphasizing personal ties rather than the virtues of loyalty to state.' Braddick, *State formation*, p. 387.

[70] Anthony McCormack, *The earldom of Desmond 1463–1583: the decline and crisis of a feudal lordship* (Dublin, 2005), pp. 145–92.

[71] Canny, *Elizabethan conquest*, pp. 142, 80; Brady, *Chief governors*, pp. 52, 172.

[72] Nicholas Canny suggests that 'Fúbún fúibh' may in fact date from the seventeenth century. Canny, *Making Ireland British*, p. 421.

competing cultural norms per se, but the 'degenerative' willingness to favour those novel norms on the part of those they felt should have known better.[73] And, indeed, Irish lords did not simply acquiesce to surrender and regrant agreements, but sought them out and believed they were in positions to bargain terms.[74] The great example is the O'Donnells. Successive chiefs pursued negotiations with the Crown to convert their traditional titles to English-style ones. No deal was struck, but the fact that the conversation was pursued by both sides, spanning numerous regime changes in London, Dublin and Donegal, suggests that in spite of the hardening of socio-cultural difference, and the emergence of exclusivist notions of faith and fatherland, there were plenty of people who thought there was still much to compete for in the new polity called into being by the emergent Tudor multiple monarchy.

This chapter began by discussing a historiography fixated upon Gaelic-English cultural differences; it has argued that those differences have been drawn too starkly and that the reality in sixteenth century Anglo-Irish elite culture was one of blending and bricolage. Anglicising hard men could still foster their children to native families, as in the case of Sir Nicholas Malby; 'collaborating' Irish lords could still govern their 'bona fide' Gaelic towns armed with Crown charters while styling themselves barons.[75] Ciaran Brady has written that '[m]uch to the frustration of modern historians, the Tudors were, for the most part, remarkably incurious about Gaelic Ireland'.[76] If in fact these people were as strange and terrifying to English eyes as the prevailing literature tells us, then that lack of interest does indeed seem remarkable. Perhaps the surprise lies with our own anachronistic expectations: conditioned as we are by centuries of racialized propaganda from Spenser to *Punch*, we expect the English experience in Ireland to mimic that in the Americas, India, or the South Pacific. Quite possibly at the heart of what Brady described was not that the English lacked curiosity, however, but that

---

[73] On the practical failures of a faith in English cultural supremacy see Canny, 'The permissive frontier: social control in English settlements in Ireland and Virginia, 1550–1650', in K. R. Andrews, N. P. Canny and P. E. H. Hair (eds.), *The Westward Enterprise: English activities in Ireland, the Atlantic, and America 1480–1650* (Detroit, 1979), pp. 17–44.

[74] Canny points out that few answered these 'calls for purification'. *Making Ireland British*, p. 136. Indeed, Christopher Maginn posits that some Leinster elites went through something of a process of 'reGaelicization' in the later sixteenth century not on account of such bardic browbeating, but rather out of frustration with the Crown's seeming unwillingness to honour the promise of surrender and regrant. *Civilizing Gaelic Leinster*, pp. 187–90.

[75] Edwards, 'Collaboration without anglicisation'.   [76] Brady, *Chief governors*, p. 245.

the Irish did not strike them as curious. As Willy Maley has argued, proximity rather than distance may have been the most important factor driving English-Irish relations, and therefore that the act of forgetting served as the once-and-future colonists' primary tool in making the proximate alien.[77] It was the cultural affinities between Gael and Gall that allowed the Crown to envision a process of elite formation for 'common social and political interests'[78] and at the same time allowed the Gaelic Irish and 'English–Irish' to go along with it. The active forgetting by the government and its 'men on the spot' of those points of similarity allowed the language of barbarity to dominate the relationship.

The story of sixteenth-century Anglo–Irish relations, then, is not simply one of the painful working out of cultural encounter; it is also one of two societies losing touch with significant points of contact. Forgetfulness was never total, however. Appeals to status and honour would continue to afford the means to cut across divisive lines of religion, ethnicity, culture and nation. Forgetting was also something of a luxury of power. The Irish had more to gain by remembering the points of contact that had made surrender and regrant possible. How they defined honour and nobility in the midst of New English ascendancy is the subject of the next chapter.

---

[77] Willy Maley, 'Nationalism and revisionism: ambiviolences and dissensus', in Scott Brewster, Virginia Crossman, Fiona Becket and David Alderson (eds.), *Ireland in proximity: history, gender and space* (London, 1999), pp. 12–25; Maley, ' "The name of the country I have forgotten": remembering and dismembering in Sir Henry Sidney's Irish *Memoir* (1583)', in Thomas Herron and Michael Potterton (eds.), *Ireland in the Renaissance c. 1540–1660* (Dublin, 2007), pp. 52–73.

[78] Brady, *Chief governors*, p. 44.

CHAPTER 2

Gaelic honour in Tudor Ireland

In 1553, Domhnaill Mac Bruaideadha, latest in a long line of Mac Bruaideadha poets who served the O'Briens, composed a poem to mark Connor O'Brien's elevation as Earl of Thomond. Like all such Irish court encomia, this would have been performed during the ceremony accompanied by music. In it he noted the attendance of New and Old English elites: Thomas Butler, 10th Earl of Ormond; Richard, 2nd Earl of Clanricard; Gerald Desmond, 15th Earl of Desmond; and even the Lord Deputy Sussex himself. The occasion was a 'brave gathering of Goill and Gaoidhil', the arrival of whom was preceded by 'banners of different colours'.[1] The poem is curious for the confusion it displays over just what the event was and what was the nature of the authority that Connor was to wield. It appears like the inauguration odes Irish poets traditionally wrote to Gaelic chiefs; but this, of course, was no installation of a chief to a lordship, but rather the conferral of an earldom.[2] And yet Mac Bruaideadha, when answering his own rhetorical question of why had these worthies descended upon Limerick, answered that they had come to witness the appointment of the 'right one as King over the plain of Tuadhmhumha'.[3] He did not ignore the fact that this was a new sort of ceremony, however, for he later recited that Connor would, in fact, have been called O'Brien were it not for the discontent of the Dal Cais.[4] Presumably he meant here that Connor would be accepted by the extended O'Brien family (the Dal Cais) as the rightful inheritor of both the earldom and the lordship were there no contention

---

[1] Lambert McKenna (ed. and trans.), *Aithdioghluim dána*, 2 vols (Dublin, 1935 and 1939), poem 27, stanzas 7 and 11, pp. 63–4. For discussion of this and ensuing poems I will be using the relevant editor's translation. Exceptions will be noted.

[2] The poem's generic novelty has been commented on by a number of scholars. Leerssen writes that it 'reads like a court calendar in *The Times* rather than like a bardic inauguration ode'. Leerssen, *The contention of the bards (Iomarbhagh na bhFileadh) and its place in Irish political and literary history* (London, 1994), p. 37. Ellis sees it as something wholly different from inauguration verse. Ellis, *Ireland in the age of the Tudors*, p. 257.

[3] McKenna, *Aithdioghluim*, stanza 19, p. 19.   [4] Ibid., stanza 30, p. 65.

44

about the latter. But, of course, there was and so it was only the former authority that went unquestioned. Undeterred, Mac Bruaideadha then went on to announce that Connor's installation as Earl of Thomond would bring fertility to the land.[5] A customary conceit attached to Gaelic inaugurations; this trope was deployed here in spite of the fact that the object of the panegyric was not a Gaelic king but merely the uncontested holder of an English-style earldom, as the poet himself had already acknowledged. We could perhaps see this poem purely as an example of trying to square new anglicized authority with traditional Gaelic socio-cultural expectations were it not for the last stanza in which the poet finally refers to Connor as an earl. He does so, however, in a way that points to the primacy of local dynastic concerns over larger ones of social and political transformation in the wake of Tudor reform, for he wrote that 'any from the North who do not come [to witness the ceremony] will be full of fear for our earl'.[6] Mac Bruaideadha seems to have been confused over a number of things: the ceremony he described, the nature of Connor's power and place, and what function his poem was to serve.[7]

Mac Bruaideadha's apparent confusion is understandable. Surrender and regrant had created a complicated mosaic of authority and political legitimacy in Ireland. On the one hand, the Crown sent mixed signals in its social engineering: was primogeniture a necessary characteristic of the new Irish peerage? Did surrender and regrant arrangements hold when English monarchs changed? On the other hand, the Irish themselves could now mobilize any one of a number of languages of legitimacy in their pursuit of power: Murrough O'Brien could latch on to primogeniture, his nephew Donough could appeal to the contractual nature of the original agreement, Domhnall could resort to arms in the traditional manner of Gaelic succession. Mac Bruaideadha, for his part, was representative of a class that, as the arbiters of political legitimacy, social status and noble honour, sought to make sense of this chaos; his poem, with its pastiche of the new and old, was merely one example of how members of that class attempted to balance change with continuity when doing so.

One constant in all this political, social and eventually religious upheaval was the importance of noble status and the honour that went with it. The frequency with which discussions of honour appear in Gaelic writings from 1541–1600 – even as Ireland devolved from kingdom to colony – demonstrates the concept's

---

[5] Ibid., stanza 31, p. 65. [6] Ibid., stanza 33, p. 65.
[7] His relationship to the Earl, too, would have caused confusion. For the Earl, and his successors, both patronized and persecuted the poets – Connor himself having three hanged in 1572. Ellis, *Ireland in the age of the Tudors*, p. 257.

continued importance in Anglo-Irish culture and politics. What remains to be determined, however, was whether Gaelic commentators altered their notions of honour to fit a new British context of elite politics or simply defined it as they had always done.

This chapter explores some of the ways in which Irish intellectuals reworked traditional notions of Gaelic honour to fit rapidly and radically changing social, cultural, political and religious circumstances. It focuses on annals and bardic poetry and is intended to serve a dual purpose. First, it will present the lexical background to the rest of the study, introducing us to the sorts of words used in the Irish language to connote honour and nobility, to the sorts of contexts in which those words appear, and to the more specific descriptions of individuals as men of honour. Second, it attempts to chart change or continuity in how noble honour was conceptualized by Irish intellectuals in the wake of surrender and regrant. The study is based on three texts: *The Annals of Loch Cé*,[8] the *Duanaire Mhéig Uidhir* (Poembook of the Maguires),[9] and the poems of Tadhg Dall Ó hUiginn.[10] Although the sentiments displayed in these works are by no means uniform, they nevertheless share three connecting themes: the attempt to explain and navigate changed circumstances through reference to issues of status and rank; the understanding that the same basic precepts of honourable conduct and comportment were recognizable and applicable to Irish and English alike; and an evolving distancing from Crown and Castle arising not out of inherent national, confessional or ethnic difference but rather from the authors' anger and frustration that the honour principles that underpinned surrender and regrant were too frequently proving hollow.

GAELIC RESPONSE IN ANNALS AND POETRY: INTRODUCTION

A study of noble honour in sixteenth century Ireland must take account of annalistic and bardic sources. The importance of the annals is perhaps obvious, providing as they did record and comment upon the great events and personages of the day. Bardic verse is equally important. Here it must be borne in mind that the 'bards' were not itinerant rhymers, harpers or entertainers but rather the intellectuals, historians, genealogists and court

---

[8] William M. Hennessy (ed. and trans.), *The annals of Loch Cé: a chronicle of Irish affairs from A.D. 1014 to A.D. 1590*, 2 vols (London, 1871).
[9] Greene, *Duanaire Mhéig Uidhir*.
[10] Eleanor Knott (ed. and trans.), *The bardic poems of Tadhg Dall Ó hUiginn*, 2 vols (Dublin, 1922).

poets of this society, for Gaelic and Old English elites alike. These were the *ollúna* (*ollamh* in the singular), the intellectual class of Gaelic Ireland. By Brehon law, they were the status equals of Gaelic lords and thus inhabited the same honour circle as the men and women they praised. In this they constituted something of a *noblesse de robe*: non-martial, highly educated elites whose status was actuated by the 'state', here meaning local lords. Yet they were not simply dependents, for no Irishman could be a lord without retaining the services and enjoying the praise of an *ollamh dána* (*ollamh* of poetry).[11] If *ollamh* denotes office and status, *file* (*filí* in the plural) refers to the chief professional duty: the composition of eulogistic verse for aristocratic patrons.[12] In Joep Leerssen's words, the *file*'s primary task was 'to be the main arbitrator of nobility, of honour': not only in present terms (individual actions), but in historical terms (it is worthy if it matches historical precedent).[13] Changes to prevailing concepts of honour and nobility would thus affect them intimately, not only in material patronage terms, but also in terms of relative status. For this reason, their writings offer an extremely sensitive barometer for measuring change or continuity in contemporary ideas of honour.

Gaelic writing of this period, however, has not always been accepted as something capable of reflecting historical change. Moreover, it is only in the last twenty years or so that Gaelic source material has been used at all by historians.[14] Deemed of dubious empirical reliability, these works – poetry and prose works alike – have traditionally come under the bailiwick of antiquarians and philologists who have read them as simplistic tales of the collapse of Gaelic Ireland. For example, Robin Flower, an English folklorist and philologist, wrote of an Ireland that 'lay panting and exhausted', only to be dealt a 'death blow to all her hopes and the old order of things' by the flight of the Ulster earls to the continent in 1607.[15] Gaelic authors' subsequent writing of histories and the compiling of saints' lives, Flower considered as last-ditch efforts to record for posterity the achievements of a culture passing into oblivion.

---

[11] For a general understanding of the relationship between *ollamh* and lord, see Breatnach, 'The chief's poet' and James Carney, *The Irish bardic poet; a study in the relationship of poet and patron as exemplified in the persons of the poet, Eochaidh Ó hEoghusa (O'Hussey) and his various patrons, mainly members of the Maguire family of Fermanagh* (Chester Springs, PA, c1967).

[12] These terms are more accurate than 'bard'. In the interest of variety, however, all three will be used throughout the text.

[13] Leerssen, *Mere Irish*, p. 180.

[14] The first concerted attempt to use Gaelic material, particularly the poetry, to answer questions about changes over time in political ideology is to be found in Brendan Bradshaw, 'Native reactions to the westward enterprise: a case-study in Gaelic ideology', in Andrews, Canny and Hair (eds.), *The Westward enterprise*, pp. 65–80.

[15] Robin Flower, *The Irish tradition* (Oxford, 1947), p. 166.

Curiously, once historians and historically minded literary scholars did turn their attention to Gaelic sources, their interpretations of the material differed little from Flower's. T. J. Dunne, for one, argued in 1980 that the Gaelic intellectual classes were unaware of the true scope of the Crown's efforts at centralization and that they interpreted the political and military crises of the period through traditional filters.[16] On the one hand, so the argument went, Gaelic commentators saw all threats as purely local problems, as challenges to the authority of a particular local lord; and on the other that this new threat could be assimilated into a traditional narrative of frequent invasions, followed by the assimilation of the invaders into a Gaelicized status quo.[17] Neither of these scenarios, however, accurately described the Tudor project – a fact not appreciated by Gaelic commentators, Dunne concluded, until Crown supremacy had put paid to the existence of a viable Gaelic cultural system. Faced with this fait accompli, the now patronless bards went about producing histories and saints' lives as 'monuments to a doomed civilization'.[18] The extension of this argument came from Michelle O Riordain whose book *The Gaelic mind and the collapse of the Gaelic world* traced an immutable Gaelic tradition over 400 years, from the Norman invasions to the early seventeenth century.[19] She denied even that little bit of awareness and agency Dunne had granted the poets, claiming instead that these commentators were solely concerned about their own professional standing, and stubbornly refused either to chronicle change or adapt to it, heedless of the reality that the social structure that supported them was imploding.

Other scholars have countered this view of Gaelic political blindness and cultural ossification. Breandán Ó Buachalla and Katherine Simms have convincingly dispensed with the notion of a static Gaelic culture, arguing instead that Irish society was constantly in flux and that any attendant cultural change was registered in Gaelic annals and poetry. Exploring the phenomenon of Gaelic support for James I, Ó Buachalla shows how traditional poetic motifs and tropes could be reworked to register innovative socio-political positions. This depiction of 'change within continuity' in the bardic corpus not only significantly altered how Gaelic political thought in

---

[16] Tom Dunne, 'The Gaelic response to conquest and colonization: the evidence of the poetry', *Studia Hibernica* 20 (1980), pp. 7–30.

[17] This immigration narrative was transmitted primarily through *An Lebor Gabála* (*The Book of Invasions*), a medieval Irish origin legend describing waves of invaders and their eventual Gaelicization.

[18] Dunne, 'The Gaelic response', p. 19.

[19] Michelle O Riordain, *The Gaelic mind and the collapse of the Gaelic world* (Cork, 1990).

the early Stuart period is understood, but also how those sources are read and interpreted.[20] Simms brings a similarly critical eye to the annals. Regarding the Tudor period, she sees medieval notions of Irish kingship falling into desuetude to be replaced by depictions of Irish chiefs as mere warlords. As she argues, the shift from *rí* (king) to *tighearna* (lord) occurred over the fifteenth and sixteenth centuries and seems 'a half-way house on the road towards the *tighearna talmhan*, the landlord'.[21] The English presence in Ireland is central to Simms' narrative, but it lies largely in the background of her analysis. Joep Leerssen, Brendan Bradshaw and Marc Caball have been more explicit in exploring the role of Tudor centralization on changing Irish mentalities. Leerssen sees a retrenchment in culture as the prevailing reaction of Irish *filí* to the twin pressures of English migration and anglicization: 'The Gaelic order is defined [in the poetry], not as a politikon opposing the political advance of English expansionism, but as a set of cultural values, and economy of honour and nobility which guaranteed a historical continuity from the olden days down to the present.'[22] Bradshaw, by contrast, has read the Irish reaction in manifestly political terms. In a provocative analysis of poems written for the O'Byrne lords of Wicklow, he argues for the bardic articulation of a sense of national consciousness defined largely in opposition to a notion of usurping Englishness.[23] Caball offers the most fully developed picture of Irish intellectual flexibility in the period between the accession of Elizabeth and the death of James I. He detects the emergence of a 'confident sense of national identity … within a discursive framework of rival and oppositional ethnic identities' and sees the Gaelic intelligentsia as couching their setbacks in providential terms, the result of divine disfavour brought about by their own impiety and pride.[24] Inherent in the theme of providence was the potential for salvation, which gave rise to a new theme in the poetry – that of the Irish as the Israelites awaiting a new Moses. The twin themes of providence and salvation, he suggests, reveal the existence of a 'proactive and dynamic' Gaelic worldview,

[20] Breandán Ó Buachalla, 'James our true king: the ideology of Irish royalism in the seventeenth century', in D. G. Boyce (ed.), *Political thought in Ireland since the seventeenth century* (London, 1988), pp. 7–35, quote p. 8.
[21] Simms, *From kings to warlords*, p. 40. [22] Leerssen, *Mere Irish*, p. 189.
[23] Bradshaw, 'Native reaction'.
[24] Caball, *Poets and politics*, p. 81; Caball, 'Providence and exile in early modern Ireland', *IHS* 114 (1994), pp. 174–88. In arguing intellectual and cultural flexibility to the Irish, Caball goes a provocative step further and suggests that the charge of a static culture applies more fittingly to the New English. Although they too believed in providence and believed themselves chosen, he argues that the colonists' confidence in their holy selection led them to regard the Irish as beyond redemption, and so ceased in their efforts to 'expand their social and political horizons' through contact with Catholics. Ibid., p. 187.

the 'faith and fatherland' ideology of which served as the basis for an emergent national consciousness.[25]

While it may seem that the arguments and ideas espoused by Dunne and O Riordain, on the one hand, and Ó Buachalla, Simms, Leerssen, Bradshaw and Caball, on the other, are mutually exclusive,[26] I wish to suggest that this is not entirely the case and that we must address the insights of all of the above when reconstructing bardic mentalities in the wake of the constitutional changes of 1541. From the latter we must take the notion that the Irish learned classes were more intellectually, socially and politically adaptable than previously given credit for; from the former we must accept that issues of class, status and reputation were often forefront in contemporary minds. By combining these two perspectives it is hoped that we will be able to see not only the agency of Gaelic intellectuals but also how their concerns were related to the status issues and promises of socio-cultural integration into a larger 'British' polity inherent in the programme of surrender and regrant.

In attempting to demonstrate this I will, as noted above, restrict the study to three sources: *The Annals of Loch Cé*; the poembook of Cú Chonnacht Maguire, Lord of Fermanagh; and the collected poems of Tadhg Dall Ó hUiginn. But before embarking on that inquiry it may be useful to briefly discuss the selection of texts. *The Annals of Loch Cé* is a natural choice for two reasons. First, because I wish to explore how annalists, and not just the *filí*, dealt with honour. Investigations of early modern Irish thought tend to focus on poetry or the annals alone; here I wish to see them in comparison. Second, this particular collection covers nearly the whole of the sixteenth century, ending at 1590. As for the Maguire poems, I am interested to see if poets were consistent in how they praised a particular lord over the course of his career and in the terms they employed when doing so. The Maguire poems cover a crucial span of the sixteenth century, 1566–89. As such, they offer a rare chance, perhaps the only one, to look at encomia to one Gaelic lord in this period. Finally, I chose the Ó hUiginn collection for the opposite reason that I chose the Maguire poems: instead of poems all *to* one person, these are poems all *by* one person. His oeuvre spans roughly the same period as the other two works under consideration (*c.* 1570–91) and allows the opportunity to consider, over the course of more than forty poems, the range of one man's treatments of honour

---

[25] Ibid., p. 13; Caball, *Poets and politics*, p. 152.

[26] For a recent survey of the debate which draws this distinction, see Natalie Mears, *Queenship and political discourse in the Elizabethan realms* (Cambridge, 2005), p. 205.

and nobility. All three of these works, it should be added, are connected with the same geographic region: Ulster and Connaught.

These texts will be considered in their entireties as they relate to the chapter's chronological focus,[27] a methodological choice I believe to be of vital importance for the study of contemporary Gaelic mentalities. As the anthropologist Frank Henderson Stewart has argued, one of the surest ways to get at a society's ideas of honour is to closely track the terms it uses for the concept across time and genre.[28] There has been some lexical work on bardic verse and annals by historians and literary scholars, most prominently within the seminal studies of Simms, Leerssen and Caball. Yet there has been no systematic and sustained exploration of the words denoting honour, and how their usage or meaning may have changed, or remained the same, over the tumultuous second half of the sixteenth century. Here it is hoped that by restricting the inquiry to just three, if rather sizeable, texts and dealing with each instance of selected terms, we may get a greater sense for the full panoply of Gaelic definitions of honour in the fraught sixteenth century.

Although I will consider these collections in isolation, each will be subjected to the same two-part analysis. First, I will provide a lexical survey of words used to denote honour and explore the contexts in which they appear. The focus will be on the two words most commonly used to connote honour: *eineach* and *onóir*. *Eineach* literally means 'face', and its importance to Gaelic society was enshrined in the concept of the *eineachlann*, or honour-price. By Brehon law, the *eineachlann* was set according to one's status and place in society. *Onóir*, by contrast, was a Latin loanword (as is the English word 'honour'). To complement the discussion of *eineach* and *onóir*, the chapter also considers a number of related words and their usage – chief among them *féile* (hospitality), *clú* (fame, reputation), *glóir* (glory), and *uasal* (noble) – as well as terms denoting royalty, noble titles, office and office-holding, ideas of lordship, and sovereignty. Having studied closely the deployment of particular terms, I will then consider more generally the ways in which various elites are described, praised and criticized. Attention will be paid to how all elites are treated, not just the Irish. Coming from these two angles – the lexical and the descriptive – this chapter aims to shed light on the variety of ways in which social, political and cultural change in the wake of Tudor state expansion was registered by Gaelic intellectuals.

---

[27] I will consider the poetry collections in their entirety. However, I will for the most part only be considering those sections of *The Annals of Loch Cé* that fall between the years 1541 and 1590.

[28] Stewart, *Honor*, p. 5. It should be noted that he does not include Ireland, Iceland or Scandinavia in his discussion of 'Western European' notions of honour. See p. 34.

THE ANNALS OF LOCH CÉ

The various Irish annals are generally taken to be the most reliable sources of contemporary Gaelic mentalities. For this reason, Simms made exclusive use of annals in her groundbreaking book on changing conceptions of kingship in medieval Gaelic Ireland, *From kings to warlords*. The intention here is to extend our understanding of Gaelic views of status and rank through investigation of how honour appears in the sixteenth-century entries of *The Annals of Loch Cé* (hereafter *ALC*). It is hoped that the close reading of just one set of annals will reveal the small details and contours of the changes in how Gaelic intellectuals registered, or failed to register, social and cultural change post-1541. Moreover, I consider how these terms are used for non-Irish persons. This chapter section argues that the compilers of the *ALC* did not increase their glorification of the martial virtues of the warlord, but rather revealed an increasing tendency to praise their subjects in the civil terms of nobility and humanity. As such, they may have been projecting their subjects to appear as much members of an international nobility, sharing the interests and characteristics of social elites throughout Europe, as petty warlords.

Eineach is the most commonly used word for honour in these annals.[29] Moreover, it occurs more often than any other term for describing Irish lords, with the possible exception of *uasal* (discussed below). It provided one half of the standard eulogistic tagline on a lord's death, typically paired with *uasal*. So, for example, under the entry for 1544 we read of the passing of Murchadh, son of Mac Suibhne na Túath,[30] 'a most eminent man in *eineach* and nobility' (… *soi a neinech ocus a nuaisli*).[31] Standard as it may have appeared by this date, however, this encomiastic formula's first appearance in these annals seems to have come less than one hundred years previous, in 1457, after which it quickly became common.[32] Prior to that, *eineach* was variously combined with terms connoting martial

---

[29] All Irish words will be first introduced in their modern, dictionary forms. Alternate spellings found in the text are given in the original in parentheses or quotations. Thus, for example, *eineach* is the nominative form, but other spellings occur below according to case or spelling variation as found in *ALC* (for example, '*einig*', the genitive singular of *eineach*).

[30] A note on names: I will give names as they appear in the editor's translation rather than attempt to 'modernize' them. Although this may result in alternate spellings throughout this book, it allows easier reference to the text under immediate consideration.

[31] *ALC*, pp. 346–7. For longer sections I generally rely on the editor's translation; exceptions will be noted. Regarding the page numbers, I have in most cases provided both the page containing the original and that containing the editor's translation, thus the frequent double-page referencing in this section.

[32] This comes on the death of O'Conchobhair Failghe in 1457. Ibid., pp. 162–3.

valour – such as *gaisce* when referring to the death of James, Earl of Desmond, in 1463[33] – or modifiers suggesting hospitality – as in the description of Aedh Buidhe, son of Brian Ballach O'Neill, as a 'man of general bounty to everyone' (*fer einig coitcenn da gach aon*).[34] In the 1580s there is a very curious shift in that tagline: the order is reversed and *uasal* precedes *eineach*, noble and honourable. There is one example of this altered construction in 1566, and not again until the 1582 entry.[35] But from there forward *uasal* enjoys almost exclusive precedence over *eineach*.[36] Could this suggest a move away from honour as something based in Brehon law (that is, the *eineachlann*) and towards a more generic notion of aristocratic status (*uasal*) with greater translatability to larger British or continental contexts?

Moreover, the definition of *eineach* itself seems to have been changing over this period. It has been suggested that in the sixteenth century the word was coming more often to connote generosity – its secondary meaning in the medieval period.[37] However, it is often difficult to decouple these definitions: on the one hand, there is overlap in the notions (that is, to be generous and hospitable was to be honourable); on the other, it often seems pure guesswork to determine when honour or hospitality is meant.[38] A significant difficulty in analysing *eineach*'s use in *ALC* is that it is rarely attached to any particular actions or traits. When it is generically deployed to eulogize the passing of an Irish lord, its importance may be clear but its definition elusive. How to translate the standard eulogistic tagline *eineach agus uasal*? As 'honour and nobility', or 'hospitality and nobility'? There really is no guide, and the preference of modern translators for the latter may derive less from sensitivity to textual and historical context than from a greater relative comfort with the idea of hospitality over honour. Nevertheless, a difference can at times be clearly established. Under the entry for 1579, for example, Sean O'Maelmocheirghe was eulogized as 'the most eminent man in Érinn for keeping a general house of hospitality (… *a noinech thighe*) for the men of Érinn, and of the world'.[39] In the entry for 1582, by contrast, the annalist laments the passing of the Old English Earl of Desmond, killed by forces of the Crown, and comments that 'there was no one in Éire whose equal he was not in nobility, honour, and powers

---

[33] Ibid., pp. 166–7.   [34] Ibid., p. 158.   [35] Ibid., pp. 390–1, 456–7.
[36] The entries for 1584 and 1586 each contain one instance of the *eineach* preceding *onóir*. Ibid., pp. 460–1, 468–9.
[37] Simms, *From kings to warlords*, p. 110.
[38] On the close relationship between honour and hospitality, Simms notes that the 'ultimate dishonour' was lack of hospitality. Simms, 'Guesting and feasting', p. 79.
[39] *ALC*, pp. 424–5.

(... *duaisle ocus doinech ocus cumachtuib*), and by whom more Saxons fell, and who put the Queen to greater cost'.[40] Moreover, he mentions that the English reconquest had put the collective honour of the men of Ireland under strain: 'All Erinn was occupied by the foreigners this year, so that they put back the honour and nobility (*Oinech agus uaisle*) of the men of Eirinn.'[41] Clearly, generosity is one of the main components of noble honour in Gaelic Ireland – particularly to the bards whose livelihood was dependent upon lordly largesse – but from the evidence of *ALC* it is unclear, even into the 1580s, that the word *eineach* was moving in the direction of meaning exclusively generosity at the expense of valour and an obligation to protect people and territory. A significant continuity with past usage, however, was that it remained reserved for Gaelic and Old English subjects; no New English were men of *eineach*.

Onóir appears far less often than *eineach* in the *ALC* and carries a greater sense of being externally generated and defined. Often it is used in a religious setting; for example, we read of Christmas festivals and bishops that are deemed honourable.[42] Curiously, the term is never applied as a personal descriptor to an Irish lord. Rather it designates something received, often from the hands of Crown representatives. For instance, O'Donnell is greeted 'with great honour' (*onóir mór*) by the Lord Deputy in 1541;[43] the Earls of Desmond and Ormond are similarly received upon coming to court to make their submissions in 1542;[44] and even the lesser lords O'Connor Sligo and Ruadhri MacDiarmada are welcomed with *onóir* '*mór*' by the Irish council in Dublin.[45] This exchange was reciprocal from Irish to English, too, as is demonstrated in the 1585 description of the English governor of Connaught's having spent a night 'with great honour and excessive enjoyment in Brian Mac Diarmada's house'.[46] The use of *onóir*, then, seems a sign of acceptance of the English monarch as the fount of all honour, even in the Kingdom of Ireland. Its reciprocal and cross-ethnic applicability also suggests a certain cultural/social/political convergence – enough of one, anyway, to ensure that elites of all ethnic backgrounds were treated, or were expected to be treated, in accordance with their station.

Of the remaining contemporary terms for honour and nobility, two stand out in importance: *uasal* and *daonnacht*. *Uasal*, as the discussion above would suggest, seems at first to be of secondary importance to *eineach*, a sort of generic descriptor that gives precedence to the more culturally specific and time-honoured *eineach*, the definition of which was provided

---

[40] Ibid., pp. 456–7.   [41] Ibid., pp. 460–1.   [42] Ibid., pp. 328–9, 428–9.
[43] Ibid., pp. 328–9.   [44] Ibid., pp. 342–3.   [45] Ibid., pp. 422–3.   [46] Ibid., pp. 464–5.

by legal tracts and the literary tradition. But as noted above, *uasal* assumes
precedence over *eineach* by the mid-1580s, a shift that may suggest an
attempt by the annalists to cast their subjects in such terms as to make
their nobility seem less provincially contingent and more in line with
international standards. At times *uasal* seems to have appropriated some
of the traditional meaning attached to *eineach*, particularly the sense of
status generated by successfully fulfilling the obligations of protecting
clients and family. O'Connor Don, for one, was noted at his death in
1587 as a noble man (*duine uasal*), a designation that seems to have been
derived in part by his being one who 'subdued and humbled his enemies the
most, and who plundered and destroyed his adversaries the most in every
quarter'.[47] There seems in this example a clear connection between martial
prowess and his status as a true bearer of nobility.[48] More frequently,
however, the term is attached to criteria of blood and lineage. Those of
good names/families are generally described at their deaths as *uasal* with no
mention of any particular deeds or actions that could have justified such a
description. The occasional mention of 'noble blood' (*fuil uaisle*) offers, of
course, the clearest example of this sense of nobility by pedigree. By the
1580s, then, it is not the valour of these men, or their standing vis-à-vis
Gaelic law that determines their claim to nobility, but rather their bloodlines and proper behaviour commensurate with their social standing in the
new dispensation. It has been argued that continental aristocrats were
shifting emphasis from 'valor to pedigree' in their definitions of noble
honour; Ireland seems to have followed this trend.[49]

The appearance of *daonnacht* (humanity) is the most interesting lexical
development in the *ALC*. While there are examples of its use in the
fourteenth- and fifteenth-century entries, it disappears almost entirely in
the sixteenth century. This seems to confirm the devolution of Gaelic elite
society to mere warlordism. But then it appears again in 1586, used to
eulogize one of the Clanricard Burkes (Richard Og, son of Rickard, son of
Shane-in-termuinn), hanged on the orders of the provincial president of
Connaught, Richard Bingham. The term is added to the standard
couplet of nobility and honour, inserted between *uasal* and *eineach*,
to read 'noble, humane, most honourable' (... *ocus fa uasal doennachtach*

[47] Ibid., pp. 480–1.
[48] Leerssen stresses the connection between Gaelic nobility, as signified by *uaisle*, and the willingness to
take up arms against the 'foreignor'. Leerssen, *Mere Irish*, p. 183. Such a connection is absent from
ALC, outside of this one example, for the term is used for Irish, English and continental personages
alike, and generally bears no martial character.
[49] Schalk, *From valor to pedigree*.

degoinigh).[50] Three years later the term is used to praise four men in death, and is paired with a variety of complementary adjectives. Thus, the death of John Ruadh O'Maelchonaire is recorded as marking a great loss to 'humanity and science';[51] similarly, the passing of Brian, 'the best cleric in Ireland', son of Maelrunaidh, son of Ferghal, was lamented as a loss regarding 'humanity and learning'.[52] *Daonnacht* could, however, bear pairing with more martial terms, as in the eulogizing of Aedh MacDiarmada as a man of 'prowess and humanity'.[53] In one instance it was even linked with *eineach*: the death of Bishop Mac Conghaile, a man of great 'humanity and honour/generosity'. As that final eulogistic couplet suggests, the later sixteenth-century entries in the *ALC* seem to suggest a shift in conceptions of noble honour to again include humanity. Could this suggest a mental shift more inclusive of European-wide trends that we tend to associate with the Renaissance? Brendan Bradshaw in his study of the antiquarian efforts of Manus O'Donnell, chief of the O'Donnells (1537–55), argues that humanistic influences were creeping not only into the actions and behaviours of Gaelic elites but also into how these men's auras of authority and legitimacy were constructed.[54] The revival of *daonnacht*, humanity, in this annalistic collection may offer support to that supposition.

From words meaning honour and nobility, let us now turn to consider terms used to identify elites. Of common use is some variation of *duine maith*, literally 'good man' (or 'good person'). This appears in a variety of settings, including references to the chiefs of the MacSweeneys,[55] the death of the O'Byrne,[56] to the participants in the Baltinglass revolt,[57] to those Gaelic lords who participated in the Dublin Parliament of 1585,[58] to the Gael and Gall of Roscommon who go to meet the Crown representative Captain Brabazon in 1582,[59] to the Gael and Gall of the Saxons and of Connaught,[60] and finally to the Lord Deputy and council in 1589.[61] Thus, there seems little hierarchical or ethnic specificity inherent in this term. Also very common, and again usable for Gael and Gall alike, are variations of *duine uasal* and *uaisle*. For example, the Irish lords who go to England in 1542 to offer their submission under surrender and regrant – O'Neill, Burke, O'Brien, Kildare, Ormond and Desmond – are described as '*urmhór*

[50] *ALC*, 2, pp. 470–1. A similar commentary followed on the death of Diarmaid Dall MacDiarmada in 1590, noted as 'a noble, honourable, humane man' (*uasal deigheinigh daonachtach*), *ALC*, pp. 510–11.
[51] Ibid., pp. 496–7. [52] Ibid., pp. 502–3. [53] Ibid., pp. 496–7.
[54] Bradshaw, 'Manus "the Magnificent"'. [55] *ALC*, 2, p. 341. [56] Ibid., pp. 378–9.
[57] Ibid., pp. 446–7. [58] Ibid., pp. 466–7. [59] Ibid., pp. 448–9. [60] Ibid., pp. 472–3.
[61] Ibid., pp. 498–9.

uaislibh Erenn' (the majority of the nobles of Ireland).[62] The term is also applicable to decidedly less august personages, such as a minor fellow of the Geraldines and the lesser Connacht lord O'Connor Don.[63] It also describes English officials. Nicholas Malby, provincial president of Connaught, for instance, enjoys the following eulogy despite his aggressive actions against the holders of local authority: 'and there came not to Eirinn in his own time, nor often before, a better gentleman (*duine uasal*) of the Foreigners than he; and he placed all Connacht under bondage'.[64] And finally, this word that is appropriate for O'Connor Don and Malby is also perfectly acceptable for speaking of the greatest of continental dignitaries, thus Don John of Austria is noted at his passing as 'the greatest nobleman to come in Christendom'.[65]

One last common term is *tiarna*, loosely translated as 'lord'. Like *duine maith* or *duine uasal* it is applicable to both Gael and Gall, aristocrat and lesser gentry or official. A bit of additional adjectival modification serves to distinguish the relative status of these various *tiarnaí*. Thus, the head of the O'Connor Sligo lordship is termed simply '*tigerna*' in the entry for 1552, as is the head of the Ulster lordship of Clandeboye.[66] The O'Neill head, by contrast, is described as '*tigerna*' of the province of Ulster (*tigerna an chóigidh Ulltaigh*).[67] In a similar ascending differentiation, both Malby and Bingham are known as lords of Connacht (*tigerna Chonnacht*, and *tigerna … cuigedh Connacht*, respectively), while the O'Neills and O'Donnells are known as *airdtigerna*, or overlords, in the entry of the same year.[68] Surveying these terms employed to identify elites, then, it appears the annalists did not use distinctive terms for Gaelic, Old English and New English subjects.[69]

Curious in the *ALC* is the use of royal terminology to refer to Irish, English and continental elites alike. The Irish word *rí* and its derivatives appear over thirty times in the text in the entries between 1541 and 1590. This is significant in light of Simms' claim that 'the annalists tend to avoid the use of the word *rí* altogether in entries for the sixteenth century, with the following exceptions – AU (*Annals of Ulster*) 1510; ALC (*Annals of Loch Cé*) 1509, 1510; AConn (*Annals of Connacht*) 1510, 1536, 1539'.[70] This disappearance of royal terminology from the various annals is vital to her argument that Irish elites experienced a socio-cultural slippage from 'kings to warlords'. The use of *rí* did not end, however, and the term's continued appearance and the promiscuity of its

---

[62] Ibid., pp. 342–3.   [63] Ibid., pp. 444–5, 480–1.   [64] Ibid., pp. 458–9.   [65] Ibid., pp. 430–1.
[66] Ibid., pp. 358–9, 394–5.   [67] Ibid., pp. 394–5.   [68] Ibid., pp. 414, 460, 462.
[69] The one notable exception is the use of '*déchtaibh móra*', which appears in the entry for 1546 and refers to one Thomas Faránta as having been 'of the great notabilities of his sept'. Ibid., pp. 348–9.
[70] Simms, *From kings to warlords*, fn. 104, p. 39.

usage argues against the social devolution to warlordism. For the entry year 1567, Toirdhealbhach O'Neill is labelled 'royal heir of Ireland without dispute' (*adhbar rí Erenn*) and almost directly afterwards Elizabeth I is introduced with the feminine of the word as the 'queen of the Saxons' (*bainrigan Shaxanach*).[71] The term covers other international monarchs, too: Henry VIII, James VI of Scotland and Philip II of Spain, to name a few. Even Mary Queen of Scots appears as '*banrigan Albanach*'.[72] In spite of that august company, *rí* also applies to those Irish below the level of the great Gaelic overlordships – the lesser lords MacDiarmada and O'Reilly are described with *rí*, to take but two examples.[73] 'Gaelicized' Old English lords can also bear the designation, as do successive heads of the MacWilliam Burkes of Sligo. Similarly, the designation *mac rí* ('king's son') applies to the sons of Irish lords, great or small, Gael or Gall.[74] There is, however, an interesting use of the term from 1568 whereby a conflict is described in which many of the 'princes and nobles' of the Gaels were slain (*macaibh rígh ocus deghdhaoinibh*), perhaps signifying a shift to a greater distinction between the sons of the main line and those of collaterals. This would be in keeping with surrender and regrant's emphasis on primogeniture.[75] Even if such a shift at that point in time were provable, however, it would remain significant that the compiler saw fit to refer to members of the main branch using the traditional terms of royalty, which by the logic of surrender and regrant should have been a meaningless anachronism.[76] In spite of arguments that posit that Gaelic annalists were aware of the distinct lack of regality accruing to Gaelic lords and thus phased the attendant vocabulary out of annalistic compilations, *ALC* bears strong witness to the continued currency of a language of kingship amongst annalists up to the turn of the seventeenth century.

In spite of this promiscuous use of royal terminology across Irish, English and continental contexts, there are certain terms connoting royalty that are applied only to English and continental actors. *Cing*, most notably, refers to English monarchs alone. And while this word is somewhat imprecisely deployed – as when Queen Mary is referred to as *cing Maria*[77] – it is never applied to a Gaelic or Old English subject. Likewise, the term *prinnsa*

---

[71] *ALC*, 2, pp. 394–7.   [72] Ibid., p. 476.   [73] Ibid., pp. 390, 396, 398.
[74] Thus the sons of the MacWilliam Burkes (1545), MacDiarmada (1553) and O'Connor Don (1583). Ibid., pp. 346–7; 362–3; 452–3.
[75] Ibid., pp. 402–3.
[76] Given the frequency of *mac rí*, the rarity of *flaith*, or prince, is surprising. It shows up only once, in 1568, to refer to the head of the Maelrunaidh clan. Ibid., p. 398.
[77] Ibid., pp. 350–1.

(prince), which although it is used in reference to both Elizabeth I (as the prince of the Saxons, *prinssa na Saxana*)[78] and the Earl of Leicester ('a most powerful prince of the people of the English queen', *iarla o Lestar .i. prinnsa ro chumachtach do mhuinntir Banrigan Saxan*), it is never attached to an Irish personage, Gael or Gall.[79] Thus, a distinction between Europe's 'crowned kings' and local *ríthe* was at times made, if not always so.

An interesting mixing of the language of royalty and lordship appears in discussions of territory, sovereignty and election. At times, *tiarnas* is used to connote lordship or sovereignty; one instance from 1585 sees the compiler noting how 'the sovereignty (*tigernus*) of each Gaelic lord (*tigerna*) was lowered by them [the English]'.[80] But at other points, *flaitheas* (deriving from the word for prince, *flaith*) or *ríocht* (from *rí*) are preferred, the latter being applicable to Gaelic and continental examples, as in the 'sovereignty' (*righeacht*) of Portugal. At times the verb *gair* (to name, or inaugurate) is the preferred one to discuss elections to Gaelic and Gaelicized lordships. Thus, we read of Richard-an-iarann being proclaimed MacWilliam,[81] and later how the same title was bestowed upon Ricard son of Oliver (*MacUilliam do gairm do Risderd mac Oilueruis*).[82] More commonly, the verb *rígh*, to crown or make king, is used. Thus, when the head of the O'Dubhda clan died, one Edmond O'Dubhda was 'Inaugurated in his place' (*do rígadh na ionadh*).[83] Likewise, one Toirdhealbhach is noted as having been made king (*ríogadh*) of the Maelrunaidh in 1568 'with the consent of the church and the laity, of ecclesiastics and ollamhs'.[84] The reliance of the annalists upon traditional royal terminology thus remained strong over this period, despite the fact that in the same year's entry (1569) it is noted how the *rí* O'Connor Sligo has come from England with a patent from the Queen (*banrigan*) for his lands – a clear sign both of the traditional hold of the term *rí* on the annalistic imagination, and of the siphoning from the term of any sense of Irish 'regal' independence of action or legitimacy. Kings they may have been, but Irish lords like O'Connor Sligo owed their authority to the legal niceties afforded them by their English *ardrí*, the Queen of England.

As for terms referring to gentry and nobility, while there was not any real sense of distinction between Gael and Gall, as we have seen above, perhaps in the wake of surrender and regrant we should expect an increasing attention to honourific titles and titles of office. Regarding the former, the Old English earls are typically, and correctly, referred to by their titles, thus Ormond, Desmond, and even the original twelfth-century Anglo-Norman

---

[78] Ibid., pp. 472–3.   [79] Ibid., pp. 486–7.   [80] Ibid., pp. 466–7.
[81] Ibid., pp. 432–3.   [82] Ibid., pp. 452–3.   [83] Ibid., pp. 448–9.   [84] Ibid., pp. 404–5.

invader Strongbow himself, appear in the text as earls. There is a bit of a lag, however, before those Irish lords who have taken anglicized titles are referred to accordingly. For instance, once Hugh O'Neill receives the earldom of Tyrone, he is incorrectly referred to as the earl of Ulster (*iarla Ullaidh*) – the very title the request for which had so upset Henry VIII.[85] But that confusion is quickly straightened out since he is correctly and consistently introduced from that point forward as the Earl of Tyrone (*iarla Thire hEoghain*) or, more simply, as the earl (*iarla*). As for titles connected with office-holding – governor, treasurer, captain, sheriff, and so on – the frequency with which they appear increases in seeming relation to the socio-political changes attendant with Tudor expansion. These are not always correct, as in the consistent reference to the Lord Deputy as the justice (*giuisdís*),[86] but, nevertheless, there is an effort to reflect the creation of new governmental positions, as when Bingham is described as 'governor, that is lord of Connacht (*guibhernóir .i. tigerna Connacht*)'.[87] Not only was the changing face of Ireland's political structure reflected in *ALC*, so too was there an effort to interpret those changes for the reader through the modification and manipulation of existing terms and concepts of authority and lordship.

This brief lexical study of one volume of Irish annals supports arguments that Gaelic annalists were cognizant of the socio-political changes attendant on Tudor reform and were engaged in a process of concordance between the 'new' British system and the 'old' Gaelic/Gaelicized one. Certainly the attention to English-style titles of honour and office reflects a sensitive eye for the changing political landscape and, if not a sloughing off by these commentators of Gaelic forms of social organization, then at least a fledgling synchronization of cultural forms. Consequently, we should be cautious before attributing too much change to these annals. For as we have seen, the terminology used to discuss various elites slides back and forth between the pragmatic (that is, reflective of current socio-political realities) and the customary. That both the chief of the Maelrunaidhs and the monarch of England can appear as *rí* reveals that the vocabulary, and perhaps even the concepts, of the Gaelic intelligentsia have not quite caught up with the realities of state centralization.

---

[85] Ibid., pp. 498–9. Regarding the controversy over the earldom of Ulster, see Connolly, *Contested island*, p. 43.

[86] This was the medieval term for the position, but in this period it was only applied to those who held interim authority in Dublin between governorships.

[87] *ALC*, pp. 464–5.

However, before damning these chroniclers for their limited ability to notice and adapt to changing times, it should be remembered that traditional terms can still have currency and meaning when their original definitions are no longer applicable. Were this not the case, would the current President of the Republic of Ireland be known as *Uachtaran* and the Prime Minister as *Taoiseach*? Moreover, there is intellectual and lexical change apparent in this text and given the usage of words for honour, nobility, lordship, humanity, and so on, it seems that that change is towards a model of noble honour in line with that recognizable in England and on the continent. Rather than suggesting a social fall into warlordship, the prominence of terms denoting nobility and humanity, and the application of the words for lord and lordship (*tiarna* and *tiarnas*) to Irish and English authorities alike, might also suggest a transition from independence to vassalage, from kingship to provincial nobility.

To test that impression, we must move beyond the lexical to consider actual descriptions of Irish and English elites in *ALC*. Although annalistic description is fairly laconic, there is ample enough editorializing from which to draw some sense for just what constituted honourable behaviour in the chroniclers' eyes. The following discussion of a wedding feast brings out the ideals of hospitality and regality that were so fundamental to the definitions of *eineach* and *rí*:

> The great, regal (*righdha*), wedding feast of the lord of the Rock, and of his wife, i.e., Medhdh, the daughter of Domhnaill O'Conchobhair, i.e., daughter of O'Connor Sligo, was celebrated together by Brian, son of Ruadhri Mac Diarmada, at which large quantities of all kinds of stock, and of all descriptions of treasure and valuables, were presented and dispensed, according to their wish, to every one of the men of Éire and Alba (Scotland) that came to solicit them during that year.[88]

Hospitality alone did not ensure authority in Gaelic Ireland, however, and the sons of Tadhg MacDiarmada were reported in 1565 to have held great sway over much of Connacht 'owing to the quantity of their horses and armour, of their men and flocks, and the power of their friends in every place'.[89] Noble honour in this society was also generated by successful border raiding – the practice of which appears to have been as respectable as it was common even through the 1580s – and by the extraction of vengeance against one's transgressors.[90] Wanton violence may have been frowned upon (as will be discussed below) but in the service of revenge it

---

[88] Ibid., pp. 446–9.   [89] Ibid., pp. 388–9.
[90] Thus the poetic *caithréim*, or 'battle roll', was not just an archaism, but a description – as traditionally stylized as it may have been – of a practice that remained quite common.

was an acceptable action, as seen in this report on the killing of a 'great Scot' by O'Connor Sligo and some 'Saxons' in revenge for the killing of Cathal Og O'Connor and others:

And though some say that the deed was not right, it cannot be said that O'Conchobhair [O'Connor] was not justified in his own share of it, for his anger against them had not cooled since the fall of his brother, and his constable, and his good men, by them before that ...[91]

These 'medieval' ideals of lordly largesse and valour find their opposite in the conduct of the merchant, or so we may speculate given the eulogy for one John son of Eoghan O'Craidhen who was recorded to have died in Sligo in 1590, 'the least wicked merchant that was in Ireland'.[92] Taken together these examples may suggest a Gaelic and Gaelicized north and west of Ireland that was more stereotypically medieval than early modern.

Nevertheless, the authors also seem to describe a certain cultural mingling of Gael and Gall. Tellingly common is the theme of treachery that runs through these entries, suggesting that the authors were very keen to point out when acceptable norms of behaviour common to Gaelic Irish, 'English-Irish' and New English alike had been transgressed. This evidently happened with alarming frequency. It could happen amongst the 'English-Irish' and Irish themselves. Thus, we read of fratricide amongst the Clanricard Burkes, the stain of which, the author notes approvingly, was erased with a revenge killing.[93] The killing of Tomaltach MacDiarmada by O'Flannagain and the sons of O'Conchobhair Ruadh in 1589 is noted as 'breach of conference' on the part of the killers.[94]

But this was most spectacularly a theme of English/Gaelic and New English/Old English interactions. Numerous historians have recently urged scholars to remember the brutality of the English in sixteenth century Ireland and the frequency of treachery in English dealings with their newly minted subjects.[95] The reportage of the Loch Cé annalists eloquently attests to the

---

[91] *ALC*, 2, pp. 444–5. This is a particularly interesting example in that it shows how Englishmen could be involved in a dispute that concerned an Irishman and a Scotsman. Revenge killing in this case was the working out of social tensions. Such actions could, however, also bear the imprint of providence as in the 1589 murder of the French king by a 'friar'. This event was noted as the will of God for the King's having killed the Duke of Guise, pp. 500–1.

[92] Ibid., pp. 512–13. See Canny, *Elizabethan conquest*, pp. 4–5, for a discussion of the dislike of the 'grey merchants', travelling peddlars and credit-lenders, in early modern Ireland.

[93] *ALC*, 2, pp. 444–5.

[94] According to the editor, this term 'was used to signify a treacherous attack made by one party on another, whilst engaged in a conference for the arrangement of mutual differences'. Ibid., p. 504.

[95] Brendan Bradshaw, 'Nationalism and historical scholarship in Ireland', *IHS* 28 (1993), pp. 227–55; Edwards, 'Escalation of violence', in Edwards, Lenihan and Tait (eds.), *Age of atrocity*, pp. 34–78.

appropriateness of this reminder. To take one powerful example, a censure of John Bingham and his troops reads thus: 'there never came into Connacht such wicked people as were in that army; for there was not a man in the world to whom they were faithful, in church or territory'.[96] This focus on faithfulness, on the keeping of one's word, as a guarantor of good conduct amongst elites is found throughout the text. At numerous points, Gaelic Irish and Old English lords are described as heading off to Dublin or England to meet with the Crown or its representatives only to find themselves imprisoned upon arrival. The extreme example of this is Red Hugh O'Donnell's having accepted the offer of hospitality to sample Spanish wines on board an English ship only to find himself placed in shackles and transported to imprisonment in Dublin Castle. In telling this story, the annalist draws a clear parallel between 'honour' and 'hospitality'. A man's offer of the latter was a sure sign of his possession of the former, and his successfully following through on the offer performed an important social function in a legally underdeveloped society in which order was partly ensured by the internalization of such un-codified codes. The false and treacherous offer of hospitality, by contrast, made a mockery of customary forms of social engagement and reduced their social functionality by making people wary of engaging in them. Treacherous action could also serve to undercut faith in the law. Along these lines, Richard Bingham was decried as having presided over a reign of terror in Connaught.[97] Deemed particularly egregious was his not respecting the very law he had been sent to represent and uphold, the most graphic example of which being when he and his sheriff Richard Mapother oversaw the hanging of Mac Maghnusa of Tir-Tuathail despite his possession of a governmental pardon. In these discussions of treacherous actions, the authors of Loch Cé highlight not merely instances of generic violence, but ones in which mutually comprehensible patterns of legitimate social and legal interaction were violated.

Interestingly, then, the compilers of these annals inveighed not so much against English encroachment as against officeholders seeking to enrich themselves behind the screen of law. Consequently, men like Bingham are seen not as enemies of the Irish exclusively but of the Crown as well, an authority served and respected, at least in theory, by Gaelic Irish, Old English and New English alike. For this reason the relation of Toirdhealbhach O'Brien's hanging in 1587 is followed by the comment that 'he [Toirdhealbhach] along with themselves [the

---

[96] *ALC*, 2, pp. 498–9.
[97] Remarking on Bingham and Perrot's treatment of the O'Neills, the author writes that it would be 'impossible to count, or reckon, or relate, all the injuries and oppressions the Foreigners committed upon these men'. Ibid., pp. 462–3.

officials responsible for his execution], [were] in the queen's service'.[98] An interesting extension of this argument of English officers as false guardians of the law casts the actions of men like Bingham and Lord Deputy Perrott as serving to turn people against the Crown and the rule of law to which they otherwise would acquiesce. Speaking again of Bingham, the text notes that 'all of the Clann-William whom he did not hang, he set at war with the queen'. This is followed by a list of other families driven by Bingham's harsh treatment into war against himself and the queen.[99] This juxtaposition between law-abiding (that is, English law) Irish elites and corrupt and lawless English officials and soldiers is well demonstrated in the story of the sons of Walter Fada Burk, Old English patriarch of the MacWilliam Burkes of Sligo. The text relates how Burke entertained Bingham honourably upon his arrival in Connacht (as noted above) only to see his own sons soon after 'wickedly taken prisoners by the governor, and sent in irons to the town of Ath Luain'.[100] Less an assault on some sort of ethno-cultural Gaelic purity, such actions are presented as serial abuses of the honour due men of pedigree, status and loyalty to the Crown and as undercutting the established authority of the monarch in Ireland.

The compilers of *ALC* were aware that they lived in momentous times and they feared the discord those times might bring. Three examples should suffice to demonstrate this. The first is the treatment of Hugh O'Neill in these annals, which carries the foreboding sense that the opportunistic and arbitrary actions of men like Bingham could be replicated by local elites to disastrous effect. For O'Neill is depicted as playing by rules of his own making. The most damning example of this is his killing of a rival, one Aedh Geimhlec O'Neill, on trumped up charges. It is noted that Aedh Geimhlec was treacherously seized by a son of the Maguire, whom Hugh afterwards rewarded for his 'evil service'.[101] More conversant with local custom and forms of power, or to put it more crassly, more 'native' than Bingham, and yet also bearing the title of earl, O'Neill was able to manipulate both his traditional powers and those conferred by the Crown to act as he wished. The second example comes in the recognition of the initial percolation of a resistance theory grounded in national consciousness and faith. On the death of James Fitzmaurice Fitzgerald in 1579 (leader of the first Desmond Rebellion, 1569–73), it is noted how he had endured great hardships in France and Spain preparing for this fight and 'performed great bravery, and warlike deeds, in those foreign countries, for the sake of his own land, and of

---

[98] Ibid., pp. 480–1.   [99] Ibid., pp. 494–5.   [100] Ibid., pp. 464–5.
[101] Ibid., pp. 506–7. On O'Neill's local oppressions, see Hiram Morgan, '"Slán Dé fút go hoíche": Hugh O'Neill's murders', Edwards, Lenihan and Tait (eds.), *Age of atrocity*, pp. 95–118.

the faith' (*a chríche ocus an chreidimh*).[102] This is the sole example of reference to the defence of patrimony and religion, but its appearance is significant for that very fact. The third is the opinion that the troubles in Ireland are but an extreme example of those affecting all of Europe. When discussing conflict between O'Neill and O'Donnell in the early 1580s, the chronicler regards this not as the contemporary manifestations of a centuries-old rivalry between Ulster lords, but rather as just one more example – if particularly troubling for its being local – of pan-European unrest: 'But truly, the evils and lamentations of that year throughout all Europe, and Ireland especially (*ocus a nErinn go háiridhe*), would be excessive to relate'.[103] An attention to local troubles and conflicts was complemented by at least some awareness of the larger British and European contexts in which these problems could be situated.

What does *ALC* tell us about Gaelic reactions to Tudor centralizing efforts? As the previous paragraph has demonstrated, these annals suggest that the Irish learned classes were aware that major events were unfolding across Europe and that the troubles in Ireland were but one example of a pan-European tumult. But with that said, the authors of Loch Cé do not attribute those troubles solely to nationalistic or confessional struggles. There is but a single discussion of patria and faith in this text, connected to the Desmond rebellion. In fact, there is little on offer as to why the problems described occur – description not explanation being the forte of the annalist. Nevertheless, the reportage of those problems, and on the actors involved in them, can suggest how these troubles were conceptualized. The character of the text suggests a certain level of socio-political and cultural convergence between native and newcomer. The terms used to denote elites are largely uniform, suggesting an outlook that saw Gaelic Irish, Old English and New English lords – all of whom bear the title *tiarna*, or lord – as variations on a common aristocratic theme. The increasing prominence of terms like *uasal* (noble) and *daonnacht* (humanity) reinforces the sense that Gaelic and Old English conceptions of noble honour were coming to look much like those current in England and elsewhere in Europe. The apparent acceptance of the English monarch as the fount of honour only strengthens that opinion. And it is the reality of that social concordance, fledging as it may have been, that lends gravity to the theme of treachery so strong in this text: without cultural understanding, violence is simply violence, not treachery. The problems here, then, are not attributable to a clash of cultures or political systems, but to the breakdown between

---

[102] *ALC*, 2, pp. 426–7.   [103] Ibid., pp. 440–1.

Gael and Gall of a system of un-codified patterns of behaviour and inter-action essential to the keeping of the peace in an environment with under-developed legal and political institutions and precedents.

GAELIC RESPONSE IN POETRY

To get a more comprehensive understanding of sixteenth-century Gaelic conceptions of noble honour requires attending to bardic poetry. This is notoriously difficult territory and, as discussed above, the suitability of these works to historical inquiry has been the focus of extended debate. Here it is sufficient to acknowledge both the difficulties and the possibilities inherent in using this material. Thus, while the annals are generally taken to be more historically reliable than the poetry and so to serve as more traditional 'historical' sources, attention to the empirical authority of verse works seems more a concern of modern commentators than of contemporaries. In spite of their near-ossified style and hyperbolic flattery, bardic poets were deemed vital arbiters of noble honour throughout the sixteenth century. Not only were they employed throughout this period by Irish and Old English elites, but by newcomers as well.[104] Remarking on that relationship between patron and poet, however, Tom Dunne has recently noted that the poets 'articulated the viewpoint of the patrons, whose propagandists in part they were, positioning them politically to survive in an increasingly difficult environment'.[105] And yet that can only be correct up to a point, for many of these poems are complaints and chastisements. It should be added to Dunne's statement that Irish court poets were also engaged in attempts to position their patrons in a way that would ensure the latter's own political relevance, albeit done with an eye to their (the poets') own well-being. Not mere yes-men, the bards could shape the viewpoints of their noble patrons, not simply parrot them.

I wish in the following two sections of this chapter to explore some of the ways in which traditional poetic motifs and tropes may have been deployed to fit changing social, cultural and political circumstances. It has been argued that the way to get at the contemporary commentary of bardic compositions is to winnow the wheat of present-centred bardic reportage from the chaff of traditional motifs.[106] This procedure is empowering in

---

[104] See Chapter 5, below.
[105] Tom Dunne, 'Ireland, Irish and colonialism', *Irish Review* 30 (2003), pp. 95–104, quote p. 98.
[106] Simms, *From kings to warlords*, pp. 1–9; 'Bardic poetry as a historical source', in Tom Dunne (ed.), *The writer as witness: literature as historical evidence* (Cork, 1987), pp. 58–75.

that it promises the means by which historians can plumb one of the few sources available for Irish views of early modern events. But it carries certain difficulties. To tease out the novel from the stock requires an incredibly detailed knowledge of the extant corpus of bardic poetry, medieval to early modern. Barring that, how is one to tell what is new or not? Even with that expertise – one, it should be added, to which I make no claim – one has to contend with the fact that the vast majority of poems from the period has disappeared. From the piecemeal remains of that tradition that have come down to us, how are we to tell what were its dominant motifs? So while this method offers our best step forward in using bardic poetry to make sense of the early modern Irish and Anglo-Irish pasts – and I will try my hand at it here – I wish to suggest that we should also be sensitive to the ways in which traditional themes may have been deployed to comment on new circumstances. Therefore, at the risk of giving too literal readings, I wish also to attempt a matching of traditional motifs with contemporary contexts in the hope of offering some thoughts on the ways in which time-honoured tropes in court poetry may have remained functional in changed social, cultural and political circumstances.

THE MAGUIRE POEMBOOK

The Maguires were lords of Fermanagh, an Ulster lordship subordinate to the O'Neills and O'Donnells. Cú Chonnacht Maguire was Lord of Fermanagh between the years 1566–89 and it is his poembook that is considered here. His rise to the lordship offers a case study in the shifting alliances and political possibilities ushered in with Tudor centralization, and of the available strategies for such a provincial lord when cultural convergence gave way to aggression and treachery. His continued association with Dublin, even if strained at times, served him well and he was able to hold the castle of Enniskillen for his entire reign, something neither his predecessor (brother Sean) or successor (son Hugh) was able to accomplish.[107]

Cú Chonnacht's *duanaire*, or poembook, offers a unique window onto the shifting fortunes and outlooks of a lord and his *fili* operating on the knife-edge between areas of government and Gaelic control. Every Gaelic lord would have collected a *duanaire* of manuscript copies of poems

---

[107] David Greene (ed. and trans.), *Duanaire Mhéig Uidhir*, viii (*DMU* hereafter). Unless otherwise stated, I will use the editor's translations.

composed in his honour.[108] Few, unfortunately, survive. For present purposes, what makes this particular one important is that it allows analysis of poems directed all to one person. Commentaries on this collection have generally focused on its traditional nature. Its editor and translator, David Greene, states that the poems reveal none of the precariousness of Cú Chonnacht's political situation, situated as he was between the English and the O'Neills. '[O]n the contrary,' he writes, 'all of them assume that the Lord of Fermanagh is supreme over Ulster, and that all the rest of Ireland willingly pays tribute to him.'[109] Greene's comments echo the pronouncements of the great scholar of the bardic tradition, James Carney, who believed that in composing their paeans to tradition the poets were merely doing what was expected of them. Carney's sense was that only one poem revealed any awareness of the shakiness of Cú Chonnacht's hold on local authority, and this because it was written by an outsider to the lordship.[110] Indeed, these poems are remarkable – or unremarkable as much of the historiography would tell us – for their static quality. And yet it seems unlikely that a native lord under the pressures faced by Cú Chonnacht Maguire would keep poets about his court merely for sentimental value and ego-stroking. Marc Caball's recent study of the poembook confirms the presence of age-old motifs, but argues that they are deployed in such a way as to register change, particularly toward the articulation of a sense of national consciousness.[111] This section builds on Caball's findings by highlighting two further aspects of the *duanaire*: the collection's attention to status issues and its use of pacific motifs – those favouring justice and peacekeeping – at the expense of martial ones. These aspects were intimately connected: the Maguire poets saw their patron's political survival to rest in negotiation not violent resistance.

As done with *ALC*, let us begin exploration of the Maguire *duanaire* by considering the uses of *eineach* and *onóir*. Of initial note is the mere fact that *eineach* appears more frequently than *onóir*. As in the *ALC*, *eineach* here encompasses notions of honour as obligation and as simply hospitality.[112]

[108] For background on this collection, and comparison with the contemporaneous O'Hara poembook, see Caball, *Poets and politics*, pp. 14–17. On the *duanaire* generally, see Brian Ó Cuív, *The Irish bardic duanaire or poem-book* (Dublin, 1973).
[109] *DMU*, p. ix.
[110] Ibid., p. ix. The 'outsider' was a Munster poet coming to seek Maguire's patronage. The poem is number nineteen in the collection.
[111] Caball, *Poets and politics*.
[112] A clear example of the latter comes in the first line to the twelfth poem in the collection: 'The Maguires are a spring of true generosity who do not grudge riches to poets' (*Tobar fíreinigh Fir Mhanach, maoine ar chléir ní choiclid súd*). *DMU*, pp. 110–11.

But whether its definition was moving over the course of Cú Chonnacht's career towards a more exclusive attachment to ideas of generosity and bountifulness, thus signalling a shift in expectations of lordship and noble honour, is difficult to gauge since it is not always clear just how to render the word. The clearest example of this ambiguity comes in a verse the first line of which is 'The Maguires have always been the Rome of *eineach*' (*Mhancaigh riamh 'na Róimh oinigh*). When the author, Fearghal Og Mac an Bháird, announces that it was the fame that the Maguires had earned for their *eineach* which brought him to Enniskillen, it seems most probable that patronage and generosity are intended.[113] But in the eighth quatrain, the poet laments that the *eineach* of the Gaels has been under fetters to the Gall and that Cú Chonnacht was thus under honourable obligation (*do chuing einig*) to restore it to its initial lustre.[114] *Eineach*'s broader meaning of status, or of honour as claim-right, seems appropriate in this case. To complicate matters, the poets had recourse to another word, *féile*, the exclusive meaning of which was generosity. This and *eineach* could at times be paired, as they are in an encomiastic couplet in which the poet claims that Ireland is due to Maguire on account of his *féile* and *eineach*.[115] Synonyms or complements? It is difficult to decide, but at least this example suggests that we should think of *eineach* as it is used in these compositions as encapsulating particular features of noble comportment. For, unlike simple generosity (*féile*), *eineach* is something that is possessed and can be lost, and so we see Maguire praised elsewhere for his 'possession of *eineach*' (*sealph an oinigh*).[116] Evidence from a further poem suggests that that possession derives from attaining a certain rank and status, namely, that Cú Chonnacht has gained *eineach* on account of becoming a king, head of his family and territory.[117] And interestingly, the next stanza claims that he received *bladh* (another, but infrequently used, word meaning fame or reputation) by sharing his wealth. Thus, his *eineach* derives not from wealth and largesse, but rather from rank and status. Here is a direct link to the sense of *eineach* which produced the *eineachlann* of Brehon law: something dependent upon rank and recognizable as such, and requiring careful management and defence.

Onóir appears less frequently in these poems and bears the sense of something received from a lordly patron, and not as something pertaining to him. Thus, the poet Conchubhair Crón Ó Dálaigh states that in return for the honour (*onóir*) he gets from Cú Chonnacht he will give his

---

[113] Caball renders this as 'hospitality'. *Poets and politics*, p. 18.   [114] *DMU*, poem 14, stanza 8, pp. 132–3.
[115] Ibid., poem 20, stanza 16, pp. 186–7.   [116] Ibid., poem 18, stanza 17, pp. 162–3.
[117] Ibid., poem 24, stanza 9, pp. 228–9.

best poems.[118] In a similar instance, the poet Muiris Ó hEoghusa announces how Cú Chonnacht has shared his *onóir* with the Maguires, the sense being that while Cú Chonnacht derives much of his status by virtue of ancient lineage, he is an individual of sufficient honour to bring further glory to the line.[119] *Onóir* can also come from attaining titles, as when a parallel is drawn between Alexander the Great and Cú Chonnacht: as the kingship of the world was sufficient honour to the former (the 'King of Greece'), so the highkingship of Ireland should satisfy the King of Fermanagh.[120] And, finally, *onóir* is not something restricted to individuals, for Ireland itself also enjoys this sense of honour. It is, however, tied up in notions of the highkingship and is an element of the literary conceit in which lords are 'wedded' to the female Ireland in a marriage of sovereignty. The example of this comes in a poem written most likely by Ferghal Óg Mac an Bháird – '*Cia re bhfuil Éiri ac anmhuin?*' – in which Ireland is said to have no honour since she lacks a high-king.[121] The implication here being that it lay upon Maguire to restore that honour. *Eineach* and *onóir* share overlapping meanings, but there is no definitive evidence that the former is giving way to the latter as the preferred term in court panegyric.

In trying to determine change or continuity in conceptions of noble honour in these poems, we must consider one further term, *clú*, for it enjoys by far the greatest usage in this collection. By contrast, it appears but once in the *ALC*, presumably because its basic meaning is fame or reputation and it was the job of the court poet, not the annalistic compiler, to increase that of his patron.[122] Consequently, it was the most hyperbolic term at the *file*'s disposal. One poet had the hubris to claim that Cú Chonnacht's *clú* was known throughout Europe; another compared it to that enjoyed by the mythical Ulster hero Cú Chulainn.[123] Chiefly, *clú* is won on the field, if not exclusively so.[124] And though it is not specifically tied to rank and status, the

---

[118] Ibid., poem 19, stanza 21, pp. 176–7.   [119] Ibid., poem 21, stanza 21, pp. 196–7.
[120] Ibid., poem 22, stanza 22, pp. 210–11.   [121] Ibid., poem 2, stanza 2, pp. 16–17.
[122] The example tells how John, the son of Domhnall Caech O'Maelmhuaidh, fought hard against his slayers, an action which added to his *clú*. *ALC*, pp. 328–9. There is possibly also a metrical consideration behind the frequent use of the word in verse. A single-syllable word, it could be worked easily into quatrains at a variety of places. Moreover, it provided a useful internal-rhyming partner with the commonly used word *crú*, meaning blood, an important term in historical and genealogical themes.
[123] *DMU*, poem 17, stanza 30, pp. 156–7.
[124] Ibid., poem 4, stanza 20, pp. 38–9; poem 6, stanzas 3, 14, pp. 52–3, 56–7. But it is not necessarily something that is only connected to force, as in the case when the poet modifies the term to reflect its connection to conflict. He notes Maguire's possession of *clú troda* (fame for fighting), with which he returned from battle. Ibid., poem 11, stanza 28, pp. 106–7.

possession of *clú* did serve to distinguish the lord from the commoners (*coirrphobal*).[125] But like any possession, it could be lost and so required guardianship. In one poem Cú Chonnacht is told to 'remember the defence of your fame, it is imposed on you as a duty'.[126]

Clú seems to have an even more exclusively exterior quality than either *eineach* or *onóir*, a fact demonstrated in some rather naked discussions of an economy of fame. Valour on the battlefield is only translatable to lasting *clú* if it is put to verse by a bard, warns the poet Giolla Riabhach Ó Cléirigh.[127] For the possession of true *clú*, however, both valour and bardic praise are necessary because one can get false *clú* from the poet's art by simply paying for it. Cú Chonnacht's fame, Ó Cléirigh confirms, is 'not fictitious' for he has won it in the field.[128] A still stronger articulation of this arrangement occurs when the Maguire warriors are lauded for having defended their *clú* against their enemies, and in doing so having 'bought theirs [their *clú*] without bestowing their jeweled ornaments'.[129] But, of course, it is only by parting with his wealth that Cú Chonnacht ensures his lasting glory, valorous actions notwithstanding. The giving of gifts should match the desire for fame, writes one poet,[130] while another states the system elegantly in the following lines:

> The fame of a lord, to which all
> should defer, is a signpost;
> fame follows a good name,
> it will be marked out by being without wealth.[131]

Fame, then, was perhaps the highest ideal of Gaelic lords and bards. One beautifully evocative line from a contemporaneous poem penned for Pilib O'Reilly, chief of the O'Reillys, would also apply to Cú Chonnacht Maguire and all Gaelic lords (at least as their mentalities are depicted in bardic verse): 'well did he understand the proverb that glory is more permanent than life'.[132]

Fame, as represented by *clú*, is not synonymous with honour, as expressed in either *eineach* or *onóir*. There are certainly overlaps, not the

---

[125] Ibid., poem 11, stanza 30, pp. 108–9.   [126] Ibid., stanza 21, pp. 104–5.
[127] Ibid., poem 8, stanza 32, pp. 76–7.
[128] Ibid., poem 18, stanza 5, pp. 158–9. The theme of this poem is a comparison between the fame of two historical figures named Cú – Cú Chulainn and Cú Raoi – and that of Cú Chonnacht, thus the discussion of fictional versus earned fame.
[129] Ibid., poem 11, stanza 9, pp. 102–3.   [130] Ibid., poem 9, stanza 33, pp. 86–7.
[131] Ibid., poem 8, stanza 1, pp. 68–9.
[132] 'maith do thuig sé an seanfhocal / gur buaine bladh ná saoghal'. James Carney (ed.), *Poems on the O'Reillys* (Dublin, 1997), poem 8, 2, stanza 32, p. 47. Translation mine.

least of which is a heritable predilection to all three. We have already seen the connection of lineage to *eineach* and *onóir*, and *clú* too is said to follow the blood of the Maguires. But the bequest is merely a tendency not a guarantee, and the relationship between familial and individual *clú* is a dialectical one: whereas the collective fame of the family benefited each new chief, the conduct of the latter could jeopardize that of the former.[133] Heritable or not, however, *clú* lacks the internal qualities of *eineach*, and the attachment to rank and status of *onóir*. A clear demonstration of this point is the fact that lords can derive *clú* from their *eineach*, meaning that they can earn fame for being honourable. *Clú*, then, is more often the term chosen to cover the martial fame of the warrior.

Having looked at the words used for honour, nobility and fame, let us now consider how Cú Chonnacht was actually described by his various panegyrists. Do these descriptions change over the course of his career? How sensitive are they to changing circumstances? Does he come across as king, warlord or Renaissance noble? Given the nature of the evidence, it is difficult to offer iron-clad answers to these questions. Nevertheless, there is enough evidence here to suggest that the noble honour demonstrated by Cú Chonnacht was less martial in origin than we may perhaps expect. In the above discussion of the origins of *clú*, the indisputable importance of militarism to its construction has been noted. Further examples abound. His charter, for instance, is said to rest in physical force: at one point it is said to come from the sword, at another from the number of foreigners' tombs he is responsible for.[134] At the same time, however, one composition tells us that that sort of activity is not the stuff of kings, for a king is not a warrior. And although aggressive behaviour may have befitted Cú Chonnacht at an early stage in his career, once elevated to the lordship he must act according to different criteria. In the words of this particular bard, 'although he has pacified the gap of danger, a warrior's activity is not work suitable for a king'.[135] This is echoed in a composition by Maoilín Ó an Cháinte who notes how Cú Chonnacht has given up raids in exchange for his present title.[136] This does not mean that he is unwilling to fight when necessary, and in the poem in which Mac an Bháird compares Maguire to

---

[133] Ibid., poem 11, stanza 22, pp. 106–7. And the poet adds, unsurprisingly, that the bard is needed in order to stitch those two together. There is a similar usage in poem 12, stanza 10, pp. 132–3, in which Cú Chonnacht's name serves as a stand-in for his fame. An interesting nod to that distinction between worth of the individual and the fame of the family appears in Mac an Bháird's answer to the rhetorical question, 'why do I advise Cu Connacht as high king?' He does so, he claims, on account of the lord's disposition, not on account of his blood and lineage. Ibid., poem 2, stanza 17, pp. 20–1.
[134] Ibid., poem 22, stanza 4, pp. 204–5; poem 6, stanza 9, pp. 54–5; poem 10, stanza 25, pp. 96–7.
[135] Ibid., poem 1, stanza 13, pp. 6–8.   [136] Ibid., poem 22, stanza 40, pp. 214–15.

the 'Rome of honour', it is added that like Cú Chulainn, Cú Chonnacht is prohibited from suffering insults.[137] Cú Chonnacht, then, as Mac an Bháird writes in another composition, has the disposition of both prince and soldier;[138] once attaining the status of *rí*, however, it appears that he should be guided by the former.[139] Consequently, we see him praised most often for the goodness of his lordship: for his upholding of the law;[140] for his honouring of oaths and love of good ordinances;[141] for his reasonable ambition and lack of covetousness for others' lands;[142] for his lack of argumentativeness and his steadfastness against angry pride;[143] for his accessibility and the frequency of his assemblies;[144] for his chastity, worship of God, and protection of holy places;[145] for his learning, as much as any poet we are told;[146] for his desire to collect only reasonable tribute, the result of which is an increase in the number of his followers;[147] and for his respect for sanctuaries and avoidance of combats.[148] As the Munster poet Conchubhair Crón Ó Dálaigh claims, Cú Chonnacht 'conquers by refraining to fight'.[149] It has recently been suggested that honour claims in England stressed the ability to keep the peace; the same could be said of claims made in Fermanagh.[150]

Undoubtedly, the compositions considered here are constructed almost entirely from time-honoured tropes and themes, but they may still reveal something of the discourse of noble honour in the contested border lordship of sixteenth-century Fermanagh. On the one hand, the move towards a more modern-looking sense of nobility encompassed in the terms *tiarna* and *daonnacht* (as revealed in *ALC*) is almost entirely absent here. *Eineach* in this *duanaire* retains its prominence as an arbitrator between individual

---

[137] Ibid., poem 14, stanza 17, pp. 134–5.   [138] '*míleadh*' and '*flath*'. Ibid., poem 2, stanza 36, pp. 24–5.

[139] He is referred to variously as *rí* and *ardrí*.

[140] Ibid., poem 20, stanza 15, pp. 186–7, where it is mentioned how the gallows are bent from all the criminals Cú Chonnacht has hanged.

[141] Ibid., poem 22, stanza 12, pp. 206–7.

[142] Ibid., poem 1, stanza 36, pp. 12–13; poem 4, stanza 6, pp. 34–5.

[143] Ibid., poem 2, stanzas 32 and 29, pp. 24–5. Curiously, this sense of measured behaviour extends to actions on the field, for it is claimed that he refrains from shaming (*náir*) his enemies when subduing them, stanza 21, pp. 20–1.

[144] Ibid., poem 2, stanza 31, pp. 24–5; poem 22, stanza 13, pp. 206–7.

[145] Ibid., poem 2, stanza 34, pp. 24–5.

[146] Ibid., poem 8, stanza 14, pp. 70–1. A similar sentiment occurs in poem 10, stanza 12, pp. 92–3, where it is written that he read books of history before raiding. It also shows up in poem 21, stanza 30, pp. 200–1, where he claims that the *clú* of a learned man is greater when Cú Chonnacht is in the hall; and in poem 21, stanza 35, pp. 200–1, when he is praised for being able to understand scholarly activity and to decipher genealogies quickly. His reading of books is also claimed in poem 2, stanza 35, pp. 24–5.

[147] Ibid., poem 1, stanza 36, pp. 12–13. In poem 22, stanza 17, pp. 208–9 it is stated that in spite of his ability for 'manly deeds' he prefers to unite people.

[148] Ibid., poem 22, stanza 17, pp. 208–9.   [149] Ibid., poem 4, stanza 19, pp. 38–9.

[150] Pollock, 'Honor, gender and reconciliation'.

conceptions of worth and community expectations for legitimate authority, superseded neither by *onóir* or *uasal.* The retention of royal terminology and the trope of the highkingship also mark the traditional character of these verses. Moreover, the lack of discussion of the English presence is remarkable. Lest we make too much of that, however, it should be borne in mind that there is little mention, positive or negative, of the O'Neill presence either – the major power broker in the region and the one to whom the Maguires traditionally owed obeisance.

What in the end really stands out in these poems is the privileging of good lordship over martial valour in the calculus of noble honour. If these poems were mere sentimental artefacts, we should expect greater discussion of Cú Chonnacht as vanquisher of his neighbours. Could the dominance of the opposite sentiment in this collection represent, in fact, an awareness of the very precariousness of the Maguires' socio-political position? Remembering Nicholas Canny's suggestion that bardic compositions are the closest thing to state papers that Gaelic Ireland has to offer,[151] and the fact that the *filí* were seen as indispensable advisors and not just hangers-on of Gaelic and Gaelicized lords, then perhaps we should be a little more sensitive to the implications of this repetitiveness.

Seen in this way, the empirical reality of these compositions is not so important, and the novel is not necessarily any more significant than the stock. Of more moment is the exercise of choice and the use of repetition. Given the range of traditional motifs at the poets' disposal to characterize noble honour, the consistency with which they chose to highlight good lordship over aggressiveness and warlordism seems significant. The serial recitation by these *filí* of a socio-political *via media* may have served, in fact, to advise Cú Chonnacht to expend his energy in an attempt to keep a low profile and safely navigate treacherous political waters rather than try to exploit the fluidity of the time for his own or his family's aggrandizement. If so, then Ó Dálaigh's pronouncement that Cú Chonnacht 'conquers by refraining to fight' might be better understood to mean that his patron *survives* by avoiding conflict, which undoubtedly was the case sandwiched as he was between O'Neill, on one side, and the forces of an expansionist government centred in London, on the other. Rather than telling Cú Chonnacht what he wished to hear and so ensure his patronage, perhaps

---

[151] Nicholas Canny, 'The formation of the Irish mind: religion, politics and Gaelic Irish literature 1580–1750', *P&P* 95 (1982), pp. 91–116; reference is to p. 111. To this we can add Simms' conclusion that bardic compositions are concerned with current events and have 'the immediacy and individual touch of a letter or diary in other cultures'. Simms, 'Bardic poetry as a historical source', p. 60.

these men were telling him what they thought he *should* hear, and this done with an eye to sustaining his lordship without which they may have had no patron at all. Gaelic honour here has undergone change, not in the emergence of new terms or definitions, but in the prominence of certain traditional elements at the expense of others.

THE POEMS OF TADHG DALL Ó HUIGINN

The Ó hUiginn poems provide a useful complement to those addressed to Maguire. If the Maguire *duanaire* reveals the full range of treatments of noble honour directed toward one person, the collected poems of Tadhg Dall Ó hUiginn give a similarly comprehensive tour through one poet's handling of the subject. These compositions are directed to a variety of Gaelic and Old English lords representing a broad range of social and political situations and must be seen within the context of the vagaries of Ó hUiginn's own career and personal circumstances. Born *c.*1550 into a long-standing Sligo bardic family, Tadhg Dall became the chief poet to Cormac O'Connor Sligo, head of the powerful O'Connor Sligo lordship of north Connacht. Although he would remain attached to the court of O'Connor Sligo, Tadhg Dall, as did most *filí*, wrote encomia to numerous other lords, most notably the Ulster chiefs O'Neill, O'Donnell and Maguire, and to the O'Haras and Old English MacWilliam Burkes of Connacht. Given the large number of compositions (forty-one), the breadth of subjects and patrons, and the broad chronological period covered, Tadhg Dall's oeuvre offers an excellent place to explore bardic conceptions of honour and nobility in the last third of the sixteenth century.

Once again, let us start simply with the words used to denote honour and nobility. *Eineach* and *onóir* register nearly the same number of appearances, and there is overlap in the way they are deployed. There does seem to be a difference, however, in the way the two words are used, most notably that *eineach* seems to connote something more internal and heritable. Thus, while the word can be translated as 'generosity' or 'hospitality', the sense is not of simple largess but of something akin to a virtue, a tendency to hospitality passed by blood. Speaking of the O'Neills he claims that the family's *eineach* was given them originally by Saint Patrick, but realized in its maturity in the person of the present O'Neill, Toirdhealbhach Luineach.[152] The sense of *eineach* as heritable and encompassing obligation comes out more

---

[152] Knott, *Bardic poems of Tadhg Dall Ó hUiginn* 2, poem 7, stanza 49, p. 32 (hereafter *BPTD*). Unless otherwise stated I will be using the editor's translations.

The politics and culture of honour

strongly in those instances when 'honour' is clearly the best translation: when Tadhg Dall requests something of O'Donnell, he reminds O'Donnell that by his *eineach* he is required to answer him;[153] and when seeking the protection of Cormac Ó hEaghra, the poet appeals to the latter's *eineach*.[154] The faith (or hope) Ó hUiginn places in the power of Maguire's status as a man of honour is such that he claims it extends to protect a person even when in an English-style court of law.[155] And, of course, *eineach* is attached to the *eineachlann*, the honour-price, which is mobilized most often to atone for insult. In these poems we read of insults to *eineach*, never to *onóir*.[156]

In contrast to *eineach*, *onóir*, while it can on occasion carry the sense of a heritable trait or predilection (as when the MacSweeny Fanadh is said to obtain *onóir* from his ancestors/ancestry),[157] it more frequently connotes action. Generally, this means the bestowing of honour on someone by a lord. At other points, *onóir* pertains to unique privileges enjoyed by certain persons. Two components of the *onóir* of the Maguires, for instance, were the right to bathe and receive sleeping arrangements first amongst a lordly host.[158] Related to this usage was *onóir* as a mark of the limited homage the Maguires owed the Ulster high-kings O'Neill and O'Donnell.[159] One curious use of the term appears in a poem to Cathal Ó Conchobhair in which Ó hUiginn declares his inability to list even half of what he has received 'from appealing in thy honour'.[160] Here *onóir* assumes the sense of obligation to, or predilection for, hospitality otherwise reserved in these poems for *eineach*.[161] Outside of this one example, however, *onóir* retains a more external, transitive quality than *eineach*. Gaelic ideas of noble honour continue in these poems to be discussed chiefly in terms of *eineach*, much as they did in the poems to Maguire.

Clú and *glóir*, although not often used by Tadhg Dall, are called upon when the sense of fame or good reputation is desired.[162] *Clú*, which of the two appears more often, could be gained for a variety of positive things – fighting,[163] hospitality[164] and wealth[165] prominent among them – and

[153] This could perhaps also be taken to mean that given O'Donnell's *eineach*, Ó hUiginn fully expects that the request will be addressed. Ibid., poem 3, stanza 43, p. 17.
[154] Ibid., poem 30, stanza 3, p. 143.   [155] See, for example, poem 22a, 1, pp. 160–8.
[156] See, for example, ibid., poem 3, pp. 13–18; and poem 22a, 11, stanza 16, p. 107.
[157] Ibid., poem 27, stanza 25, p. 132. The MacSweenys were one of the most powerful sub-lords in the O'Donnell overlordship.
[158] Ibid., poem 9, stanzas 31, 32, p. 41.   [159] Ibid., stanzas 15, 22, pp. 39, 40.
[160] Ibid., poem 14, stanza 19, p. 39.   [161] Ibid., poem 14, pp. 62–5.
[162] Knott translates it as fame. Ibid., poem 32, stanza 68, p. 158, as one example.
[163] Ibid., poem 10, stanza 10, p. 45.   [164] Ibid., stanza 14, p. 45; and poem 29, stanza 25, p. 141.
[165] Earned on account of 'surpassing treasure'. Ibid., poem 11, stanza 3, p. 49.

was something to be broadcast throughout Ireland.[166] And while it could be derived from the family name,[167] it needed to be upheld by each generation.[168] By attaining *clú* the individual, regardless of how illustrious his bloodlines, could achieve lasting fame as one of the paragons of his line. With this conceit in mind, Ó hUiginn compared the *clú* of various patrons to the mythological warriors Cú Chulainn and Hercules. However, that which could be gained could also be lost or tarnished, and the poet was the force driving both. To the Maguires, for instance, Tadhg Dall laments the poets' having over the years 'harmed' the *clú* of the Maguires by dispraising it in the course of praising the seed of Conall.[169]

Glóir shares *clú*'s basic range of meanings, with one difference being that *glóir* appears once in a collective sense, whereas *clú* never does. The example is curious in that it states that the *glóir* of the Gaels has over recent times gone into decline. However, while this suggests awareness of the effects of the political and social pressures occasioned by Tudor state formation, the reason for this eclipse of glory is ascribed to the jealousy amongst Irish lords which keeps them in conflict with one another. Perhaps here we are seeing one of the first seeds of bardic complaint over lack of co-operation amongst their patrons to resist subordination to Westminster and Whitehall. This is quite possible, but there is only one example to support the supposition. Typically these two terms are used much as they always had been, and as they were used in the Maguire poems: to signify the fame deriving from individual traits or actions.[170]

Like the poets whose work comprises the Maguire collection, Ó hUiginn too makes frequent use of royal vocabulary. He employs the full panoply from *flaith* (prince), to *mac rí* (king's son), to *rí* (king) and even *ardrí* (high-king). Descriptive forms of *rí* are not uncommon either, as when O'Hara is said to come from 'royal stock' (*ríoghda*), and the household of MacWilliam is described as of the queen (*ríoghna*).[171] Royal terminology is also employed to describe territory, as in '*roflaithis*', or princedom, to denote the territory of the Gaelicized Old English lord, Eamonn Burc.[172] Although the usage of *rí* is somewhat loose – Ó hUiginn applies the term to Gaelic overlords such as the

[166] Ibid., poem 7, stanza 14, p. 29; poem 25, stanza 32, p. 123; and poem 33, stanza 13, p. 153.
[167] Ibid., poem 22a, II, stanza 8, p. 106.   [168] Ibid., poem 32, stanza 79, p. 159.
[169] Ibid., poem 3, stanza 4, p. 13.
[170] One thing worth considering, however, is why these words appear so much less often in this collection than in the Maguire *duanaire*.
[171] *BPTD*, vol. 1, poem 29, stanza 2, p. 209; poem 20, stanza 61, p. 149.
[172] *BPTD*, vol. 2, poem 18, stanza 8, p. 87.

O'Neills, lesser Gaelic lords like the Maguires, and Gaelicized Old English lords like the MacWilliam Burkes alike – the depiction of a patron as *rí* has its limits. When enumerating the rights of Mac Suibhne Fánad, head of one of the main subordinate families to the O'Donnells, Ó hUiginn states that while the Mac Suibhnes were kings they could not be high-kings. The head of the clan could serve as *ardrí* on an interim basis between the death of the old and the selection of the new, but he could never be a candidate for the permanent post. Consequently, part of his status was derived by privileges he claimed vis-à-vis the high-king, such as the right to keep watch over the couch on which the latter was reclining. This example suggests that while royal terminology was applied to a variety of Gaelic and Old English elites, it was not indiscriminately bandied about.[173] If it is correct to see in bardic poetry not the recitation of ossified archaisms, but rather the manipulation of traditional tropes to suit present demands, then perhaps the effectiveness of that manipulation was derived in part from the poets' fealty to that tradition's constraints of hierarchy and the rights it described.

Looking below the level of royalty – fictitious or not – Ó hUiginn uses a number of terms when speaking of the gentry and nobility. Most commonly, he speaks of *uaisle*, nobles, a term typically covering unspecified groups of elites. Thus, we encounter amongst these poems the nobility of Ireland, of Sligo and various nobles present at Gaelic lordly courts all introduced as *uaisle*.[174] Only once does he speak of *maithe*, a term favoured in *ALC* and generally rendered as 'gentlemen' or 'nobility'. Of note is the occurrence of *laochra*, meaning heroes or warriors, a term entirely absent from *ALC* for the entry years 1540–90 and so suggestive of the more hidebound outlook of the poets relative to that of the annalists. Beyond that observation, the interchangeable use of these terms makes difficult any effort to determine change in notions of noble honour strictly by lexical consideration.[175]

Perhaps we can gain some sense of Ó hUiginn's understanding of the difference between European nobilities and Irish lords, and the tropes used to describe the latter, by looking at the appearance of peerage titles and titles

---

[173] It should be noted that subordinate status to a greater lord was not incompatible with noble honour. Tadhg Dall, in the course of praising the O'Neills, writes how it is no disgrace or shame to other Irish lords to follow the O'Neills. Curiously, this represents the single mention of shame or disgrace in the collection. Ibid., poem 7, stanza 51, p. 33.

[174] Ibid., poem 14, stanza 33, p. 65; poem 16, stanza 46, p. 76; and poem 11, stanza 26, p. 51.

[175] Complicating matters, as is always the case when dealing with this material, is the possibility that choice may have been determined as much by metrical demands as anything else.

of office in his work. Unfortunately, for present purposes, this is infrequently done. In fact, Tadhg Dall only once refers to someone as an earl, MacWilliam Burke, and this is done in a historical context, for the MacWilliam Burkes did not hold an earldom in this period. The reference is instead to the Norman earls from whom the family descended, and the appearance of the term in the poetry is part of a laudatory pedigree.[176] As for discussion of the proliferating titles of colonial offices, there is but a single mention of a sheriff. Seen from this angle at least, Ó hUiginn was not speaking the language of cultural and political awareness, let alone convergence.

Taking stock at this point, a purely lexical study of Ó hUiginn's verse reveals a very traditional outlook. Occasional snippets give a sense of aware-ness and concern for changing socio-political circumstances, but these are greatly outweighed by stock phrases and terminology. Working strictly from frequency of use, *eineach* remains the primary word encapsulating Gaelic notions of noble honour: the connection to Brehon law and the honour price, the sense of obligation and protection, and the need to defend it. *Onóir*, by contrast, is reserved for those situations when the bestowing of honour by one person upon another is in question. *Clú* and *glóir*, in turn, cover references to simple fame and glory. But while the discussion above has displayed the range of meanings and contexts of the words available to a *file* like Ó hUiginn for discussing concepts of honour and nobility, it has not given a sense for change over time. If change is to be found here, it must come from exploration of individual poems – their themes, subjects and dates and how the terms we have already explored appear in them.

If these are men of the highest ranks of *eineach*, then what are the characteristics and patterns of behaviour unique to them that set them up as such? In short, what does a man of honour look like in the work of Ó hUiginn? Much of the description in these poems is as traditional as the vocabulary. It often seems hyperbolic at best, but by no means uniformly so. For instance, the homes and affinities of Gaelic lords are referred to as courts, even as a king's court (*cúirte an ríogh*).[177] This terminology is not a total conceit, however, for these men were surrounded by advisors, other elites, officers and various hangers-on who would have filled a lord's house. On offer too are some fascinating, if perhaps idealized, descriptions of courtly life. In describing Lifford Castle, Ó hUiginn writes 'Beloved is the

---

[176] Ibid., poem 23, stanza 18, p. 113; and poem 25, stanza 11, p. 121. Their southern rivals in Galway, the Clanricard Burkes, beat them to this honour; being made Earls of Clanricard through the policy of surrender and regrant in 1543.

[177] Ibid., poem 11, stanza 30, p. 52.

castle in which we used to spend a while at chess-playing, a while with the daughters of the men of Bregia, a while with the fair books of the poets'.[178] When speaking of Enniskillen Castle, seat of the Maguires, he speaks of nobles in a 'thronged court' dividing treasure and of the presence of those who knew the genealogy of the Grecian Gaels (*Gaoidheal nGréag*).[179] Of continued currency are the ancient tropes of physical beauty, ancient pedigree and hospitality. This last is one of the most important, revealingly demonstrated in the sentiment that 'beloved are the two who keep that house without excess, without lack'.[180]

Unsurprisingly, these poems are also replete with reminders of the bard's ancient and necessary role in the calculus of Gaelic noble honour. On the one hand, a lord could not be a lord without a chief poet. Thus, we read how the Maguire lords always have a poet at their 'right hand',[181] and, more explicitly, of how the presence of a poet at a man's elbow 'ennobles' him.[182] On the other, and as we have touched upon briefly above, if the presence of the poet was necessary to confirm status, so his art was needed to bring a lord's claim to honour before its final jury, the wider public.

A poem to Cormac Ó hEaghra nicely parses out the workings of the Gaelic economy of honour. Ó hUiginn praises Cormac as a good merchant, shrewd in his cattle dealings. But, he continues, Cormac passes on this worldly wealth in favour of honour since praise of 'his noble, ruddy countenance shall endure eternally'.[183] The bulk of the composition is then given over to a didactic analogy in which Ó hUiginn portrays his patron as a good merchant, namely one who bargains panegyric for baubles.[184] Ó hUiginn laments that few are buying poems these days, and, consequently, their price has plummeted. Cormac, however, has a good eye for the market and is wise to stock up on this commodity when the price is low. For his own part, Ó hUiginn refers to himself as a 'trafficker in the gold of poesy'.[185] Wealth here did not guarantee honour, for the latter could only be called forth by public confirmation. It did, however, play an important role in sustaining the patronage relationship with those who would spread the lord's deeds and pedigree abroad and thus confirm his honour. This connection between a lord's inherent, God-given, tendency towards honour and the role of the *file* in finding an audience before which that virtue could be actuated comes in the poem's last quatrain:

---

[178] Ibid., poem 5, stanza 7, p. 24.   [179] Ibid., poem 11, stanza 14, p. 50.
[180] Ibid., poem 5, stanza 2, p. 24.   [181] Ibid., poem 11, stanza 26, p. 51.
[182] Ibid., poem 27, stanza 20, p. 132.   [183] Ibid., poem 31, stanzas 4 and 5, p. 146.
[184] Ibid., stanza 10, p. 147.   [185] Ibid., stanza 40, p. 149.

> From God above he hath
> excellence of truth and constancy;
> in the house of election
> he hath triumphed in generosity and prowess.[186]

What of violence as grounds for noble honour? Again, in the literature dealing with Gaelic notions of honour, martial activity and autonomy of action have been offered as its most vital elements. The praise of valour and noble freedom of action certainly appear in Ó hUiginn's verse. To take but one example, he admonishes O'Donnell, telling him to avenge insult to his family, territory and lordship before making peace with rivals in Connacht.[187]

It is too simple to suggest, however, that an unqualified preference for militarism lay at the heart of Gaelic notions of honour. A fascinating poem addressed to Brian na Murrtha Ó Ruairc suggests not only the acceptable parameters within which violence could be legitimately wielded, but also contrasts the inherent civility of the Gael who understands and respects those constraints upon physical force with the 'foreigner' who indiscriminately resorts to violence in pursuit of personal interest. The general thrust of the composition is that since the only thing the English understand is violence, one must deal with them through force not diplomacy. This sentiment is pithily declared in the first stanza: 'only a fighting man finds peace'. Brian is urged to forget his differences with other Gaelic lords and oversee a unification of strength that will overturn English incursions. Of interest here is how Ó hUiginn chastises Brian for being too civil, not because that is a dishonourable character trait, but because it is one that, given present circumstances, invites extinction. '[T]he Gaels of civil behavior will not get peace from the foreigners', he exhorts. Later he adds that the English do not respect terms of peace and so it is necessary to resort to arms if Brian wishes to maintain his authority and the greater honour of the Gaels, regardless of how reluctant he may be to do so. Moreover, Tadhg Dall contrasts the Irish taste for peace against continental trends toward militarization. He laments that

> It is because of their weakness
> in fighting men against the foreign battalions
> that beyond those of any land in Europe
> this wounded and unfairly-used people lack peace.[188]

Thus, he exhorts Brian with the promise that the people will follow a king (*rígh*) who will banish the foreigners.

---

[186] Ibid., stanza 62, p. 151.   [187] Ibid., poem 2, stanza 16, p. 8.   [188] Ibid., poem 16, stanza 8, p. 72.

Here, then, is what to the cursory eye may appear the classic articulation of proper kingship/authority arising from the exercise of physical force. And given the fact that Brian is recorded by Lord Deputy Sidney to have been 'the proudest man he ever dealt with in Ireland',[189] this would also seem to be an archetypal expression of telling a patron what he wanted to hear. Yet, curiously, this appeal to martial valour as a basis for authority, status and noble honour appears innovative, created out of the pressures caused by English centralization and possibly intellectually influenced by the European military revolution.[190] Completing this picture of Irish virtue and English vice, Ó hUiginn cautions his patron against the inevitable bribes of the newcomers:

> Their robes of satin, their precious treasures,
> they will bring to the host of ancient Sligo,
> whose nobles will be plied with golden rings
> by the surly, impatient band.[191]

Echoing the concern for treachery demonstrated so forcefully in the *ALC*, the poet warns that Brian will be asked to come to court, an invitation to be avoided since no Gael who has accepted such an invitation in the past has returned thence 'safe from treachery or betrayal'.[192] As the poem begins, so it ends – in praise of peace, but declaring that only military mobilization against the English will secure that peace:

> Then will the Saxon tribe be vanquished
> by the seed of keen-weaponed Gaedheal
> so that from the proclamation of war
> there will never be any save Irishmen over the land of Fódla.[193]

If this was Ó hUiginn's view of Gaelic tendencies – that the Gaels were peaceful by nature and so needed goading to defend 'their' homeland – how then do we make sense of the next poem in Knott's collection, which in its declaration that Irish land belongs only to the strongest seems to make a mockery of Gaelic territorial claims? This famous poem – a work of praise to the Gaelicized Old English noble, MacWilliam Burke – is perhaps not so difficult to explain as often claimed if we bear in mind the Gaelic tradition of Ireland as a society created by the assimilation of waves of invaders and whose constitutional claims rested upon conquest. The opening line of the poem is

---

[189] Quoted by Knott (ed.). Ibid., vol. 2, p. 251.
[190] See Leerssen, *Mere Irish*, and Bradshaw, 'Native reaction', for excellent discussions of this phenomenon. On the European military revolution generally, see Geoffrey Parker, *The military revolution: military innovation and the rise of the west, 1500–1800* (Cambridge, 1988).
[191] *BPTD*, vol. 2, poem 16, stanza 30, p. 75.   [192] Ibid., stanza 43, p. 76.   [193] Ibid., stanza 68, p. 78.

arresting, for it states boldly that Ireland is 'but swordland: let all be defied to show that there is any inheritance to the Land of Fal save that of conquest by force of battle'.[194] This has generally been taken as clear evidence of the mercenary aspect of the bards and their lack of interest in anything more grandiose than their own personal and professional survival.[195]

At a certain level that is undoubtedly true, but the poem should not be read as such a cynical piece. Rather than generically stating that Ireland is merely up for grabs for the strongest, the verse instead provides a justification for the legitimacy of the 'English-Irish' MacWilliam Lords of Sligo, who, like all Irish lords, saw their constitutional claims anchored in conquest. The poem, in fact, reads like a versification of the *Lebor Gabála* (*The Book of Invasions*), the mytho-historical ur-text of seventeenth-century Irish national consciousness which described the growth of Irish society out of the assimilation of successive bands of foreign invaders. According to this line of thought, the Anglo-Norman invasion of the twelfth century was a crucial component of the diverse Irish polity that was under threat from Tudor, and later Stuart, centralization.[196] Moreover, what generally is not mentioned by commentators on this poem is the attention given to the peaceful and legitimate rule of the Burkes following their medieval forays into western Ireland. Burke is praised for his honesty, justice and the respect afforded him by Gael and Gall.[197]

This poem may be better understood, perhaps, as an effort to compare the historical Anglo-Norman conquest favourably against the contemporary Tudor effort. As Caball has argued, the poem is 'aimed at effecting ethnic coalescence among both historic communities on the basis of language and culture'.[198] There may be a further level of political theorizing at work here, however. Rather than simply an effort to unite the island's two historic communities in the face of unwanted political interference, this verse may serve as a disquisition on the process by which physical power becomes legitimate authority. Whereas both incursions were potentially legitimate – conquest offering the ideological underpinning of nearly all land holding in this period, as argued by Gael and Englishman alike – only the Norman invaders further justified their authority through just and honourable rule.

---

[194] Ibid., poem 17, stanza 1, p. 80.

[195] See Richard McCabe, *Spenser's monstrous regiment: Elizabethan Ireland and the poetics of difference* (New York, 2002), p. 48; Palmer, *Language and conquest*, pp. 212–14. It also appears in the title of the second chapter of Connolly, *Contested island*.

[196] On the knitting of the Old English into a new sense of Irish identity as *Éireannaigh* (Irish), see Ó Buachalla, 'James our true king', pp. 16–23; and Brendan Bradshaw, 'Geoffrey Keating: apologist of Irish Ireland', in Bradshaw, Hadfield and Maley (eds.), *Representing Ireland*, pp. 166–90.

[197] *BPTD*, vol. 2, poem 17, stanzas 64–7, pp. 85–6.   [198] Caball, *Poets and politics*, p. 47.

By contrast, the English of the sixteenth century followed up their physical incursions with martial law, corruption and self-enrichment and so forfeited their claim to legitimate rule in spite of their charter by conquest. Swordland or not, Ireland was a place where conquest brought power, but justice and good lordship brought legitimacy.

The connection between honourable character and comportment, on the one hand, and legitimate political authority, on the other, is made over and over again in these poems. For instance, Ó hUiginn praises Maguire's fostering of unity with other lords:

> Banbha [that is, Ireland] is guarded, though it be difficult,
> without violence or enmity;
> no man has accused the blood of Odhar
> of spoiling the Gaels.[199]

More extraordinary is the warning to Eamonn Burc not to pursue a first-strike military strategy. Ó hUiginn asks,

> What war has there ever been
> in which he that first started it
> was not vanquished?
> That is the way in wars.[200]

He then goes further, adding that

> Those who enkindle dissension
> are ever defeated in requital
> for making war, a work
> that does not meetly go unpunished.[201]

In a poem to MacWilliam Burke, Ó hUiginn makes his clearest statement that true lordship lies in finding a balance between aggressiveness and humility. The first quatrain states:

> Much circumspection is due to the title of king,
> it must be guarded both from
> headstrong arrogance and lack of vigor,
> it is truly difficult to defend it.[202]

For as Ó hUiginn goes on to explain, a headstrong man seeks wars, which in turn draw competition for the kingship, out of which he typically loses some or all of his lands. No better is the humble and servile man who is despised. Between these extremes lies the golden mean of kingship. Ó hUiginn then

---

[199] Ibid., poem 10, stanza 38, p. 47.   [200] Ibid., poem 18, stanza 16, p. 88.
[201] Ibid., stanza 20, p. 88.   [202] Ibid., poem 20, stanza 1, p. 93.

enumerates those traits that render Burke's lordship legitimate: he seeks nothing from others, yet leaves none wanting;[203] he has won 'every territory' and
thus assumed the kingship, yet his ambitions are no larger than to 'be as before,
Richard, son of MacWilliam';[204] he is the best of candidates since he is the
eldest and so can answer for his comrades;[205] he is temperate in spirit;[206] he is
prudent, but not humble or submissive;[207] and yet he is arrogant enough not to
be plundered.[208] The bulk of the remainder of the composition is dedicated to
illustrating the superiority of the middle way through a telling of the story of
Daedalus and his two sons. As in the Greek legend, so in the politics of Tudor
Ireland: he who flies between extremes prospers.[209]

As the above samples suggest, Ó hUiginn's verse is concerned more to
decry the persecution of just rulers than to create battle-rolls for assorted
patrons. We should not be surprised, then, to see in a composition to
Toirdhealbhach Luineach Ó Neill[210] the Irish likened to the Israelites:
morally sound and deserving of territory of their own but under threat
from a physically superior, if morally inferior, foe.[211] Cleaving to custom,
Toirdhealbhach Luineach is called *rí*, while the O'Neills generally are
praised for being most numerous in the rolls of Irish kings. Seven stanzas
in the middle of the work are given over to a classical description of O'Neill
as a king: he has never allowed the other men of Ireland to outdo those of
Ulster; he rules without envy or causing war; he keeps his word and despises
'evildoers'; he is a rigid upholder and enforcer of the law; he is unaffected by
the charms of wealth or the wiles of greed.[212] These all seem fairly standard
bardic descriptions of the Gaelic *rí*. What makes them seem less like
sleepwalking through the demands of a fossilized poetic form is the very
next stanza (number twenty-eight in Knott's edition) in which Ó hUiginn
remarks that these traits of Toirdhealbhach Luineach are surprising given
that Ireland outside the O'Neill lordship is but a 'wave of depredation'.[213]
Rather than a perfunctory trotting out of traditional tropes, this run of regal
descriptors functions to set up O'Neill as a new Noah who will deliver

---

[203] Ibid., stanza 7, p. 93.   [204] Ibid., stanza 8, p. 93.   [205] Ibid., stanza 9, p. 93.
[206] Ibid., stanza 11, p. 94.   [207] Ibid., stanza 12, p. 94.   [208] Ibid., stanza 13, p. 94.
[209] A similar preference for the *via media* is expressed in a later poem (no. 21) to one of the younger
Burkes, Maoilir. The first stanza states unequivocally to 'rein in your arrogant spirit and stop
plundering the children of Conn'. Ó hUiginn then reports that many are blaming him for recent
troubles between Ulster and Connacht septs. Moreover, he cautions Maoilir to get control of the
'troublesome, careless-minded' men among his followers. These young men live for the foray, but
once Maoilir becomes King of Connacht, he will regret not having tamed them. Ibid., stanzas 1, 12
and 15, pp. 99, 100.
[210] Ibid., poem 7, pp. 28–33.
[211] See ibid., poem 9, stanza 3, p. 38, in which the Maguires are styled '*clann Israhél na hEirionn*'.
[212] Ibid., poem 7, stanzas 22–7, p. 30.   [213] Ibid., stanza 28, p. 30.

Ulster out of the deluge of lawlessness that threatens to overwhelm Ireland. Duly, Ó hUiginn launches into an adaptation of the story of Noah in which the English 'reformers' are the deluge, the Plain of Conchobhair (O'Neill's patrimony) the ark, and Toirdhealbhach Luineach is Noah.[214] This poem with its creative use of traditional terms of lordly praise thus offers a fascinating example of how customary forms and tropes could, and were, adapted to fit present socio-political circumstances.

The appeal to a patron for 'deliverance' could be much more concrete, however, as a poem to one of the MacWilliam Burkes demonstrates.[215] This particular piece is a play to the lord's traditional obligation to protect his clients, inherent in the concept of *eineach*, when the supposed protections of the new order fail. Here Ó hUiginn describes going to a court of law (which one is unstated) in order to protect his belongings from seizure. He claims he was put off and his complaint passed on first to the sheriff, then to the lord president of Connaught.[216] And yet as far up the chain of command he pursued his grievance, he could get no satisfaction. Most galling was the fact that the patent he held for his lands – the supposed gold standard of ownership in the reformist Ireland of the Tudors – turned out to hold no weight with any of the officials he encountered.[217] Whereas many others in similar straits have despaired and accepted the loss of their goods, Ó hUiginn states that he has chosen to stay put in the hopes that MacWilliam will sort things out for him.[218] The poet had tried to play by what he thought were the new rules, but those rules kept changing. In the end he was forced, as he depicts it, to fall back on the protection of his traditional local lord and patron.

A more dramatic example of this sort of need for lordly protection in the face of a rather intrusive political authority comes in a poem to Cormac Ó hEaghra.[219] Ó hUiginn begins with a standard piece of praise, referring to Cormac as the 'chief royal of Cian's race'.[220] The next line is of more interest for here he appeals to Cormac for protection, asking specifically for Cormac to 'accept me on thy mercy and honour (*eineach*), protect me'.[221] Tadhg Dall craves this protection because of ordinances put in place by the English to curb the prevalence in Ireland of what they deemed masterless men. He then walks his patron through the practicalities of Tudor census/ethnographic efforts and their local implications. The government desires to 'know who every man is and his native place'; information which they

---

[214] Ibid., stanza 42, p. 32.   [215] Ibid., poem 22, pp. 104–5.
[216] Ibid., stanza 4, p. 104.   [217] Ibid., stanza 7, p. 104.   [218] Ibid., stanza 19, p. 105.
[219] Caball suggests that the background to this poem may be the composition of Connacht, a programme that set rents, payable to the government, on Irish-held land. *Poets and politics*, p. 36.
[220] Ibid., poem 30, stanza 2, p. 143.   [221] Ibid., stanza 3, p. 143.

will then record on rolls of parchment. Each man thus identified is to accept an overlord, who will serve as guarantor of that man's good conduct. It is for this reason that Tadhg Dall seeks the patronage of Ó hEaghra.[222] This scenario is quite curious in that poets seeking patrons were in Ireland a historical commonplace, but in this instance the catalyst for the request comes not from pursuit of the traditional *ollamh*–lord relationship, but out of a need to abide by the legal demands of an anglicizing local authority.

What can Ó hUiginn offer in return for this protection? He can tender his traditional skills as public relations man and genealogist. Giving a taste of those skills, he assures Ó hEaghra that since both Gael and Gall have chosen him (Ó hEaghra) for the 'title of righteous king', he (Ó hUiginn) will devote the best of his verse to you to make others envious.[223] Lest we think that the poet was bargaining from a position of weakness, that this was a mercy plea to a superior, we should note that Ó hUiginn placed great store in the power of his profession. He expected that were the pact agreed upon, Cormac would offer his 'life and body on my behalf if I be captured'.[224] Still, to sweeten the deal, he throws a final flattering line at Ó hEaghra's honour:

> Even were one on trial for his life in a courthouse,
> while depending on thy honour (*eineach*)
> neither he nor thou need tremble;
> here, Cormac, is the guarantee[225]

The honour of Ó hEaghra as described in this poem is something confirmed by Gael and Gall alike, something to which one could appeal for protection, and of sufficient stature to override the wishes of English and/or anglicized officials who may drag one through the new legal system. Idealized pleadings of the bard or not, these quatrains demonstrate the continued importance of traditional concepts of honour as enshrined in the notion of *eineach*, defined as an obligation to protect those to whom one is pledged. For even if the appeal worked solely as a rhetorical move, it still showed that quite serious legal and social predicaments could be navigated by playing upon customary honour obligations.

Throughout his career Ó hUiginn attempted to straddle the social and political changes brought to Irish society in the wake of the island's union to the English crown. Let us end with a poem that nicely illustrates the complexities of the contemporary scene: a complaint to Riocard Óg Burke

---

[222] Ibid., stanzas 11 and 12, p. 144. [223] Ibid., stanza 23, p. 145.
[224] Ibid., stanza 24, p. 145. [225] Ibid., stanza 25, p. 145.

not to accept an anglicized title or office.[226] Ó hUiginn begins by telling Burke he should not forsake his old appellation, 'Richard son of MacWilliam', in favour of a new rank. The old name is not only comfortable, like an old cloak or home, but it has done so much for him. The new title can make no such claims:

> as for the foreign title thou hast
> got, never didst though gain any
> advantage from it that the fame (*clú*)
> of the former title did not outdo.[227]

In a play to tradition, Ó hUiginn admits that an *eiric* (monetary compensation demanded by Brehon law) was leviable against him for reproaching Burke in this way. Nevertheless, he presses on with the reminder that

> Not happily didst thou
> obtain the strange title,
> or the horrid outlandish right,
> about which I made bold against thee.[228]

His tone turns more aggressive in two later quatrains:

> In the name of poetry
> we forbid thee to change thy title;
> thou shouldst renounce the new appellation
> rather than lose thy patrimony.

> Thou wert the sinew of Banbha's land
> until thou didst get the outlandish title;
> the sheriffship of Conn's seed would not compensate
> for leaving sinewless the fair hunting-field of Ior.[229]

This is then followed formulaically by a didactic tale, in this case the story of a French knight tempted by the offer of kingship. The story details a knight errant who comes to a land whose people annually choose a new king. Each year some flattered noble agrees to forsake the lordship of his local territory for the prize of monarchy. Equally predictably, that noble then finds himself stripped of office or authority, supreme or local, come the end of that year. But, as the story goes, one astute French knight refused the offer, understanding that the temporary elevation in status will result in his permanent

---

[226] Ibid., poem 22a, pp. 106–11. The actual title or office in question is unclear. As Knott points out, the only clue in the verse suggests possibly a sheriff, or perhaps seneschal. An honourific title appears not to be intended, however. Ibid., p. 263.
[227] Ibid., poem 22a, stanza 8, p. 106.   [228] Ibid., stanza 12, p. 107.
[229] Ibid., stanzas 19 and 21, p. 108.

banishment to a purgatory of no name or title once his turn at kingship is complete. Ó hUiginn exhorts Riocard Óg to be equally clear-headed and so resist the lure of an English-style title in favour of retaining his claim to the chieftainship of the MacWilliam Burkes. It is difficult to know just what was the difficulty Ó hUiginn saw between one's holding a lordship and serving as sheriff, for the latter by no means invalidated the former. Perhaps he saw the post as beneath the dignity of a *rí*. Whatever the reason, he clearly felt the move impinged upon that highest marker of Gaelic honour, the attainment of position as chief of the name. And, here, perhaps, we can perceive a more aggressive retention of, or perhaps retreat to, customary socio-cultural factors in the construction of Gaelic notions of noble honour.

Ó hUiginn's career was a long one, over the course of which he attempted to navigate the changes brought to his profession, his own social standing and that of his would-be patrons, and to Irish culture and society generally. If at times his deployment of the ancient forms and tropes of Gaelic courtly praise poetry seems archaic and out of step with evolving socio-political conditions, his suspicion regarding the taking of English titles by Irish lords and his astute comments on the dangers of warmongering and aggression reveal an intimate understanding of contemporary changes and a desire to control them, or at least negotiate them, as best he could. And while there is really no consistency to his positioning, aside from a desire to protect his standing, a general pattern does emerge of his favouring only a limited cultural assimilation. Like many bards before him, he was happy to sing the pedigrees and exploits of Gael and Gall alike. But the exchange of the Gaelic 'name' for an English title of office was one he looked upon with suspicion and trepidation. The former was a fundamental element of Gaelic honour, and thus one of the cornerstones of Irish social and political stability, and so not to be discarded or diluted.

The texts considered above give three different impressions of Gaelic conceptions of noble honour in the wake of Henry VIII's being proclaimed King of Ireland in 1541. *The Annals of Loch Cé* present a picture of nascent cultural and social convergence. Whereas *eineach* remained in common use, it seems to have been largely supplanted by a notion of nobility encapsulated in the definitions of *uasal* and *daonnacht*. And while royal terminology remained applicable to Gaelic and Old English subjects, the language of monarchy (*cing*, for example) was reserved exclusively for English and continental potentates. As Simms has argued, the *rí* was starting to be styled *tiarna* – but so too were incoming English officials and planters. Traditional terms were starting to change their signification in important ways in *ALC*.

The poems in the Maguire *duanaire*, even allowing for difference of genre, appear to take a more traditional approach to honour. It is still largely determined by the obligation to protect and entertain as expressed in the idea of *eineach*, and very little explicit attention is paid to external political influence. Nevertheless, the preponderance of themes addressing good lordship at the expense of martial ones seems significant.[230] On the one hand, it contradicts historiographical convention that Gaelic notions of honour were derived solely from militarism and touchiness.[231] As in England at the time, honour in the Maguire poems frequently derived from being willing and able to maintain peace; honour thus could foster social stability. On the other, it suggests that external factors, even if not explicitly addressed, could help determine which discourses of honour took precedence. It may not be the case that honour in Ireland became more pacific and 'civilized', but rather that certain traditional themes fitting particular socio-political situations were stressed, while others, deemed likely to exacerbate matters, were passed over. The previous chapter argued that Irish elites could be plotted along a continuum of European nobilities, if occupying a somewhat more marginal position. Here it seems that the arbiters of honour in Gaelic Ireland, the *filí*, by focusing on virtue over militarism, were attempting to move their patrons more towards the middle of that range.[232]

Ó hUiginn's verse is less traditional than that addressed to Cú Chonnacht Maguire, and more aggressive in its articulation of a culturally specific sense of honour as a means to cope with the realities of Tudor expansion. *Eineach* here retains its customary attachment to the lord's duty to protect, but is seen as relevant and functional in spite of the introduction of English common law. Ó hUiginn's complaints with the English are not concerned with the law or other elements of anglicization, however, but over the seeming inability or unwillingness of the newcomers to keep their

---

[230] By means of contrast, see Nicholas Canny's comments on Spenser's fixation with violence. Canny, *Making Ireland British*, chapter 1.

[231] For other commentaries on bardic cautions against foolhardy militarism and in support of lordly virtue, see Cunningham, 'The anglicisation of East Breifne', p. 63; Simms, 'Bardic poetry as a historical source', pp. 64, 69; and Simms, 'Bards and barons', p. 179.

[232] We can perhaps see the poets as part of a broader European trend of nobilities attempting to use virtue as an alternative language of social legitimacy in preference to martial valour. For continental parallels, see Schalk, *From valour to pedigree*; and H. C. Erik Midelfort, 'Curious Georgics: the German nobility and their crisis of legitimacy in the late sixteenth century', in Andrew C. Fix and Susan C. Karant-Nunn (eds.), *Germania illustrata: essays on early modern Germany presented to Gerald Strauss* (Kirksville, MO, 1992), pp. 217–42. Moreover, we can perhaps see this tutelary verse as partaking of a broader European trend of educating the aristocracy towards moral improvement. See J. H. Hexter, 'The education of the aristocracy in the Renaissance', *The Journal of Modern History* 22 (1950), pp. 1–20.

word, to uphold the laws they themselves have introduced, or to respect basic precepts of social trust.

Linking these disparate texts is an interpretation of events through a lens of honour. While they offer intimations of a growing concern for the defence of faith and fatherland, and demonstrate clearly an emergent pan-insular political awareness, their authors were not unilaterally favouring an ethnically or confessionally exclusive vision of Irish society: Gaelic Irish, Old English and even English lords and monarchs appear as (potentially) legitimate authorities. Rather they were speaking in terms of an interplay of culture and politics that was at times exclusionary – forcefully articulated in some of Ó hUiginn's verses[233] – but more often than not applicable to natives and newcomers alike. It is important to remember that the study of Gaelic writings, particularly bardic poetry, is not the study of 'discourse'. Verse eulogies were performed live and were vital components of a lord's legitimacy; they were, to invoke Canny's and Simms' comments again, akin to state papers and letters. Attention to matters of honour in the poetry reveals signs of pan-British cultural and political concerns.

In the wake of 1541, therefore, the politics of honour played a vital role in Anglo–Irish relations. The successes of surrender and regrant, and the frequency with which Gaelic commentators framed Tudor policies in terms of honour imperatives, revealed the potential of melding honour systems as a means to effect what had never been accomplished in the long history of those relations: an integrated nobility, loyal to one executive authority and partaking of common social and cultural patterns. This is not to argue that the transition was smooth, uncomplicated or to everyone's liking, but merely that appeals to honour were used by allcomers in competition for place and power in 'British' Ireland. As Ó hUiginn in his more revanchist moods demonstrated, however, that which could build could also tear apart. If Anglo-Irish relations could come together along lines drawn by honour, they could split apart at the very same seams: just as Henry VIII could turn on his new subjects when his honour was bruised, so could those subjects resist their new monarch when they felt dishonoured. That is precisely what happened during Tyrone's Rebellion and the ensuing Nine Years' War, the effects of which would reverberate through England as well as Ireland.

---

[233] See Palmer, *Language and conquest*, pp. 212–16, for discussion of the spectacular ethnic violence encouraged in Ó hUiginn's 'poem of instigation' to Brian O'Rourke.

CHAPTER 3

'British' honour and the Nine Years' War

This book's previous two chapters have argued for honour as a factor in Anglo-Irish politics of the sixteenth century. While considering both English state and Irish elite perspectives, they have nonetheless focused largely on Ireland and Irish society. Moreover, Chapter 2's extended attention to language (deemed necessary because a sustained study of Gaelic terms for honour and their uses is vital for the rest of this project and none existed) and consequent focus on literary sources begs a very pertinent question: were discussions of honour merely discourse and only tangentially related to 'real world' activities? This chapter aims to broaden the investigation of British honour politics by, first, returning the discussion of honour to the realm of people and events, and, second, attempting to show the effects of Anglo-Irish honour politics on England as well as Ireland.

Let us set the stage with a brief exploration of perhaps the most famous example of the intersection of honour imperatives and high politics in sixteenth-century Ireland: the fizzled duel of 1571 between James Fitzmaurice Fitzgerald and Sir John Perrot. Fitzmaurice was the instigator and initial leader of the so-called Desmond Rebellions that raged in Munster in the 1570s and early 1580s; Perrot was the aging English knight and ex-soldier sent by the Crown to suppress them. Fitzmaurice proposed to settle matters through personal combat, a proposal to which Perrot gladly agreed, even allowing Fitzmaurice to set the conditions of combat. They arranged to meet outside of Killmallock to fight with the sword and target while clad in 'Irish tresses'. But if Fitzmaurice's challenge represents the high point of the politics of honour in Anglo-Irish affairs, his failure to show on the day suggests its rapid demise. He justified his absence by saying that were he to kill Perrot, the Queen would simply send a new president to crush him.[1] Whether this was sincere or not, it certainly showed a concern

---

[1] For an extended discussion of the honour principles at stake, see Palmer, 'The insolent liberty'.

for the limits of honour politics: how could Fitzmaurice be sure that the Queen would abide by the extra-legal agreement made between himself and Perrot, two gentleman commanders? Following a period of self-exile on the continent, the would-be-duellist returned to Munster and with the aid of a small papal force attempted to raise a holy war against the forces of the Crown – marking the first time that a mature ideology of faith and father-land appeared on the Anglo-Irish landscape, an ideology that would dom-inate that relationship, arguably, into the present.[2] In his abandonment of honour principles for the stronger stuff of faith and fatherland as a basis of resistance, Fitzmaurice may not have shown himself the bravest of rebels, but he certainly demonstrated political vision.

That Anglo-Irish politics in the wake of the Desmond rebellions revolved around ideological differences of religion and national determination is now a historical commonplace. Its most eloquent expression is found in the work of Hiram Morgan, who has argued that the 'faith and fatherland' rhetoric of the Nine Years' War was not only a product of the ideological turn in Anglo-Irish relations in the 1580s, but also marked its ascendancy as political motivator.[3] Its most wide-reaching treatment appears in Susan Brigden's recent survey of Tudor history.[4] The genealogy of these ideological posi-tions as a political trump card in early modern Ireland is thus carefully drawn and widely propagated. But does it explain everything? Did the appeal to honour as a means to practise politics die in a field near Killmallock, the only victim of a cancelled duel?

The point of this chapter is to argue 'no' to both of those questions. The presumed death of honour politics was premature because the two, having been so vital to Anglo-Irish relations for at least the previous forty years, were not so easily decoupled. The appeal to honour would remain a powerful political tool well past the date that Fitzmaurice failed to show at his own duel. To make the case this chapter focuses on the Nine Years' War, the conflict that marked the emergence of faith and fatherland as the ideological axis points on which Anglo-Irish relations would turn well into the modern era. Quite striking in the materials pertaining to the war is the frequency with which the principal combatants on both sides spoke in

---

[2] Anthony McCormack's analysis of the Earls of Desmond's intrigues with Francis I of France and Charles V, Holy Roman Emperor, however, demonstrate the longer lineage of 'faith and fatherland' ideology in Ireland and in Anglo-Irish relations. Nevertheless, Fitzmaurice's landing in Munster accompanied by papal troops and carrying a banner bearing the cross marks the first appearance of this ideological position in the field. See McCormack, *Earldom of Desmond*, p. 68.

[3] Morgan, *Tyrone's rebellion*; 'Hugh O'Neill and the Nine Years War in Ireland', *The Historical Journal* 36 (1993), pp. 21–37.

[4] Susan Brigden, *New worlds, lost worlds: the rule of the Tudors, 1485–1603* (New York, 2000), pp. 262–3.

terms of honour. Chiefly, of course, this meant describing one's own actions as honourable, and one's opponent's as dishonourable. And while it is difficult to parse out when these appeals may have been sincere and when merely rhetorical, the important task seems not to separate the truth from the hypocrisy – even if such a thing could be done – but to figure why this was such a popular discourse. For it seems clear that Irish and English leaders alike believed that such a stance might prove effective to their audiences; this suggests that the concept of honour encapsulated a complex of behaviours and notions that was recognizable to leaders on either side. If this is so, the war then becomes not so much a conflict between irreconcilably different worldviews but rather something of a – if not exactly a civil war – then at least an internal 'British' struggle in which the proper relationships between members of a nascent inter-realm aristocracy, and between provincial aristocrats and the state, were being worked out.

It is useful, I wish to suggest, to see the Nine Years' War as just such an internal struggle, the contours of which are discernible through the appeals to honour made by its participants.[5] I build the case by exploring the words and actions of the primary players in this drama: Elizabeth I; Robert Devereux, 2nd Earl of Essex; the Crown's Irish allies the Earls of Thomond and Clanricard; and, of course, the leaders of the Irish confederacy themselves: Hugh O'Neill, Earl of Tyrone, and Red Hugh O'Donnell, Lord of Tyrconnell. Although honour provided a fundamental frame through which each of these players could interpret events and interact with one another, there was significant disagreement as to what constituted true honour, and even honourable behaviour between allies. Thus, I wish to argue that among the many things being hammered out in the course of this conflict were the definition and role of honour politics between monarch and noble, and noble and noble, in an emerging 'British' political nation.

As a bit of historical background on the conflict proper, the Nine Years' War pitted the Elizabethan government against an Irish confederacy led by Hugh O'Neill, the once and future Earl of Tyrone, and Red Hugh

---

[5] Aspects of the internal 'British' context to this conflict have been charted by Morgan, in *Tyrone's rebellion*, and by John Morrill, among others. Here I wish to explore the cultural aspects of this relationship. In doing so I find useful John Morrill's suggestion to view the conflict as a *bellum sociale*, one pitting 'members of polities associated in a system comprising a multiplicity of states' and characterized by 'the violent demand of a peripheral region for a redefinition of its relationship with, but not separation from, a metropolitan center'. Here, however, I am less interested in seeing O'Neill and O'Donnell's demands as representative of 'regional' concerns reflective of a broader local opinion and rather as expressions of aristocratic entitlement and expectation. Morrill, 'The British problem', p. 27.

O'Donnell. It was the most expensive campaign of Elizabeth's reign and nearly bankrupted the Crown.[6] More seriously on the Irish side, the disastrous loss at Kinsale in 1601 marked the beginning of the end for the Gaelic political order.[7] O'Donnell fled to Spain to seek additional help from Philip III, only to die there shortly after. O'Neill, although he returned to Ulster and recovered most of his pre-war authority, would flee to the continent in 1607 – the famous Flight of the Earls – never to return. Their territories were seized by the Crown for the massive plantation of Ulster, so marking the effective end of Gaelic Ireland as a political challenge to the Crown.

This conflict has typically been discussed through some combination of the following interpretations: it was driven by competition for, and competing notions of, sovereignty, between the Gaelic lords O'Neill and O'Donnell and the Crown; it was the last great cultural clash between the Gaelic and English systems; and that it marked the birth of a very 'modern'-looking ideology of the defence of faith and fatherland as the grounds for resistance of English expansionism. These interpretations provide vital insights on contemporary motivations and mentalities: the refinement of Fitzmaurice's Catholic resistance theory as demonstrated in Tyrone's appeals to would-be allies – Irish and continental – is undeniable; the sterner stuff peddled first by Fitzmaurice and later by O'Neill was mirrored in the harsher 'civilizing' language of Edmund Spenser's *View of the present state of Ireland* written during the course of the war; and the 'literary' musings of Spenser on civility and savagery were matched by the poetic exhortations of certain Irish *filí* for Gaelic lords to banish the foreign host from Ireland. Anglo-Irish relations were certainly hardening along ideological lines – religious, national and, to a point, ethnic – and the grey areas between them were shrinking. Nevertheless, these analyses fail to explain fully the conflict in its contexts, for there were other motivating factors in determining the character of the Nine Years' War.

We may take Philip O'Sullivan Beare as our guide to what some of those other factors may have been. O'Sullivan Beare, scion of one of Munster's great families and later historian of Catholic Ireland, wrote to Philip III of

---

[6] John McGurk estimates the war effort cost the Crown nearly £2 million. Quoted in Canny, *Making Ireland British*, p. 66.

[7] For an important and persuasive case that it was the course of events in the battle's immediate aftermath as much as the actual military route which dictated the course of the war, see Ciaran O'Scea, 'The significance and legacy of Spanish intervention in west Munster during the battle of Kinsale', in Thomas O'Connor and Mary Ann Lyons (eds.), *Irish migrants in Europe after Kinsale, 1602–1820* (Dublin, 2003), pp. 32–63.

Spain in December 1601 and offered to transfer his allegiance from Elizabeth I to the Spanish prince. He made the offer on the grounds of fictive kinship links between Gael and Spaniard and because Philip had provided, and could continue to provide, 'great wealth of provisions and armaments against our enemies who are diabolically suppressing the Catholic faith, vindictively killing our nobles, and unlawfully coveting our patrimony'.[8] By O'Sullivan Beare's reckoning, then, the confederates' troubles with the Crown were driven by issues related to religion and patria, but also by concerns over the trampling of ancient privilege and the eclipse of the native nobility. Consequently, his appeal to Philip played not only on religion and national consciousness but also on precepts of family honour and notions of aristocratic rights and privileges.[9]

This chapter explores that neglected aspect of the conflict we know as the Nine Years' War in order to uncover the role played by honour imperatives in provoking, prosecuting and settling the war. In doing so, the intention is not merely to shed new light on the Irish theatre of the war but to look at some of the ways in which these honour conflicts affected English society too. Financial drain was not the only danger England faced in this conflict. The creation of knights in the field, the negotiations between the Earl of Essex and O'Neill, and Elizabeth's fraught relations with her aristocratic and gentleman officers all combined to produce something of a crisis of honour at home. Just what it meant to be an English man of honour, or what was the proper relationship between prince and aristocracy, were fraught questions in England in the 1590s. The rivalry between Essex and the Cecils, between the Earl's circle of neo-chivalric Protestant hawks and the pen-pushing subjects of the Regnum Cecilianum, brought faction back to the Tudor court.[10] Tensions within England's domestic honour culture and political nation fed each other and worsened symbiotically. The Irish

---

[8] Quoted in O'Scea, 'Spanish intervention in west Munster', p. 39. O'Sullivan Beare's history of the war is awash with the theme of English efforts to eliminate Ireland's natural (and naturally Catholic) elites. Philip O'Sullivan-Beare, *Ireland under Elizabeth*, ed. and trans. Matthew J. Byrne (Port Washington, NY, 1970).

[9] For an extended discussion of Irish appeals to the Spanish court on the grounds of blood, and O'Sullivan Beare's role in those appeals, see Declan Downey, 'Purity of blood and purity of faith in early modern Ireland', in Alan Ford and John MacCafferty (eds.), *The origins of sectarianism in early modern Ireland* (Cambridge, 2005), pp. 216–28. This focus on war as the defence of lineage can, however, be taken too far. See Debora Shuger's writing of 'the dangerous *clan revolts* of the 1590s' (emphasis mine) – a comment made with no reference to the fact that this series of actions is typically referred to as the Nine Years' War. Shuger, 'Irishmen, aristocrats, and other white barbarians', p. 506.

[10] Simon Adams, 'Favourites and factions at the Elizabethan court', in Ronald Asch and Adolph Birke (eds.), *Princes, patronage and the nobility: the court at the beginning of the modern age c. 1450–1650* (Oxford, 1991), pp. 265–87.

events of 1594–1603 would only increase those tensions. England's honour crisis of the 1590s was very much a British affair.[11]

In exploring this crisis of British honour, it makes sense to consider the English case first since in the historiography the Crown is credited with pursuing honour imperatives during the course of the war. Hiram Morgan, in his study of the early years of the conflict (*Tyrone's rebellion*), states that once war seemed inevitable Elizabeth, with 'her honour and sovereign claims at stake, found it impossible to compromise'.[12] He also demonstrates how Thomas Lee, in a series of tracts on how to pacify Ireland, equated military defeat to the Irish with dishonouring the queen.[13] This acknowledgement of the importance of the defence of honour in Elizabeth's queenship has recently gained support in the work of Natalie Mears who argues that it 'was, ultimately, issues of trust and personal intimacy with the monarch, backed by social and familial networks, that defined Elizabethan politics, not institutions or institutional status'.[14]

The queen's honour was certainly engaged in her dealings with her rebellious subjects in Ulster, and her interest to safeguard the same explains many of her decisions. Of particular importance to her was the manner in which negotiations were conducted between her representatives and the rebels. Repeatedly she showed as much concern for their form as for their content. It was imperative that O'Neill and the other Irish should at all times negotiate from a position of social inferiority. Thus she informed Thomas Butler, 10th Earl of Ormond and supreme commander of the Crown forces in 1597, that while he was to seek terms for the rebels' submission he was to be sure

to have the same implored in such reverent forme as becometh our vassalls, and such heynous offenders to use with bended knees, and harts humbled, not as if one Prince did treat with another upon even tearmes of honour or advantage, in using words of Peace or war, but of Rebellion in them and mercy in us, for [?] rather than ever it shall appeare to the World that in any such sorte we will give way to any of their pride, wee will cast of ether sense or feeling of Pitty or Compassion, and upon what pryce soever prosecute them to the last hower.[15]

---

[11] For this reason, I believe that the frequent commentaries on the inherent 'conservatism' of the Irish lords misses the point that it was a conservatism shared by ancient nobilities (self-styled or otherwise) throughout Europe, faced as they were by challenges to their privileges.

[12] Hiram Morgan, *Tyrone's rebellion*, p. 167. See, too, R. Dunlop's comment that the Queen's harsh treatment of her commanders in Ireland was because by their fecklessness 'her pride was touched'. Dunlop, 'The plantation of Leix and Offaly', *English Historical Review* vi (1891), p. 74.

[13] Morgan, 'Tom Lee: the posing peacemaker'.   [14] Mears, *Elizabethan queenship*, p. 71.

[15] Queen to Ormond, 29 Dec 1597, Carew MS, v. 601, p. 147r.

A more dramatic example of the regal obsession with form over content (or perhaps form *as* content) in the theatre of honour, dates from May of 1596 when Elizabeth instructed the Lord Deputy (Sir William Russell) to arrange a submission of the Ulster lords that would be completed for 'our' honour and 'with such conditions as we may find to be derived only from public respect and not for particular end'.[16]

Indeed, Elizabeth's concern to see her and England's honour emerge unblemished from the conflict was so great as to justify any means for effecting that end. Very early in the conflict, in October 1594, she wrote to Russell:

We hold it strange that in all this space, you have not used some underhand way to bring in the Earl; and we think that by setting division in his country, wherein full many there are which would be glad to be maintained against him, and by other sound means, he may be disabled and reduced to obedient conformity, which were more honorable to us and commendable in you than to be put to trouble for such a base person.[17]

This seems at first glance an extraordinarily Machiavellian comment, but it was not necessarily outside the bounds of honourable conduct. First, lying to deceive seems to have been an acceptable activity by holders of noble honour. In this sort of strategic lying, one's word was never engaged and thus the honour bonds that that pledge should have created were not applicable.[18] Second, the labelling of the Irish as rebels would have served to jettison them from the protections and privileges of honour. In defining the Irish confederate leaders as rebels, Elizabeth absolved herself of the obligation to treat them according to the precepts of the vertical honour bonds that connected monarch and noble. So important was the maintenance of the public face of honour that it overrode concerns to adhere to ostensibly 'honourable' modes of conduct.

This desire to protect the Queen's honour at all costs from potential sullying at Irish hands was, unsurprisingly, taken up by many of her servants, most of whom also focused on ends at the expense of means. Thus, one anonymous author of a discourse on Ireland noted that if the Queen's honour were to be saved 'without blemish, like unto an unspotted virgin herself', any and all possible tactics should be used to draw the Earl

---

[16] Queen to Lord Deputy Russell and Council, 25 May 1596, *Cal. Carew*, 3, p. 176.
[17] Queen to Russell, 31 Oct 1594, ibid., p. 101.
[18] Julian Pitt-Rivers, 'Honour and social status', in J. G. Peristiany (ed.), *Honour and shame: the values of Mediterranean society* (Chicago, 1966), p. 32; and James, 'English politics and the concept of honour', pp. 399–400.

into his 'former obedience'.[19] In his own 'discourse on Ireland', Sir George Carew presented to Robert Cecil a more specific programme for the defence of the monarch's honour through settlement of the conflict:

> To avoid this present mischief, one of two ways must be taken, either a peace with Spain or a pacification with the rebels here, and both of them, in wise men's opinions, easy to be wrought if they are attempted. The first upon indifferent terms, he being so great a monarch, and heretofore desired by himself, is far from dishonour, and the other may be handled as it may be no less honorable … Whereby the Queen's honour (which is most religiously to be guarded) is not only preserved, but increased by the abundance of her mercy to so famous an offender.[20]

As great a threat as O'Neill posed to the Queen's honour, his submission, if staged correctly, could in fact increase it.

However, Elizabeth's honour was not challenged solely by the actions of the rebels, for those of her subordinates could be seen as calling her honour and the Crown's into question. This was particularly the case when the latter followed their own notions of honour which ran counter to the Queen's. One observer, a certain Francis McShane, cautioned against too priggish an attachment to the defence of honour. This could lead the government to drive too hard a bargain with the rebels, and so run the risk of compounding the Crown's dishonour in the conflict. For although he agreed that granting concessions to the rebels would be distasteful, it 'would not exceed the dishonour of the loss of a kingdom held these 430 years'.[21] This tension between definitions of honourable conduct was exacerbated most spectacularly by the actions of the Earl of Essex. Essex, according to his most recent biographer, was driven by an ideology that posited the proper relationship between noble and monarch, and thus of the state, as one in which the former first earned glory for himself, his nation and his monarch, preferably in the field, after which it was incumbent upon the monarch to bestow the commensurate reward upon him.[22] At odds with this, however, were competing notions of honour based on unquestioning loyalty to the monarch and government, and service to the commonwealth through the holding of civil office.[23] These were concepts embodied by Essex's great rival, Robert Cecil, and were ones he had a difficult time abiding by, especially when in Ireland. Indeed, the post in Ireland allowed

---

[19] *Cal. Carew*, 3, p. 106.   [20] Ibid., 4, p. 169.   [21] Ibid., p. 202.

[22] Paul Hammer, *The polarization of Elizabethan politics: the political career of Robert Devereux, 2nd earl of Essex, 1585–1597* (Cambridge, 1999).

[23] The exemplars of this being, of course, the Cecils. See ibid., pp. 297–8; and James, 'English politics and the concept of honour'.

him to act on honour impulses frowned upon by Elizabeth and Cecil.[24] Actions in Ireland, however, were still actions taken within the bailiwick of the Tudor dynastic state and their effects would be felt throughout the British political nation.

This clash over honour precepts plagued Essex's tenure in Ireland. It did so in large part for the simple reason that this was a theatre of war, and war foregrounded certain aspects of the honour code followed by Essex and which put him at odds with his prince. For command in war assumed an even heightened level of noble autonomy, the most dramatic example of which was the ability to create knights, a privilege unheard of in peacetime. It is likely too that this focus on the military commander's freedom of action was intensified under a female monarch, a sort of exercise in the maximization of masculine agency under a prince who by her sex would have been a stranger to the military arts. Elizabeth made it clear in her instructions to Essex prior to his departing for Ireland that defence of her honour was a priority: 'We find it necessary, both in regard of our honour and the safety of Ireland, to end the rebellion there by a powerful force.'[25] But she was less responsive to the fact that he had honour principles of his own. She was, for instance, furious that he had named unqualified noblemen rather than men of proven military merit to positions of military leadership.

The *cause célèbre* of this disagreement was Southampton's appointment to general of the horse on grounds no firmer than his friendship with Essex. The Queen took exception to this appointment, which elicited a shrill defence from her general. Essex supported himself by reference to his commission, which allowed him to choose his own officers and commanders as he saw fit. Although he did admit remembering a conversation at Richmond in which Elizabeth had shown displeasure at the suggestion of Southampton's elevation, he nevertheless dug in his heels and challenged her to revoke his commission if she wished to control military appointments. Otherwise, he would continue to prosecute his commission as he understood it, adding that 'Whereas, if I had held myself barred from giving my Lord of Southampton place and reputation someway answerable to his degree and expense, no man I think doth imagine that I loved him so ill as to have brought him over.' As a parting shot, he claimed he would gladly acquiesce in the dismissal of his general of the horse if it would mean nothing more than Southampton's 'disgrace and my discomfort', but that he could not do so since the act would, in fact, spell the end of

---

[24] As Nicholas Canny has pointed out, Essex saw his role in Ireland through the lens of honour. Canny, *Making Ireland British*, p. 76.

[25] *Cal. Carew*, 3, p. 292.

his authority among the friends who had followed him here. Worse still, he claimed, the rebels would 'start to circle me as a carcass, seeing my serial disgrace'. If Essex owed his commission to his monarch, he, nevertheless, believed the naming of military sub-officers to be the sole preserve of a military commander. The Crown's feckless military presence in Ireland was thus further hamstrung by domestic quarrels over the privileges of monarchical prerogative and aristocratic honour.[26]

That tension would only be exacerbated by Essex's creation of knights in the Irish field. The creation of knights was one of the traditional privileges of a military commander. Moreover, the potential for such summary elevation was one of the most effective recruiting tools for early modern military ventures. The flood of letters Essex received by men desiring to pursue their honour under his command in Ireland eloquently attests to this aspect of armed service. The demand for posts in Essex's army was most likely so high in part because of the queen's by then notorious parsimony in creating new knights and peers. The Irish theatre thus offered something of a safety valve for gathering social pressures created by frustrated expectations for social advancement.[27] Time-honoured though it may have been, the practice nevertheless rankled with the queen. On the one hand, she was gravely disappointed with Essex's lack of success in subduing the Irish rebels. That the only result of his activities was a clutch of new knights infuriated her. On the other, she was scandalized over the sheer number of men he had knighted and was of the opinion that many of them were undeserving and that others lacked the means to lead a life commensurate with the honour. This was not a new concern for her. In the instructions to Lord Burgh on his appointment as Lord Deputy in 1597, the Queen noted how she considered herself to 'have been much dishonored in the proceedings of Divers Deputies' in the granting of knighthoods. Thus, she issued the warning that Burgh was not to 'give the order of knighthoode to any but such as shalbe both of blood, and livelyhood, sufficient to mayn tane that callinge, except at some notable day of service to bestowe yt for Reward upon some such as in the field have extraordinaryly deserved it'.[28]

---

[26] Essex to privy council, 11 July 1599, ibid., pp. 312–14. This issue would appear again in 1600. In a letter to Carew, Dowdall asked 'Why are the forces so weak and poor?' His response to his own hypothetical was as follows: 'One cause is the electing of captains rather by favour than by desert, for many are inclined to dicing, wenching, and the like, and do not regard the wants of the soldiers'. Dowdall to Cecil, 2 Jan 1600, ibid., p. 353.

[27] This bottlenecking of elevation was in part responsible for the spate of creations following the accession of James I. We will return to this issue in Chapter 6, below. More generally, see Lawrence Stone, *Crisis of the aristocracy* (Oxford, 1965), particularly chapter 3, 'The inflation of honours', pp. 65–128.

[28] Carew MS, v. 601, p. 140v.

Essex received a similar caution, and was expressly told not to confer knighthood on the undeserving, or on those who 'have not in possession or reversion sufficient living'.[29] That he then, in 1599, awarded knighthoods to scores of individuals whose lack of military success did not justify this ennoblement, sent the Queen into a rage, as noted above.[30] Elizabeth may have seen the defeat of the Irish in terms of the defence of honour, but she was also sensitive to the possibility of the Irish theatre creating social discord at home by dumping a regiment of ignoble rebel-fighters into the ranks of the domestic elite. The English homefront thus faced an honour crisis among the members of its political nation, and it was one created by an 'Irish' conflict.

GAELIC AND OLD ENGLISH HONOUR AND THE NINE YEARS' WAR

So far we have seen that the actions of English participants in this conflict were driven in part by concerns for honour. But what of those of the Irish? According to English commentators, unsurprisingly, their actions were not honour-driven; at least not in the field. The Irish relied on ambushes, and avoided pitched battles and set pieces. Reporting on one such ambush, Lord Deputy Russell could not help but opine that such tactics would bring dishonour to continental commanders. Following the initial sortie, he wrote, the Irish had fled to the woods. To this, Russell claimed that 'If such a running away had been in France or Flanders, either of the French king's army or the King of Spain's, the mightier of them could not have showed himself again in the field within one year following, and must of necessity have lost towns and territories.' The Irish, however, unhindered by a 'civilized' sense of honour and shame, continued to band together.[31]

Similarly, the Irish actions at Kinsale were seen to fly in the face of honourable military conduct. Here the confederates' English detractors had a continental captain – and rebel ally, no less – as witness to Irish pusillanimity. According to Carew, in his 'A short relation of the siege of Kinsale', the Spanish leader, Don John de Aguila, described the conflict's combatants thus:

… having found the Lord Deputy (whom he termeth the Viceroy), although a sharp and powerful opposite, yet an honorable enemy, and the Irish not only weak and barbarous, but (as he feared) perfidious friends, he was so far in his affection

---

[29] *Cal. Carew*, 3, p. 295. His successors, the Lords Justice Sir George Carew and Archbishop Adam Loftus, were similarly told not to bestow knighthoods. Queen to the lord justices, lord lieutenant and council, 6 Oct 1599, ibid., pp. 339–41.
[30] BL Harleian MS 983.   [31] *Cal. Carew*, 3, p. 117.

reconciled to the one and distasted with the other as did invite him to make an overture of such a composition as might be safe and profitable for the State of England, with least prejudice to the King of Spain, by delivering into the Viceroy's power the town of Kinsale, with all other places held in Ireland by the Spanish, so as they might depart on honorable terms, fitting such men of war as are not by necessity enforced to receive conditions, but willingly induced for just respects to disengage themselves and relinquish a people by whom their King and master had been so notoriously abused, if not betrayed.[32]

De Aguila's words of martial camaraderie to the English, however, were followed by the assurance that he and his men were 'thoroughly resolved to rather to bury themselves alive and to endure a thousand deaths than to give way to one article of accord that should taste of baseness or dishonour'.[33] This threat was given teeth by the added claim that the peninsula, already naturally defensible, had been strengthened and could hold out until, as Carew paraphrased it:

Spain (being so deeply engaged) did in honour relieve them; which would draw on a more powerful invasion than the first, being undertaken upon false grounds at the instance of a base and barbarous people, who, in discovering their weakness and want of power, have armed the King, my master, to rely upon his own strength, being tied in honour to relieve his people that are engaged, and to cancel the memory of our former disaster.

Carew did not believe this honour talk to be mere rhetoric or bluffing, for he feared that were the expeditionary force able to hold out, in time 'their succours out of Spain in all likelihood would have come unto them, the King being so far engaged in his honour to second his enterprise'.[34] This anxiety must have been somewhat mollified by the pleasure undoubtedly provided by de Aguila's parting shot at the Irish leaders:

But to conclude our business. I was sent by my King to assist the 'Condees O'Neale and O'Donnell', only to see them broken, and scattered, 'so as now I find no such Condees in rerum natura' (for those were the very words he used) as I came to join

<hr/>

[32] Ibid., 4, p. 195.
[33] This was echoed in the later boast that 'he and all his would rather endure the last of misery than be found guilty of so foul a treason against the honour of his prince and the reputation of his profession, though he should find himself unable to subsist'. Ibid., p. 195.
[34] Ibid., p. 198. He would repeat this concern in a letter to the privy council in April, stating that the King of Spain was young, 'and given the violent affections that possess young princes, the importunity of the Irish and their agent O'Donnell (whose estimation, by all intelligences, is great in Spain), together with the dislike held of Don John, as is reported, are motives sufficient' to suggest that he may just finance another assault. Carew to privy council, 11 April 1601, *Cal. Carew*, 3, p. 225. See O'Scea, 'Spanish intervention in west Munster', on the possibilities of further Spanish involvement and de Aguila's role in frustrating them.

withal, and therefore have moved this accord the rather to disengage the King, my master, from assisting a people so unable in themselves that the whole burthen of the war must lie upon him, and so perfidious as perhaps might be induced in requittal of his favour at last to betray him.[35]

We should not, however, take de Aguila's words as evidence of a mentality that invariably saw the English and Spanish as civilized and the Irish as some sort of barbarous 'other', incapable of inclusion in an honour circle at whose centre sat the Spanish monarch. First, he was in a position where it made strategic sense to present himself and the rest of the Spanish as being like the English, and unlike the Irish, and as having been also deceived by the 'rebels'. On this point it seems likely that the massacre of Smerwick (1580) may have weighed on the Spanish commander's mind, for there an entire garrison – man, woman, child, Irish, Spanish and Italian – were slaughtered after having surrendered on terms.[36] Moreover, if we take his comments to in fact be generalizable observations on the civilization of the Irish, are we then to assume that they were to be applied equally to Thomond, Clanricard and the other Irish (Gaelic and Old English) who were fighting on the side of the Crown? De Aguila's seems a very opportunistic deployment of the rhetoric of savagery, and should not be taken at face value as a harbinger of racial classification.

Nor did Elizabeth, in spite of her fuming over 'rebels', believe that the Gaelic Irish lacked a sense of honour. Quite the contrary, she believed them so obsessed with hierarchy and enamoured with their traditional lords that she banked on the maintenance of the latter – on Crown terms, of course – as the key to maintaining local authority and peace. At least this is how she approached the handling of the Desmond earldom during the period of the war. One of the three great Anglo-Norman earldoms, the Fitzgerald Earls of Desmond held great sway over vast swathes of Munster and its population. As noted above, that power could be used for rebellion (that is, the earlier Desmond Rebellions). But given that the earldom continued to have significant influence in the locality, it was also hoped that the tremendous social capital of the Desmond earldom could be harnessed in the effort to bring stability to the area on terms satisfactory to the Crown. As Cecil wrote to the current Earl, 'I am right glad to find by your letter that some one of your followers hath made it appear that your name and person are like to

[35] *Cal. Carew*, 4, p. 197.
[36] Vincent P. Carey, 'Atrocity and history: Grey, Spenser and the slaughter at Smerwick (1580)', in Edwards, Lenihan and Tait (eds.), *Age of atrocity*, pp. 79–94.

prove of use to her Majesty's service'.[37] The attempt to re-install a Crown-approved Earl of Desmond was one of the great subplots of the war's southern theatre.

Two things complicated the Crown's designs for the Desmond earldom. First was the fact that there were two claimants to the title. The Crown's choice was James Fitzgerald, son of the last, the 14th, Earl.[38] The other was Fitzgerald's cousin, one James FitzThomas. FitzThomas staked his claim to the earldom on the grounds that it should have devolved to his father on the rebellious 14th Earl's death, and so in turn to himself. Against Fitzgerald's claim, he noted that their common grandfather had married twice and that he, FitzThomas, was descended from the first union and thus of the elder line. Inconveniently for him, however, was the fact that that union was generally considered null and void.[39] In a very strange statement for a future 'Gaelic' rebel, FitzThomas argued as early as 1584 that his grandfather's second wife was but 'a base and bloody Irish woman' and that her son had 'usurped' the title. Thus, he petitioned Lord Deputy Perrot to restore his father and him to their 'right and lawful inheritance and patrimony'. In turn, the petitioner promised, he and his father would see off the pretended earl and so restore order to the queen's territory.[40] The Crown favouring his rival, and he still coveting the earldom, FitzThomas eventually took the route of declaring himself Desmond. In spite of the declaration's lukewarm reception from the Geraldines (that is, the extended Fitzgerald family), it was enthusiastically supported by Tyrone, whose sending of armed support gave the claim a certain *de facto* legitimacy. In official correspondence FitzThomas was generally referred to as the 'titular earl', but has come down to us as the *sugán*, or straw-rope, earl. Once again, a succession dispute would determine the personnel on either side of an Anglo-Irish conflict.

The second problem was that the Crown's man, Fitzgerald, had no stomach for the role in which the Crown had cast him. FitzThomas may have enjoyed only limited support amongst the Fitzgeralds, but he enjoyed a wide popular support[41] – wide enough that O'Donnell was rumoured to be seeking an alliance with him in the autumn of 1599, and that the government was desperate for information on 'how the titulary Earl of Desmond

---

[37] Cecil to Desmond, 25 Jan 1601. *Cal. Carew*, 4, p. 11.   [38] Executed in 1583.
[39] Cyril Falls, *Elizabeth's Irish wars* (London, 1950), p. 223.
[40] 'Petition of James FitzThomas of Desmond to Lord Deputy Perrot', *Cal. Carew*, 3, pp. 489–90.
[41] Even at the time of FitzThomas' capture in 1601, Carew explained to the privy council that he was shipping the rebel 'earl' to England since he was so well-loved in Ireland it was dangerous to keep him imprisoned there. *Cal. Carew*, 4, p. 77.

would be had, whereupon depends the good of Mounster'.[42] Fitzgerald, by contrast, had almost no local prestige. Worse still, he showed precious little desire to assert himself to gain any. Through the early years of the war he was resident in England, successfully resisting Elizabeth's near-desperate desire to see him returned to Ireland. Evidently he was right in his reluctance, for the reaction to his re-introduction to the 'patrimony' was, in G. A. Hayes-McCoy's term, 'derisory'.[43] Local loyalties were as much to the man as to the title. It was surely on account of this weakness that O'Donnell could raise the stakes in his bid for local influence in Munster by floating a potential match with Fitzgerald's sister Joan. But while he proved a good servant by informing the Crown of the proposed union, Fitzgerald continued to balk at the queen's plans to repatriate him as a means to counter any rebellious accretions around pretenders to the title. By March of 1601 he was back in England, far more eager to seek the repair of his fortune in the safety of London than to serve as the government's 'earl' in Munster. As Carew would report to Cecil, Fitzgerald preferred a small plot in England to the 'best man's living in Ireland. So far is his humour and religion different from the Irish as that he thinks all time lost which is spent among them.'[44]

What is interesting in this tale of the Crown's management of the Irish nobility is how it contradicts the contemporary English rhetoric of an Irish lack of respect for hierarchy. One of the justificatory discourses of reform was that Irish society was not one of orders but rather a near-anarchic environment in which the strong oppressed the weak. It was supposed that among anglicization's many benefits would be the freeing of commoners from the tyrannical yoke of their overlords.[45] And yet here was Elizabeth not only fearful to offend the locals' support of their traditional leaders, but also desperate to harness it. Far from not understanding hierarchy, the Irish appear to have had an obsession with it – an obsession that needed to be factored in to political and military calculations. Elizabeth, for her part, knew perfectly well the intricacies of the relationships between nobles and their local communities and the important role such hierarchical bonds played in the structure of politics throughout the British Isles, and even Europe. Ireland was no different, and her interest in managing the earldom of Desmond was not some sort of accommodation of Celtic social peculiarities but a well-reasoned strategic move to establish local control through something of an informal surrender and regrant arrangement.

---

[42] 'Queen's instructions "for one to be sent into Ireland"', ibid., p. 342.
[43] T. W. Moody, F. X. Martin and F. J. Byrne, *A new history of Ireland*, 3 (Oxford, 1984), p. 130.
[44] Carew to Cecil, 22 March 1601, *Cal. Carew*, 4, p. 33.
[45] This was, for instance, an article of faith in Spenser's *View*. See Canny, *Making Ireland British*, p. 46.

Nevertheless, the attempt to cultivate the loyalty of a section of the populace to a nobleman, as opposed to the Crown, was a curious one; made possible only because of the particular circumstances of wartime Ireland. In England such an action would have been unthinkable, viewed as something tending dangerously toward subversion. But given the Crown's tenuous hold on power in Ireland this was a gamble worth taking. Carew, too, shared some of his Queen's concerns, for as he explained to the privy council his shipping of the recently captured FitzThomas into England alive was a necessity born of his fear that, were the 'usurping earl' to die, his brother John would immediately assume the title and potentially prove as dangerous a rebel, 'Whereas (whilst he lives) he cannot make any pretence to move the actual followers and dependents of the house of Desmond to assist him.'[46] But even if this 'love' of the Irish for their lords were little more than some sort of early modern Stockholm syndrome, effected *en masse*, Fitzgerald was not a willing volunteer for the task of de-programming the misled. For him, his honour and nobility were truly gifts of the Crown and things to be displayed and confirmed before an *English* audience.

The Irish leaders' own words paint, of course, a very different picture of Gaelic and Gaelicized notions of honour and honourable conduct. As much as did Elizabeth, Essex, or even Don John de Aguila, O'Neill and O'Donnell were operating out of a concern for the defence of honour: in their respective decisions to enter into open rebellion, in their actions during the course of war, and in the way they described their actions and motivations and those of their counterparts. They did so, however, in often very different ways, showing that there was no monolithic sense of Gaelic honour that was engaged here. Like so many other things in this chaotic period, what it meant amongst Gaelic lords to act with honour was being fiercely contested.

Let us consider O'Donnell's case first, since he seems to have been acting on the demands of an old code of honour. Asked by Crown commissioners why he had taken up arms given that his ancestors had been so loyal to the Crown, he responded flatly that it was on account of his illegal imprisonment by that very same government.[47] In 1587 he had been treacherously

---

[46] *Cal. Carew*, 4, p. 77. It should also be noted that in his confession, given on 3 June to Carew, FitzThomas claimed he was pushed to rebel because of religion, the encroachment upon gentlemen's lands, fear of English juries (the execution of Redmonde FitzGerald given as an example of how life-and-death issues were decided upon on the basis of inconclusive or incomplete evidence), and the rate of composition. Ibid., p. 78. After Essex left he let it be known that he was happy to lay down arms if the Queen would confirm his earldom and lands. Ibid., p. 79.

[47] Commissioners (Wallop and Gardiner) to the Lord Deputy and Council, 23 Jan 1596. *Cal. Carew*, 3, p. 142. The commissioners' answer was very curious, and worth noting: 'Touching the imprisonment

kidnapped by agents of the Lord Deputy and deposited in Dublin Castle, where he languished until escaping in 1591. Even the English captain Thomas Lee felt the manner of O'Donnell's taking to have been 'most dishonourable and discommendable, and neither allowed before God nor man'.[48] Traditional Gaelic notions of honour as enshrined in centuries of prose and poetry would have demanded immediate response to cleanse the shame of this disgraceful capture, and O'Donnell's participation in rebellion seems to have been fed by this concern for restoring lost honour.[49] But if we accept, even in part, Joep Leerssen's argument that Gaelic poets were over the course of the sixteenth century increasingly coming to equate honour with defeat of the foreigners, then perhaps he should be seen not as living in the past but acting in the cultural and political vanguard.[50]

There certainly was no shortage of neighbouring Irish lords who believed just that; that his actions were innovative in an absolutist sort of way. O'Donnell's penchant for installing his own candidates to the chieftainships of subordinate lordships seems in his mind to have been merely a prerogative of rank. Yet to his Gaelic detractors, his actions smacked of tyranny, and thus a violation of the responsibilities incumbent upon lords in a system of vertical honour. This tension would in turn prove crucial in the war; Donough O'Connor Sligo's spells of loyalty to the Crown throughout the war, for instance, were driven largely by his anger over what he felt were O'Donnell's unwarranted claims to authority over northern Connaught and by his need to garner support to fend them off. As proof that he 'honours and esteems [the Queen] above all others' he forwarded to Cecil a letter O'Donnell had

of you, O'Donnell, and of O'Relye, if there were no cause to touch you in disloyalty, yet all princes in policy may and do use to take their subjects in pledge for the peace of their countries, and you both, being but subjects, do use the like, and therefore should the less dislike of that course'. Thus when dealing with the Irish, the activities of the Crown, at least in this case, were determined by local conditions. Here is a good example of how a certain action or behaviour may be understandable, indeed honourable, if effected by someone who was a part of a particular cultural milieu but seen as purely illegal and mercenary when done by an outsider.

[48] McGettigan, p. 43.
[49] Even as he lay on his deathbed O'Donnell was absorbed by matters of precedence and place. In his will he noted the following agreement between himself and O'Neill: 'The stipulation was that one had no pre-eminence over the other and that in walking or travelling together whichever was the elder should be on the right hand'". The will stated that this arrangement should also apply to his brother, as successor to the head of the family, and that any support from the Spanish King should be shared equally between the two Irish leaders. J. J. Silke (ed.), 'The last will of Red Hugh O'Donnell', *Studia Hibernica* 14 (1984–88), pp. 51–60.
[50] Leerssen, *Mere Irish*, pp. 157–93. It may be worth bearing in mind Helen Coburn Walsh's comments that antipathy to outsiders was a characteristic shared by many European revolts of the period. If this is so, then O'Donnell looks even less like a medieval Gaelic anachronism. Coburn Walsh, 'The rebellion of William Nugent, 1581', in R. V. Comerford, Mary Cullen and J. R. Hill (eds.), *Religion, conflict and coexistence in Ireland: essays presented to Monsignor Patrick J. Corish* (Dublin, 1990), p. 51.

sent him in which he spelled out terms on which the two could settle their rival claims to Sligo. O'Donnell offered to forgive the entry of his predecessors on Sligo's lands. But the strings attached were strong, for O'Donnell promised

> he would give me [O'Connor Sligo] the arbitrement of four of my men and four of his men, conditionally that I should forego any prince and help him and any the rest of the Irishry. Unless I consent to this offer, I shall undo myself and my posterity for ever; and by my means I shall be an instrument to undo the rest of all those that defend their own right ... Also he sent me, if the Irishry were overthrown by my means, that I shall be after less esteemed of any man and dispossessed of all that Her Highness bestowed upon me at this present. Therefore consider with yourself how hardly you were dealt withal by those ungodly officers that coveted my life and lands and were sent for our wars in Ireland, you should not be restored to your living during your life, nor none of your name. If these my great offers which I offer you may not move you at this present, which was never offered to any of your predecessors, or any of my predecessors, I will place another of the Connors in your place, and call him O'Connor Slyggoe, and will maintain him, not doubting but I shall be assisted of others that will maintain myself and him.[51]

An appeal to honour by a Gaelic lord, then, did not equate to an appeal to some sort of monolithic notion of Gaelic honour, and the conflict over honour imperatives affected inter-Irish dynamics of the war as much as it did Irish-English or English-English ones.

O'Neill's actions represented a very different take on the politics of honour to O'Donnell's, in part due to his peculiar position in Anglo-Irish society and politics. Although of ancient Gaelic stock, he had been fostered by a Pale family, bore an English-style title, had visited the court twice, counted members of the English privy council among his friends, and had done much to anglicize the north. Thus, he was on the one hand very much a provincial Tudor nobleman, and on the other represented the most advanced amalgamation of Gaelic Irish and English nobility in late Tudor Ireland.[52] The running conflict between O'Neill and the Crown and its Irish officers must then be seen as very much an internal British affair, and one in which a major sticking point was the proper relationship between the monarch and her provincial nobility in an evolving multiple monarchy.

---

[51] O'Connor Sligo to Cecil, *Salisbury MS*, 6, p. 437. O'Donnell's reference to 'ungodly officers' is, of course, an interesting example of his use of religious affiliation in the definition of honour.
[52] On the 'Machiavellian' character of O'Neill and his ability to play to multiple political identities, see Morgan, 'Hugh O'Neill's murders', and Canny, 'Taking sides in early modern Ireland', especially p. 115.

For here was an outlying lord who had had his honour claim validated by an earldom, and who, in turn, had attempted to anglicize his territories, and yet by the early 1590s sensed that the privileges that should have come naturally to him as a result were being serially abused from above and below. His grievances can be boiled down to these three: first, he was resentful of the Crown for installing, as he said, low-born and greedy men to serve in Ulster; second, he was convinced that such men sought to undermine his position, effect his disgrace, and end up in possession of his lands; third, he was then further angered with the Crown for not heeding his complaints and instead continuing to allow base-born men to serve in or around his territories. O'Neill's growing sense of injustice was to peak in dramatic fashion when, in 1593, he challenged his personal nemesis, Henry Bagenal, marshal of the army, to a duel. But, more generally, it served to make him question the integrity of the Crown and the English privy council. Writing to the Lord Deputy in 1594, he complained that the presence and actions of such men had poisoned his relationship with the local population who he claimed were ready to kill him for his dealing with a lying state.[53] The Crown's false dealings were thus not only a flouting of the honour claim he felt confirmed by his earldom, but they also had the practical effect of damaging his local reputation, and so his ability to govern effectively. And this in turn, he astutely argued, only served to reduce Crown authority in Ulster.[54] If a monarch was made legitimate by his/her fulfilling the obligation to protect inferiors (a concept explored at length in the last chapter) then Elizabeth as *ardrí* had failed in her *eineach*. This conflict, then, was not entirely one of incompatible notions of sovereignty, but rather one driven in part by the fury that derives from having an overlord who refuses to stop certain of her servants from preying on others.

In contrast to the false dealings of Bagenal and other allegedly low-born servants, and by extension the Crown, O'Neill was always careful to portray himself as a man of his word. When petitioning for pardon in the winter of 1597 he demanded equivalent terms for his allies, as he had sworn an oath to them that he would make no treaty that did not also apply to them.[55] Two years later he would tell the Dublin administration that he was unable to proceed with negotiations for a truce until he spoke with O'Donnell; they had agreed to make decisions jointly and O'Donnell had been greatly offended over his (O'Neill's) having previously floated terms without consulting him first.[56] Granted this was to some extent a stalling tactic, designed to buy more time in the hope that the arrival of Spanish troops would strengthen his bargaining and/or military position. However, there are scattered pieces of

---

[53] *Cal. Carew*, 3, p. 89.   [54] Ibid., p. 87.   [55] Ibid., p. 274.   [56] Ibid., pp. 337–8.

correspondence that reveal Tyrone's understanding that the reputation for honesty was one of a nobleman's greatest assets.[57] For example, he sent a letter to Con O'Neill in which he counselled the latter to release the Bishop Richard Power, with whom he was feuding over lands. 'Howsoever desirous your people are to get gain,' he cautioned, 'hazard not your own scandal or reputation for any benefits.'[58] One of the best ways to decline a person's claim to honourable status was to question his word, and O'Neill, who was actively impugning that of his opponents, was diligent in trying to protect himself from counter-claims of a dissembling and untrustworthy character.

Challenging the word of the Crown, even if done indirectly by implication, was of course a dangerous strategy, and so O'Neill was careful always to comport himself with deference when negotiating with the Crown's representatives. Again, a vertical honour system is built upon the internalization of unquestioning obedience to authority, the flouting of which is deemed a serious transgression. And whereas O'Donnell was consistently described by English commentators as arrogant and insolent and his demands as affronts, O'Neill, understanding that form was as important as content when negotiating with the Crown, showed a calculated obsequiousness in his correspondence and live performances. In his submission of 17 August 1594, for example, he wailed how 'Her Majesty's displeasure has been my greatest grief, for she it was who advanced me to high title and great livings; and I know that her Majesty, who by grace has advanced me, by force may pluck me down'.[59]

What then to make of his rejection in 1595 of his earldom in favour of the chieftainship of the O'Neills? Does this mark the true end to the utility of a politics of honour in Anglo-Irish relations, the final nail in a cultural-political coffin constructed by Fitzmaurice? Obviously 'yes', for it is a rejection of the monarch as the fount of all honour in favour of a status system rooted in ancient Gaelic tradition. But also 'no', in that many of the examples used above demonstrate that shared, if contested, Anglo-Irish

---

[57] The Crown had long attempted to have Tyrone stand as pledge for O'Donnell and various sublords in Ulster, something for which Tyrone had in fact petitioned. On this point, Elizabeth had written Tyrone on 26 July 1592: 'Whereupon as we perceive from our deputy the said Hugh O'Donnell, your son in law, offereth to submit himself to such good orders as shall become him to live like a good subject, nevertheless considering he is your son in law and in all men's opinions dependeth upon you to be ruled, We cannot but earnestly charge you, as you will have our favour, by which you know how from your first beginning you have been maintained, that you use your whole credit or rather your active service, as you shall be required, to reduce your said son to his dutiful behaviour as our Deputy and council shall require of him.' *Salisbury MS*, 4, pp. 218–19. If for no other reason, this exchange is interesting for the discussion of 'reducing' O'Donnell to 'dutiful behaviour'. The language of 'reduction' thus was not the sole preserve of the likes of Spenser.

[58] *Cal. Carew*, 3, p. 297.   [59] Ibid., p. 96.

honour principles still proved useful in negotiations after that date. Submission remained an option up until Kinsale in 1601 and, of course, the war ended with O'Neill again taking up the earldom as part of his surrender. And 'no' again in that the taking of the Gaelic title was done simultaneously with a turn toward the continent, primarily toward the Spanish. His actions should be seen less as an attempt to reconstitute the Gaelic political system and more as a calculated fashioning judged most likely to garner international sympathy and support. Even if he cast off his English-style title in favour of his Gaelic title, he nevertheless held onto the need, even right, to be referred to as 'Lieutenant', an office and title completely foreign to Gaelic tradition. Warren's comments on this matter offer a fascinating insight into the multiple 'identities' manipulated by the erstwhile earl:

> Whilst I was there with him I saw a letter sent unto him out of Connaught with this superscription, 'To the Right Honorable my very good Lord O'Neyle, chief Lieutenant of Ireland;' at which I laughed; and he, perceiving me to laugh, asked what it was. I answered, 'To see so strange a superscription.' He then read the same, not marking it before he opened the letter. I asked to whom the devil he could be Lieutenant. He answered me, 'Why should I not be a lieutenant as well as the Earl of Ormond?'[60]

Hardly a retrograde motion, then; the taking of the chieftainship was a necessary move to re-fashion himself for a European audience as a man whose claim to nobility and office rested foremost in long lineage and local authority.

ARISTOCRATIC VERSUS MONARCHICAL HONOUR
IN THE NINE YEARS' WAR

Nowhere does O'Neill's sense of himself as European aristocrat come more clearly into view than in his dealings with Essex. With Essex, O'Neill believed he was conversing with a member of his own honour circle, an aristocratic man-at-arms. Essex, too, seems to have had some of the same respect for O'Neill. Elizabeth, for her part, let her patience with Essex snap in the autumn of 1599 when he, instead of engaging with Tyrone's forces, chose instead to negotiate one-to-one with the Ulster leader. This episode is worth exploring a little further for it elegantly demonstrates the triangulation of honour politics between the monarchy, the English nobility, and

---

[60] 'William Warren's report of his third journey to see Tyrone', 13 Nov 1599, ibid., pp. 348–9.

the Irish nobility. Let us begin with Elizabeth, who was furious over Essex's action for the simple reason that her representative was not to ennoble the rebels or their cause by speaking with them on anything like equal terms. Her concern that this point be impressed upon her commanders is most starkly laid out in her instructions to Essex's predecessor as general, the Earl of Ormond, in 1597 (noted above). Essex not only received the same instructions, but was ostentatiously concerned to ensure that his own subordinates understood them as well. Thus he instructed Chief Justice Saxey of Munster in August of 1599 that in making parleys, receiving submissions or granting protections he was to have some subordinate sound out the other party first, since open parleys and treaties with them 'are dishonorable to her Majestie'.[61] The rebels too were made to understand the honour constraints placed upon parleying with the Crown's representative. When the Wicklow rebel Phelim McFeaghe O'Byrne sent an 'Irishman' to tell the Lord Lieutenant that he wished to speak with him, with condition that he may have the lieutenant's word for his safe return, Essex responded that

if he sent to Arcloe for a passport only to come as a repentant rebel, to tender his absolute submission to her Majesty's servant and minister, authorised by her royal commission, he should have safe conduct; but if he sent in any other form, or to any other purpose, he would execute the messenger; for he would never suffer his commission to be dishonoured by treating of parleying with rebels.[62]

How then could Essex have justified his parley with the chief rebel, Hugh O'Neill, erstwhile Earl of Tyrone? Part of the reason was chance, for the appearance of O'Neill took Essex and his forces by surprise. And with O'Neill looking for dialogue, not ambush, the Lord Lieutenant obliged. Famously, Essex would speak alone with O'Neill for half an hour. But contingency was at best a partial explanation, for there was more than one meeting between the leaders. Reporting on the second meeting, Essex was eager to impress upon his sovereign that the conversation had been conducted in such a way as to reflect and respect the power differentials involved and so protect the honour of the Crown. He assured Elizabeth that O'Neill and his companions – for this time they were both accompanied – had 'stood with their horses up to their bellies in water, [and] we on hard ground', and that O'Neill 'spake a good while, bare headed, and saluted with a great deal of respect all those that came down with the Lord

---

[61] Instructions from Essex to Saxey, 16 Aug 1599, ibid., p. 321.
[62] Proceedings of Essex, 1 July 1599, ibid., pp. 311–12.

Lieutenant'.[63] In the end, as the Queen would describe it later to Sir Geoffrey Fenton, Secretary of Ireland, Essex claimed that O'Neill's willingness to negotiate and submit was largely a product of his confidence in dealing with him specifically, 'in respect of the opinion he had of him … Tyrone professing, as it seemed by Essex his words, that such was his affection for his father's sake, as he would not draw his sword against him, but he would do that for him which he would not do for any other'.[64]

This is an important point, for in this meeting and the truce it produced we see on display not only O'Neill's sense that as an Irish peer he was entitled to such negotiations, but also Essex's belief that as a noble commander he was able to pick his parleys as he wished. And so in the fateful parley, conference and truce of 1599 we see a curious third vector of honour politics, one graphed along a line drawn according to the relations between individual nobles. That is to say that the potential success of the Essex–O'Neill truce was, according to both negotiating parties, dependent upon the respect that they had for each other. Essex's circle of people deserving his honourable treatment was not ethnically restrictive, and dealing with an earl of the Tudor crown, Gaelic or not, would have been well within respectable bounds.[65] This, then, was a gentlemen's agreement, related to state affairs, but one in which the actual prestige of the monarch was cut out.

Elizabeth made it abundantly clear that she had no interest in negotiations and truces made between her inferiors who believed themselves acting in her name. To Essex she thundered that of course O'Neill had offered a parley for he had done so every time a force approached, 'having often done it to those who had but subaltern authority'. Moreover, she was incredulous that Essex had spoken with the chief rebel in private, especially given that he had been so careful to 'have testimonies to all your actions up to this point'. The final insult for her was Essex's trying to mollify her with the assurance that during the ensuing conference, attended also by his subordinates, the power differentials had been respected in how the negotiations had been physically conducted:

Furthermore, we cannot but muse that you should recite that circumstance of his being some time uncovered, as if that were much in a rebel when our person is so represented, or that you can think that ever any parley (as you call it) was upon less

---

[63] Proceedings of Essex in the north, 9 Sept 1599, ibid., p. 324.

[64] Queen to Fenton, 5 Nov 1599, ibid., p. 343.

[65] In his instructions to Dunkellin and Art Savadge (10 Aug 1599), Essex asked for word on the state of O'Connor Sligo. They were to assure Sligo that if he could just hold out a while longer Essex would 'march in person and set up my rest to free him, to have a revenge for my worthy friend, and especially to recover her Majesty's honour'. Ibid., p. 318.

terms of inequality than this, when you came unto him, and he kept the depth of the brook between him and you; in which sort he proceeded not with other of our ministers, for he came over to them. So as never could any man observe greater form of greatness then he hath done; than more to our dishonour that a traitor must be so far from submission as he must first have a cessation granted, because he may have time to advise whether he should go further or no with us.[66]

Done with Essex, she fumed to Fenton that he should make O'Neill understand that while it had been fine for him to address his complaints to Essex – for that was how provincial subjects' grievances were transmitted to the Crown – he was to be made to understand that he was

our subject born, and raised to honour by us only, and not born to depend upon any second power (as long as he shall carry himself as a good subject) so if, after his offences known to the world so publicly, this submission of his shall not as well appear to the world by all clear circumstances to proceed simply out of his own grief and sorrow for his offences against us, and from his earnest desire only to satisfy us his Sovereign, but that it must be bruited abroad, that for any other man's respect whosoever he takes the way, wither sooner or later, to become a good subject, or that it shall be conceived that Tyrone would forebear to draw his sword against our Lieutenant rather than against us, we shall take ourselves thereby much dishonoured, and neither could value anything that shall proceed from him on such conditions, nor dispose our mind to be so gracious to him hereafter as otherwise we might have been induced.[67]

At stake in this episode was not only the tenor of relations between Crown and nobility, both English and Irish, but also the status of aristocratic relationships and extra-legal guarantees in the eyes of the state.

In appointing a successor to the disgraced Essex, Elizabeth was determined to put her stamp on actions and negotiations taken in the field. The opening lines in the instructions to the new commander, Charles Blount, Lord Mountjoy, would have horrified the honour-obsessed Essex had he seen them: 'We commit to you the government of Ireland, wherein we have received dishonour and consumed infinite masses of treasure through the errors of those to whom we formerly committed it'. And while she held out the possibility of ending the conflict through accepting the submission of 'even the worst conspirators', she warned Mountjoy that 'this has been so indiscreetly used that in showing mercy we have punished our best subjects and dishonoured ourselves'.[68] Moreover, she instructed him not to bestow

---

[66] Queen to Essex, 17 Sept 1599, ibid., p. 326.   [67] Queen to Fenton, 5 Nov 1599, ibid., p. 343.
[68] Instructions for Mountjoy, Jan 1600, ibid., p. 356. In an earlier letter to Mountjoy, she had also discussed bringing O'Neill to heel by means of a pardon, but with the following reservations: 'But forasmuch as his petitions consist of many considerable circumstances, wherein we must have regard to our honour above all things, we will delay our answer for some few days'. Ibid., p. 359.

knighthood upon any person without asking permission, a point driven by her concern for the effects of the Irish conflict on English society. For, as she explained,

the excess which other governors have used in that particular hathe not only made that degree soe Common, as the Honorable Callinge it self is generally become more contemptible. But it hathe wrought an opinion in dyvers gentlemen of bloode and gentilitie heere, that they are disgraced soe much when they doe meete in publique place ... as they are wholie discouradged ... in the same.[69]

To this she added that although she held Mountjoy to be of 'soe much discretion' as to be allowed to create knights, his recommendations would only be approved 'provided always that you make none that are not of years because our right in the wardship of their bodies is often called in question thereby'.[70] In Elizabeth's Ireland, the subaltern may have been able to speak, but he was not to parley. Nor, for that matter, was he to bestow knighthoods.

HONOUR POLITICS AND THE WAR'S CONCLUSION

If honour imperatives affected the character and trajectory of the war, they also coloured the fates of the *dramatis personae* as the conflict wound to a conclusion. On this count, Essex was the first casualty. Having unceremoniously dropped his Irish command and returning to court to re-ingratiate himself with Elizabeth, he abandoned what little ground existed to keep him in the queen's good graces. For her part, the queen felt that 'For our honour's sake we can do no less than in some measure to chastise him'.[71] Faced with what he thought was no chance at reconciliation with the fount of honour – a situation he believed to be exacerbated by the lobbying of his ignoble enemies at court, primarily the sedentary and decidedly non-martial Robert Cecil – Essex tried one last-gasp effort to restore his status by leading a band of retainers and hangers-on in a rebellion in London against the Queen's evil councillors. Often seen as the last of the baronial honour revolts,[72] the Essex rebellion graphically demonstrated the ways in which the English presence in Ireland greatly affected the intersection of honour and politics at home.

---

[69] Carew MS, vol. 632, p. 208r.   [70] Ibid.
[71] 'Queen's instructions to one being sent into Ireland', Oct 1599, *Cal. Carew*, 3, p. 342.
[72] James, 'At a crossroads of the political culture: the Essex revolt', in James (ed.), *Society, politics and culture*, pp. 416–65.

The fate of the Irish leaders, O'Neill and Rory O'Donnell (Red Hugh's brother and successor), offered a different take on the role of British honour in politics at the end of the Tudor period. For in spite of the efflorescence of a faith and fatherland ideology in the prosecution of the war, the settlement was carried out according to blueprints drawn up in the 1540s. The rebels' reconciliation with the government was effected through a version of surrender and regrant. O'Neill, who had ostentatiously cast off the title of earl in favour of the O'Neillship in 1595, was constrained to reverse that action and so accept restoration to the earldom of Tyrone. More interesting was the fact that Rory O'Donnell was made to accept an earldom as well, that of Tyrconnell. This marked the end of an era, for the O'Donnells were the only Gaelic overlords not to have taken part in surrender and regrant under the Tudors. But now they too were incorporated into the feudal structure envisioned by Henry VIII's ministers sixty years prior. However, this was surrender and regrant with a bite; a measure implemented for punitive rather than assimilative purposes.[73] The web of honour, structured upon that feudal network and controlled by the person of the monarch, was still deemed the most expedient means by which to bring stability to Ireland. But the notion that this was a process of social convergence, that the granting of titles was merely the exercise of a transfer of authority, was gone. Honour politics as a means of connecting the Crown to its Irish subjects was not dead, but it had been greatly altered.

This fact was not lost upon the Irish, at least if we take the poet Eoghan Ruadh Mac an Bhaird's sentiments as in any way representative. Mac an Bhaird, a *file* from a family long attached to the O'Donnells, composed a poem on the occasion of Rory's journey to Dublin to negotiate the taking of the title. He well understood that the event was different to previous ceremonies of surrender and regrant; that this was not a voluntary self-incorporation into a British web of aristocratic honour but rather a condition of surrender. The roads O'Donnell had so recently trodden in 'the clothes of war' (*i treallaibh coguidh*) he now walked in peace.[74] And although the 'anger and hate' between the enemies had now turned to 'love' and the 'warrior faces and cruel hearts of Englishmen turn to good spirits', Mac an Bhaird worried for O'Donnell's safety and the long-term

---

[73] For an indispensable discussion of the Crown's efforts to curtail O'Donnell authority through the imposition of constraints on the earldom, see R. J. Hunter, 'The end of O'Donnell power', in William Nolan, Liam Ronayne and Máiréad Dunleavy (eds.), *Donegal: history and society* (Dublin, 1995), pp. 229–66.

[74] Thomas Ó Raghallaigh (ed.), *Duanta Eoghain Ruaidh Mhic an Bhaird* (Galway, 1930), poem 6, stanza 7, p. 88.

fate of those under his protection. Indeed, times had changed. This study's previous chapter explored a hybrid bardic inauguration address for one of the O'Brien Earls of Thomond, a composition in which traditional Gaelic lordship was wedded to the heightened authority that came with being the Crown's earl. But Mac an Bhaird saw little to gloat over in this ceremony. He lamented how every knee used to bend before the lord of Tyrconnell,[75] and, more tellingly, referred to the English monarch in a way that up until this point had been missing in Gaelic discussions of the monarchy but which accurately captured the reality of the situation. For he referred to the Lord Deputy as the representative of the high-king of Ireland, not as the *cing* of England or the *rí na Saxan*, but as the '*áirdríogh Eireann*'.[76] If the Irish lords had been stitched into the elaborate tapestry of the British feudal system over the last sixty years, now the English monarch was finally entered into the hierarchy of Gaelic notions of hierarchy and overlordship. The internal British nature of the forces driving the Nine Years' War was thus at last reflected in the Irish poetry.

There were, of course, Irish 'winners' in this story and they used an honour politics to advance themselves. However, this was not done in a strictly local context, in the pattern of those who had participated in surrender and regrant in the sixteenth century, but rather in such a way as to advance themselves on an emerging British stage. On the Irish side this included the Gaelic Irish Donough O'Brien, Earl of Thomond, and the Old English Richard Burke, Earl of Clanricard. Thomond was an anglicization success story. When Fenton recommended him to Burghley for a position of leadership against the rebels, he noted how in addition to his record of service in the government's interest,

his Lordship affecteth English customs, both in ordering his private house and family, and reducing his country to the rules of law and justice; and is willing upon all occasions to answer any employment that the State doth call him unto; and is of good valour and judgement to perform the same.[77]

Fenton's faith was well-rewarded as Thomond proved to be a leader of great merit, especially during the fateful campaign in Kinsale. Clanricard did not come so highly recommended, given that members of the Burkes had created chaos in Connaught and headaches for Irish officials during the last decades of Elizabeth's reign, the so-called Mac an Iarla (son of the earl) revolt. However, he too was able to secure a military command, and he too distinguished himself against the Irish rebels in the field. Ironically, both of

[75] *Do feactha glún gach Gaoidhil*. Ibid., stanza 19, p. 92.   [76] Ibid., stanza 18, p. 92.
[77] Fenton to Burghley, 8 Jan 1598, *CSPI*, 23, vol. 8, p. 12.

these Irishmen succeeded where the English favourite Essex had failed: they were able to achieve military glory in the Irish wars which they then used to advance themselves in British social and political circles.

A discourse of honour thus pervaded many aspects of the Nine Years' War. It was operable in all theatres, appealed to by all parties, and applicable to all audiences. The particular shape or character of honour, however, was highly flexible; there was a range of available positions from which one could pick and choose. Again, just like 'religion' and 'law', 'honour' was a vital ordering principle in this period. Its contested nature was merely a tribute to its cultural importance and social power, which is to say that it was ground worth fighting over. And in that contest O'Neill distinguished himself as a remarkably astute manipulator of the available discourses of honour, able to master the rhetorical demands of provincial, national, metropolitan and even international audiences, not to mention confessional ones. His use of a 'faith and fatherland' rhetoric merely shows how capable he was at assuming a number of different stances when addressing different audiences and, like similar actions by Desmond before him, need not be seen purely as a significant leap forward toward the 'modern'.

It should be noted that there were those who saw the events of the Nine Years' War in terms of their local ramifications. George Carew, for example, wrote to Mountjoy of a horseman in his troop who went into rebellion just prior to the Battle of Kinsale. As Carew described it,

This blind traitor is at this present of his own followers the strongest man in Munster. His ambitions thirsted after the title of McCartie More, unto which dignity, although many of the Carties are in blood nearer than he, yet he, seeing himself to be the most powerful of all the Carties, he thought by his own strength and by the favour of the Spaniards to carry it.[78]

Even Rory O'Donnell could take a detour in his and his troops' horrific long-walk from Munster back to Ulster to settle old scores. *The Annals of the Four Masters* notes how Rory took his followers on a detour to ravage Breifne and so avenge the insult and dishonour he had suffered previously at the hands of Brian O'Rourke.[79]

These were exceptional instances, however, for clear to all was the fact that the fates and fortunes of those in Ireland and England were more closely intertwined in the wake of the Nine Years' War than they had ever been previously. And in spite of O'Neill's mimicking the evolution of his rebellious forerunner Fitzmaurice and re-fashioning himself from honour

[78] G. Carew to Mountjoy, 18 Aug 1602, *Cal. Carew*, 4, p. 307.   [79] *AFM*, 6, p. 2341.

warrior to holy warrior, the simple matter of honour claims proved just as important to the trajectory of this conflict as did the ideological positions of faith and fatherland or the defence of culture. In spite of O'Neill's propaganda missives, the Nine Years' War did not take on the character of religious war. This is not how Elizabeth saw things, nor did any of the other major players: not the fervent Protestant Essex, the ambiguously 'Catholic' O'Donnell, the Protestant Thomond, the Catholic Clanricard, or even the Spaniard de Aguila. The correspondence of these people was suffused with discussions of honour, discussion of religion and patria proving less common, and of culture rarer still. Faith and fatherland had undoubtedly emerged during this conflict as the basis for an ideology of resistance. Nevertheless, as O'Sullivan Beare had made explicit to Philip III in 1601 (as quoted at the beginning of this chapter), they still shared the political stage with the pursuit of honour principles. Unsurprisingly, then, the settlement of 1603 was not a winner-take-all example of the continental wars of religion, but rather an internal settlement accommodating of religious difference and effected through the restoration of the sociopolitical hierarchy by means of the granting of honour titles.

Although the 1603 settlement resembles the surrender and regrant policy of the previous century, albeit with a punitive element that was previously absent, it was implemented in circumstances very different from those of the 1540s. Whereas the original programme was largely uni-directional in influence, designed to structure Irish society and politics in such a way as to make them peaceful and palatable for English centralization schemes, this latest series of creations was done to restore order to a larger British polity. And just as with the conflict itself, its aftermath would be determined in large part by the demands of honour imperatives. As R. J. Hunter has described it, the Gaelic earls had pushed during the conflict for some sort of 'aristocratic constitutionalism' as the basis for Irish governance.[80] This, of course, had proven unsuccessful. Post-Mellifont they would again find their claims to honour rejected by the larger British aristocratic honour circle and so they would attempt in the early seventeenth century to direct that claim toward a continental audience. For these men, honour had evolved from an assimilative tool into grounds for resistance theory; honour politics here would meet and combine with the ideology of faith and fatherland, and honour culture would now stretch towards Madrid and Rome, not London. Conversely, for those Irish who had sided with the Crown, men like Thomond and Clanricard, honour provided a ladder for advancement in

[80] Hunter, 'The end of O'Donnell power', p. 257.

the Stuart multiple monarchy. Thomond would become a leader of Lords in the Irish Parliament; Clanricard would become the first Irishman post-1541 to attain a peerage title in England. Members of the English political nation had to accommodate not only these men but also myriad men who had been knighted during the conflict or who had purchased titles in the re-colonized Ireland post-1607. The early Stuart period was not yet an age when ideology dominated Anglo-Irish relations. To return once more to Fitzmaurice (the 'rebel' with whom this chapter began), while he may have been a better prophet than a duellist, it would take another forty years for his vision of an Irish faith and fatherland movement to come fully into focus and dominate Anglo-Irish relations. Until then, one could still navigate those relations by pursuing the claim to honour. How that was done – for the Irish losers, Irish victors, and the English political nation – is the subject of the following three chapters.

CHAPTER 4

Making the Irish European: Gaelic honour after the Nine Years' War

INTRODUCTION

So far, this study has traced the evolution of the honour culture spanning the kingdoms of England and Ireland from 1541 to 1603. It has attempted to show that honour imperatives greatly influenced the interactions between not only native and newcomer, but also between native elites and their traditional inferiors once the existing social order was disturbed by Tudor centralization. The previous chapter closed with the suggestion that honour politics remained relevant even in the wake of the Nine Years' War and that it did so in three general forms. First, Irish intellectuals used a language of honour to re-cast exiled Gaelic lords as European aristocrats. Second, honour remained a relevant political language and tool for those Irish (Gaelic and Old English) who remained in Ireland to compete for status and place in the very novel setting of early Stuart Britain. Third, the creation of Irish peers and the frequent assaults in Ireland upon the honour of the Crown's viceroy combined to make Anglo-Irish honour politics an issue that affected England as well as Ireland.

This chapter follows the first of those threads, the fashioning of Gaelic elites as members of an international aristocracy. It focuses on two pieces of Gaelic prose. The first is Tadhg Ó Cianáin's manuscript chronicle of the Ulster lords' travels through Europe between 1607 and 1609, a text commonly known as *The Flight of the Earls* (hereafter *Flight*). This manuscript is generally ignored by historians, but here I will argue that it reveals a very progressive and imaginative attempt on Ó Cianáin's part to re-cast Gaelic notions of noble honour to fit a European, Catholic context. The second is Lughaidh Ó Cléirigh's *Beatha Aodha Ruaidh Uí Dhomhnaill* (or *Life of Red Hugh O'Donnell*; *Beatha* hereafter), the only prose biography of a Gaelic lord, written sometime between 1616–32.[1]

---

[1] On attempts to date the text, see Pádraig Breatnach, 'Irish records of the Nine Years' War: a brief survey, with particular notice of the relationship between *Beatha* and the *Annals of the Four Masters*', in Pádraig Ó Riain (ed.), *Beatha Aodha Ruaidh: The life of Red Hugh O'Donnell: historical and literary contexts* (Dublin, 2003), p. 127.

Like Ó Cianáin's *Flight*, the *Beatha* is a generically innovative text which defines Gaelic honour in the context of continental – here Spanish – norms and reads events from the early part of the century as in large part driven by concerns over honour. But unlike Ó Cianáin's, Ó Cléirigh's discourse of honour is more in keeping with the militaristic and lineal traditions of medieval Gaelic convention, and shows much less of the post-Trent religious precision, or the careful social taxonomy, displayed by Ó Cianáin. This chapter suggests, then, that Gaelic notions of honour were transformed not only through the influence of Tridentine Catholicism but also out of concern for a larger continental dimension in the affairs of the Irish. Traditional Gaelic aristocratic honour – with its hierarchical and militaristic emphases – could in fact work quite well in concert with more religiously inflected notions of honour.

TADHG Ó CIANÁIN'S GRAND TOUR OF THE EARLS

If the submission of Hugh O'Neill at Mellifont in 1603 suggested the end of Gaelic Ireland as a functioning socio-cultural system, the so-called Flight of the Earls of 1607 seemed to confirm it. The self-exile of the Ulster lords Hugh O'Neill, Rory O'Donnell and Cú Connacht Maguire, accompanied by many of their relations and retainers, produced shock amongst the native intelligentsia. The classic expressions of a Gaelic sense of loss and despair come from two well-known poems: Eoghan Ruadh Mac an Bhaird's 'The Sorrows of Eire', with its metaphor of the Egyptian captivity, and Fear Flatha Ó Gnímh's 'After the Flight of the Earls', with its painful evocation of an Ireland desolate and defenceless before the forces of 'the foreign host'.[2] With historical hindsight, we know that the Flight allowed for the plantation of Ulster, and thus the effective end of the Gaelic system. Conditioned by that hindsight, the haunting, even wrenching, poems of Mac an Bhaird and Ó Gnímh strike us as, quite simply, natural reactions to the *fait accompli* of the collapse of the Gaelic order. That these poems continue to make the selection for anthologies of Irish poetry attests not only to their popularity as examples of early modern Irish courtly verse, but also, and perhaps more importantly, to their ability to shape popular conceptions of English treachery and its role in the end of a Gaelic Ireland.[3]

---

[2] In Lughaidh Ó Cléirigh, *Beatha Aodha Ruaidh Uí Dhomhnaill*, 2 vols, ed. and trans. Paul Walsh (Dublin, 1948), 2, pp. 137–47; Thomas Kinsella (ed. and trans.), *The new Oxford book of Irish verse* (New York, 1989), pp. 162–4.

[3] This theme of irreversible loss is often replicated in the historiography, see Cathal Ó Háinle, for example, who sees this as indeed the end of an era, and that the poetry had no more function but to

But if we look beyond the poetry, we find that not all contemporary Gaelic commentators depicted the Flight in such harrowing terms. Here I wish to explore one extraordinary example of an alternative reading of events to that proposed by the Mac an Bhaird/Ó Gnímh school: Tadhg Ó Cianáin's chronicle of the earls' travels from Lough Swilly to Rome, a text – although it bears no title in manuscript – generally referred to as *The Flight of the Earls*.[4] It has made little impression on historians' readings of this period, and even less upon popular ones. The one exception is Micheline Kerney Walsh who made extensive use of this text in her biography of Hugh O'Neill, Earl of Tyrone. But she used it as a travelogue, largely as a mine for nuggets of local colour to adorn her retracing of the earls' footsteps. For as Tomás Ó Fiaich explains in his foreword to the 1996 edition of Kerny Walsh's book: 'Ó Cianáin … a simple unsophisticated scribe, somewhat naïve and medieval in outlook, was obviously not *au fait* with the political chicanery which revolved around his master's destination and wrote like an Irish country lad seeing the Taj Mahal for the first time. We have to go to Ó Cianáin, therefore, for the little personal touches on "the path to Rome" '.[5]

I wish to suggest that this text is more than the travel journal of a simple 'country lad'. First and foremost, as already indicated, it paints a far less tragic picture of the Irish lords' journey to Rome than one finds in other Gaelic sources, such as the poems of Mac an Bhaird and Ó Gnímh. In doing so it complicates our views of Gaelic mentalities on the eve of the Ulster plantation. Moreover, in constructing his narrative of the Flight, Ó Cianáin reworks the traditional bardic language of praise in the course of his descriptions of the Irish lords and their interactions with continental elites. The text seems, therefore, to be an attempt to re-cast not only the language of, but also the criteria for, Gaelic notions of honour and nobility along the lines of contemporary European norms. It also offers one of the clearest expositions of the multiple contexts in which the interests of Gaelic elites were fought out. In the poetry, which has proven so influential to both professional inquiry and popular perception of the Flight, the self-exile of these lords was an event that played out on an English-Irish axis. But

bewail the passing of the old world: 'Ní raibh an t-athaoibhneas i ndán d'Eirinn. Ní raibh le déanamh ag na filí anois ach Éire mharbh a chaoineadh agus beannacht a chur lena hanam, rud a rinneadar. An saol ina raibh na filí sin beo, bhí deireadh leis; an phatrúnacht ar ar mhaireadar, níorbh ann di feasta. Bhí ré nua ag tosú, ré na sráid-éigse'. Cathal Ó Háinle, 'D'fhior chogaidh comhailtear síothcháin', *Léachtaí Cholm Cille* 2 (1971), p. 72.

[4] Paul Walsh (ed. and trans.), 'Tadhg Ó Cianáin's Flight of the Earls', *Archivium Hibernicum*, appendix to vols 2–4 (1913–15). (Hereafter, 'Flight of the earls').

[5] Micheline Kerney Walsh, *An exile of Ireland: Hugh O'Neill, Prince of Ulster* (Dublin, 1986), p. 10.

Ó Cianáin's manuscript not only draws upon the larger European context of Anglo-Irish relations – it is after all a chronicle of events that took place on the continent – it also reminds us of the inter-Irish dynamic behind these events. For I believe that we can see Ó Cianáin as being concerned not merely with English designs on the territory and powers of the Ulster lords, but also with the motives and actions of those lesser Irish lords who sought to capitalize on the instability brought on by war and plantation in order to usurp the authority of their traditional superiors. Ó Cianáin's text, I wish to suggest, was an attempt to make the Irish European, the point of which was to solidify the claim of the Ulster earls to rule their traditional territories against those of New English and Gaelic Irish competitors.

Let us briefly consider the text itself and its author. Ó Cianáin was of a bardic family that traditionally produced poets for the Maguires, lords of Fermanagh. As for the text, it is written in a very clear scribal hand – evidently Ó Cianáin's – covering nearly 140 pages. For centuries it existed only in a single manuscript, written it seems in Rome by Ó Cianáin himself. At some point in the seventeenth century it was brought to Louvain and housed in the library of the Irish Franciscan College of St Anthony's. In 1872 it was brought to Dublin, where it remains. The Reverend Paul Walsh prepared an annotated dual-language edition of it that was serialized between the years 1913–15 as an appendix for the journal *Archivium Hibernicum*. It was published as a book the following year.[6] Although the manuscript bears no title, Walsh dubbed it 'The Flight of the Earls'.

In spite of Walsh's choice of title, the text gives no sense that the earls' travels were a flight from persecution. It offers no discussion of what occasioned the decision by O'Neill and the others to leave for the continent, and their journey from Loch Swilly to the shores of Normandy is quickly dispatched within the first few pages. Once there, they appear to be less in flight than on tour. One could perhaps even think of the text as the record of a noble's progress through the Catholic states of western Europe. But if it was such a 'record', it did not pretend to objectivity. In spite of its general accuracy on names and dates, it grossly misrepresents the journey's atmospherics.[7] That contemporary Gaelic commentators saw in the 'Flight' a profound tragedy is made clear by the following quatrains from Mac an Bhaird and Ó Gnímh:

---

[6] Tadhg Ó Cianáin, *The flight of the earls*, ed. and trans. Paul Walsh (Dublin, 1916). (Hereafter, *The flight of the earls*).

[7] Kerney Walsh has checked the accuracy of dates and places and found them largely in concordance with other sources.

Eóghan Ruadh Mac an Bhaird: 'The Sorrows of Eire'[8]

> Lonely is Ireland tonight:
> The outlawry of her native stock
> Fills with tears the cheeks of her men and her fair women:
> That the land should be desolate is unusual.
>
> Lonely tonight is Connla's Plain,
> Though crowded with a foreign host:
> The strong, vigorous land's complement
> Have been banished to Spain.

Fear Flatha Ó Gnímh: 'After the Flight of the Earls'[9]

> Her nobles and freemen dead,
> She cannot cure her shame.
> It is a shameful step for the Gael,
> If we dare presume to say it.
>
> By a blow of Balor's eye,
> Her lovely land is sickened,
> Her corn blossomless in the clay
> – and I pray God rest her soul.

Moreover, Walsh's extended footnotes to the text detail numerous forces actively working against the earls' efforts to reach Rome, and reveal the frequent reluctance with which even supposed allies assisted them.

Ó Cianáin's narrative, however, has none of the gloom of Mac an Bhaird and Ó Gnímh's poems; nor does it reveal the earls' trials and tribulations discussed by Walsh. Rather, Ó Cianáin's earls seem to be more on an early version of the grand tour – albeit one taken in dangerous times – than flying into exile. With but rare exception, Ó Cianáin describes the earls as travelling from place to place and being honourably received by princes and prelates from Normandy to the Vatican. They are put up in palaces and feted at grand banquets. The Duke of Lorraine – who entertains them in his 'chief city' of Nancy – goes so far as to proclaim that 'under severe penalty, that no one should accept gold or silver of them while they should be in the city, but that all their expenses during that time should be borne by the Duke'.[10] They are shown the great guns of Milan by the Spanish governor the Duke of Fuentes, a security clearance, we are told, granted only to the

---

[8] Walsh (ed. and trans.), *Beatha*, vol. 2, p. 139.
[9] Kinsella (ed. and trans.), *New Oxford book of Irish verse*, p. 164.
[10] Walsh, 'Flight of the earls', pp. 78–9.

Spanish and the Irish.[11] They are taken to churches and cathedrals and shown holy relics. When they arrive at the Catholic College of Louvain, the 'Assemblies of the colleges received them kindly and with respect, delivering in their honour verses and speeches in Latin, Greek and English'.[12] The Pope himself gives them presents of 'a silver basket, a bottle full of wine, and a gilded loaf of bread'.[13]

In a world dictated by codes of honour and rules of precedence, where one sat at a banquet, or walked in a procession, was perhaps more important than the fact that one was there at all. And Ó Cianáin was often quite explicit on just where the Irish were placed amongst the assembled dignitaries. The most striking example of this comes from the seating arrangements in the house of the Marquis Spinola: the Marquis has seated '… O'Neill in his own place at the head of the table, the Papal Nuncio to his right, the Earl of Tyrconnell to his left, O'Neill's children and Maguidhir next the Earl, and the Spanish ambassador and the Duke of Aumale on the other side, below the Nuncio. The rest of the illustrious, respected nobles at table, the Marquis himself, and the Duke of Ossuna, were at the end of the table opposite O'Neill'.[14]

The extraordinary privilege shown the Irish earls could at times even cause jealously amongst the nobles of other nations. This we see in Ó Cianáin's description of the lords' participation in a Corpus Christi procession in Rome. He writes how the Irish were chosen,

and never before did Irishmen receive such an honour and privilege. The Italians were greatly surprised that they should be shown such deference and respect, for some of them said that seldom before was any one nation in the world appointed to carry the canopy. With the ambassadors of all the Catholic kings and princes of Christendom who happened then to be in the city it was an established custom that they, in succession, every year carried the canopy in turn. They were jealous, envious, and surprised, that they were not allowed to carry it on this particular day.[15]

The earls, in turn, showed their respect for this hospitality and generosity by constantly touring churches, hearing special Masses and completing brief, local pilgrimages.

Not only is the tone of these passages surprising, so too is the criteria by which the Irish lords are held up as nobility. Absent are the traditional markers of Gaelic honour and nobility: martial prowess, hospitality, ancient lineage, physical beauty, and so on. In their place appear two new criteria: an

[11] Ibid., p. 97.   [12] Ibid., p. 36.   [13] Ibid., p. 187.   [14] Ibid., p. 47.   [15] Ibid., pp. 189–91.

adherence to a post-Tridentine Catholicism, and the simple acceptance these lords received from European elites.

Perhaps more surprising when we compare Ó Cianáin with poems like those of Mac an Bhaird and Ó Gnímh is the difference in language used to refer to the Irish Lords. Gone is the royal terminology. These men are not *flatha* or *prionsaí* – terms which mean prince – nor, significantly, are they *ríthe*, or kings. It is not that these terms are absent from the text, it is just that when they are used they refer to internationally recognized monarchs and princes. Thus, for example, we encounter the contemporary *rí na Spáinne* (the king of Spain)[16] and *ríg Saxan* (the king of England),[17] and the historical *Rí na Persia* (king of Persia)[18] and other *rígha paganta* (pagan kings), introduced in the course of a long aside about the holy house of Loreto.[19] As we saw in Chapter 2, the meanings attached to words of royalty were changing in Gaelic prose over the sixteenth century. Here they are simply dropped altogether.

Ó Cianáin instead makes use of status designations more in keeping with European norms when discussing the Irish. Those who have titles are often referred to accordingly: O'Donnell, for example, is almost always *an t-iarla*, or the earl, and O'Neill's son, the baron of Dungannon, is typically met as *an barún*. This is not entirely a break from bardic tradition, for peerage titles do show up in bardic poetry and annals, just not always quite correctly. For example, *The Annals of the Four Masters*, which dates from the 1620s, refers at various points to the 'Earl O'Donnell' (*Iarla ua nDomhnaill*).[20] In doing so its compilers combine the Gaelic practice of referring to a chief by the name of his family (thus, 'the O'Donnell') with the English/European custom of designating nobility by peerage titles based on territorial markers (say, the Earl of Essex). While this is an interesting mix of lineal and heraldic/territorial identifiers of nobility, it is a bastard construction not at home in either system. Ó Cianáin, by contrast, gets it right. With him it is either 'O'Donnell', or *'an t-íerla Tíre Conaill'* (the Earl of Tyrconnell), and never a combination of the two.[21]

When speaking of a group of elites – some title-bearing, others not – Ó Cianáin employs a number of terms that can mean noble or gentlemen: these include *maithibh* or *daoine maithe* (gentlemen), *daoine uaisle* (noble people) and *tiarnaí* (lords). These words are all of traditional usage in Gaelic

---

[16] Ibid., p. 104.   [17] Ibid., p. 10.   [18] Ibid., p. 112.   [19] Ibid., p. 114.   [20] *AFM*, 6, p. 2369.
[21] Which is not to say that he always gets it right when speaking of the new socio-political dispensation. See his reference to Chichester, the Lord Deputy, as *giústís na hEirenn* (justice of Ireland). Walsh, 'Flight of the earls', p. 60.

writings, but here they are given a greater specificity simply by the fact that they are no longer synonymous with the royal designations *rí*, *flaith*, and so on. These men, then, are not royal, but noble, or gentle, and referred to as such. Moreover, Ó Cianáin seems on occasion interested to produce a more exact, European-style taxonomy of relative status positions for his Irish elites. Thus, at one point in the text when we encounter O'Donnell in the company of a host of lesser lords, Ó Cianáin introduces them not as an undifferentiated mass of *daoine maithe*, but rather as '*an t-ierla*' (O'Donnell), followed by assorted '*tighernaidhe*' (those just below the Earl in status), and finally the '*maithibh*' (those lower still, but yet worthy of mention).[22] This is not always exact – *maithibh*, for example, can at times refer to the earls themselves – but it seems to mark a greater concern for status hierarchies than one generally meets in other Gaelic writings of the time.

Changed, too, is the language used to praise the Irish. Gone entirely are the bardic stock words *clú* and *glóir*. *Clú* can mean fame, reputation, perhaps even honour in certain contexts, and was one of the most commonly used words to praise an Irish lord. Significantly, I have seen it show up more frequently than anywhere else in the Maguire *duanaire* (analysed in the previous chapter).[23] That Ó Cianáin came from a family of poets to the Maguires makes the complete disappearance of the term all the more surprising. *Glóir* in bardic verse and annalistic compilations accords closely to the meaning of its English cognate, glory: lords, thus, are traditionally praised for their glory and fame, generally arising from military victory. Although the word does appear in the *Flight*, it does so only three times and always in a religious context – the glory of Mary, God and heaven, to be exact.[24] Most dramatic, however, is the utter disappearance of *eineach*. Throughout the late medieval period *eineach* was the term most commonly used to denote the honour of an Irish lord,[25] and here it is gone entirely.

Eineach is replaced in the *Flight* by *onóir*, an obvious cognate with the English word 'honour'.[26] It has a long history in Gaelic verse and prose, but was often used in a religious sense – to refer to the honour of God, the honouring of Mary, and so on. But here it has taken on a sense that used to be fulfilled by *eineach* – that is, to refer to an individual's personal

[22] Ibid., p. 20. [23] See Chapter 2, above.

[24] Walsh (ed. and trans.), 'Flight of the earls', pp. 150, 156, 160.

[25] This judgement is based on the reading of the poetry of the late medieval and early modern periods that is available in print.

[26] The eclipsing of *eineach* by *onóir* in the Irish lexicon is discussed more generally in Simms, *From kings to warlords*. See also the discussion of this development in Chapter 2, above.

honour – and, simultaneously, one more in keeping with 'honour' as used in contemporary English to mean an extra-legal complex of attitudes and behaviours that regulated social behaviour.[27] And whereas honour, I would argue, functioned this way in Ireland, it was not usually described as such by Gaelic authors. That is to say that it would be rare to see in Gaelic writing the discussion of someone pledging his honour, whereas it would be a commonplace occurrence in English. Ó Cianáin, however, is right at home with the language of the 'pledging' of honour, which we can see in his discussion of the King of France's vowing *as focal* and *as onóir* (on his word and on his honour) to ensure the Irish lords safe passage through his territories.[28]

Why would Ó Cianáin's language and descriptions differ so radically from the Gaelic tradition, a tradition in which he was not only raised but trained? Most immediately there is the reason of genre. This work is something new in Irish writing. Nothing like it appears until the 1640s,[29] or at least nothing like it has survived. In style it is something of a modified annalistic compilation: it is arranged chronologically, is primarily a catalogue of facts (trustworthy or not), and is concerned with the actions of great men. But structurally it is not organized by years, rather by Roman numerals that mark off short episodes ranging in length from a day to a few weeks. There is also a tremendous indulgence of miracle tales and such, which would seem alien in standard Irish annals. Given that the *Flight* is part annals, part panegyric in prose, and part travelogue, perhaps we should not be so surprised to see within it novel uses of vocabulary and rhetoric.

We can, however, find some generic similarities if we look outside the Gaelic tradition – a search that offers some further clues to explain the peculiarities of this text. Most likely it is in the long tradition of secretarial recordings of foreign expeditions. Keeping the Irish context in mind, we may think of Gerald of Wales, who kept such a record while accompanying the Norman invaders to Ireland in the 1180s, or of Fynes Moryson, secretary to Lord Deputy Mountjoy, whose observations of the Nine Years' War represent one of our best sources for the period.[30] Both of these men not only kept a record of the movements and actions of their superiors, but also took notice of local customs, landmarks, political systems, geography and natural wonders, miracle tales and the like. And so did Ó Cianáin. Recent research supports the idea that Ó Cianáin may have served in a secretarial

---

[27] On the shift from *eineach* to *onóir* in Gaelic discourse, see Simms, *From kings to warlords*, pp. 106–10.
[28] Walsh (ed. and trans.), 'Flight of the earls', p. 30.
[29] Tadhg Ó Donnchadha (ed.), 'Cín Lae Ó Mealláin', *Analecta Hibernica* 3 (1931), pp. 1–61.
[30] Gerald of Wales, *The history and topography of Ireland*, trans. with intro. John J. O'Meara (London, 1982); Fynes Moryson, *An history of Ireland, from the year 1599, to 1603…* (Dublin, 1735).

role to Hugh O'Neill. Feargus Ó Fearghail has discovered an Italian reference to the 1610 death of 'il segretario del Principe d'Ibernia'.[31] Ó Fearghail's suggestion that this refers to Ó Cianáin supports the notion of the *Flight* as secretarial record.

If this was in fact a secretarial chronicle, who was supposed to see it? Nollaig Ó Muraíle has noted that the text was housed in the library of St Anthony's, the Irish Franciscan college in Louvain, in the later seventeenth century.[32] This suggests the Irish community in Louvain as likely readers. A further step in the potential circulation of this text seems likely, however, namely that it was intended for an Irish audience in Ireland. O'Neill, up until his death in 1616, attempted to return to Ireland;[33] Ó Cianáin, like those other secretaries Gerald and Moryson before him, also most likely expected to return whence he set out. His ultimate audience, then, was likely a domestic Irish one. This would largely explain the disparity between Ó Cianáin's narrative of a stately progress through foreign parts and the much less exalted lived reality of the earls' experience on the continent, as reconstructed by Paul Walsh. If the intended readership was to be Irish supporters of the Ulster lords, it seems understandable that the delays and general discouragement the earls received from their supposed counterparts on the continent were downplayed. Moreover, it would explain why the text is written – as it has recently been suggested – in a way that suggests it was meant to be read aloud.[34] Those in Louvain were literate, they could read it themselves; many of those at home in Ireland were not and could not, and so would need the benefit of public recitation to gain access to Ó Cianáin's text.

The identification of an Irish audience may also help explain why there is so little discussion by Ó Cianáin of events leading up to the Flight. On this point Walsh, in his introduction, suggests that those events were so

---

[31] Feargus Ó Fearghail, 'The tomb of Hugh O'Neill in San Pietro in Montorio in Rome', *Seanchas Ard Mhacha* 21 (2007–08), pp. 69–85. Quotation, p. 73. I wish to thank Dr Nollaig Ó Muraíle for this reference.

[32] Nollaig Ó Muraíle, 'Cuntas Thaidhg Uí Chianáin ar Thuras Deoraíochta na dTaoiseach Ultach, 1607–09', *History Ireland* 15 (2007), pp. 52–5.

[33] See Kerney Walsh, *An exile of Ireland*.

[34] The suggestion is John McCafferty's, and was noted by Nollaig Ó Muraíle in his talk 'An insider's view of the "Flight of the Earls" – Tadhg Ó Cianáin's contemporary account of the exile of the lords of Gaelic Ulster', Louvain, 22 May 2007. I wish to thank Dr Ó Muraíle for the text of this talk. I should also note that I place more emphasis on this aspect of the text than does Dr Ó Muraíle. He sees the text more as the basis for a propagandistic instrument in support of the earls, and less as something intended for oral presentation. While I agree, and argue here, that the Flight was a secretarial chronicle with propagandistic intent, I do not feel that these purposes are mutually exclusive. It certainly could have served as the basis for a political tract, and could also have been used for oral presentation in and of itself.

well-known that they did not require discussion.[35] I would argue instead
that the silence is not due to the fact that everyone knew what precipitated
the Flight, but rather to short-circuit any in-depth discussion of the matter.
Whether or not the earls were intriguing against the Crown and had to flee
because the state caught wind of their designs has been a historical controversy for the last 400 years. And it was certainly a very lively one at the
time. Therefore, I would suggest that Ó Cianáin intended to obliquely leave
the impression that the Flight was occasioned by English oppression – since
there are occasional, if understated, references to how the earls were driven
from their patrimonies by the forces of greed and religious heresy – without
providing too much information or commentary on the subject.

We are still, however, left with the question of why he wished to say the
things that he did, and said them in the way that he did, to his particular
audience. As one possibility, he may have been partaking in a bit of political
theorizing. We know that the Irish intellectual classes were deeply engaged with
trying to make Gaelic lordship compatible with monarchical rule; Fearghal Og
Mac an Bhaird's poem 'Three crowns in James' charter' is the most famous
such attempt.[36] Ó Cianáin's intense interest in the political oddities of the Swiss
system – the only political system he comments on – suggests that perhaps
there is a little of that same project going on in the *Flight*. The following quote is
representative of the remarks he makes on the Swiss political reality:

… and no supremacy, rule or claim to submission by any king or prince in the
world over the inhabitants. In themselves they form a strange, remarkable,
peculiar state. They make their selection of a system for the government
of the country each year. They have fourteen important cities. Half of them
are Catholics and the other half heretics, and by agreement and great oaths they
are bound to one another for their defence and protection against any neighbour
in the world who should endeavour to injure them or oppose them in upholding
the public good with moderation and appropriateness … It is said of the people
of this country that they are the most just, honest, and untreacherous in
the world, and the most faithful to their promises. They allow no robbery or
murder to be done in their country without punishing it at once. Because of
their perfect honour they alone are guards to the Catholic kings and princes
of Christendom.[37]

---

[35] From the introduction to the 1916 book edition: Ó Cianáin, *The flight of the earls*, p. x.
[36] See the discussion of this poem in Ó Buachalla, 'James our true king', and Caball, *Poets and politics*,
pp. 85–9.
[37] Here I have used Walsh's translation. Curiously, Walsh renders the original *ffirinne* as 'perfect
honour'. 'Perfect honesty' or 'truthfulness' is more literal. Nevertheless, I agree with Walsh that,
given the importance the text places on the keeping of one's word to a sense of honour, 'true',
or 'perfect', honour is what Ó Cianáin has in mind here. Walsh (ed. and trans.), 'Flight of the earls',
p. 93.

Is there some lesson here to be applied to the Irish situation? It is certainly possible, and his use of *naisiún* throughout the text does suggest that he was thinking along the lines of some sort of incipient national consciousness.[38] This could also be a simple and suggestive description of the fact that there are other political modes by which Catholics and Protestants may co-exist.[39] It may even be something of a rebuke to the Irish and English themselves for not upholding those precepts of honour which not only allowed the Swiss system to run, but allowed the Swiss themselves to be the guardians of Christendom. I think it is on this last point that we can see, if not exactly what Ó Cianáin was intending with this text, at least how he went about trying to make the case.

A return to Ó Cianáin's use of language may reveal what is really going on here. He radically reworks the criteria for, and language of, Gaelic honour and nobility. This becomes apparent when we consider what words he uses to denote Gaelic nobles, nobility and honour, and then look at what other things he describes using the same terms. On the one hand, the same terms used to refer to the Irish lords – *duine uasal, maithibh*, and *tiarnaí, iarla*, and so on – are used to describe the continental elites they encounter. The impression we are to take from this, it seems, is that these men are all members of a European aristocracy. Stripped of its connection to a mytho-historical Age of Kings, and more carefully stratified according to relative status position, Ó Cianáin's language of a social hierarchy of Irish elites is more in line with European norms than Irish traditional ones. It marks a concerted effort to create an image of the Irish as participants in a post-Trent European polity whereby their nobility and honour is no longer determined chiefly by martial valour and praised using terms derived from Brehon law. Rather it is also constructed in part by their adherence to a proper reformed Catholicism and their respect for rigid social hierarchy.

This, I believe, is something new. For Ó Cianáin's subjects are not Gaelic kings, in the tradition of bardic panegyric; nor are they Mac an Bhaird and Ó Gnímh's tragic, end-of-an-era scattered nobles; nor still are they mere warlords, the term Katherine Simms uses to describe the petty lords of early modern Gaelic Ireland.[40] Instead these are nobles, *daoine onóracha* (men of

[38] On the emergence and implications of the use of 'nation' in Ó Cianáin's text, see Mícheál Mac Craith, 'From the Elizabethan settlement to the Battle of the Boyne: Literature in Irish 1560–1690', in Margaret Kelleher and Philip O'Leary (eds.), *The Cambridge history of Irish literature* (Cambridge, 2006), vol. I, pp. 191–231.

[39] There were those in Ireland thinking of a republic future for the island. See Canny, *Making Ireland British*, p. 419, and 'The attempted anglicisation of Ireland in the seventeenth century: an exemplar of "British history" ', in Julia Merritt (ed.), *The political world of Thomas Wentworth, earl of Strafford, 1621–1641* (Cambridge, 1996), p. 183.

[40] Simms, *From kings to warlords*. For a discussion of Simms' thesis, see Chapter 2, above.

honour), whose social equals are to be found throughout the Catholic states of Europe. And yet Ó Cianáin, it seems, is eager to downplay the novelty of his classification; an attempt that comes into focus if we once more look at how he uses the words *onóir* (honour) and *uasal* (noble). For both of these words are also deployed to refer to inanimate objects. Thus we read of stones, grottos, banquets, churches, ceremonial progresses, palaces, napkins, cemeteries and many other things that are *onórach* (honourable) or *uasal* (noble).[41] The meaning here seems to be that those things which accord to their own nature are honourable and/or noble. And given the fact that contemporaries often made the distinction between gentlemen – a class constructed through education, Crown patronage, or some other third party means – and aristocrats – mankind's natural elites – Ó Cianáin's terminology suggests the organic and undeniable nobility of his Irish subjects.[42] What is new in his text, then, is masked by a rhetoric of antiquity and naturalness.

When constructing this new description, or definition, of Gaelic honour and nobility, Ó Cianáin undoubtedly was drawing a distinction between his patrons (O'Neill and O'Donnell) and the New English officers and settlers who stood to take possession of their property in Ulster. As well, and perhaps even more importantly, he probably had in mind those lesser Irish lords who remained in Ulster and stood to profit from the Crown's redistribution of the earls' territories. We tend to think of the conflicts and interactions of this period in Anglo-Irish history as revolving exclusively around an English-Irish axis. In doing so we lose sight of the inter-Irish dynamic, which to contemporaries was just as real, threatening and exasperating as relations with the New English. Rory O'Donnell's troubles with Niall Garv O'Donnell, and O'Neill's with his traditional inferiors the O'Canes, remind us that there was a world-turned-upside-down element to the changes that were facing Gaelic lords in this period. Poems like 'Faisean Chlair Eibhir' and the anonymous prose work *Parliament Clan Thomas* lampoon the pretensions of those Gaelic upstarts who sought to benefit from the social chaos occasioned by war and plantation to rise above the status of those who were traditionally their superiors.[43] Ó Cianáin's

---

[41] See the following examples in Walsh (ed. and trans.), 'Flight of the earls': *cloch uassal*, p. 172; *dá leic onóracha*, p. 200; *Cavarello i. inadh aoibhinn onórach*, p. 208; *eaclus onórach*, p. 192; *prosesion onórach*, p. 176; *palas ro-onórach*, p. 168; *naipicín uassal*, p. 176; *reilic is ferr 7 is onóraighe*, p. 34; *bangcéd onórach*, p. 68.

[42] See, for instance, Cust, 'Catholicism, antiquarianism and gentry honour', and Stone, *Crisis of the aristocracy*, pp. 21–128. For an opposing view which posits nobility moving from being defined as a profession to being seen as an aspect of blood, see Schalk, *From valor to pedigree*.

[43] Both of these works will be more extensively analysed in the next chapter.

depiction of O'Donnell and O'Neill was most certainly intended to remind these upstarts that not only were his patrons the natural rulers of Ulster – and perhaps of all Ireland – but that they were accepted as such by the pre-eminent social, political and religious figures of Catholic Europe.

In his preface to the printed edition, Walsh claimed that the oddity of the text was due to the fact that Ó Cianáin was not privy to decisions made by the earls.[44] Quite possibly this is true, but, as I have maintained, there is probably more to it than that. Although the *Flight* did serve as a chronicle of the earls' travels through Europe on their way to Rome, its purpose was a larger one. It was, in my opinion, a concerted propaganda effort that broke from existing generic forms in Irish. In making that break it also split from bardic language in adopting a new criteria for and language of lordly praise. Moreover, the author cleverly situated his argument within a larger European context, trying to damn the incursions of the Crown into Ulster not by reference to any particular theory of Irish sovereignty, local or national, but by damning it as the unlawful, perhaps immoral, encroachment upon the rights and property of noblemen. And so I do not think we can look at Ó Cianáin's text as the curious scribblings of a Gaelic innocent awed before the majesty of Renaissance Europe – as suggested by Ó Fiaich – but rather as a determined attempt to move the Ulster lords squarely into the court of the European nobility and so portray them as members of an international cohort of aristocrats. For that reason it seems to make more sense to see in this manuscript not the description of a flight into decline, obscurity and loss – as we see in the poems by Mac an Bhaird and Ó Gnímh – but rather as the grand tour of a pair (trio, if we include Maguire) of aristocrats in temporary exile, seeking support to return home to claim their rightful *dúchais* (patrimonies) from rival claimants, English and Irish alike.

AVANT-GARDE TRADITIONALISM? *BEATHA AODHA RUAIDH UÍ DHOMHNAILL* AND THE EUROPEANIZATION OF 'MEDIEVAL' GAELIC HONOUR

Like Ó Cianáin's *Flight*, Lughaidh Ó Cléirigh's *Beatha Aodha Ruaidh Uí Dhomhnaill* (or *Life of Red Hugh O'Donnell*)[45] is a generic oddity. Seen from one angle, the *Beatha* is an aggressive piece of archaism. It is constructed in the traditional form of annals – headings by years, coverage of the deeds of great men, and so on – and the style and vocabulary have more in common

---

[44] Ó Cianáin, *The flight of the earls*, p. x. [45] The discussion below relies on the editor's translation.

with works of, say, the fifteenth century than of the seventeenth.[46] Yet the text is also highly original in that, to the best of my knowledge, the production of annals as personal memorial was entirely unique. Moreover, it is less sparse than the typical annals and engages with intimate questions of good lordship and practical politics – the bulk of the narrative following Red Hugh's fortunes post-inauguration as chief of the O'Donnells, focusing particularly on his role in the Nine Years' War. Also like the *Flight*, the themes of honour and nobility pervade the text. Indeed, these twin themes form the central thrust of Ó Cléirigh's argument as to why O'Donnell prosecuted the war as he did. The way in which Ó Cléirigh constructs these themes, however, is markedly different from Ó Cianáin's treatment. The presence of religion in honour's definition is significantly muted here, if not absent. In its place appear the more traditional criteria of blood, militarism and good lordship. Yet, as I hope to demonstrate, these honour codes are not so in conflict as they may appear. For like Ó Cianáin, Ó Cléirigh sees his honourable Gaelic lord as one attentive to both religious reform and continental, aristocratic modes of conduct.

The language Ó Cléirigh uses in the *Beatha* marks a return to much of the traditional bardic terminology eschewed by Ó Cianáin. He makes full use of royal terminology, regularly referring to the Ulster lords as prince (*flaith*) and king (*rí*), and to their territories as kingdoms (*flaithiusa*) and to their local authority as *righe* (sovereignty).[47] For matters of personal and/or family honour he uses *eineach*, while he typically reserves *onóir* – Ó Cianáin's choice when addressing such matters – for demonstrations of external respect, such as the honour due religious figures or the deceased.

Ó Cléirigh also resurrects much of the traditional criteria of Gaelic honour dispensed with by Ó Cianáin, proving on some points to be more retrograde even than Mac an Bhaird and Ó hEoghusa. The role of lineage, important to Ó Cianáin but never explicitly discussed, takes centre stage in the *Beatha*. It colours nearly every description of people, political units, and even the land itself: O'Donnell is repeatedly referred to using genealogical identifiers, for example, as the 'scion of Conall', the mytho-historical ancestor of the O'Donnells and founder of the dynasty; his political position is described as head of the Cenel Conaill, literally 'the people of Conall'; and the territory over which he governed is referred to as Tir Connaill, or the land (*tír*) of Conall.[48]

[46] See Damian McManus, 'The language of the *Beatha*', in Ó Riain (ed.), *Beatha ... historical and literary contexts*, pp. 54–73.
[47] For examples, see Ó Cléirigh, 1:33, 129, 319 (*flaith*); 55, 265, 337 (*rí*); 275 (*flaithiusa* and *righe*).
[48] To reinforce the point, it should be noted that new persons in the narrative are almost never introduced by first name alone but rather trailing a full complement of ancestors. A wonderful example of this comes in Ó Cléirigh's description of the MacWilliam succession of 1595. The

In addition to high birth, the holder of noble honour in this text had to demonstrate autonomy of action. The word *saor*, or free, occurs over twenty times as a means to define Gaelic elites and implies that the person or family was free from paying tribute to superiors. It also implies that others were to obey the free noble unquestioningly and O'Donnell, we read, was a 'lion in strength and force, with threatening and admonishing so that it was not allowed to gainsay his word, for whatever he ordered had to be done on the spot'.[49] This judgement is driven home in the following description of O'Donnell's treatment of certain lords who had not attended his inauguration as chief of the name in 1592. Ó Cléirigh writes that since 'it was no honour or glory (*niruo miadh no maisi*) to him that one chief of his people should be in opposition and enmity to him', Red Hugh immediately set out to physically remind absentees of the honour due him.[50]

An honourable noble was to be sensitive regarding insult to his name and personal honour and quick to defend the same. This, according to the *Beatha*, was a near obsession for O'Donnell, 'a man who did not allow himself to be injured or afflicted, cheated or insulted without repaying and avenging it immediately'.[51] Even O'Donnell's military decisions, at least as Ó Cléirigh explains them, were made as much over concerns for the protection of his personal and family honour than overall military strategy. His setting an ambush for a certain Captain Martin (a commander under Sir Richard Bingham, governor of Connaught) in order to 'teach him a lesson' for his insolence is but one, though representative, example.[52]

As the Captain Martin excerpt suggests, true honour as described in the *Beatha* flourished on the battlefield. The importance of war and militarism to Irish notions of honour, as depicted by O'Cléirigh, can hardly be over-estimated. He praises Irish lords above all for their warrior qualities: O'Donnell was 'a determined, fierce and bold invader of districts; a warlike, predatory aggressive plunderer of others' territories; and a destroyer of any of the English and Irish that opposed him', and 'a powerful war-dog' whose anger and wrath even the great O'Neill was afraid to rouse.[53]

But Gaelic honour was not founded purely on good lineage and martial valour, and Ó Cléirigh was careful to show that the militarism and freedom of action of the Gaelic lord was constrained on the one hand by certain

---

MacWilliam Burkes were lords of territory in north Connacht, in present-day County Mayo. Out of a large field of claimants, two emerged as the front runners. Claimant number one, Ó Cléirigh introduces as William Burke of Shrule, claimant number two as Tibbot, son of Walter Ciotach, son of John, son of Oliver. It is a clear sign of who is going to win the election, and claimant number two duly prevails. Ó Cléirigh, *Beatha*, pp. 113–19.

[49] Ibid., p. 345.   [50] Ibid., p. 57.   [51] Ibid., p. 347.
[52] Ibid., p. 105; this will be discussed further, below.   [53] Ibid., pp. 347, 243.

duties and responsibilities grounded in notions of good lordship and, on the other, by obeisance owed higher secular authorities in Europe, namely the King of Spain.[54] And, as will be discussed below, Ó Cléirigh believed a lord's actions were bounded ultimately by the threat of providential displeasure.

What constituted good lordship should not look odd to anyone with a passing familiarity with medieval notions of good kingship.[55] There was the need to look after the common sort, and O'Donnell was 'their pillar of support, their bush of shelter, and their shield of protection against every trouble'.[56] Evidently he discharged these duties with gusto, for O'Cléirigh claims he was known as the 'legal executioner' for his readiness to hang robbers and outlaws.[57] The good lord was also a generous one. The word for generosity in Irish makes this connection clear: *flaithiúil* (generous) deriving from *flaith* (prince). As chief of the O'Donnells, Hugh showed hospitality to people across the social hierarchy commensurate with their place, thus, '… he gave entertainment throughout his territory in his farm-houses and land-holdings to the wretched poor people, to the inhabitants and to the weak and feeble'. When Alonzo Cobos, the representative of Philip III, arrived he feasted him for three days.[58] With his social peers he was steadfast and true to his word. Once he entered into a bond of friendship, that bond was eternal. For example, after Feilim Ó Tuathail helped O'Donnell escape Dublin, the two men, through bidding farewell and giving blessings, cemented a friendship between them and their descendants that 'would last to the end of time'.[59] There was also the need to patronize the learned classes and, as the fount of honour, preside over the naming of new chiefs in neighbouring lordships. To reiterate the importance of good lordship to Gaelic honour, Ó Cléirigh includes something of an anti-hero in the text, the north Connaught lord O'Connor Sligo[60] – one-time loyalist, reluctant rebel and traditional foe of the O'Donnells – the negative depictions of whom serve to reinforce the presentation of O'Donnell as a model governor.

Despite his depiction in the *Beatha* as a man of royal blood, O'Donnell did have superiors to whom he owed deference, most importantly, the King of Spain. Ó Cléirigh describes a clear trickle-down of legitimacy leading

[54] Darren McGettigan, in fact, claims that it was O'Donnell, not Hugh O'Neill, who engineered the Spanish alliance during the Nine Years' War and that he wished to transfer Irish sovereignty to the Spanish king. McGettigan, *Red Hugh O'Donnell*, pp. 125–6. Hiram Morgan, however, is of the opposite opinion. Morgan, 'The real Red Hugh', in Ó Riain (ed.), *Beatha … historical and literary contexts*, pp. 1–35.
[55] For more on this subject, see Chapter 3, above.   [56] Ó Cléirigh, *Beatha*, p. 113.   [57] Ibid., p. 123.
[58] Ibid., pp. 113, 121.   [59] Ibid., p. 26.   [60] For more on O'Connor Sligo, see Chapter 2, above.

from Philip, to O'Donnell and O'Neill, to the lesser lords allied with them, and down finally to the soldiers. When in 1600 Spanish support of the war effort came in the less than princely sum of £6,000, instead of a hoped-for army, the Ulster lords 'fear[ed] their people and friends will be distrustful of them once they learn how little concern the King of Spain has for them'. At first they decided to refuse the money, but changed their minds as they did not wish to 'awaken the wrath of the King of Spain. For there was no true friend to whom they could complain of their trials and troubles, who had power to aid them in the straits they were in but the King of Spain. They took the money for that reason and not for avarice or a desire for wealth.'[61] O'Donnell appears in the *Beatha* to have been well aware of the need to treat his only international ally with proper respect and deference. Moreover, he echoes the European-wide sense that to show too great an interest in money was to act ignobly. Thus, the claim by some historians that Gaelic honour was all about might-makes-right and the maximization of individual autonomy cannot be sustained by a reading of the *Beatha*.[62]

The most curious aspect of O'Cléirigh's construction of Gaelic honour was the muted role played by religion. As we have seen above, Ó Cianáin would place reformed Catholicism at the centre of his definition of Gaelic honour. O'Cléirigh, by contrast, approached religion more with a sense of medieval piety than of post-Reformation confessional certainty. He was not blind to the confessional nature of the conflict between the Ulster lords and the Crown, as his eulogy to the fallen Hugh Maguire, Lord of Fermanagh, demonstrates: Maguire, he writes, 'killed and defeated many parties both gentle and simple of the foreign race with whom he contested and fought to protect his faith and native land until he fell by them then'.[63] But this is the text's only sustained discussion of the defence of a confessionalized faith – and this in spite of the fact that O'Donnell and O'Neill themselves made a great play to faith and fatherland in the course of the conflict.[64] Red Hugh instead appears in the pages of the *Beatha* as having been content to follow the time-honoured religious devotions and practices of clerical protection and patronage adhered to by Gaelic lords throughout the medieval period: 'a dove in meekness and gentleness to privileged men of the church', and not an adherent to Tridentine certainties and a defender of the faith against heretics.[65]

---

[61] Ó Cléirigh, *Beatha*, pp. 284–5.
[62] See Palmer, 'That "Insolent Liberty"'; Leerssen, *Mere Irish*, pp. 151–202.
[63] Maguire was killed in a skirmish in 1600. Ó Cléirigh, *Beatha*, p. 241. [64] See Chapter 1, above.
[65] Ó Cléirigh, *Beatha*, p. 345. On this point, Darren McGettigan writes that O'Donnell did not make any concerted use of Counter Reformation rhetoric and that he was more concerned with military affairs. McGettigan, *Red Hugh O'Donnell*, p. 124.

In trying to explain the *Beatha*'s sepia tone, one could perhaps argue that the language and criteria of noble honour deployed by O'Cléirigh is simply a function of the fact that he was writing about a period prior to the conclusion of the Nine Years' War. Individual Gaelic lordships still existed, as did the time-honoured relationship between *ollamh* and lord, and so perhaps it only stands to reason that he should speak of Gaelic kings, ancient dynasties, and so on.[66] Writing on the same events and about the same time as did Ó Cléirigh, however, the compilers of *The Annals of the Four Masters* followed a different approach.[67] They placed far greater importance on the role of proper religion in the actions of O'Donnell and O'Neill. For instance, they write how Red Hugh sought the assistance of the King of Spain because he 'was the person who could render him [Red Hugh] most relief, and who was the most willing to assist those who always fought in defence of the Roman Catholic Religion'; in the *Beatha*, by contrast, there is no mention of matters of faith when describing Red Hugh's mission to Spain.[68] Nor does the *Four Masters* play up O'Donnell's touchiness as Ó Cléirigh does. When they introduce the skirmish with Captain Martin (discussed above) they merely note that he was a proud and haughty youth who could not bear to be in eye contact with his enemies without attacking them; remarking on his death, they simply record that he was struck, carried off by his men, and later died.[69] In the *Beatha*, by contrast, Martin is first introduced as a captain and then described as 'crying out and blustering against Aodh Maguire continually and against every one of the Irish whose name, fame, or repute for skill, especially in the matter of skill in horsemanship, he had heard of – a clear series of honour challenges.[70] On the subject of Martin's death, Ó Cléirigh details how the javelin 'pierced his heart in his breast as his misdeeds deserved; for he who was wounded there was a merciless rogue, and his hatred of the Irish was very great, and his evil deeds many wherever he had been throughout the whole province from Limerick to the Drowes, on account of his relative'.[71] Nor does the *Four Masters* claim, as Ó Cléirigh does, that a nasty wrangle between O'Neill and O'Donnell over who should march at the front of the troops in to battle was largely to blame for the disaster at Kinsale (that is, that God punished them

---

[66] On the continued poet–*ollamh* relationship into the seventeenth century, see Carney, *Irish bardic poet*.

[67] I include this brief comparison also to counter the notion that the *Beatha* and the *AFM* offer near-verbatim descriptions of the same events. For this claim, see Falls, *Elizabeth's Irish Wars*, p. 378. The question of the relationship between these two texts has recently been explored by Breatnach, 'Irish records of the Nine Years' War'.

[68] *AFM*, 6, p. 2291.   [69] Ibid., p. 1977.   [70] Ó Cléirigh, *Beatha*, p. 105.   [71] Ibid., p. 107.

for their pride). The focus on aristocratic honour, good lordship and Gaelic cultural tradition, then, was a matter of choice for the author and not determined solely by the historical setting of his subject.

But nor was that choice determined by insular, Irish contexts alone, since the language of honour here seems constructed quite consciously within a European context. The obsession with lineage set the stage for Ó Cléirigh's couching of international relations in terms of kinship responsibilities and family honour. O'Donnell's appeal for Spanish aid for the war effort was, according to Ó Cléirigh, based upon the supposed common ancestry of the two peoples. In May of 1596 the Ulster lords entertained a Spanish envoy, Alonzo Cobos, who had come to Ireland

to confer with and get information from the Gaels, for the Gaels of Fodhla were friendly to and united with the King of Spain on account of their having come from Spain long before, and a number of learned men and historians of the Irish had set down in remembrance and recollection for the King the doings and history of the sons of Mil, and besides, the people that were driven into exile by the English from the island of Erin, after their patrimony had been filched from them, used to go to complain of their hardship to him and his ancestors for a long time.[72]

The Spanish, as Ó Cléirigh described it, thus had a responsibility to assist the Irish lords because of blood connections, not as we might expect because of concerns over defence of the faith or matters of international realpolitik.[73]

The focus on honour imperatives also offered an explanation for the evolution of military events at Kinsale. There the Irish abandoned a strategy of ambushes and limited engagements, tactics which they had pursued successfully since the start of the war six years earlier, and chose instead to meet the English in pitched battle. The results were, of course, disastrous. But in a pre-emptive answer to questions regarding the change in military strategy, Ó Cléirigh explained the switch as the only honourable option available at the time. Looking at the situations of the various forces prior to the battle, those of the Irish and Spanish were vastly superior. Although the Spanish were pinned down in the town of Kinsale by besieging English troops, once the Irish arrived from the north the English were caught in a vice. Strong on paper as this situation may have been for the Ulster lords, it was weakened by the fact that the Spanish were suffering terribly under siege conditions. The two Irish lords were split on how best to proceed.

---

[72] Ibid., p. 121.
[73] McGettigan offers further evidence on this point by noting that O'Donnell was ashamed by the state of his lodgings in the presence of these Spanish envoys and thus set about refurnishing them so as to make a better impression during any future negotiations. McGettigan, *Red Hugh O'Donnell*, p. 76. More generally on the Spanish-Irish politics of lineage, see Downey, 'Purity of blood and purity of faith'.

O'Neill, confident that the Spanish could hold out, favoured starving out the English; O'Donnell felt it was a matter of shame to leave their allies to suffer in that way. Moreover, O'Donnell held pitched battle to be more honourable than O'Neill's plan of victory by privation. His case was strengthened by the fact that the Spanish had sent messengers appealing to them to attack the English and lift the siege. This request played strongly on O'Donnell's belief that it was 'a shame and disgrace to be taunted with the great straits Don Juan and the Spanish were in, without making an attempt to relieve them though his death would come of it, and besides, lest the Irish be thought little of and despised by the King of Spain, if they suffered his soldiers to be in hardships and straits from their enemies without being aided as they requested'.[74] Whereas O'Neill's proposition may have been the more strategically sound, O'Donnell's was more in keeping with honour principles – and it was his that prevailed in the end.

Providence was predictably brought in to show why a properly honourable military strategy could have ended in defeat. In the early days of O'Donnell's lordship, Ó Cléirigh wrote, the young chief had enjoyed nothing but success: he had banished the English from Tyrconnell; he had returned peace and order to his patrimony; he had made successful raids into Connaught and chastised those who resisted his authority. But 'as worldly power without reverses and happiness without eclipse are not pleasing to the one God, he gave a reverse of fortune to the success of the race of Lughaidh, son of Setna for a while'. And why was this done? '[L]est pride or haughtiness, desire or self-will, should turn O'Donnell aside from the straightness of his judgment, his probity in ruling his kingdom, and lest by reason of his leadership and victory over the neighbouring territories he might set his mind and thoughts on his own strengths and powers, rather than on the decrees and gifts of the Lord of Heaven and earth, who is able to humble the valiant and exalt the miserable …'[75]

Although generally seen as antithetical to one another, in the *Beatha*, martial prowess and good governance were, in fact, complementary traits of the good ruler.[76] Thus, Red Hugh O'Donnell's martial valour appears prominently in the text not merely because this is a telling of life during wartime, or because Ó Cléirigh may have pined for the days of autonomous Gaelic warlords, but also because such a description echoed the text's generic models. As Damian McManus has posited, the models for this

[74] Ó Cléirigh, *Beatha*, pp. 329–31.   [75] Ibid., p. 275.
[76] See, for instance, Leerssen's discussion of the increasing militancy of Gaelic verse in the late sixteenth century, in *Mere Irish*, pp. 164–89.

sort of king-hero biography were the sagas, and thus Red Hugh was bound to appear in the *Beatha* as model of both warrior and good lord.[77]

But if the sagas provided the model, what was the audience? This remains a matter of conjecture. Mícheál Mac Craith has suggested that the text was intended as propagandistic support for a potential military campaign in Ireland by Red Hugh's nephew, assisted by Spanish troops.[78] If that is correct, it would explain Ó Cléirigh's depiction of the decline of Gaelic honour in Ulster. For if honour was so vital a feature of legitimate rule, then he had little choice but to highlight its loss from Ireland in the wake of the Ulster plantation and the eclipse of O'Donnell imperium. Only the return of the O'Donnells would restore honour to the region, and with it justice, good government and some approximation of the Gaelic cultural order. Moreover, the focus on honour would seem a wise strategy when pursuing Spanish assistance since it played on the contemporary Spanish obsession with the same. As John Elliott has noted, the Spanish had a very highly developed sense of honour in this period.[79] Consequently, they may have been sympathetic to appeals for its restoration. And here Ó Cléirigh would prove particularly clever, for by pushing the bonds of fictive kinship, and thus the duties of family honour, and by blaming the military disaster of Kinsale in part on the honourable decision of O'Donnell to assist the besieged Spanish, he implicated the honour of the Spanish crown and people in the fate and future of Irish honour.

Mac Craith's thesis, while suggestive, is speculative and therefore the question of audience remains open. Language alone suggests an Irish audience (be it in Ireland or in exile) rather than a continental one. Nevertheless, the themes Ó Cléirigh deals with suggest intellectual and ideological concerns common throughout aristocratic, confessionalized Europe. And, thus, while we cannot at present identify with any certainty the intended audience for the *Beatha*, we can at least look for some potential generic comparisons. Fulke Greville's *The Life of the Renowned Sir Philip Sidney* seems a likely candidate: the two texts were written around the same time, the *Beatha* between 1616–32, the *Life* between 1609–14; they are both reflections on events that took place during Europe's *fin de siècle* wars of religion; and they also share a sense of despair that true honour had gone to the grave with their protagonists.[80] At first sight, the end of honour as

[77] McManus, 'The language of the *Beatha*', pp. 72–3.
[78] Mac Craith, 'The *Beatha* in the context of the literature of the Renaissance', in Ó Riain (ed.), *Beatha Aodha Ruaidh: The life of Red Hugh O'Donnell: historical and literary contexts* (Dublin, 2003), pp. 26–53.
[79] John Elliott, *Imperial Spain 1469–1716* (New York, 1973), pp. 20, 215–16.
[80] Fulke Greville, *The life of the renowned Sir Philip Sidney* (1652): a facsimile reproduction with an introduction by Warren W. Wooden (New York, 1984).

described in these books – personified in the deaths of those paragons Sidney
and O'Donnell – closely mirrors modern historiographical arguments of
'medieval' chivalric codes of personal honour retreating before the advance
of the 'modern' state.[81] But we may be able to read the evidence more subtly,
as testimony to the continued relevance of such 'older' forms of conduct on
an emerging stage of honour occupied by elites of different nations. Lineage,
for example, was important to both Greville and Ó Cléirigh, and both
favoured action over passivity. We may think of Sidney, for instance, as
being foremost a man of letters, but as Greville saw it, 'the truth is: his end
was not writing, even while he wrote; nor his knowledge moulded for tables,
or schooles; but both his wit, and understanding bent upon his heart, to
make himself, and others, not in words or opinions, but in life, and action
good and great'.[82] Touchiness and the quick defence of one's good name
were requisite for the man of honour, and whereas O'Donnell punished
those who dishonoured him by their absence from his inauguration, so
Sidney challenged the Earl of Oxford for insult delivered on the royal tennis
courts.[83] Both authors claimed their subjects also held proper respect for their
honourable betters: Sidney for Elizabeth, O'Donnell for Philip II and III.
And, finally, there was a supra-national religious element to both authors'
depictions of honour, as evidenced by Sidney's fighting in the Low Countries
for the Protestant cause and Ó Cléirigh's celebration of Maguire as a defender
of the Catholic faith. Both of these works, then, in spite of their culturally
specific influences and inflections, appear products of European-wide neo-
chivalric thinking – a phenomenon which would fuel the revival of the Court
of Chivalry under Charles I and the proceedings over honour and reputation
in both London's Star Chamber and Dublin's Castle Chamber during the
1620s and 30s. And, thus, if Greville's hagiography was a critique of the low-
born of the Jacobean court, so Ó Cléirigh's may have been a critique of those
who allied themselves with Crown and Castle in the wake of the Flight. Like
Ó Cianáin's *Flight*, the *Beatha* too may have been aimed at competitors for
authority in Ulster – Irish and English alike.

MAKING THE IRISH EUROPEAN

Ó Cianáin's *Flight* and Ó Cléirigh's *Beatha* are two very different texts.
Nevertheless, there are interesting links between them. First, they show a
dynamic response to the changes to Gaelic culture and society occasioned

---

[81] See, for example, Mervyn James, 'English politics and the concept of honour'; Neuschel, *Word of honour.*
[82] Greville, *Sir Philip Sidney*, pp. 20–1.   [83] Ibid., pp. 73–81.

by anglicization and Crown centralization. These works are hardly records of a 'Gaelic mind' in collapse.[84] Rather, they are examples of ways in which genre and *mentalité* could be reworked to prepare Irish elites for an international stage. Second, they highlight the theme of honour. Gaelic lords and intellectuals were very concerned to preserve their own status and authority as Anglo–Irish relations took a colonial turn; the language of honour was well-suited to that project. Third, they demonstrate the willingness to push generic boundaries.

Most interesting in the end, however, is the intellectual trajectory these works chart when read together. Both Ó Cianáin and Ó Cléirigh seem to have been interested to re-cast Gaelic nobles as members of an international aristocracy. This is important to bear in mind given the current emphasis on the development of faith and fatherland ideologies amongst Gaelic elites in this period. Undoubtedly, these ideologies figured prominently in the thinking and actions of those with political agency. Nevertheless, we must be cautious in assigning too 'modernizing' a character to these changes: national consciousness is not nationalism, and Tridentine Catholicism was not a levelling religion. Those who advocated these new ideas envisioned them working in concert with traditional patterns of social differentiation: 'faith and fatherland' may have required defence, but it was traditional elites who felt entitled to do the defending. If the Irish were thinking in terms of an Irish nation, it was a 'dynastic nation'. And as political and religious conceptions became internationalized in this period, so too were the criteria of aristocratic honour which marked the natural ruler from the low-born interloper.

These two texts, then, demonstrate the sorts of politically charged prose pieces Irish literati penned in support of Irish nobles who not only physically moved between Ireland and the continent, but also thought outside of an Irish-English axis and within a pan-European context. Gaelic honour, then, was by necessity affected by these larger contexts and began to take on a more confessional tone. But of course not all Gaelic and Gaelicized lords rebelled against the Crown, and of those that did, the majority did not go into exile. In the wake of the Nine Years' War they too attempted to navigate Anglo-Irish society and politics aided by appeals to honour. It is to their tales that we turn next.

---

[84] See Nicholas Canny, 'The formation of the Irish mind'; Michelle O'Riordan, *Gaelic mind*. More generally, however, much of the work done on Gaelic Ireland simply assumes the existence of a monolithic Gaelic worldview. This, for example, is the impression given in Palmer, 'That "Insolent Liberty"'.

CHAPTER 5

Gaelic and Old English honour in early Stuart 'Britain'

The appeal to definitions of honour and nobility was not strictly a strategy for Gaelic exiles but was also employed as a means to compete for place and status by those who remained in Ireland and England during the early Stuart period. This chapter considers the deployment of a language of honour by those Irish lords and intellectuals concerned with affairs at 'home'. It consists of three parts, constructed so as to provide perspectives reflective (if not necessarily representative) of the main sites of British honour culture in Ireland: bardic/intellectual, Gaelic aristocratic, and Old English.

The first section focuses on three Gaelic works produced after the Flight of the Earls (1607) and considers the authors' fears of social inversion. The second section consists of a case study of one Gaelic lord's construction of honour in post-Mellifont Ireland. The subject here is Donough O'Brien, 4th Earl of Thomond, who parleyed loyalty to the Crown during the Nine Years' War into dramatic social and political advancement. Well-known to history as the most 'English' of native lords, Thomond was faced with his own crisis of authority as he tried to make the transition from ancient Gaelic lord to anglicized aristocrat. By focusing on his use of genealogy and pedigrees, I aim to demonstrate the continued importance placed on traditional markers of nobility – here specifically the claim to ancient lineage – by a fully collaborating Gaelic earl. The third and final section looks at the other extraordinary example of successful transition from pre- to post-Mellifont authority – that of Richard Burke, 4th Earl of Clanricard. Like Thomond, Clanricard also sided with the Crown against O'Neill and O'Donnell. And again like Thomond, he was amply rewarded for his assistance. What makes Clanricard's case so spectacular is that he was the only Irish noble (although Old English, he certainly could be considered 'Gaelicized') to gain a title in the English peerage, having been created Earl of St Albans in 1628. This study of that most adaptable of Anglo-Irish lords argues that Clanricard's construction of honour and nobility was not a matter of uni-directional anglicization: while he worked assiduously to rise through the English social and political ranks, he simultaneously strove to retain his honourable standing in Ireland.

Overall, this chapter argues for, one, the importance of honour and nobility as a means by which to interpret post-Mellifont Anglo-Irish society and to navigate its uncharted waters and, two, that despite the collapse of the Gaelic order, the sense of honour developed by anglicizing nobles like Thomond and Clanricard was influenced as much by the traditional as by the new. The chapter ends, however, on a cautionary note. A brief consideration of the 1626 precedence dispute between Clanricard and the 5th Earl of Thomond (Henry O'Brien, Donough's son) raises the spectre of socially disruptive and politically crippling wrangles over status fought by those who seemingly were aiding the process of making Ireland British. Whereas honour imperatives could very well aid the cultural and political amalgamation of Irish and English social systems, it could equally serve to break that unity down.

GAELIC FEARS OF SOCIAL INVERSION

The theme of honour was as important to those authors writing about Anglo-Irish events as it was for those whose subject was Gaelic lords in exile. The authors discussed in the previous chapter may have been concerned about social inversion in post-Mellifont Ireland, but their primary concern was to modify Gaelic nobility so that it conformed more closely to continental, Catholic norms. By contrast, Gaelic intellectuals who remained in Ireland, and whose main concerns were contemporary Anglo-Irish affairs and the place of the native aristocracy in them, were obsessed with this topic. The collapse of the Gaelic system had left a gaping vacuum of authority, particularly in Ulster, into which rushed allcomers. The ensuing competition for place, status and fortune was greeted with horror by some amongst the Irish intellectual classes.

I will consider three works in this section. The first is a very short (three quatrains in length) and well-known poem – 'Faisean Chláir Eibhir' ('Fashion of Ireland') – that pithily describes the disgust of old elites with the ostentation and immoderation of Irish upstarts.[1] The second – Muiris mac Dáibhí Dubh Mac Gearailt's 'Mór idir na haimsearaibh' ('How great the difference between the ages') – is a much longer work that uses an

---

[1] Pádraig de Brun, Breandán Ó Buachalla and Tomás Ó Concheanainn (eds.), *Nua-Dhuanaire* I (Baile Átha Cliath, 1971).

Ovidian periodization of the ages of the world to describe the decline of humanity and the concomitant debasement of honour and nobility in Ireland.[2] The last is a satirical prose work entitled *Pairlement Chloinne Tomáis* (The Parliament of Clan Thomas) in which the author, in the mode of Sebastian Brant or Rabelais, lampoons the pretensions of those native Irish – be they of Gaelic or Old English stock – who attempted to capitalize on the social instability occasioned by the collapse of the Gaelic order to rise in status above their traditional betters. All three of these works reveal that in the minds of Irish contemporaries the enemies of honour, nobility and hierarchy could be native opportunists as well as English and Scottish Protestant interlopers.[3]

The author of 'Faisean Chláir Eibhir' – the best guess for which is Brian Mac Giolla Phádraig, member of an Ulster family of poets[4] – decries the material immodesty of his fellow Gaels. As the title might imply, he focuses largely on sartorial excess. Thus, he acidly notes the wearing of bright cuffs (*cufa geal*), flashy rings (*fáinne aerach*), bracelets (*bráisléidibh*) and scarves and garters (*scairf is gáirtear*) by those who should know better. But fashion here is not purely sartorial. He also bemoans the rage for tobacco ('*S gach mogh nó a mhac … a stoc tobac 'na chlab*), the disdain for the learned classes (*… gan scot ag neach le fear den dáimh éigse*), and the rejection of euphonious Irish in favour of broken English (thus the reference to *fear an smáilBhéarla*). Here, it seems then, is the quintessential expression of dismay over the disappearance of the old ways before the deluge of new fashions and consumer products of the metropole. In that respect, this is not a novel work; commentators in the sixteenth century took aim at social-climbing churls.[5] But I include this poem here because the message seems slightly more complex. For while the author abuses these parvenus for their pathetic attempts at anglicization, he simultaneously chides them for parading around as if they were princes of O'Brien blood from the Ireland of old ('*… mar gach flaith d'fhuil Chais dár ghnáth Éire*'),

[2] Nicholas Williams (ed.), *Dánta Mhuiris Mhic Dháibhí Dhuibh Mhic Gearailt* (Baile Atha Cliath, 1979), pp. 48–57. Translations mine unless otherwise noted.

[3] For incisive comments on the native Irish intelligentsia's snobbery and continued fascination with honour in the face of Jacobean derision, see Canny, *Making Ireland British*, chapter 7, and Raymond Gillespie, 'Negotiating order in early-seventeenth century Ireland', in Michael Braddick and John Walter (eds.), *Negotiating power in early modern society: order, hierarchy and subordination in Britain and Ireland* (Cambridge, 2001), pp. 188–205.

[4] De Brun, et al. (eds.), *Nua-Dhuanaire*, pp. 11, 97.

[5] See, for example, Laoiseach Mac an Bhaird's 'A fhir ghlacas a ghalldacht', in Osborn Bergin, *Irish bardic poetry* (Dublin, 1974), pp. 49–50.

the O'Briens having produced Ireland's last effective high-king, Brian Boru.[6] The situation he describes, then, is more complex than the simple aping of English fashions. Rather he hints at a tense syncretic character to the social changes he describes, one in which the old status symbols (Irish aristocratic bloodlines) are mixed with the new (fashions of London as displayed by planters) by opportunistic Gaels of base blood.

Muiris mac Dáibhí Dubh Mac Gearailt takes up this theme of inversion in his poem 'Mór idir na haimsearaibh', but does so at greater length. Although of Old English stock, Mac Gearailt chose to write in Irish. This particular poem, dating from the 1610s, begins with the author re-casting the Ovidian periodization of the ages of the world to fit the Irish context.[7] Following the ages of gold, silver and brass – each succeeding one having ushered in a period of further moral decline – the world was now wallowing in an age of iron, the stage of greatest moral turpitude. The poem then goes on to lament the disappearance of the true nobility from Ireland and to describe the debased socio-cultural environment that has sprung up in their absence. In a pattern very like Brant's 'The Ship of Fools', Mac Gearailt catalogues the follies of the denizens of this iron age: the god-lessness of contemporary society; the rise of professional classes who exist mainly to enrich themselves by bilking the ignorant; the greed and pettiness of tavern-keepers and labourers; the horror and shame of rampant usury; and humanity's all-consuming passion for material goods. Depicted here is fundamental and total social inversion. The last quatrain leaves the impression that Mac Gearailt doubts this travesty will improve any time soon, for in those closing lines he declares that, given the state of the world, he had no wish to be young again.[8]

What defines honour and nobility for Mac Gearailt is only partly answerable by reference to his discussion of these themes, for his direct attention to them is limited. Their flourishing, we know, is one of the defining characteristics of the golden age. But what they entail goes unaddressed.[9] Nor do we get much help by analyzing his discussion of the nobility itself, for such

[6] The actual comparison employed here is with the Dál Cháis, clan of the greatest of Irish high-kings, Brian Boru, and of the O'Briens, Earls of Thomond. De Brun, et al. (eds.), *Nua-Dhuanaire*, p. 11.

[7] Williams (ed.), *Dánta Mhuiris … Mhic Gearailt*, stanzas 2–6, p. 48. For Mac Gearailt's background and his English and continental literacy influences, see Williams (ed.), pp. 7–30. I wish to thank Mícheál Mac Craith for his advice on these poems and on dealing with Irish syllabic verse more generally. Responsibility for translation and interpretation remains, of course, solely with me.

[8] I dtuatacht ná i lorgántacht / i seascaireacht ná i gcomhól / ar mbeith dhamh im' óganach / níor chuireas dúil go romhór. Ibid., p. 57.

[9] Aimsear órdha an chéadaimsir / ar bhoige, ar uaisle 's ar aoibhneas. 'Uaisle', here to be taken as 'nobility', is a feature of the first age of man: the golden age. Ibid., p. 48.

discussions are rare. The poem, after all, is concerned to describe the age of iron in which the presence of the nobility is slight. It is not that the Gaelic aristocracy are completely absent from the verse,[10] but that when they do appear their social presence is judged to be almost imperceptible, besieged as they are in the current environment of so-called progress:

> O poor nobles of honour,
> Your journey is truly foolish;
> For alas, it is a cruel game
> That leaves honour with no power
>
> Without office, patrimony,
> Cattle or ready money,
>
> There is no point in you, who are the people
> of true prowess, not being in decline[11]

By Mac Gearailt's reckoning, the native gentry and nobility are in permanent free fall since there is little chance they will be able to secure their lands and the rents that come from them in the face of the Crown's centralizing and anglicizing policies. The author closes his brief discussion of the fate of the Gaelic aristocracy by lamenting his own social decline, a result of his having foolishly stuck to traditional loyalties and not following the times:

> Like a fool I went
> With you [the old nobility] into the deluge;
> If I were to get a second chance.
> Not for my life would I go again.[12]

It is clear, then, that Mac Gearailt feels honour and nobility to be dead in contemporary Ireland. But to better understand what defines them we must analyse their opposites, for he spends considerably more energy describing ignoble traits and actions. Through attention to these

---

[10] Of this age he writes how it has been a long time since he has laid eyes on one of the true nobility. (Gaol dá ghaire is fioruaisle / ní fhacas riamh le fada). Ibid., p. 49.

[11] Is fíorleamh bhur dturas-sa / a uaisle bochta an oinigh / oineach gan bheith cumasach / mo thruagh, is cruaidh an cluiche; Gan oifig, gan seanoidhreacht / gan stoc, gan cheannach láimhe / sibhse an dream re síoroirbheirt / ní gar dhíbh gan bheith tráite. Ibid., p. 51.

[12] Do-chuaidh mise mar amadán / libhse fá uisce an cheatha / dá bhfagainnse an athanál / ní reachainn arís rem beatha. Ibid., p. 51. The phrase 'fá visce an cheata' was probably intended to resonate with Catholic readers, many of whom have been familiar with the story regarding the Oath of Supremacy, a common didactic tale among Catholics. The tale concerns a group of wisemen who had predicted a deluge that would drive those caught in it insane. They hid in a cave; their sceptical listeners stayed outside and were reduced to fools by the showers. When the wisemen re-emerged, the populace believed them to be the mad ones. The point of which being, of course, that simply because the majority is doing something or because a king demands it, does not make it right. See Mícheál Mac Craith, *Lorg na hlasachta ar na Danta Grá* (Dublin, 1989), pp. 139–46.

deficiencies we may work backwards to construct the outlines of his concepts of honour.

Of chief concern to Mac Gearailt is the godlessness of contemporary society. Interestingly, he does not condemn the upwardly mobile lower orders for converting to the reformed faith but rather for their opportunistic atheism. He speaks of the ministers of Munster and how the lower-born fill the temples to hear them. But it is not out of any sense of piety that they do so:

> It is not out of love for the minister,
> No more than out of love for the Pope,
> That these things are done,
> But rather from a desire to scrape together money.[13]

These Church of Ireland Gaels, then, are irreligious – loving neither Pope nor reformed minister – and only pack the church as a means to cosy up to their new masters whose favour they seek. Later in the poem Mac Gearailt returns to this theme of the godless Gael (the functional atheists) when he accuses those about him of being a 'cheerless, morose and clod-hopping bunch, with no love for God or man'.[14] Protestantism, then, does not represent a competing belief system (it standing to reason that a committed Catholic would not wish to legitimize the reformed faith, preferring to view it as false and heretical), but rather an irreligious cover for earthly covetousness and greed. True nobles, by default, are followers of Rome – something vehemently insisted upon by Ó Cianáin as we saw in the last chapter. Mac Gearailt was likewise coming to equate honour with confessional attachment.

Like the author of 'Faisean', Mac Gearailt, too, dwelt on the sartorial and material excesses of the lesser-born. He lampoons the peddlers of wares who promise bargains better than those found in London.[15] But whereas the author of 'Faisean' seems to have been speaking of the lower-born – thus his lament that it seems every beggar woman's son is fashionably attired[16] – Mac Gearailt makes specific mention of the changed behaviour of the sons of the gentry. Instead of protecting their patrimonies and keeping to traditional ways, they are losing their lands, and thus Ireland, in payment to those who sold them those trinkets.[17]

---

[13] Ní mar ghrádh don mhinister / ní mó is mar ghrádh don Phápa / do-níthear na neithese / acht d'fhonn airgid do scrábadh. Ibid., p. 50.

[14] dream ghéar ghruama gharbhchosach, gan grádh Dé ná grádh duine. Ibid., p. 54.

[15] go reacfadh riot earraidhe, seoch mar bhíd ar sráid Londan. Ibid., p. 50.

[16] … ar mhac gach mná déarca. De Brun, et al. (eds.), *Nua-dhuanaire*, p. 11.

[17] Do mheall uaibh an ceannaidhe / go lór bailte d'iath Eibhir / fá dheoidh ag an sladaidhe / biaidh an fearann le chéile. Williams (ed.), *Dánta Mhuiris*, p. 50.

This lament for the end of a system of moral economy – one in which hierarchical bonds of deference and responsibility, and the system's attendant sartorial and behavioural rules for those at different levels, were well-defined – is expanded upon in Mac Gearailt's discussion of the professions and other classes. To him, the world of the common law hardly represents the march of progress and civility, rather it means the end of promise, good word and noble arbitration.[18] The spread of English law merely serves to multiply disputes and create an increasingly litigious society. Worse still are the actions of the professional lawyers, for they are more interested in their clients' money than in justice.[19] This theme of the decay of basic trust-worthiness in society runs through the rest of his discussions of the professions: doctors trick you with false potions, schoolmasters with empty lessons; tavern keepers encourage people to drink on credit and so indebt themselves; and usurers are thick on the ground.[20] Mac Gearailt, thus, not only decries the rise of a cash economy in this age of iron, but laments the simultaneous decay of faith in an individual's word and promise and of the social regulating function of a properly stratified society of orders.

How might these themes appear in a work of prose? Are the social critiques of Mac Gearailt and the anonymous author of 'Faisean' purely poetic conceits? A reading of the anonymous prose work *Parliament of Clan Thomas* (hereafter *PCT*) reveals similar concerns. As with many Gaelic texts of this period, *PCT*'s author, date of completion, intended audience, and circulation are matters of conjecture and debate.[21] It cannot be read as representative of contemporary mentalities. It can, however, suggest ways in which at least one early seventeenth-century Gaelic commentator reacted to the social and cultural changes initiated by the completion of English hegemony over Ireland post-1607. The text is thought to date from the 1610s and there is speculation that it may have been influenced by the ineffectual, and often uproarious, packed-Parliament called by Lord Deputy Chichester between 1613–15.[22] As for its audience, the text's editor and translator, N. J. A. Williams, suggests that the work may be a satirical answer to 'Mór idir na haimsearaibh'.[23] Its central theme is certainly the

---

[18] Ibid.

[19] So an fear dlighe dúthrachtach / do-ní don chóir éagcóir / mo mhallacht dá ghúnasan / do mheall uaim mo dheich *jacob*; Ar feadh fichid groidthéarma / go hAth Cliath leis go scíosmhar / do-chuaidh mise ar boidéarma / 's gan liom acht *nisi prius*. Ibid., p. 53.

[20] Ibid., pp. 53–4.   [21] See discussion below.

[22] Williams suggests that perhaps the author is one of the O'Dineen family, traditional *ollúna* to the MacCarthy Mor. Ibid., p. 54.

[23] N. J. A. Williams (ed. and trans.), *Pairlement Chloinne Tomáis* (Dublin, 1981) (*PCT* hereafter). I use the editor's translation unless otherwise noted.

same as that of Mac Gearailt's poem: the social inversion of post-Flight of the Earls Ireland.

The text follows the fortunes of an Irish family of minor lords, Clan Thomas, from their origins in the distant past through the early seventeenth century. The family descended from Beelzebub's union with a mortal woman. On account of their partial human blood, the members of Clan Thomas were allowed to stay when St Patrick banished the demons from Ireland. However, Patrick laid strict conditions upon them: their lives were to be spent in menial agricultural labour and service and they were to wear coarse clothes and eat poor food. Until the time of Elizabeth I the family members wavered back and forth between following St Patrick's commands and trying to better themselves. After the Nine Years' War they would move decidedly in the direction of self-improvement. Once having attained wealth and relatively high status, however, they were dismayed to see how quickly their fortunes diminished as they attempted to follow the lifestyle requisite of gentry/minor noble status. To address this concern they called a Parliament in which they argued the merits of going back to their old ways, as commanded by St Patrick, against the advantages to be had from prosecuting a course of individual self-fulfilment. With that question still unresolved, the text closes with one of the delegates, having failed to get redress for an insult he received from one of the other MPs, storming out of the assembly. As he trudges off to his corner of Ireland, he lays a curse on the extended family that they may never prosper. The last line of the text assures the reader that this request was indeed fulfilled.

Williams suggests that the work is a satire upon Gaelic commoners, or 'churls', who embraced the new dispensation as a means by which to end their traditional social subordination.[24] Marc Caball, however, makes a persuasive argument that the lower gentry are the satire's victims. The text's descriptions of Clan Thomas as uncouth bores best suited to a life of menial agricultural labour seem to justify Williams' thesis. Caball, however, has challenged this interpretation on two fronts. First, he argues that given the structure of society at the time, it makes little sense to think that those classes identifiable as 'churls', that is, true commoners, would have been in any position to advance their place and standard of living to the point where they could have entered the ranks of the nobility, no matter the level of social instability and mobility. Second, he connects the text to a real historical place – north

---

[24] Ibid., p. xxiii.

Kerry – and to two families – the Gaelic O'Mores, and the settler Crosbies – locked in a tussle for local authority and status.[25] This interpretation is bolstered when we recall the family's origin, for they descend in part from lordly blood, that of Beelzebub, and thus have a certain claim to nobility. Granted it is a claim twisted by its demonic origins, and given St Patrick's mandate for the family to live wretchedly, it is a claim that would signify a gross inversion of proper social order were it to be fulfilled. It is the fear of that claim being fulfilled that drives the text of *PCT*.

It takes the Nine Years' War for Clan Thomas to finally commit to a programme of social improvement. The text implies that the social disruption caused by the war was of a scale unseen in the annals of Irish history: only then did the bonds of authority and order diminish to the point that Clan Thomas could confidently turn their back on St Patrick's centuries-old commandment to live wretchedly. The window for their social better-ment was initially opened on account of the war's having greatly reduced the numbers of native nobility and the consequent rendering of wide swathes of land ownerless. This was a once-in-a-millennium opportunity and the family seized it: 'with the scarcity of population, they began to take holdings and to seek marriage alliances that were unseemly for them to seek or get; and gradually they became village headmen, and they began to make land expensive for the nobility, and set to dyeing their clothes stylish colours and to cutting them stylishly'.[26]

Under James I, the members of Clan Thomas both reach the zenith of their social advancement and witness the first pitfalls to sustaining their gains. James is credited with having brought 'peace and prosper-ity' that allows the family to build on gains initially made during the chaos of the Nine Years' War. But sustaining that success quickly becomes a challenge, for they soon overextend themselves by sending their children off to learn rhetoric and natural philosophy (*rhetorique 7 le feallsamh nádúrtha*),[27] the costs of which cut deeply into their wealth. This represents the critical juncture in the text: after centuries of servitude to the noble and pious, they have now arrived at the top of the social heap and must act swiftly to stave off descent back into social obscurity and poverty. To address these matters the heads of the various Clan Thomas branches call a family parliament to convene in

---

[25] Marc Caball, 'Pairlement Chloinne Tomáis I: a reassessment', *Éigse* 27 (1993), pp. 47–57.
[26] *PCT*, p. 83.   [27] Ibid., p. 23.

1632.[28] The ensuing descriptions of the parliament, which meets over three sessions, offer a scathing commentary on Irish social inversion.

The description of the initial session – during which the 'MPs' attempt to establish some modicum of parliamentary procedure – reveals the author's concerns that the old markers of noble honour have been abandoned by society at large and that the old nobility are no longer respected. An MP from Limerick arrives to inform the gathered worthies that courts in his home county are hanging members of the ennobled Clan Thomas for crimes against property, stealing and the like. The news-bearer is furious because he feels Clan Thomas is paying for crimes committed by churls and the offspring of labourers. This pattern of false accusation, he declares, is a product of the courts' favouring of the lower-born and their belief that it can only be the 'idle aristocracy, the minor gentry and the scroungers among the tail-ends of noble families' who practise such 'skulduggery'. The other MPs, however, calm him by pointing out that whatever the case in Limerick, the courts generally support both Clan Thomas and the lesser-born, seeing both as loyal to the new establishment. It is the old aristocracy and gentry alone, they claim, who must fear the biases of the courts – a state of affairs brought about in part by the family's disparagement of the old aristocracy to the new authorities Crown and Castle. This, they add, has proven one of the family's most clever improving strategies, for into that vacuum of authority Clan Thomas and the Gaelic churls have rushed, with the demonically 'noble' Clan Thomas asserting themselves at the pinnacle of this new and motley social order.[29]

This theme of the enmity and competition between Clan Thomas and the old native aristocracy gets played out more explicitly later in the first session when two 'foreign' horsemen arrive at the gathering. The parliamentarians accuse one of them of having 'published a learned and very informative book on the genealogy and deeds of Clan Thomas, and he did not leave unpublished on us any blunder that we ever committed; and our reputation will live on the lips of sages and learned men until the end of the world and until doomsday because of that book'.[30] This, Williams suggests, is a reference to Muiris Mac Gearailt and 'Mór idir na haimsearaibh'.[31] Yet in spite of this enmity between Clan Thomas and the horsemen, and despite

---

[28] That this date is well ahead of the date of the text's composition has led Williams to suggest that the author is using a well-known satirical device: that of setting events in the future. Ibid., p. xviii.
[29] Ibid., p. 86.
[30] Ibid., p. 86. chuir sé leabhar feasach fíreolach amach air gheinealach 7 air ghníomharthuibh. Ibid., p. 27.
[31] Ibid., p. xxiii.

their referring to the riders as 'dilapidated gentry', some members of Clan Thomas ask the pair of foreigners to arbitrate a dispute between two of their number. The riders, Mac Gearailt and his companions, listen to both sides, yet pass no judgement in the dispute. Rather they condemn Clan Thomas as barbarians and ride off.[32]

This odd interaction between traditional, if fallen, elites – Mac Gearailt and his companion – and their newly ascendant inferiors neatly encapsulates the complexity of social relations in early seventeenth century Ireland. On the one hand, the MPs clearly dislike their traditional superiors. Their reference to them as the 'dilapidated gentry' rings with gloating over the fallen prospects of their erstwhile betters and is a piece with their earlier satisfaction at the courts' suspicion of the old nobility. Nevertheless, this is not a simple situation of social inversion whereby an inferior class makes use of the tools and markers of a new socio-cultural system to lord it over their former superiors. For clearly there is a residual acceptance that the foreign horsemen, representatives of a disappearing social elite, still wielded social authority. Otherwise they would not have been pressed to arbitrate the dispute. That Mac Gearailt and his companion failed to deliver a decision, preferring instead to curse the disputants and their family, merely highlights the distance that has grown between these classes as the Irish social hierarchy came undone under colonial pressure. Far from destroying Clan Thomas' esteem for the ancient nobility and gentry, this episode seems instead to highlight the confusion of the family's rise: in a world where the legal system's reach was still less than comprehensive and its justice suspect, and in which the age-old delineations of social order and authority had been torn apart, where does one turn for arbitration, justice and even legitimization?

Given this confusion, the men of Clan Thomas come to the conclusion that the only way to secure their new-found status is to prop it up with a claim to that greatest of pillars of Gaelic honour and legitimacy: a noble pedigree. In the parliament's last session the assembled family heads select a committee to whom all can air their grievances. The committee, in turn, is charged with drawing up a set of articles that will address the members' chief complaints. These eventually number three: that 'they were without noble surnames; and further that they used not have even half a year's provisions for the whole year; and still further that there were many of them unemployed and going to France, leaving their cattle and property behind them in Ireland'.[33] It is the first of these complaints that interests me most for it

[32] Ibid., pp. 87–8.   [33] Ibid., pp. 95–6.

reveals – as did the poem 'Faisean Chláir Eibhir', discussed above – the persistent status given to blood and name in spite of the fact that (or perhaps precisely because) the social order was in disarray. And also as in 'Faisean Chláir Eibhir', in *PCT* the name which carries the greatest social and historical gravitas is that of O'Brien:

'And as for our having noble surnames', said one of them, 'let each man invent a surname to suit himself'. 'That's all the more fitting', said Tomás an Trumpa, 'because I know many people who say they are of the Kindred of Brian, though they are of ignoble and uncouth families'. 'I'll be of the Kindred of Brian from now on', said little Brian. 'That is fitting', said Diarmuid Ó Clúmháin; and Diarmuid composed a quatrain on that subject: 'Ó Clúmháin, seemly Ó Céirín / Ó Curnáin, Ó Feoir, Ó Bruic / we shall now be of the sons of Cian / of the Kindred of Niall and the Kindred of Blod'. 'Blessing and prosperity to you', said Tomás an Trumpa, 'it is not more fitting for many others these days, now that Ó Briain is powerful, to call themselves Ó Briain, than it is for us; and do you think we'll get honour and equality before the law, as many people I know do? Now, Diarmuid, my boy, what is your surname?' 'I am of the family of Caimidil', said Diarmuid, 'that is, Caimidil Ó Briain'. 'Prosperity and blessing to you', said Tomás an Trumpa …'[34]

Like the upstarts lampooned in 'Faisean Chláir Eibhir', the men of Clan Thomas are not simply aping New English ways and manners. Their social appetite is far greater in that they wish to combine the trappings of English fashion with the assumption of the mantle of ancient Irish nobility. This, and only this, it seems will guarantee them the sort of social authority that is translatable across all political, social, ethnic and religious divides that ran through early Stuart Ireland.

Tying these three texts together is not merely the authors' fears of social inversion but the shared sense that Gaelic upstarts were constructing their social advancement through a promiscuous bricolage of new and old markers of honour and status. Clearly, honour remained of vital importance to all three authors: as they lamented the passing of traditional notions of Gaelic honour with the eclipse of the native nobility, so they decried the emergence of new, anglicized building blocks of honour. English-style fashions, religious conformity (however opportunistic it may have seemed) and the wholesale shedding of cultural forms (language, dress, forms of deference, and so on) were widespread enough to elicit the sort of acid critiques shown in these three texts. And yet the authors, in all their distaste for change and their hand-wringing over the state of the old nobility and the values they (ideally) embodied, could not help but reveal, perhaps even

---

[34] Ibid., p. 96.

unintentionally, the persistence of the authority enjoyed by those who could claim ancient lineage. Lower gentry and base-born upstarts may parade around as if they were in London, and kowtow to the demands of a new colonial authority, but in the absence of a complete, Spenserian social revolution, the ties of respect and deference that bound Gaelic Ireland were still very much alive in the Ireland of the Ulster Plantation. Each of these texts suggests that when seeking to draw a picture of the social transformations that shook early modern Ireland it makes limited sense to speak of a unidirectional and unilateral socio-cultural change, i.e., anglicisation. Rather it seems truer to contemporary complexities to posit that the construction of authority and the defence of status in an unstable colonial setting would by necessity draw upon the new *and* the old. Nowhere would that uneasy and syncretic nature of honour and nobility be more readily apparent, however, than in the real world attempts of people to straddle these complexities and contradictions – and perhaps in no family more clearly than among the O'Briens, Earls of Thomond, who were mentioned in 'Faisean' and *PCT* and to whom we turn next.

ETHNICITY, ANGLICIZATION AND ANCIENT HONOUR: DONOUGH O'BRIEN, EARL OF THOMOND, AND HIS PEDIGREES

The public articulation of a family's genealogy could greatly affect its and its individual members' social standing and cultural legitimacy. In our discussion of *PCT* we witnessed the bitterness that arose from the production and circulation of a disparaging genealogy: this was the reason that Clan Thomas bore a hatred of Muiris MacGearailt, author of that defamatory 'genealogy' in verse, 'Mór idir na haimsearaibh'. Conversely, a celebratory pedigree could act as a tool in advancing a family's standing and status, thus the attempts of Clan Thomas to create links to that most storied of lineages, the O'Briens. But it was not merely upstarts – and fictional ones at that – who appreciated the power of pedigree. The O'Briens also appreciated it, and here I wish to look at two lavish pedigrees commissioned by Donough O'Brien, 4th Earl of Thomond, in the 1610s.[35] They reveal that Thomond, like the upstarts lampooned in 'Faisean' and *PCT*, was pursuing social

---

[35] It is my assumption that Thomond commissioned the pedigrees, although there is no evidence to show that this was so. However, since it is clear that the pedigrees were made for him and that they were based on materials in his ownership, it is indeed possible that he ordered their completion. This explanation applies to all further mention of commissioned pedigrees in the chapter.

advancement in the new socio-political environment of early-Stuart Britain through the combination of personal anglicization and a claim of ancient Irish nobility.

Donough O'Brien's authority in early-Stuart Ireland derived from his loyalty to the Crown, his Protestantism, his anglicizing predilections and his noble lineage. The family demonstrated its loyalty to the Crown and willingness to adapt to changed political circumstances post-1541 when Murrough O'Brien renounced his interest in succeeding as chief of the O'Briens and took instead the title Earl of Thomond. His descendant, Donough the 4th Earl, would dramatically prove that loyalty on the battlefields of the Nine Years' War, distinguishing himself against the forces of O'Neill and O'Donnell at Kinsale. His Protestantism assured his rapid rise in post-Mellifont society and politics, and as the ranking Protestant native lord, he proved one of the Crown's best assets in the troubled parliament of 1613–15. In the controversy that surrounded the election of members to Commons, he was one of two men chosen to travel to court to brief the King and Council on the actions of the 'recusants'.[36] Two years later he was made Lord President of Munster.[37]

His accommodation of new social realities was furthered by his passionate anglicizing tendencies. He counted among his friends and allies that greatest of Englishmen-on-the-make, Richard Boyle, later Earl of Cork, and Sir George Carew described him 'as truly English as if he had been born in Middlesex'.[38] Another contemporary observed that 'In the ordering of his house or the governing of his country, his course has always been English, striving to bring in English customs and to beat down all Irish barbarous usages, that he might in time make his country civil and bring the inhabitants in love with English laws and government. So much so, that he is held to be more English than Irish'.[39] To quote the historian John McCavitt, 'Thomond was clearly attempting to "out-English" the English'.[40]

None of this advancement, however, would have been possible had Thomond not been of ancient Gaelic noble blood. Gaelic commoners – regardless of their loyalty, faith or willingness to ape English cultural forms – stood no chance of promotion to the ranks of the nobility; Gaelic entry into the Irish peerage was a process of noble transference, not of social

---

[36] John McCavitt, *Sir Arthur Chichester: lord deputy of Ireland 1605–16* (Antrim, 1998), p. 86.
[37] For a fuller discussion of Thomond's anglicizing efforts, including a detailed exploration of its financial aspects, see Cunningham, 'Political and social change', pp. 210–46.
[38] Quoted in Victor Treadwell, *Buckingham and Ireland 1616–1628: a study in Anglo-Irish politics* (Dublin, 1998), p. 107.
[39] McCavitt, *Chichester*, p. 80. [40] Ibid.

elevation.[41] A number of Englishmen of lower birth – most notably Richard Boyle, the Earl of Cork – managed to work their way into the Irish peerage, but this was not a feat accomplished by any Irish commoners. Thus, in spite of his 'Englishness', Thomond's social and political prominence in early Stuart Ireland was as much a product of his noble, if Gaelic, pedigree as it was of his ostentatious religious and political loyalty. And in spite of his aggressive anglicization, Thomond would prove an energetic promoter of his rank and the Gaelic genealogy upon which it was grounded.

That Thomond was obsessed with the respect due men of rank is suggested by his conduct towards representatives of the lower house of Parliament in 1614. During the session, a meeting had been called to defuse a dispute that had arisen between the two houses over knights' wages: the members of Commons were dissatisfied with the level of the wages; the members of Lords with how those wages were determined.[42] Annoyed that the Lord Treasurer (representing Commons) would present the demands of political office as a burden, Thomond demanded to know 'which of you all were chosen against your Wills?' To this the Treasurer gasped, 'O! My Lord! It might seem a strange Question if one of us should ask your Lordships, which of you were made a Bishop or a Baron against your Wills'.[43] Seeing this as an attack on the dignity and privileges of nobility itself – a crass concordance of lower house parliamentary duty with the privileges of nobility – Thomond and the rest of the representatives from Lords rose and departed in silence.[44] For all his anglicizing efforts and political and confessional loyalties to the forces of centralization (perhaps even because of them), Thomond was still not one to brook insult to his rank.

No one, in fact, worked more assiduously than Thomond to construct a sense of personal authority and power through the welding of ancient pedigree and privilege to accommodate the new social realities. As the Lord Treasurer's comments suggest, there was emerging in this period a sense of authority and status based largely upon office-holding and ideological compatibility with the forces of a centralizing state[45] – the potentially distasteful effect (to men like Thomond, at least) of which was that Commons, however gerrymandered in its selection, was the socio-political equivalent of Lords. Put another way, this implied that membership in Commons was as prestigious as that in Lords. However, as Thomond's

---

[41] A fact which in part explains the power of Caball's argument that *PCT* is aimed against opportunistic gentry and not Gaelic churls. Caball, 'Pairlement Chloinne Tomáis I: a reassessment'.

[42] The following discussion is drawn from *Journals of the House of Commons of the Kingdom of Ireland, 1613–1791*, 25 vols (Dublin, 1753–91), vol. 1 (hereafter *CJ*).

[43] Ibid., p. 73.   [44] Ibid.   [45] On this point, see James, 'English politics and the concept of honour'.

wordless exit from Chancery in the wake of those comments suggests, his sense of honour and authority was one in which title and blood stood for much, even in the labile world of colonial social uncertainty. In the next three years he would commission two expansive pedigrees to prove it.[46]

The pedigrees

Thomond commissioned what appear to have been the two most elaborate illustrated pedigrees in early-Stuart Ireland.[47] Read together they provide not only an exhaustive illustrated and annotated lineage of his own house, but also for all of the Gaelic nobility. Moreover, they provide spectacular material evidence of the importance placed by the leading Protestant Gaelic noble of the period on ancient lineage as a fundamental element of noble honour.

The first pedigree dates from 1614 and details the descent of the O'Brien lords within the context of the collective origins of the Gaelic Irish. The breadth of the text's intentions is made clear by its introduction:

This Arbor, or genealogicall tree, brancheth forth, the pedigrees, and lyniall malse' lines; and descentes in blood; not only of the ye Right honourable, Donat, Lord Obrien, baron of Ibreakan, Earle of Thomond &c: But also of Sondry other antient Irish familys. Issued and Sprung, wth their continuance, (from Breach a nobell gretian;) Untill this preset yeare of Grace 1614, beinge in this table mentioned the issue of Hiberus-fynn: 3 son of Milo.[48]

The ensuing pedigree consists of four separate, though related, sections. The first, reproduced on p. 174 as Figure 5.1, consists of one enormous page, measuring roughly 2' in width by 3' in height, which depicts the male descendants of Hiberus, third son of Míl, a descendant of Breach and the first Gaelic invader of Ireland. The names of succeeding eldest sons are

---

[46] In these same years he supported the antiquarian investigations of Florence MacCarthy Reagh and saw a poet in his (possible) employ and living in Dublin instigate a poetic dispute over the relative merits of Ireland's southern and northern halves. See Leerssen, *Contention of the bards*.

[47] G.O. MS 158, National Library of Ireland; Carew MS vol. 599 (consulted mainly on microfilm at Firestone Library, Princeton University, Princeton, NJ). This opinion comes after having searched the records of the Irish Genealogical Office, National Library, Trinity College Dublin library, and the Irish and English State Papers, including the Carew Papers. Although there may be a document to rival the extravagance of the Thomond pedigrees elsewhere, the fact that there is no heraldic work of a Gaelic family to rival these two of Thomond's makes the possibility of finding a more lavish production seem remote. The uniqueness of this production has been confirmed by the Office of the Chief Herald, Republic of Ireland. Private correspondence with Micheal Ó Comáin, 17 April 2008.

[48] G.O. MS 158, NLI. This is included on an unpaginated, fold-out sheet that appears at the front of the book.

written out within small, red-shaded circles. At some point (the manuscript here is torn) this singular trunk splits into three, each of which represents the bloodlines of the three progenitors, all brothers, of the nobility of Munster. Again, the names appear in small circles, except here they are colour-coded to identify the brother from whom they descend: Eoghan Mór's, the eldest son's, line is red; Kien's, the middle son's, is yellow; and the youngest son's, Cormack's, is green. The branches follow the male lines into the present, that is, the early seventeenth century. Although afforded no visual pride of place on the 'tree', we see that Donough O'Brien, the Earl of Thomond, represents the present state of Cormack's line. Within this final green circle is written 'Donat Earl of Thomond is living 1614', and it is graced with a four-pointed coronet.

The next section laboriously traces out the lineage of Hiberus' descendants. The names found in the circles of the first section are presented in boxes, accompanied with titles (if any) and death dates.[49] This section, the entirety of which covers over 100 manuscript pages, concludes with an illustration of the O'Brien family arms, above which a banner reads 'The Armes of the right honorable Donat Lord Obrien, baron of Ibreaken, Earl of Thomond & cat: whose genealogie; is before declared'.[50]

This is followed by two more comprehensive 'arbours' that track all the Gaelic nobility. The introduction to the first laconically states the breadth of the text's intentions: 'This table shewith ye liniall malle descents of Sondry Irish families continued unto this tyme ano Dm 1614; and sprong from Ire, the fift sonne of Milo, sonne of Bilius, sonne of Briogan, who was the Sonne of Brach, a noble gretian'.[51] The succeeding tree traces the descendants of Hermon, Míl's seventh son. These trees are made easier to read through visual and textual annotation. Thus, when the branch of the 'posterity of Hermon' arrives at Rory O'Donnell, his arms and their crowning coronet are drawn tilted downward and 'Rory O'Donell, Earle of Tirconnell a Traitor' is penned in the box below his name (see Figure 5.2 on p. 175). Comparable heraldic depictions of the fall of the O'Neills Earls of Tyrone

---

[49] That these two sections are well co-ordinated is demonstrated by the fact that next to the circles of the first section is written the number of the page where that particular person's name appears on the second section's extended 'arbour'. Although the numbering may be a later addition – given that the numbers appear very lightly in black ink in a hand that does not match that of the rest of the text – it does nicely illustrate the tight concordance of the two trees.

[50] Ibid., p. 148.

[51] Ibid. This too is an unpaginated, fold-out document. Interestingly it is not just Irish nobles whose pedigrees are to be traced here, for it is also shown that the O'Manus family of Scotland descends from Ireland.

are reproduced in Figure 5.3 and Figure 5.4, pp. 176–7).[52] These pedigrees are not mere catalogues of ancestors, but records of conduct and loyalty on the part of the major Gaelic families as well.

Finally, the manuscript traces the succession of Irish high-kings. The accompanying introduction accurately describes the table's goals and appearance:

A cathalogue of all the Monarchs that have reigned in Ireland, of the issue of Hiberus-fynn, Ire, and Hermon, sonnes of Milo; And are here set downe not according to their liniall progretion, in the severall steemmes; but as they succeeded one ye other; he ruling; (for ye most parte) that could by force or otherwise get possession; and are distinguished, by colours: Viz those from Hiberous by [red]; Those from Ire by [green]; and those from Hermon, by [yellow]; as hereafter folowith.[53]

The 'cathalogue' consists of one contiguous line of circles, within which appear the kings' names and dates of their reign. In total 168 circles appear, representing 163 monarchies (the disparity because some ruled jointly), spanning the years 1368 BC to 1086 AD. Only 32 of these are red, that is, in the O'Brien line. But they are red when it counts, namely, at the end of the line. The last monarch of Ireland to appear in the list is one Murierth O'Brien who died in 1086. Next to his circle is a box in which it is written 'In anno Dm 1086: the monarchs in the Irishrie took ende, The Last of them being of the O'Briens'.[54]

The second pedigree under consideration dates from 1617 and is a shorter and slightly different affair. The two do share some basic commonalities: both contain genealogies of the O'Briens and other Gaelic noble families, and a listing of Irish high-kings. Nevertheless, how these basic tasks are carried off in each one is very different, and suggests that whereas the earlier text represented an attempt to draw the ancient descent of the O'Briens in the context of the wider history of the collective origins of the Gaelic Irish, the latter appears more a present-centred, general ethnographic survey of all Irish families, their origins and fortunes. It is introduced thus:

In this booke is contayned, the descents of ye meere Irishe families with ye severall Monarchs of them which ruled in that Lande, whose government continued untill ye Henry ye Second King of England conquered, & suppressed them: The same was formed by sundry collections of the Earl of Thomond, and was converted by divers of ye nation, according ye true ortographie of ye Irishe writtings. This Booke

[52] Ibid., p. 148. Graphically the same is done for Hugh O'Neill, with the accompanying text: 'Hugh earl of Tyrone fledd; an liveth, a traitor, beyond the seas: a° 1614.' Ibid., p. 158.
[53] Ibid., p. 144.   [54] Ibid., p. 247.

with ye table, before annexed, was made in the yeare of Christ 1617 by commandment of [blank].[55]

After beginning with a list of successive Irish monarchs,[56] the text charts the
descent of the male descendants of Hiberus, Ire and Hermon. The final
section of the manuscript consists entirely of a series of family pedigrees,
beginning with the main branch of the O'Briens – that which produced the
Earls of Thomond and Barons of Ibracken[57] (see Figure 5.5 on p. 178) – then
moving on to other noteworthy Gaelic families. Descent is illustrated in
typical heraldic flow-chart style, with the names of successive generations
displayed within circles bearing coloured borders. On the one hand, the
pedigrees here are more complete than those of the 1614 text in that all
descendants, male and female, are noted, not merely the succeeding sons.
They also bear more extensive textual annotation. Each family is introduced
with brief explanatory comments. Thus, of the O'Neills we read, 'This
genealogie next followinge of Oneale's, of whom three were Earles of Tiron,
doth shewe the severall families of the Neals, etc.' Yet on the other hand, the
trees are less detailed in that they stretch back only to the eleventh century.
Thus, of the O'Brien Earls of Thomond we read that 'This Genealogie
followinge of the Earl of Thomond, sheweth the lyniall progretion of the
O'BRIANS familie; beinge a braunch of the auntien Irish; for this Brian
Borauie, is descended in ye 68 degree from Hiberous one of the sonnes of
Billius, sonne of Brach, who was son of Dea, a Gretian, as in page: 11
appeareth'. Whereas reference is made to the Greek origins of the Gaels,
these detailed family pedigrees only commence in the medieval period.

    Who may have produced these two documents is unknown since neither
bears attribution, yet they appear to be the work of the same person. The
handwriting is the same, the graphics are similarly constructed (circles with
shaded borders, and so on), and even the language used in the various
introductions and explanatory asides is similar.[58] An obvious candidate
for authorship is Daniel Molyneux, Ulster King of Arms in the 1610s.[59]
Yet if Molyneux was the hand behind these pedigrees, it is odd that there are
not similar productions for other families. We know that there were

---

[55] Carew MS vol. 599, fol. 1.   [56] Ibid., fols 2–22.   [57] Ibid., fol. 23.

[58] For this one, like the 1614 pedigree, comes with running commentary. And its description of the
monarchical succession is very similar. Here the 'Catalogue of the Monarchs of Ireland' is introduced
with these words: 'From these 3 brethren [Hiberus, Ire and Hermon], all the Monarchs that have
reigned in the land of Ireland are descended. Which are not sett downe heere as they are Liniallie
descended from father to sonn; but as they did succeed in government the on^after th'other; Wch was
obtained most by stronge hand. And by the 3 coulers by the 3 brethren above are distinguished; the
severall monarchies following may be distinguished'. Ibid., fol. 6.

[59] John Barry, 'Guide to records of the genealogical office', p. 20.

numerous visitations in this period to confirm arms in Ireland, with Molyneux himself having conducted just such a survey for the counties of Dublin and Wexford in 1607–10.[60] As the historian of Irish heraldry John Barry has pointed out, there may have been more visitations, the records of which have simply not survived. Additionally, we may imagine that other extensive genealogical tracts were commissioned by Irish lords other than Thomond, but which have similarly vanished. And yet it seems strange that in the collections of the Genealogical Office in Dublin, and in the State Papers in London's PRO and Lambeth Palace (the Carew papers), there does not appear a single pedigree of the size and detail of these two commissioned by O'Brien. Molyneux, therefore, as chief herald, must remain the primary authorial suspect; the texts themselves, however, seem the products of a peculiarly Thomond project.

Why these were produced, as opposed to by whom, offers a more fruitful line of inquiry. Most simply, these pedigrees were produced – as were all such genealogical collations – to demonstrate the ancient and noble blood-lines of a particular family. That the Earl of Thomond should have commissioned such a pair of manuscripts is thus, on the face of it, fairly unremarkable – such undertakings had been for centuries part and parcel of the performance of nobility. And yet Thomond's genealogical pursuits are quite interesting, and not a little unique, primarily due to the comprehensiveness and breadth of the genealogical research and the visual lavishness of their production, something almost entirely unknown to Gaelic genealogists.[61] Even in the early seventeenth century, when the commissioning of pedigrees was all the rage, multi-coloured illustrated productions covering nearly 300 pages were extraordinary.

Why would Thomond commission such gaudy pedigrees? The easiest answer, and the most difficult to prove, is by reason of personality and predilection. Donough O'Brien may simply have had a passion for genealogy and a perceived need, not to mention the financial wherewithal, to see his lineage in full graphic display. While this is probably part of the story, there is most certainly more to it. A further hint at motivation is provided by two of the texts explored in the first section of this chapter, the poem 'Faisean Chláir Eibhir' and the prose satire *PCT*. Both of these texts reveal

---

[60] Ibid., p. 31.
[61] When heraldry was adopted by the Gaelic Irish is a matter of controversy. Undoubtedly, there were occasions of visual depictions of arms by Gaelic families throughout the period following the twelfth-century Norman invasion. Only with the Tudor advent of surrender and regrant did wholesale conversion to English/continental heraldry come to compete with the oral and annalistic listings of pedigrees as practised by the Irish *ollúna*. See Chapter 1, above.

the frequency with which commoners attempted to pass themselves off as members of the nobility, in particular, as scions of the O'Brien clan.[62] Nor was this a mere literary device, for in this period it was notoriously difficult for English/Dublin authorities to prove just who was a legitimate possessor of Gaelic noble blood. Up through the 1620s, at the very least, there were continued problems with imposters trying to lay claim to noble patrimonies, titles and privileges, and Irish heralds had been active attempting since the late-sixteenth century to shore up the lists of the rightful bearers of titles.[63] And since, as the two Gaelic texts suggest, the O'Briens may have been particularly hard-hit by this traffic in fraudulent honours, these pedigrees with their exhaustive descriptions of who begot whom may perhaps have been one way to quash such chicanery.

To truly understand the motivations behind the production of these texts, however, we must see them in the context of the contemporary British fashion for pedigrees. As Lawrence Stone has described it, the interest in genealogical productions in England was a near craze.[64] It was a craze that made its way to Ireland by the early seventeenth century. The first official herald of Ireland, the Ulster King of Arms, was only appointed in 1552. Come the turn of the century, Molyneux, or Ulster (as the Chief Herald was known), was making regular visitations to confirm the arms of Irish elites. Significant documentation of those activities survives in the present Genealogical Office collections and, as they are undoubtedly but a fraction of the contemporary records, suggest a heraldic industriousness in late-Tudor, early-Stuart Ireland that echoed English practice.[65] Whether or not Molyneux himself was the author of the pedigrees under consideration here, their production must be seen as a further element of the Earl's anglicizing tendencies.

---

[62] Remember that in the poem 'Faisean' the author speaks of the base-born parading about as if they were Dal Caisians (the clan which produced Ború), and the author of *PCT* closes his account of the last session of the parliament with the MPs deciding to grant themselves Gaelic surnames, and the one example given is of a man declaring himself an O'Brien. See above.

[63] Barry notes the difficulty with which this was done, and comments that it led to the practice of 'confirming' arms in Ireland. Barry, 'Guide to records of the genealogical office', p. 31. As regards problems with imposters, the most famous example of this was the attempt to prop up a commoner's son from Galway, one Pierce Lennon, as the heir to the earldom of Ormond. See Edwards, *Ormond lordship*, pp. 126, 285.

[64] Stone, *Crisis of the aristocracy*, pp. 65–128.

[65] See Barry, 'Guide to records of the genealogical office', p. 40. In particular, Barry notes the following collections of interest in Dublin: 'ordinary of arms c. 1605 by William Smith, Rouge Dragon Puirsuivant; emblazons of Irish peers 1595–97 and of knights dubbed by the lord deputy 1566–1617; emblazon in colour of the armorial achievements of the lord deputy and Council, together with notes on their pedigrees compiled by Molyneux c. 1606; a treatise on precedence by Ralph Brooke, Yorke herald, c. 1595'. Ibid., p. 40. On Old English heraldic adoption of Gaelic 'ancestors', see Simms, 'Bards and barons'.

Moreover, there was a peculiarly Irish context to this 'British' rage for the production of genealogical works. Since the later sixteenth century, there had been concerted efforts to determine the true origins of the Gaels. Although not quite as ambitious or fantastical as the later investigations into the origins of the New World Indians, this sort of amateur ethnographic/anthropologic endeavour was a popular intellectual sub-genre to Tudor and Stuart efforts to pacify Ireland. The most notable, and quotable, of such theorists was Edmund Spenser, whose treatise of Ireland, the Irish and the best ways by which to 'reduce' them to civility – *A view of the present state of Ireland* – connected the Irish to the ancient Scythians, a barbarous people who lived menacingly on the fringes of the civilized, if pagan, world of the ancient Greeks.[66] This proto-racial classification was used by Spenser, and in turn by numerous treatise-writers and self-styled policymakers after him, to argue the inborn savagery of the contemporary Gaelic Irish and to advocate for the violent destruction of their culture as the only means capable of bringing them to metropolitan English social norms.[67] Others not necessarily sharing Spenser's ethnic-cleansing tendencies, however, also took a concerted interest in Irish pedigrees. Burghley, that supposed paragon of the new 'service' nobility, was also obsessed with bloodlines and genealogy; and, as one of the chief architects of Elizabethan policy in Ireland, he had occasion to satisfy his interest in matters genealogical in Ireland too. Thus, he kept in his own hand the genealogical trees of various Gaelic nobility and gentry.[68] And as we have already seen, the establishment of an official Irish herald initiated a process by which the armorial bearings and claims to nobility by the Gaelic Irish were systematized. Moreover, the State Papers Ireland and Carew MSS not only contain armorial collections of the Irish gentry and nobility, but also ethnographic/demographic mini-studies by which the families of particular counties were categorized by ethnicity and class.[69] The 1620 commonplace book of Sir James Ware, the famed antiquarian and Dublin official, shows

---

[66] *A view of the present state of Ireland: from the first printed edition (1633) / Edmund Spenser*, eds. Andrew Hadfield and Willy Maley (Oxford, 1997). See, for example, pp. 47–66.

[67] See Nicholas Canny, *Making Ireland British*, pp. 1–58, in which the argument is put forward that Spenser provided the framework for subsequent English policy in Ireland.

[68] Burghley's pedigrees of the Irish are mainly to be found 'tricked out' in the margins of various state papers. I thank Dr Christopher Maginn for bringing these to my attention. However, the volume of Irish pedigrees in the Carew manuscripts (vol. 626), which have long been attributed to Burghley, do not in fact appear to be in the Secretary's hand. Rather they seem to be seventeenth-century productions of Sir George Carew. I wish to thank Dr Richard Palmer of Lambeth Palace Library and Dr Valerie McGowan-Doyle for their insights and advice on properly attributing these documents.

[69] See, for example, Carew MS vol. 635, fol. 58, which marks the beginning of such a study of Connaught.

that this sort of collective genealogical research into Gaelic and Old English origins showed no sign of abating. For with Ware, too, we find rough genealogical trees, discussions of families by county and speculations upon the ancient origins of the Gaelic Irish.[70] Ware, Carew, Molyneux (Ulster King of Arms), Burghley and Spenser: the fascination of these men with Irish origins, class demographics, coats of arms and their relationship with high politics is a curious and unmistakable aspect of the cultural contact and attempted assimilation of Ireland into a larger English-centred polity.

Thomond's pedigrees must be seen as engaged with this ongoing research into Gaelic origins. They seem to serve as something of a Gaelic response to the more negative excesses of the genre. As noted above, the first of the two pedigrees traced Gaelic origins back to the Greeks – to the Greek nobility, no less. Far from representing a mere exercise in self-flattering antiquarianism, this is a crucial polemical move, for in doing so the author short-circuits the Scythian argument. By linking the Gaelic Irish lineally to the ancient Greeks themselves, to the very civilization that gave rise to the concepts of civic humanism, virtue and the commonwealth, this pedigree allowed the Gaelic Irish to challenge the opinions of hostile ethno-cultural theorists in a way that upstanding and loyal conduct in the here-and-now never could. For part of the strategy of the 'racial' depiction of the Irish as Scythians was to perpetually place in doubt their loyalty: no matter how obsequious any individual Gaelic lord or family may appear, so the argument went, their 'nature' would always incline them to rebellion and petty absolutism. But here Thomond and his anonymous herald have quashed that powerful line of critique by 'disproving' it at its source. The tracing of Gaelic roots to Greek soil was not new – such a claim was common in bardic poetry.[71] The sort of visual, heraldic translation of that motif commissioned by Thomond was new, however, and represents the continued usefulness of traditional origin narratives in very novel socio-political settings.

Thus positioned – with Gaelic loyalty and nobility no longer inherently suspect – Thomond was free to wield his ancient lineage in pursuit of his own elevated place and status. Generally speaking, these documents may have been intended to help promote the ancient O'Brien name within the

---

[70] BL Add MS 4821, 'commonplace book of James Ware'. This is, as far as I can tell, unpaginated. By my manual count, the description of Donegal (Dungall, as it is written) appears on p. 261 (this is excluding from the count the series of blank pages that appear early on in the volume).

[71] See, for example, Domhnaill Mac Daire MacBruaideadha's 'Cia as sine cairt ar chrich neill', which traces Irish origins back to the 'royal house of Greece'. Quoted in McCormack, *Earldom of Desmond*, p. 116. The Mac Bruaideadhas, it should be noted, were traditional poets to the O'Briens.

vice-regal court and political circles in the rapidly developing metropolitan centre of Dublin. Although of an ancient family, and recipients of an earldom in the early days of surrender and regrant, the O'Briens were not traditionally intimate with Dublin's power elite; their dynastic seat, after all, was in the west (Limerick and Clare) and far from the administrative/ financial centre in the east. A little genealogical self-aggrandizement may have helped 'introduce' the O'Briens to Dublin society.[72] Moreover, these texts could have helped distinguish his claims to nobility and authority from those of New English arrivistes, men like Richard Boyle. I use Boyle here as an example in part because he and Thomond were close allies, and because they occupied similarly marginal positions vis-à-vis the Protestant nobility of England: Thomond on account of his ethnicity, Boyle by virtue of his low birth.[73] Yet both enjoyed great success in post-Mellifont Ireland, due in part to their ability and willingness to pay for promotion. But whereas Thomond secured the Presidency of Munster with a £3,200 payment to Buckingham's agents,[74] Boyle had also to buy his social legitimacy through the purchase of titles of honour.[75] Thomond, by contrast, was the scion of the most noble of Gaelic bloodlines and his pedigrees were quite probably meant to distinguish himself from the Boyles of the world in what was a hyper-competitive market of socio-political advancement.

Seen in this light, Thomond was most likely engaged in a variation of the sort of practical genealogical/antiquarian research Richard Cust describes as having been practised in certain English Catholic circles. In a study of the Midlands gentry family the Shirleys and the circle of amateur historians and heralds of which they were a part, Cust has demonstrated that the English Catholic gentry, barred from office on account of their faith yet desperate to remain a part of the highest circles of gentry and noble honour, stressed the centrality of bloodlines and loyalty to the person of the monarch as the foundations of noble honour and downplayed virtue (increasingly seen as a by-product of humanist education in a Protestant vein), office-holding and

---

[72] The pedigree is presently bound between covers. While I am unsure that this was its original form, it is quite likely to have been because such 'book-pedigrees' were common in this period and were self-importantly displayed and shown to visitors to aristocratic homes. I wish to thank Richard Cust for his comments on such pedigrees.

[73] Treadwell describes Thomond as 'Cork's old ally'. Treadwell, *Buckingham and Ireland*, p. 58. McCavitt notes Michael MacCarthy-Morrogh's claim that Richard Boyle's support was crucial to Thomond's securing the Presidency of Munster. If so, McCavitt suggests it was merely payback for Thomond's having backed Boyle's successful bid for a place in the Irish privy council in 1613. See McCavitt, *Chichester*, pp. 86, 242.

[74] Ibid., p. 59.

[75] He would, however, die frustrated in his efforts for an equivalent title in the English peerage.

interest in service to the commonwealth.[76] With the same end-results in mind, Thomond similarly highlighted his ancient lineage and family's loyalty to individual monarchs as foundational aspects of his claim to honour and status in the face of intense New English competition. If this parallel is accurate, then it should come as no surprise that Shirley and Thomond commissioned what must have been the most extravagant pedigrees in their respective countries.

The comparison with the practical antiquarianism of the English Catholic Shirleys is also instructive when considering the fact that Thomond's pedigrees would have allowed him to argue his personal claims to honour and place vis-à-vis other Irish lords. As Cust explains it, men like Shirley were not only concerned with their own families' pasts, but in those of their social equals, of neighbouring English Catholics. Thus, in addition to tracing their own pedigrees, they researched and wrote county histories that were basically biographical sketches of their own families and the families of the nearby elite. These county histories, in turn, played an important part in how these men defined honour and authority, and how they couched their personal claims to the same. The template involved an initial counter to Protestant arguments of 'natural' Catholic disloyalty – accomplished primarily by equating loyalty with loyalty to the person of the monarch – followed by a comprehensive study of all the author's kindred gentry and noble competitors, the point of which being to demonstrate past loyalties and treason. Additionally, the county survey allowed the author to demonstrate the relative antiquity of local gentry bloodlines – a powerful rhetorical device amongst men who stressed that family survival over time was one of the clearest marks of divine favour against the ravages of disease and war and the uncertainties of conception and birth. Having made a case for general Catholic inclusion in the highest ranks of gentry honour, it was then upon these two criteria – antiquity of bloodline as a mark of divine favour and unbroken history of loyalty to the monarch – that these Catholic antiquarians judged their own claims for honour and status against those of their social rivals.

Thomond's annotated pedigrees work a similar strategy and taken together operate as a sort of Gaelic 'county history' on the English Catholic model. By tracing the ancient lineage of the Gaels to the unquestionably acceptable ancient Greeks, these texts argue that the criteria by which Gaelic lords should be judged as to their honour, status and fitness to govern should be made individually by family and based upon the standard criteria of traditional loyalty: length of bloodline and history of high

---

[76] Cust, 'Catholicism, antiquarianism and gentry honour'.

political authority. Naturally, the O'Briens reside at the top of the Gaelic noble hierarchy, a precedence which the 1617 pedigree effectively details. For the tree does not go into the deep past, but commences only with the greatest of Irish high-kings, the O'Brien ancestor Brian Boru (d. 1014), thus leaving the impression that in the last days before the Norman invasion, it was an O'Brien who wielded supreme political authority over the island. And like the English Catholics of the Midlands, Thomond, through his pedigrees, suggested just who among the Gaelic Irish was or was not fit to rule.

The 1617 manuscript seems particularly calculated and 'practical' as a guide to Gaelic loyalty. Most simply, this was effected by beginning with the pedigrees of the various O'Brien branches, then of other Munster dynasties, and only then moving on to chronicle the bloodlines of the nobility of Ireland's other provinces – granting in the process the O'Briens, and more generally the southern families, precedence before the lords of the other three provinces. More ingeniously, however, the author traced all the families depicted only as far back as Brian Boru. Although there are no dates included in the non-O'Brien genealogies, merely given the length of them, it seems safe to assume that each of them follows the model set by the initial O'Brien pedigree. Consequently, every one of the pedigrees included in this manuscript commences at a point at which the family in question was subordinate to an O'Brien overlord. If the 1614 text flattered the family by linking it to the Greek nobility, the 1617 text did likewise by beginning its survey of Gaelic nobility from the point of the O'Brien zenith of authority and status.

Moreover, the running commentary helps to distinguish who was and was not fit to wield authority. Donough himself was listed as not only the Earl of Thomond, but also as the Lord President of Munster. Below him his son by his second marriage – this to Elizabeth, daughter of Gerald, Earl of Kildare – is listed as Lord Ibracan and 'heire apparent'. Annotations on the O'Neills tell a very different tale:

Hugh Earl of Tiron, was restored by order from Queen Elizabeth, to ye title of Earl of Tiron in anno 1585. Wch: for many yeares had bine discontinued, and he bare only the title of Baron of Dungannon, from ye death of his father, wch was in anno 1560. He was proclaimed traitor ye 12 Junii mo 1595 (by record). In an[n]o 1598 he overthrewe nere unto black water, her Maj: army: Where Sr: Henry Bagnall marshall of Ireland generall of ye Forces, wth: many Captains.[77]

---

[77] Carew MS vol. 599, fol. 213.

Tyrone's treason was also graphically illustrated, for his earl's coronet is drawn off kilter and, more ominously, the family tree ends with him.

Finally, these pedigrees must be seen as part of an effort to accommodate Thomond's Anglo–Gaelic authority to the less anglicized expectations of his social inferiors. For all his cultural and confessional mutation, Thomond drew upon a power base of Gaelic gentry and peasants who could not have been expected to fully embrace his desire to shed tradition and custom. And whereas Gaelic fears of social inversion were strong among the elite, there was something of an analogous fear amongst the less well-placed that their superiors had sold out to the colonial authorities, jettisoning in the process their duties – as defined by time-honoured notions of good lordship – to their subordinates. This, as we saw above, was a charge Mac Gearailt levelled at some of the native gentry; and as we will see later in this chapter, it was a critique also directed at the anglicizing Earl of Clanricard. That Donough O'Brien patronized the bards – primarily the Mac Bruaideadha family, traditionally poets to the O'Briens – up until his death reveals his sensitivity to the traditional expectations of his Gaelic inferiors, as do his pedigrees.

Thomond's pedigrees, however, represented a unique attempt to employ lineage in the defence of authority. The use of pedigrees and genealogies as a means by which to legitimate somewhat novel-looking authority in the eyes of the governed was a product, and a common one at that, of the cultural fluidity occasioned by the collapse of the Gaelic order and the extension of effective English sovereignty over the island. Most famously, Fearghal Og Mac an Bhaird's genealogy in verse, 'Trí corona i gcairt Sheamuis', offered 'native' imprimatur for James I's rule in Ireland.[78] A further example, which can be seen in Figure 5.6 on p. 179, is Fear Flatha Ó Gnímh's pedigree of Randal MacDonnell, a Scotsman made Viscount Dunluce in the Irish peerage. Digging about in books from Ireland and Scotland, Ó Gnímh gathered the building-blocks of his patron's Gaelic bloodlines. This is the very same Fear Flatha Ó Gnímh discussed in the previous chapter, author of that lament to the end of the Gaelic order commonly known as the 'Flight of the Earls'. And yet ten years on he had made his peace with the new dispensation and found employment as a public relations consultant to justify the Scotsman MacDonnell's authority as Viscount Dunluce to his new Ulster underlings.[79]

It is at this intersection of high politics, noble culture and genealogical, historical and ethnographic research that we must place Thomond's

---

[78] See Ó Buachalla, 'James our true king'.
[79] See the original, reproduced here, and Jane Ohlmeyer, *Civil war and restoration in the three Stuart kingdoms: the career of Randal MacDonnell, marquis of Antrim* (Dublin, 2001), p. 75.

pedigrees. His situation was of course different to that of MacDonnell or James I in that he, alone of the three men, was indubitably of Irish Gaelic descent. Yet his faith, loyalties and predilections would still have marked him as something quite different in the march of O'Brien overlords – a novelty that could not help but benefit from a little pre-emptive justification. What is interesting about Thomond's pedigrees relative to those produced by Ó Gnímh and Mac an Bhaird, however, is their visual sophistication. Mac an Bháird's genealogy of James was a traditional bardic ode in praise of the lineage of a rightful lord, something more traditionally performed than displayed as a text. Ó Gnímh's genealogy of Dunluce, on the other hand, was but a list of who begot whom, the sort of textual listing one encounters regularly in Gaelic annals.[80] With Thomond's pedigrees, however, we see the full integration of Gaelic annalistic pedigrees and the visual sophistication of English/continental heraldry (the visual sophistication of the Thomond pedigrees can also be contrasted with the simplicity of the pedigree of the O'Briens found in Figure 5.7 on p. 180). Justifiably, much has been made of the faux-Gaelic lineages produced for James I and Dunluce,[81] and yet they represent merely the aiming of traditional tools of legitimization at new holders of power. By contrast, Thomond's pedigrees, while they are engaged in a similar project, are not traditional constructions in and of themselves. Rather they are examples of just the sort of cultural amalgamation they were meant to justify. Grounded in Gaelic genealogical knowledge, yet adopting the visual power of the highly decorated contemporary English pedigrees and adding textual commentary, these unique texts offered an illustrated and annotated guide to early-Stuart Gaelic nobility.

Thomond's pedigrees caution us against viewing this period of Anglo–Irish relations as one in which ethnic boundaries hardened in the face of a sort of proto-nationalist conflict. Undoubtedly there was an increasing sense of ethnic exclusivity in some contemporary writings: the anthropological tirades of Spenser and the increasingly anti-English tenor of some of the contemporary Gaelic poems suggest that the often blurred lines between English, Old English and Gaelic Irish were coming into much clearer focus. The case of Thomond and his historio-genealogical work reveals, however, that the ethnic divides could be navigated in more strategic ways, and done

---

[80] Dunluce (later Antrim) maintained a retinue of bards and poets in his castle of the same name, and undoubtedly the verbal recitation of this lineage would have been far more impressive than the simple textual transcription of it that survives in the Carew Papers. See Ohlmeyer, *Civil war*, p. 75.

[81] Ibid., p. 75; and Ó Buachalla, 'James our true king'.

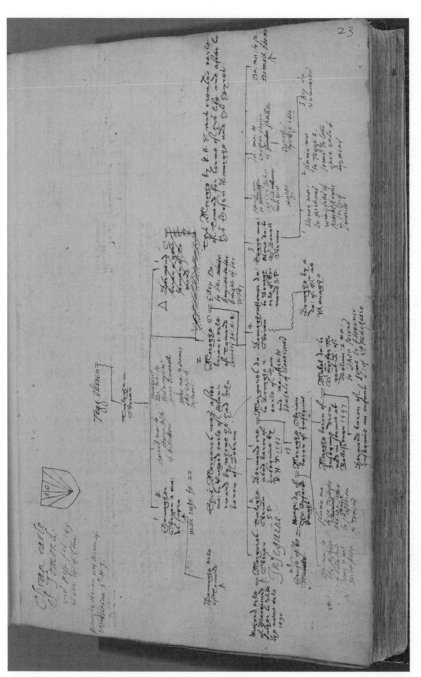

Figure 5.1. Carew MS 635, fol. 23, Lambeth Palace Library: Genealogical tree of the O'Brien Earls of Thomond. The simplicity of this pedigree offers a stark contrast to the later illuminated pedigrees made for Donough O'Brien, 4th Earl of Thomond.

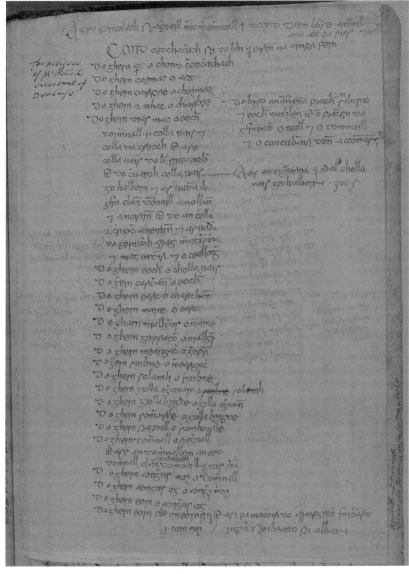

Figure 5.2. Carew MS 635 fol. 139, Lambeth Palace Library: Fear Flatha Ó Gnímh's pedigree of Randal MacDonnell, a Scotsman made Viscount Dunluce in the Irish peerage. This traditional, non-pictorial pedigree was produced contemporaneously with the lavishly illustrated O'Brien pedigrees (MacDonnell having been created Dunluce in 1618).

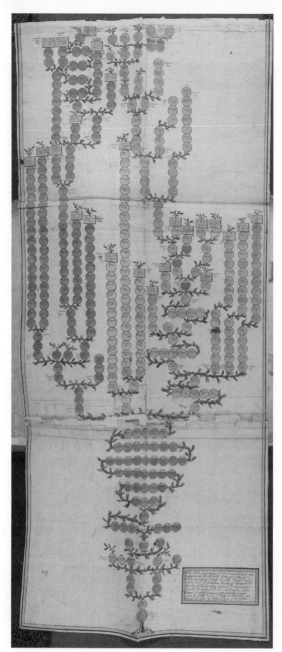

Figure 5.3. NLI G.O. MS 158: Pictorial representation of the heads of noble lines descended from Hiberus, third son of Milo. The circles in the upper two thirds of the pedigree are colour-coded to show the lines of various noble houses: red for that of Eoghan Mór; yellow for Kien; green for Cormack. At the penultimate level of Cormack's branch a circle bears the inscription 'Donat Earl of Thomond is living 1614' and is graced with a four-pointed coronet denoting his earldom. A later hand has attempted to carry forward the pedigree with additions of later O'Brien descendants. Image courtesy of the National Library of Ireland.

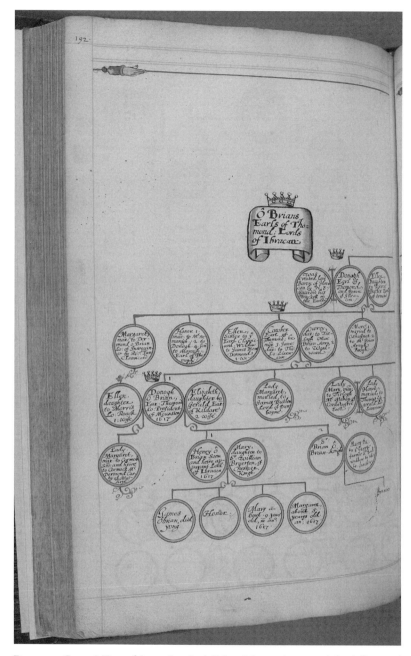

Figure 5.4. Carew MS 599 fol. 192, Lambeth Palace Library: A more subdued illustrated pedigree of the immediate family of the O'Brien Earls of Thomond taken from a collection of Gaelic pedigrees produced from records in Thomond's possession and completed in 1617.

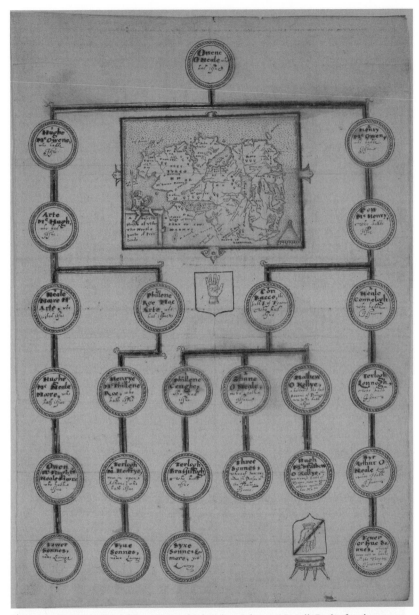

Figure 5.5. Carew MS 635 fol. 139a, Lambeth Palace Library: Not all Gaelic families were as successful as the O'Brien Earls of Thomond in making accommodation with new political and social realities. This pedigree shows descendants of Owen O'Neill, a map of Ulster, and the apparent end of the O'Neill claim to nobility with the 2nd Earl of Tyrone's 'open actione' against the Queen.

Figure 5.6. Pictorial representation of the disgrace of the O'Donnell Earls of Tyrconnell. This image appears in Donough O'Brien's 1614 genealogy of Gaelic families. Image courtesy of the National Library of Ireland, NLI G.O. MS 158 fol. 148.

in such a way as to further muddy the distinctions.[82] Rather than attempt to downplay his past, Donough O'Brien attempted to highlight it as proof of his ancient lineage and loyalty, both of which could then be mobilized to increase his own authority in the new dispensation of post-Flight of the Earls Ireland. A cultural and confessional convert to English ways, Thomond, nevertheless, had to fight for his authority. Whereas his Protestantism allowed him into the ring with New English pursuers of place and status – men like Boyle – it was his lineage which gave him advantage over these parvenu rivals. His means of navigating between cultural, confessional, national and ethnic fault lines was as unique as it was successful, and the massive pedigrees finished at his request in 1614 and 1617 were but one of the many tools he brought to the task of maintaining, or even increasing, his and his family's stature

---

[82] In addition, we may bear in mind Geoffrey Keating's efforts in *Foras feasa ar Eirinn*, and even in *Trí biorghaoithe an bháis*, to create a sense of Irish national consciousness by collapsing the Gaelic Irish and the Old English under the heading of 'Irishmen' (*Éireannaigh*). See Bradshaw, 'Geoffrey Keating: apologist of Irish Ireland'; Geoffrey Keating, *Trí biorghaoithe an bháis*, ed. Osborn Bergin (Dublin, 1931), p. 171.

Figure 5.7. The fall of the O'Neill Earls of Tyrone as depicted in Donough O'Brien's 1614 genealogy of Gaelic families. Image courtesy of the National Library of Ireland, NLI G.O. MS 158 fol. 158.

in the seemingly ever-changing climate of the early modern Anglo-Irish world. He was not, however, the only Irish lord to mix old and new honour markers as a strategy to boosting status and place in the early Stuart dominions. The following case study considers the other great family of western Ireland, the Old English Burkes, Earls of Clanricard, and reveals a very different manipulation of the tools provided by an Irish lordship within an anglicising trajectory.

OLD ENGLISH AND ENGLISH HONOUR: THE CASE OF RICHARD BURKE, EARL OF CLANRICARD AND ST ALBANS

Richard Burke was a true 'British' aristocrat: 4th Earl of Clanricard in the Irish peerage and Earl of St Albans in the English. The lack of any estate records or extensive correspondence makes in-depth study of the Earl nearly impossible. That is unfortunate, for Richard was an intriguing figure, better able than perhaps any of his contemporaries to move through both English and Irish noble circles. That peerless assimilative ability has allowed historians to appropriate him as either an exclusively Irish or English aristocrat. For instance, in the Irish historian Aidan Clarke's *The Old English in Ireland*, Burke is always 'Clanricard' and his English identity is never discussed; Stone, in his *Crisis of the aristocracy*, refers to him exclusively as the Earl of St Albans.[83] Reading the two books side-by-side one could come away with the impression that two different people were under consideration.

In spite of the dearth of source material related to Richard there is enough available to reconstruct his career more fully than historians have done to date.[84] By most historical accounts, Clanricard appears on the stage ready-made as the chief Catholic noble of early Stuart Ireland. Here I would like to take time to show how that aristocratic persona was carefully constructed by Richard over the preceding decades in order to show what sort of conception of nobility and honour he may have operated under, and to argue that he was as much an English peer as an Irish one, or, perhaps more accurately, a 'British' one more than either. Historians' use of the terms Old English, New English and Gaelic Irish can leave the impression, usually unintentionally, of monolithic socio-cultural blocs – a situation exacerbated by attempts to anatomize these groups' representative mentalities.[85] Clanricard, however,

---

[83] Aidan Clarke, *The Old English in Ireland, 1625–42* (London, 1966); Stone, *Crisis of the aristocracy*, p. 552. Moreover, Stone confuses the father and son, stating that Ulick was created Viscount Tunbridge in 1624 and Earl of St Albans in 1628 when in fact it was the father, Richard, who was so ennobled. See p. 798. For yet a third take, see Natalie Mears, who calls the Burkes 'Gaelic lords'. See Mears, *Queenship and political discourse*, p. 246.

[84] Unfortunately, Bernadette Cunningham's UCG MA thesis, 'Political and social change', remains unpublished. I wish to thank Dr Thomas Brophy for providing me with a copy of this very valuable thesis. Useful as well is Bernadette Cunningham, 'Native culture and political change in Ireland, 1580–1640', in Ciaran Brady and Raymond Gillespie (eds.), *Natives and newcomers: essays on the making of Irish colonial society 1534–1641* (Dublin, 1986), pp. 148–70; and Cunningham, 'From warlords to landlords: political and social change in Galway, 1540–1640', in Gerard Moran (ed.), *Galway – history and society: interdisciplinary essays on the history of an Irish county* (Dublin, 1996), pp. 97–129. Cunningham's primary focus is on Richard as a reforming – even colonizing – figure in early modern Irish history. Here I wish merely to bring out more fully the picture of Clanricard as an English peer, the better able to understand his conception of honour.

[85] See, for instance, O'Riordan, *Gaelic mind*.

provides a tremendous opportunity to see the interplay of Old English and English, and even Gaelic, honour in one man's conduct.

Descended from Richard de Burgh, an Anglo-Norman adventurer who had come to Connaught in the thirteenth century, the Clanricard Burkes were long established as one of the great families of Ireland. As all Irish lords discovered in the sixteenth century, however, ancient lineage did not automatically confer Crown favour. At the beginning of the century, the family possessed no lands recognized in English law.[86] Undoubtedly aware of the family's exposed position, the head of the family, Ulick Burke, was an early participant in the Crown's programme of surrender and regrant. In 1543 he was made 1st Earl of Clanricard, only to die the following year. Over the next four decades succession disputes would plague the family, and cause headaches for the Crown. On the death of the first Earl, a rival, also named Ulick, asserted himself as chief of the name. When the first Earl's son, the interestingly named Richard Sassanach, came of age he took over the earldom and headship of the family. Although he would hold it until 1582, his sons Ulick and John fought a protracted battle over the inheritance. The so-called Mac an Iarla dispute – after the eldest son Ulick's appellation, meaning 'son of the earl' – blew hot and cold from 1567 to 1582 and led Lord Deputy Henry Sidney to opine how the region's lesser families desperately needed release from the oppressions of the Earl and his warlike sons.[87] Not until Ulick Mac an Iarla's son Richard assisted the Crown against O'Neill and O'Donnell in the Nine Years' War was royal favour secured. His bravery in the cavalry charge that secured victory for the Crown forces at Kinsale in 1601 earned him the sobriquet Richard of Kinsale, and, more importantly, a knighthood.[88] Also that year he succeeded to the earldom, secure in the Queen's support and blessing.

Once in the good graces of the Crown, Richard made his way to court and quickly set about fashioning himself as a member of the English nobility. This he did by assiduously and astutely working social, legal and patronage networks. As early as October 1602, the English court gossip John Chamberlain wrote to Dudley Carleton how 'The earle of Clanrikard followes the court and aspires to high favour. I have heard he was offered a great match to marrie the Lady Straunge, but yt seemes he more regardes

---

[86] Cunningham, 'From warlords to landlords', p. 99.   [87] Ibid., p. 106.
[88] J. J. N. McGurk, 'O'Brien, Donough, fourth earl of Thomond (d. 1624)', *Oxford Dictionary of National Biography* (Oxford University Press, 2004) (www.oxforddnb.com/view/article/20453, accessed 22 Feb 2007).

courtly hopes then present profit'.[89] Richard's marriage the next year to Frances Walsingham, daughter of Elizabeth I's secretary Francis Walsingham and widow of those paragons of chivalric honour Sir Philip Sidney and Robert Devereux, 2nd Earl of Essex, was just the sort of social coup he sought. There is unfortunately no record of how the match came to pass, but it did not go down well amongst many in the English court: Chamberlain noted, 'Here is a common bruit that the earle of Clanickard hath maried the Lady of Essex wherewith many that wisht her well are nothing pleased'.[90]

Nevertheless, the marriage immediately set the Irish earl in the thick of English aristocratic culture, in part by expanding his alliances – Robert, 3rd Earl of Essex, was his wife's son and would prove over time an important ally – and in part by bringing him substantially greater wealth and property.[91] At Maidstone in Kent, on land acquired by him upon marriage, he would construct the manor of Summerhill where he would spend most of the rest of his life. A letter from F. Goldynge to Viscount Lisle (Robert Sidney, later 1st Earl of Leicester), dated 1612, attests to the house's splendour. Lisle intended to build a sewer for the garden at Penshurst, and Goldynge suggested Summerhill's as a model. The builders, Fuller and Frenche, had 'mayd the lyke for the Erle of Clanrickard and [Fuller] saw a man of an indifferent stature to passe cleane thorowe yt'.[92] His building projects also extended to his Irish territories. At Portumna in east Galway he built one of the few early-Stuart estate homes in Ireland.

Keen to make improvements beyond the home as well, Richard attempted to set up an ironworks by enclosing and clear-cutting forest commonage in a place called Bishop's Wood, in Hereford. When local tenants organized to resist the enclosure, the Earl first had his servants forcibly scatter them, and then charged the group's leaders with riotous assembly in a case brought before the Star Chamber.[93] This was not the only wrangle in which he

---

[89] Norman McClure (ed.), *The letters of John Chamberlain*, 2 vols (Philadelphia, 1939), vol. I, p. 161.

[90] Ibid., I, pp. 193–4. Clanricard, who was rumoured to have been having an affair with Frances (which led to a duel between him and Essex), was reported to resemble Essex in appearance. See Vernon F. Snow, *Essex the rebel: the life of Robert Devereux, the third earl of Essex 1591–1646* (Lincoln, NE, 1970), p. 22, fn. 10. But see the more positive comments of John Manningham: 'It was said for a truth that the Countes of Essex is married to the E[arl] of Clanricard, a goodly personable gent something resembling the late E of Essex'. Robert Parker Sorlien (ed.), *The diary of John Manningham of the Middle Temple 1602–03* (Hanover, NH, 1976), p. 231.

[91] In addition to bearing the estates of her two former husbands, Frances also received the inheritance of her father, c. 1612. Chamberlain, *Letters*, I, p. 377.

[92] F. Goldynge to Viscount Lisle (4 May 1612, Penshurst), in *HMC, D'Lisle and Dudley MS*, 6 vols (London, 1925–66), vol. 5, p. 48.

[93] PRO STAC 18/84/18, 18/84/19: Burke v. Clark, et al.

became embroiled. In time he also contested property rights with social equals; from 1612 through the early 1620s he and Lisle/Leicester would clash in the courts over lands at Udiam.[94] The most spectacular contest in which he became entangled was, in fact, one he inherited. This involved two of his wife's former servants, Jane and John Daniels, and dated from when she was married to Essex. At its most simple, this dispute involved letters of the Earl and his wife which were entrusted to John Daniels in the wake of Essex's imprisonment and his (Daniels') subsequent handling of them. What made it so explosive was, of course, the high profile of the deceased Essex and the fact that Jane Daniels received permission to publish three separate tracts detailing her and her husband's rough treatment at the hands of Frances and Clanricard. In the end, these tracts were never printed and the matter was resolved in favour of the defendants.[95]

In the litigious and socially competitive culture of early Stuart England, Clanricard's actions were remarkable only in that they were successful. Socially, his rise was marked by the successful match of his son Ulicke to Anne Compton, the only daughter of Spencer Compton, 2nd Earl of Northampton, in 1622, and his own creation as Viscount Tunbridge and Baron Somerhill two years later. The pinnacle of his transformation into an English noble came with his creation as Earl of St Albans in 1628, a direct benefit of the patronage of the Duke of Buckingham.[96] From that point on, Richard moved freely and easily within the upper echelons of English society; in the 1630s he was often noted as having taken part in heraldic processions, such as at the installations of Danby, Morton and Northumberland into the Order of the Garter.[97] However, a letter from Sir John North to Leicester of 1625 wonderfully illustrates the contradictions straddled by the ascendant earl. On the one hand, North made it clear that, English titles aside, Richard was still an Irishman, and a Catholic one at that: 'The Earl of Clanricard is now in Court, and it is thought must shortly go into Ireland. There is a strict order to disarm all recusants and execute the penal statutes against them'. Yet on the other hand, North acknowledged that patronage connections could override those ethnic and religious shortcomings: 'My Lord Duke's creatures are the men that rise, the King's servants have little hope of preferment'.[98]

[94] *De L'Isle and Dudley MS*, 5, pp. 61, 415, 419.   [95] *CSPD, 1603–10*, pp. 583–4.

[96] Treadwell, *Buckingham and Ireland*, p. 109.

[97] Garrard to Wentworth (1 May 1634), *Strafforde letters*, 1, pp. 242–4; and Garrard to Wentworth (19 May 1635), ibid., pp. 426–8.

[98] Sir John North to Earl of Leicester (4 November 1625, Hampton Court), *De L'Isle and Dudley MS*, p. 441.

With his creation as St Albans, this Irish-Catholic creature of the Duke had realized the 'preferment' he had set out to achieve in 1602, and that so rankled Chamberlain.

Clanricard's English social climbing raised eyebrows in Ireland, too. Tadhg McDáire's poem 'Faghaim ceart a chlann Eibhir' pithily illustrates the exalted position the Burkes traditionally enjoyed in the Irish social universe. Having sung the praises of the great Gaelic dynasties of the south of Ireland,[99] the poet goes on to include the prominent Old English families in his pantheon:

> There sprang other lofty branch
> from the root of our fragrant tree.
> That their names are not like those of the Gael
> keeps me not from mentioning them.
>
> Count owing to their female ancestors
> as worthy brethren of Eibhear's stock,
> the Burkes, Butlers, Barrys, Roches,
> though all of foreign stock.
>
> If the powerful prince Richard were
> present now in bright-yewed Eire
> would any of the branches of the wood seem fairer,
> though you look all round the fair plain of Eire?[100]

Richard, of course, was no longer resident in 'bright-yewed Eire', but in London and Kent. The poem 'Cnoc Samhradh' – Irish for 'Summer Hill' – brings out the concern many must have had that Clanricard's residence in England meant his turning his back on Ireland and the traditional duties and responsibilities of an Irish lord. The anonymous author, a member of a religious order,[101] describes his journey to Summerhill from London as 'horrible', perhaps even 'evil' (*olc*), and expresses his disbelief that upon his arrival he found not the hospitable welcome he expected but 'little joy and a lack of love' (*beagán aoibhnis, easbaidh ghráidh*).[102] Instead of being

---

[99] The poem comes from a contest in verse – the so-called 'Contention of the bards' – in which the relative merits of the southern and northern regions of the island were argued. A line running, approximately, from Dublin across to Galway provided the traditional border between the south (Leath Mogha) and the north (Leath Cuinn). See Lambert McKenna (ed. and trans.), *Iomarbhaidh na bhfileadh: the contention of the bards* (London, 1918).

[100] *Iomarbhaidh na bhfileadh*, vol. 2, stanzas 31, 32 and 35, p. 247 (editor's translation).

[101] De Brun, et al. (eds.), *Nua-Dhuanaire*, 1, p. 7. The author does not reveal the order with which he is associated: 'Im bráthair bhocht tré bheith dhamhsa / 's im shagart do dheibhléan Dé'.

[102] Ibid., p. 7.

tossed a few bones of patronage, he was denied entrance, turned back and warned not to return.[103] Believing his reception to be in violation of the norms of patronage and hospitality extended to men of learning and religion, the author took a swipe at this Kentish lord by opining that were he the Earl of the O'Donnells or O'Neills, he, the poet, would certainly have enjoyed a proper welcome.[104] But, alas, that was not the case and so the supplicant received no solace for his pains (*ní fhuaras feóirling dhá shocar*). A fruitless journey indeed, he concludes (*turas Ghóidrisc, donas é*).[105] This is a much more practical poem than McDáire's; its author refers to Clanricard as *iarla* (earl), dispensing with the traditional bardic term of praise, *flaith* (prince), used by McDáire. If Chamberlain was concerned about an Irish upstart making inroads into English elite culture, this anonymous Irish author saw in the 4th Earl a terminal case of a once-Gaelicized lord gone native in the metropole.

Many Irish outside the circles of the literate intelligentsia must also have felt, if not betrayed by, then at least uncomfortable with, the Earl's absenteeism. Primarily that unease arose from the pressure the Earl's lifestyle put on those who paid him rent. Nobility is as much a matter of performance and presentation as anything else, and display of that kind is costly. Clanricard's efforts to live the life commensurate with his rising status meant that his expenditures constantly outstripped his revenues. Writing to his agent John Donelan in July 1623, Clanricard moaned how 'We spend so fast as all we can take hold of is little enough'.[106] Consequently, he could be a hard landlord of his Irish estates, and the need to collect rents efficiently and to arrange quick and accurate monetary exchanges constitutes one of the strongest recurring themes in his extant correspondence.

But we should be cautious before attributing to Clanricard the belief that his Irish lands served as little more than rent farms. There is strong countervailing evidence of his desire to reside in Ireland at some point in the future. This is suggested in part by his construction of Portumna Castle. Though

---

[103] 'Ar mh'aithne do lucht an dúnaidh / amach tar múraibh mé / dhá rádh leam arís gan rochtain san dúnsoin do bhochtaigh mé'. Ibid.

[104] 'Ua nó iarla dá mbeith againn / de shíol gCuinn, de chlannaibh Néill / saoilim féin go bhfuighinn fáilte / im riocht féin, gér bhráithair mé', ibid., p. 7. Cunningham notes that the 4th Earl of Clanricard may in fact not have been an active patron of the poets, although the evidence is not conclusive. Cunningham, 'Political and social change', pp. 113–14.

[105] According to the editors, 'turas Ghóidrisc' means a journey bringing no results (*turas tairbhe*). De Brun, et al. (eds.), *Nua-Dhuanaire*, I, p. 95.

[106] Richard Burke to Henry Lynch (29 July 1623). Cunningham (ed.), 'Clanricard letters: letters and papers, 1605–1673, preserved in the National Library of Ireland manuscript 3111', *Journal of the Galway Archaeological and Historical Society* 48 (1996), p. 173 (hereafter 'Clanricard letters').

for all intents and purposes he was after 1602 permanently resident in England, he built this, one of the few great Jacobean Irish houses, to serve as his Galway seat. The house bears English and continental influences, and the Earl was well-attuned to, and concerned over, the details of its construction. In May 1623, for example, he ordered Donelan to see that the garden wall about the house be finished, the Earl 'not thinking it fit to leave a thing so necessary imperfect'.[107] The following year he informed Lynch of his horror that the Lord Deputy had not been properly entertained during his visit to Galway; the Earl had been taken aback to hear that the Deputy had been put up in the inferior house of Sruhir, when he should rightly have been lodged at Portumna.[108] He also took great interest in who would fill the tenancies in immediate proximity to the estate, directing his agent Sir Henry Lynch that only the best and most trustworthy should be allowed so near.[109] But there is more direct evidence of Richard's desire to return long-term to Ireland, for he expressly said as much himself at numerous points in his correspondence. As he wrote to Donelan, however, the impetus for returning may not have been his own, or driven by any cultural or sentimental reasons: 'I never meant to remove my wife to any place without her own desire and good liking and I was never so desirous to live in Ireland as she hath been herself, both for to avoid our infinite expenses here, and to order and settle things being the main, which in our absence can never <receive> perfection'.[110] His absenteeism, then, may have been intended as temporary.[111]

Despite his absenteeism and ascension in English society, Clanricard's Irish lands and titles continued to be important to him for other than financial reasons. There his authority was greatest, and the lands linked him to centuries of family prestige and myth. When a question arose over the title and interest of Tuarin,[112] Sir Richard asked Lynch to look over all his writings concerning this business since he wished 'chiefly to satisfy myself if any part concern me that requires either consideration in honour or conscience'.[113] He fought hard to block encroachments upon his official

---

[107] Clanricard to [Donelan?] ([1] May 1623). Ibid.
[108] Clanricard to [Lynch] (24 Sept 1624). Ibid., p. 176. This faux pas would not be repeated on Lord Deputy Wentworth's tour through Connaught, but with disastrous results. See Chapter 7, below.
[109] Clanricard to Lynch. Ibid., p. 179.   [110] Ibid., p. 203.
[111] Not only did he remain in England, however, but also, following his death in 1635, his remains were laid to rest in Maidstone, Kent.
[112] A townland in Galway, near Tuam.
[113] Clanricard to Lynch (28 April 1619). 'Clanricard letters', p. 169. Likewise, he could make the case that James was bound in honour to execute the indentures promised him by Elizabeth I.

position and powers within the region – he had held the title of Governor of Galway County and City from 1616 – most notably when he scuttled Sir Oliver St John's bid to be made Lord of Galway. While he explained to St John that not receiving the title was in 'no way prejudicial in honour or profit to him', he confided to his agent Sir Henry Lynch that had the entitlement gone through it would have been a 'wrong to me, and a terror to that people of Galway'.[114] Consequently, he took great offence at suggestions that he had disregarded the best interests of the people of Galway as he manoeuvred through court. Whispers that his hand was prominent in moving forward plans to plant Connaught elicited a strong denial: 'a most abominable wicked invention, I should rather wish my hand in the fire first; it were no time now to want both honour and conscience'. These rumours he called the work of those wishing to 'lessen my power or credit in my own country, <to serve their turn the better in a broken time>'.[115]

In addition to securing his own position in the county, it was also of vital importance to Clanricard to secure positions of honour and authority for friends, family and clients, and to ensure that members of his family lived in accordance with their station. For example, he sponsored a steady stream of Galway men to the Inns of Court, and for his brother William's support he gave £40 'out of the entertainment of my company of foot so long as I hold it', and £100 'to purchase some land for his dwelling place'.[116] The Earl's largess, however, was not unconditional. Honora Burke, for one, pushed his generosity to its limits. She had repeatedly hectored him for assistance in recovering certain lands and 'commodities' kept from her by her father-in-law (Sir John McCoughlan). But she had pushed too hard, and Richard was unsympathetic: '… I confess it is against my heart to do any favour that way. I have done too much already and without question it is an ill example and a point of conscience, those kind of courses are but encouragement for women to be bad'.[117] Ferdorogh O'Kelly pushed the Earl's goodwill even further by refusing to acknowledge the legitimacy of the governor, despite the latter's legal authority and personal relationship to O'Kelly. Disappointed and angry at O'Kelly's posturing, Clanricard wrote to Lynch: 'The complaint to me was that none [w]as more adverse in coming to my courts than Ferdorogh, or more opposed against my jurisdict[ion]. It were the worse in him being my foster br[other] whose father and mother were true and faithful in all occassions a[] [] extraordinarily favoured'.[118]

---

[114] Clanricard to Lynch. Ibid., p. 171.   [115] Ibid., p. 180.
[116] Clanricard to Lynch (6 May 1621). Ibid., p. 170.   [117] Ibid., p. 171.
[118] Ibid., p. 184.

As that attitude suggests, Clanricard, in spite of his intimate partic-ipation in the Gaelic cultural practice of fosterage, was a reformer who embraced anglicization. With flair worthy of a New English speculator, he blamed the low value of his lands on the poor character of his Gaelic tenants: 'I am assured it is the drunken humours, laziness, and want of skill which they will not learn will prove the main causes'.[119] Moreover, he found the native Irish too combative, especially the O'Flahertys of western Galway, and felt keenly the need to fortify the borders of his property 'from that unruly people … not knowing when a sudden blast might come'.[120] In contrast, Clanricard envisioned himself as a man of peace, compromise and law. He may have won his 'charter' in the field – thus the name Richard of Kinsale – but he had moved on from then to legitimise his authority through good governance. This emerges quite clearly in a letter to Lynch about the settling of pending local suits: 'Now concerning the suits in general I confess I would be most glad to make a fair end of them though to my loss, rather than spend my time in wrangling, specially with such as live under my jurisdiction; and I would willingly come in peace, live in peace, and end my days in peace with all the world'. He lacked the touchiness characteristic of chivalric honour, preferring arbitration, 'solemn submissions or intention of friendly ending'.[121] A reformation of manners in that spirit of compro-mise would be assisted by importing English settlers, of whom he seems to have been fond. When the threat of war with Spain loomed in the early 1620s, he proposed to have men on constant watch over Athleague, Clare (Claregalway) and Callow (Co. Galway). One of those men was to be his 'cousin St Barbe', but the other positions he preferred to be filled by Englishmen, for 'they [the positions] are to be undertaken by sub-stantial men'.[122]

Could Irish sons be trained as similarly 'substantial men'? On this vital question the Earl encouraged his agent Henry Lynch not to make his eldest son a lawyer. The training was long and unnecessary for an eldest son. A product of Oxford himself, Clanricard assured Lynch that his eldest would have enough companions studying law to assist him in all such needs. Rather, Lynch should send him to university for one year, to be followed by a year about London 'where he may learn qualities fit for a gentleman'.[123] He (Clanricard) made a pledge to personally oversee the boy's proper education. The second son, however, should follow the law

---

[119] Clanricard to Lynch (9 March 1624/5). Ibid., p. 177.   [120] Ibid., p. 182.
[121] Ibid., p. 175.   [122] Ibid., p. 174.   [123] Ibid., p. 182.

and thus 'toil out for his living …'[124] The Earl was quite happy to see either Englishmen or Irishmen prepared as proper provincial gentlemen, fit to occupy the topmost stratum of Galway's social and political hierarchy.

That melding of concerns for the traditional duties of a regional magnate with the reforming interests of an improving and anglicizing landlord is also apparent in Clanricard's approach to titles of honour. He was intensely aware of their social importance. The example given above of his blocking St John from becoming Lord of Galway speaks not only to his sense of self-interest but also to his notion of the role reserved for the native nobility and gentry in maintaining order and stability. In a letter to Lynch on the subject, he could appeal both to heraldic and legalistic explanations and back them up with the authority of birthright and royal favour: 'The reason I used though I intimated that I could allege others was that it would be held strange that any called by any such title should have the name of both town and county my self having a title of an earl comprehended within the same nomination, reserving that King Henry the 8 did not get the lordship, chiefries, and command of that place from my ancestors …'[125]

All the same, he was simultaneously keenly aware that competition for titles had to be approached circumspectly, for excessive competition could create enemies amongst great men and families, while seeming timidity in the defence of one's claims to honour could lead to a devastating loss of reputation amongst the public at large. His commentary regarding a precedence dispute with the 5th Earl of Thomond, in which he became involved in 1625, shows the Earl trying to walk that fine line. He approached the matter very cautiously at first, writing to Richard Hadsor:

my purpose hath been always to proceed therein tenderly as most unwilling to have an difference between that house and mine, God knows how little I value the business itself, if public knowledge did not in a manner forcibly put me on to try the true state of it, and if my lord can give me by his counsel reasonable satisfaction, it shall without further noise be dashed and past over by me, and if it be my right the Earl hath no reason to take it ill at my hands rather b[lame] [those] that went afore that wronged my family so long.[126]

Yet by the following summer the matter remained unresolved. So in July he wrote to Lynch requesting 'records of order of nobility in all past times and

[124] Ibid., pp. 182–3. Cunningham notes that Lynch did not follow this advice, however. Cunningham, 'Political and social change', p. 245.
[125] Clanricard to Lynch (6 May 1621). 'Clanricard letters', p. 171.
[126] Clanricard to Lynch (6 May 1625). Ibid., p. 186.

materials related to father and grandfather, including of attempts made on his father's life'.[127] Despite Clanricard's grave concern that bad blood would follow this dispute, things had reached the point at which not defending this alleged encroachment on his privileges of precedence would have been more detrimental to his social status and authority.[128]

An English title, though desperately sought, was also potentially troublesome. He wrote to Lynch how

A title here for <privileges and other> many reasons hath been advised by divers friends, but that as it is difficult it may be so I would never entertain a higher than a viscountsy to avoid the dislike or envy of earls of Scotland or of Ireland ancienter than myself when they came hither. Of this particular you write nothing and I think it will rest without further thinking thereof, for the means that may be used to prevail I shall <not be drawn unto> though it be the common custom, and an English title is held no small matter specially for an Irish birth.[129]

Clanricard, then, was not representative of Old English honour, nor was he an exemplar of Irish conformance to a new 'modern' code of honour, as described by Mervyn James.[130] Rather he embodied the fluidity of honour as a social mechanism, for he could, and did, make use of it on a number of levels, and in a variety of guises. A man who could ride prominently in English heraldic processions, and express shock that his Gaelic foster-brother had violated the bonds enshrined in that relationship, was out of the ordinary. But not because such a cross-cultural aristocratic persona was inconceivable, but because so few people managed to realize it. He was in the practical, not the conceptual, avante garde, since the blueprint for just such a two-pronged ascension had been drawn by the programme of surrender and regrant. Clanricard was the idealization of that mostly unsuccessful Tudor programme. The Crown benefited by piggybacking

---

[127] Memorandum [from Clanricard to Lynch] (12 July 1627). Ibid., p. 189.
[128] Clanricard to Lynch (no date, 1627). Ibid., p. 204. The case was eventually determined in favour of Clanricard. Bodleian, MS Selden Supra 125, fol. 30; BL Lansdowne MS 323, fol. 67; BL Cotton Titus B XI, fol. 410. Thomond's creation was in fact older, but it was not continuous, having passed from one line to another. The matter, however, would not die there but would again be taken up after the Restoration. See, for example, Ireland. Parliament. House of Lords. *Journals of the House of Lords*, 8 vols (Dublin, 1799–1800), vol I, p. 253. Accessed electronically at www.galenet.galegroup.com/servlet/ECCO.
[129] Clanricard to Lynch (15 Oct 1623). 'Clanricard letters', p. 181.
[130] Canny, in his study of Cork, argues that Irish peers were adopting the new 'service-honour' principles of their English conterparts. Canny, *The upstart earl*, p. 132. Clanricard's conduct shows elements of that trend but also strong continuity with an honour system based on his personal/familial control of Galway and of a vast affinity within it. While Clanricard was not representative of noble honour in early seventeenth century Ireland, neither was anyone else. Fluidity and uncertainty were the rule.

its authority on that of the Earl's in western Ireland: once safely ensconced within the colonial establishment, Burke and his successors could – and did – serve as local agents of social reformation and as regional pillars of central authority. For his own part, the Earl benefited by simultaneously using royal favour to augment his traditional authority in Connaught and by making the jump into the English peerage. Unfortunately for Clanricard, however, his ability to seem different things to different audiences, while it allowed him to scale to unprecedented heights in British elite society, would also allow the future Lord Deputy, Wentworth, any number of positions from which to impugn the Earl's honour when they clashed over the Connaught plantation in the 1630s.[131]

THE SOCIAL DANGERS OF PRECEDENCE DISPUTES

Seen from one angle the case studies presented here sit oddly together: the Gaelic commentators seem impotent and nostalgic before a historical tide that has lifted the fortunes of more flexible social aspirants like Clanricard and Thomond. One could come away from this with the sense that the laments of the Gaelic learned classes were little more than the final grum-blings of a displaced social elite. There is much to recommend this view: anglicization was a fact of early Stuart Ireland, and the Gaelic order would never recover from the Flight of the Earls. In contrast to the native poets, however, Clanricard and Thomond were able to adapt to change, reconfi-guring the ancient as well as the more recent concepts of honour and nobility to maintain, though ideally to improve, their status within the new dispensation.

The socio-cultural critiques of the poets and satirists are important to keep in mind, however, for they remind us that in every honour contest there were losers as well as winners. And the losers were not only the increasingly redundant Gaelic intellectual classes and lesser lords, since with every step up the honour hierarchy taken by men like Clanricard and Thomond, there was someone who felt his place threatened or, worse still, was left to lick his wounds at having watched a rival surpass him. The precedence clash between those two 'British' aristocrats themselves, more-over, reminds us that such struggles could also create division amongst the victors.

The mobilization of a language of honour, then, was not a merely academic or abstract project but a vital tool for navigating the waters of

---

[131] See Chapter 7, below.

an increasingly Protestant and anglicised Anglo–Irish socio-political scene. With the stakes so high, the competition for honour could prove incredibly contentious. In the precedence dispute of Clanricard and Thomond we can see how such a struggle could poison the relationships between individuals and houses. Such wrangles could, however, poison politics as well, and whereas in this chapter – at least in the case studies of the two earls – we have considered how a language of honour could be used to elide ethnic, national and religious difference in Anglo–Irish high culture and politics, in the next chapter we will consider how struggles over honour could, in fact, serve to derail just the sort of assimilation between English and Irish culture so effectively realized by Thomond and Clanricard. For what may seem to the modern observer as petty squabbles over who follows whom in a parliamentary procession, or who sits where in church relative to whom, could, in fact, hinder the function of government. And after Mellifont this would not be an exclusively Irish affair, for as we will see, the amalgamation of honour systems in Ireland and in England would cause serious social dysfunction in both the colonial kingdom and the imperial metropole.

CHAPTER 6

A hierarchy transformed? Precedence disputes, the defence of honour and 'British' high-politics, 1603–1632

In the early modern period, Ireland pacified may have caused more trouble to the Crown than Ireland independent. This chapter explores the ways in which the defeat of the Gaelic order, and the resultant 'conquest' of Ireland, served to destabilize not only the society of Ireland, but that of England too, and considers the political ramifications of that destabilization. The focus falls on precedence ('precedency' to contemporaries) disputes in both kingdoms and on the political logic of the need felt by various persons from the Crown on down to defend their honour. It argues that Ireland played a fundamental role in shaping the politics of honour in the early Stuart period and ends with the suggestion that Ireland would again figure prominently in Charles I's drive to restore honour as an element of the personal rule.

The object here is not to rewrite the history of the inflation of titles in early Stuart Britain. Charles Mayes and Lawrence Stone have expertly detailed its workings in England; Mayes, and now Victor Treadwell, have equally well described the Irish story, and especially the Duke of Buckingham's role in it.[1] Rather, this chapter builds upon the excellent structural foundations laid by those studies in order to make some further suggestions. First, it attempts to link the inflation of honours in both kingdoms together. The studies mentioned above maintain fairly strict national focuses. These phenomena, however, were closely related and need to be seen more explicitly as two parts of a larger whole. Second, the chapter is not concerned with the mechanics of title inflation but rather with its social, cultural and intellectual implications. Most studies of this subject have looked at the workings of the system, leaving its social fallout unexplored, the consequences assumed as opposed to examined. By looking at the language used by contemporaries when discussing these sales – primarily at the

---

[1] Charles Mayes, 'The early Stuarts and the Irish peerage', *English Historical Review* 73 (1958), pp. 227–51; and 'The sale of peerages in early Stuart England', *Journal of Modern History* 29 (1959), pp. 21–37; Stone, *Crisis of the aristocracy*, pp. 65–138; Treadwell, *Buckingham and Ireland*, pp. 103–47.

discourse of noble honour – this chapter seeks to elicit from the sources just what the sale of honours meant to early Stuart notions of status, authority and social stability. Third, the chapter then seeks to move beyond the theoretical – that is, the discourse of honour – to explore just how the inflation of honours affected society and politics in the early Stuart multiple monarchy. This I do in two ways, first, through a focus on precedence disputes. Odd as they may seem to a modern viewer, precedence disputes were taken very seriously indeed by contemporaries. If we accept that personal relationships not institutional structures bound the political nation, then these contests do not seem 'medieval' anomalies in a world of Parliamentary procedure but rather the stuff of real politics. As this chapter shows, the social disharmony occasioned by such disputes served to greatly disrupt the workings of politics in and between both kingdoms. To demonstrate this we will look at the Irish Parliament of 1613–15 and at the English Parliaments of 1621 and 1628–9. Second, I tie these honour disputes to a growing desire on Charles I's part to defend honour. Recent scholarship has highlighted the political role played by Charles' concerns over honour in England.[2] Here I wish to highlight Caroline efforts to restore honour to Ireland and, moreover, to argue that these efforts were of fundamental importance in the slide to personal rule. Seen from this perspective, the inflation of honours looks less like a slow-burning corrosive force in Anglo-Irish relations and more like an explosive high-political matter.

BRITISH HONOUR AND THE IRISH PARLIAMENT
OF 1613–15

The defeat of the Gaelic order brought political chaos to Ireland. It was not supposed to be that way. Defeat of the Ulster lords and the Flight of the Earls was expected to usher in a brave new world of anglicization and social stability. Some leading contemporaries chose to see developments in just such terms. In 1612, gazing out over a majority-Protestant political nation and a newly planted Ulster, Sir John Davies crowed how he could envision that in a generation's time Ireland would in 'tongue and heart, and every way else, become English'.[3] He was right in the sense that Gaelic culture was heading towards permanent decline, but woefully incorrect was his

---

[2] Charles I's obsession with the defence of honour is discussed in Kevin Sharpe, *The personal rule of Charles I* (New Haven, 1992). It is also an important theme in Richard Cust's new biography of Charles I: *Charles I, a political life* (London, 2005).

[3] Sir John Davies, *A discovery of the true causes why Ireland was never entirely subdued and brought under obedience of the crown of England …*, ed. James Myers, Jr (Washington, DC, 1988), p. 217.

underlying assumption that Ireland would thus prove a readily governable Stuart province. Instead, Ireland without the Gaelic 'threat' became a political jungle. In spite of Hugh O'Neill's sporadic efforts to couch his rebellion at the end of Elizabeth's reign as a loyal one, English observers always saw Gaelic rebellion as an external threat – both in terms of the cultural 'otherness' of the Gaelic Irish and because such risings carried the threat of foreign invasion.[4] Consequently, efforts against the Gaelic Irish generally served to unite politically divergent interest groups in England and the Pale.

With that unifying threat removed, however, those interest groups – court factions, soldiers on the make, projectors and speculators, and so on – were free to turn on one another. And they did – the effects of which would wash back to disturb the metropole as well. The trouble Ireland posed to the Crown had thus transformed in the wake of the Nine Years' War into an even more readily recognizable internal one, the central struggle of which pitted members of the Old English nobility and the newly ascendant New English against one another. Far from savages or barbarians, Old English aristocrats represented something of a fifth column of social corrosion in the early Stuart polity. They were after all 'like us', so to speak, and their demands for status, privilege and rights could not be so handily managed as those made by the Gaelic Irish. Nor was it clear just what should determine honour and status in this newly conquered kingdom. Contests over that question would create enormous headaches for the Crown. At no point was this more clear than during the Irish Parliament of 1613–15.

This parliament was dominated by concerns over possible penal legislation. Earlier in his deputyship, Chichester had embarked on an aggressive policy of rooting out Catholics from positions of authority through the administration of 'mandates'. These were official letters sent to prominent Catholic nobles to attend Protestant services. When the recipients refused to obey these mandates they were fined in Castle Chamber. With the subsequent fears of pan-Catholic scheming against the government in the wake of the Flight of the Earls, it was widely expected that the government would use the Parliament to make a more concerted and sweeping move against recalcitrant Catholics.[5]

Although in the end there would be no aggressive move toward penal legislation, what was significant about this assembly was the attempt to pack

---

[4] Generally on the threat of invasion, see William Palmer, *The problem of Ireland in Tudor foreign policy, 1485–1603* (Woodbridge, NY, 1994).

[5] On the mandates, see McCavitt, *Chichester*, pp. 111–28.

Parliament – primarily Commons – with Protestant allies of the government. This was chiefly done through the creation of new boroughs and the engineering of their elections to ensure the return of Protestant candidates. In the end, therefore, we see a situation in which religion was, as contemporaries suspected it would be, a matter of overriding importance to the calling and conduct of the Parliament. But religious exclusion would not operate in the ways contemporaries expected. For in place of a frontal assault on Catholic privilege by means of penal legislation, there was instead the move to simply shift the demographics of the political nation through election-rigging. The Catholic response, then, was not based so much on matters of faith and loyalty as upon questions of fair election, noble and gentle rights to govern, and the need for resident authorities. As Nicholas Canny has commented, the Old English were angry at government efforts to cut them out as natural leaders.[6] Consequently, questions of honour, fair-dealing and noble/gentle privilege provided much of the language of this Parliament in spite of the underlying confessional tenor of the conflict between parties. Nor, as things turned out, would it be only over election issues that honour imperatives would influence this Parliament.

To consider the role played by honour concerns in the proceedings of Chichester's Parliament it may prove best to group the many instances of honour disputes into three broad categories: questions of privilege – noble and parliamentary; precedence disputes; and the defence of honour. There is certainly overlap among these categories, but this division will allow us to summarize the extent of the honour conflicts that plagued the assembly, to show some of the different ways in which such concerns manifested themselves, and to demonstrate the disruptive effect they had on the workings of politics at a moment when Ireland was supposed to be more quiescent than ever before.

The defence of noble and parliamentary privilege

Well before the session ever sat, there were signs that honour disputes would disrupt this Parliament. Irish lords complained that the government had violated a principal tenet of noble privilege by only selectively announcing the upcoming event. On 25 November 1612, six 'lords of the Pale' penned a complaint to James over the means by which notice of the legislative gathering, and the matters it was to address, were circulated. The Lords Gormanston, Trimbleston, Dunsany, Slane and Louth all claimed how 'till

---

[6] Canny, *Making Ireland British*, p. 407.

that of later years it hath been a duty specially required of the nobility of this kingdom, to advertise their princes, your majesty's most noble progenitors, of all matters tending to the service, and to the utility of this kingdom'.[7] And yet, they despaired, with this calling of the first Parliament in over a quarter of a century the matters to be discussed at the assembly had not been made known to them, or to others of the nobility.

Although this oversight was undoubtedly a personal affront to the signers, they chose to argue their case for conciliar inclusion by calling upon the collective rights and responsibilities of the nobility, generally conceived. Thus, they pointed out that such pre-notification of business dated back to the time of Henry VII, who had established a grand council of the nobility. By pointing out that they were of estate next to the monarch himself and thus knew what was best for the country and its people, they implied that the first Tudor was astute in having done so. Were this first Stuart to overlook the precedent of seeking noble counsel in the governance of Ireland, as established by the first of the Tudors, he, the letter-writers hinted, may soon face social chaos in his western kingdom. For once natural leaders were removed, the letter warned, then the lower orders and meaner sorts would eventually seize the opportunity to attempt rebellion. Raising yet a more threatening spectre, they further cautioned that this sort of general dissatisfaction could give hope to the discontented abroad which would not only bring the risk of rebellion but also serve to 'calumniate and cast an aspersion upon the honour and integrity of your highness's government' in the eyes of the international community.[8] The Crown's limited circulation of the plans to call a parliament may have been driven by matters of religion and favouritism, but the response of those excluded was to shift the grounds of debate to favour their position – Catholics that they were, they decried their exclusion as an affront to ancient privilege.

The pursuit of honour principles would continue to plague this Parliament after it sat. Once the assembly was convened, the question of which house had the privilege of deciding matters of honour served to poison relations between the lower and upper houses. In matters of honour Lords expected to reign supreme and, as Treadwell has noted, the Crown acknowledged this privilege

---

[7] William Farmer, 'A chronicle of Lord Chichester's government of Ireland …', in John Lodge (ed.), *Desiderata curiosa Hibernica or a collection of state papers* (Dublin, 1772), p. 159.

[8] Ibid., p. 161. This kind of thinly veiled threat about the consequences of ignoring noble privilege would come up again during the Parliamentary sessions. The journals of Commons notes that during the reading of a bill entitled 'Act for the Attainder of the Earl of Tyrone' some 'scrupulous consciences' wondered at the wisdom of the move given that 'the Earl was oppressed, complained and not redressed, and therefore requisite to fly out'. *CJ*, vol. 1, p. 18.

by 'introducing in the Lords important official bills for the recognition of the king's title, the attainder of Tyrone, and the general pardon, none of which met with serious opposition in the Commons'.[9] But Commons revealed it had other ideas on these matters when it took it upon itself to determine the restoration of blood of one John Heydon. The bill for restitution was hastily moved through the lower house in May of 1615, while Lords was in recess. Upon hearing of the bill, the upper house, already having felt its toes stepped on by a self-aggrandizing Commons,[10] submitted a three-part grievance to the Lord Deputy. The third complaint was over the Heydon affair. This, and the brief concluding lines of the complaint, accurately sum up the Irish peers' views of their role in policing questions of honour:

Where all Honour is derived from the King, and Matters concerning Point of Honour should properly descend from the higher House to the House of Commons, they assumed the same to themselves, as appeareth by the Act of Restitution of John Heydon to his Blood

These and other like Grievances as Matters of Disrespect, and tending to breed an utter Neglect of their Nobility and Honours in their several Places, the Lords Spiritual and Temporal of the upper House of Parliament do, with all Humility, lay down before your Lordship, praying such a Remedy as in your Noble Consideration you shall think most fit.[11]

In its defence, Commons retorted that Heydon was a commoner and thus it fell to it (Commons) to decide on the question of his restitution.[12] Whatever became of the matter is unknown, but the contention that it symbolized – which house held the privilege to determine issues of honour – served to complicate a political assembly that was already troubled with issues of religious difference and irregular elections.

Parliament and precedence disputes

Probably more disruptive still were the frequent, occasionally even violent, contests of precedence between individuals. Such disputes were simple wrangles over who held rank and place over whom. They began just prior to the session's opening, much to the exasperation of Chichester. Writing to the 'lords of the council' on 30 December 1612, he noted that whether it was due to the 'seldom calling of Parliaments here or for some other reason we do not know, some nobles starting to

---

[9] Victor Treadwell, 'The house of lords in the Irish Parliament of 1613–15', *English Historical Review* 80 (1965), p. 97.
[10] See the previous chapter's discussion of Thomond and the parliamentary debate over land valuations.
[11] *CJ*, 1, p. 81.   [12] Ibid.

contend for place'.[13] By his account the jostling for place began with the feud between the Barons of Delvin and Killeen, but that others quickly followed their lead. For fear that they would all be caught up arguing these matters instead of attending to business, Chichester and the council asked for the power to 'summarily' deal with precedence questions.[14] Although this request was granted, it did little to lessen the disruptive power of precedency disputes once the Parliament was convened.

The first, and most spectacular, squabble came on the opening day itself, occurring during the ceremonial parade to St Patrick's which was part of the convening ritual. The day was a Sunday, the 23rd of May, and the Lord Deputy, the council and the peers rode together to St Patrick's in 'very great estate'.[15] By Chichester's account, 'some of that Nobility', Gormanston the main figure, began to squabble 'more' as he wrote, 'to interrupt this great affair as we conceiv'd it, then for any sound reasons besides'. So exercised were the contestants – Viscount Buttevant being Gormanston's rival on this occasion – that they declared they would neither come into the Parliament house, nor accompany the Lord Deputy to the church, until those differences were settled.

William Farmer's contemporary account gives a fuller impression of just how virulent, disruptive and public this matter truly was:

[Viscount Buttevant and Viscount Gormanston] fell at debate for precedence of places, as who should ride foremost, or take the upper hand, &c. which strife continued between them all along the street, even till they came to the Castle gate, wherby the Lord Deputy and all that honourable company were greatly disturbed and troubled, and with much ado they were appeased for that time. And shortly after they were called before the lord deputy and the council, where each of them challenged precedency of the other by antiquity of their births and callings; but when their antiquities appeared doubtful and could not be well proved for the want of good records, it was ordered that the viscount Buttevant should have the precedency until the viscount Gormanston could bring forth more ancient records than the other.[16]

Chichester was taken aback by this disruption, finding it especially vexing given that he had been charged to hear and determine such controversies and was willing to do so at the disputants' request. Moreover, he scolded the quarrelling peers for picking this time to quarrel when other more pressing matters were at hand, namely the very public ceremonial opening of Parliament. Eventually he was able to restore peace by appealing to his

[13] R. D. Edwards (ed.), 'Chichester letterbook', *Analecta Hibernica* 8 (1938), p. 72.   [14] Ibid., p. 73.
[15] Farmer, 'A chronicle', p. 204.   [16] Ibid., pp. 204–5.

and the two men's mutual respect for the King – something he was quite eager to do in order that 'the publick Proclomation to be made in the hearing of the multitude without insinuateing some such dissensions to be'.[17] Unfortunately for the Lord Deputy, Buttevant and Gormanston were not the only peers to clash over place in this opening procession: the Barons of Lixnaus and Delvin, and of Trimblestown and Dunsany, also felt the need to dispute rank and place.[18] Chichester was eventually able to engineer an orderly procession by, first, assuring the participants that the precedence he had determined for the day was merely for convenience and not permanent and, second, by allowing that challenges to place could be made, and would be considered, at a more convenient time.[19] With these assurances, the nobility of the House of Lords attended their Lord Deputy to the church door. There the recusants waited, refusing to enter to hear the Protestant services, then they filed back 'in like order' to the upper house.[20]

Was this merely a means to disrupt the assembly orchestrated by Old English nobles whose power was being eclipsed by New English competitors? Put another way, was this the acting out of a series of social, political and religious grievances but done using a vocabulary less potentially explosive than that of religion and nation? If Chichester hoped that it was, and that this spectacle was merely a further example of Old English degeneracy, he was to be cruelly disappointed by the spectacle of English commissioners carrying on equally stubbornly about precedence later that year. Besieged by complaints over election irregularities, the Crown sent over a party of four commissioners to look into the allegations. Their arrival in September, however, merely added to the chaos of the proceedings since no directive had been sent with them detailing what precedence they were to hold. This, as Chichester described, caused great problems: 'These Commissioners do insist upon precedency of places here, before the Privy Councell of this Realm, which they on the other side do take indignation at, and are nothing inclined to yield unto, because they know no speciall cause to the contrary, nor think it to be the King's meaning'.[21] Not wishing to 'incurr the assured Envy in determineing of the difference on either side', Chichester was once again reduced to appealing to the need to respect the King and the business of Parliament. Thus, he was able to persuade the commissioners and his own council that it was an 'honor for them to separate themselves from such contentions at this time' when the monarch's business was pressing.[22] In the

[17] 'Chichester letterbook', p. 101. [18] Farmer, 'A chronicle', p. 205.
[19] 'Chichester letterbook', p. 101. [20] Ibid. [21] Ibid., p. 131.
[22] Ibid.

end, Chichester skirted the issue by holding sessions in his house and by making sure that the councillors and the commissioners were never simultaneously in attendance at public assemblies.[23] As much as he may have been piqued by the very public precedence squabbles of the native nobility on the opening day of the assembly, he was downright nervous over getting involved in a contest between his councillors and the English commissioners. He begged the lords of the council to move James to make some judgement on the matter.[24]

And still the problems continued. In November 1614 Chichester complained that despite his attention to questions of precedence, there were many who, being so adamant in their claims to place and in their unwillingness to accept his arbitration, chose not to sit in session but instead sent proxies, the better to avoid causing greater offence to the Deputy.[25] Others, he complained, 'challenge places by Antient custome and prescription only, as is alleaged which some other doe now Controvert that have any matter of Evidence to shew, so as I may justly despair to determine of them aright'.[26] Throwing up his hands, he declared that he could merely do his best on each occasion, after which he would send a report to the privy council in the hope that it may find evidence in England (this usually meant in records held in the Tower) to bring a final settlement.[27]

The chief herald of Ireland, Daniel Molyneux, Ulster King of Arms, may have been the only person more traumatized than the Deputy by the rash of precedency disputes that plagued the Parliament of 1613–15. In a letter dated 8 May 1614, the English privy council reported on a complaint it had received from the herald in which Molyneux claimed to have been grievously assaulted by one Sir William Stewart and two of his henchmen. Stewart, it appears, was furious over Ulster's decision on a point of precedence that concerned him. Thus, he tracked Molyneux down to the latter's own garden and there proceeded with the help of his men to

cruelly assault him that he received many woundes, and irrecoverall maymes, his sight being exceedingly decayed through the losse of seven or eight pounds of his bloud, the use of his right hand and arme utterly lost, and his body made so weake and tortured with such convulsions as by the opinion of phisicions he hath noe hope ever to recover, but by languishment to ende his dayes in continuall weakenes.[28]

---

[23] MacCavitt, *Chichester*, p. 83.   [24] 'Chichester letterbook', p. 131.   [25] Ibid., p. 172.
[26] Ibid.   [27] Ibid.
[28] *Acts of the Privy Council of England, 1532–1631*, 46 vols (London, 1890–1964), 1613–14, p. 429.

Unsurprisingly, the council requested the Lord Deputy and council to provide Molyneux some satisfaction for his injuries and loss. Somewhat surprising, however, was their dismissive comment on the dispute that provoked the attack. They declared that it was against the honour and justice of the state to let pass such an 'injurous and barbarous usage' of a deserving servant of the state over 'soe slight and triviall an occasion'.[29] With this comment we can hear echoes of James I's anti-duelling campaign: as James was desperate to lower the temperature of noble competitiveness in England, so he was in Ireland too.[30] But in trying to defuse the situation by lessening the gravity of precedence disputes, the men of the council seem to have been fooling only themselves. The lesson of the 1613 commissioners showed clearly that such matters were hardly trivial, amongst English and Irish alike.

In the end, it was deemed necessary to send the recalcitrant Irish barons to England to establish once and for all an order of precedence amongst them. This was a decision reached with some difficulty. In March of 1615 James was still ordering Chichester to work out some temporary settlement between, among others, the Viscounts Gormanston, Barry, and Roche; and the Barons of Slane, Courcy and Lixnaw, so that the business of Parliament could proceed.[31] More specifically, the Deputy was to place them as they were under Perrot's Parliament (1585–6), or according to 'other rolls of the best credit there'. Those who remained dissatisfied would have their cases heard later, at a time of Chichester's choosing, before the 'King's Commissioners' Marshal'.[32] Not three months later, however, the privy council was ordering Chichester to send over the barons and viscounts who, with their widespread bickering, were retarding the business of parliament. They were to be accompanied by a herald so that matters could be quickly dealt with.[33] Two weeks later the lords of the council reported to Chichester that only Lixnaw had arrived and, thus, that he should see to it that the others travelled soon.[34] Once assembled, the Irish peers would face the full wrath of their monarch. As unpleasant as that may have been, it was too little, too late: the wrangling over precedence had already badly disrupted the proceedings of Chichester's only Irish Parliament.

James I, Lord Deputy Chichester and the defence of honour

Finally, let us consider what role the defence of honour played in determining the course of events in the parliament years 1613–15. We have already

---

[29] Ibid.   [30] On the Jacobean anti-duelling campaign, see Peltonen, *Duel in early modern England.*
[31] James to Chichester (25 March 1615). *CSPI*, 15, p. 5.   [32] Ibid.
[33] Council to Chichester (12 June 1615). Ibid., p. 66.
[34] Council to Chichester (26 June 1615). Ibid., p. 79.

seen how some individuals sought to defend their honour in precedency cases, and how others like Sir William Stewart would actually resort to physical violence. But here I wish to look at the ways in which the defence of honour could serve as a point upon which distrust and ill-feeling between king and subject could crystallize. We saw in Chapter 3 of this study how the honour politics of Anglo–Irish relations could spill over into England, particularly in Elizabeth I's clash with Essex and in her concern over the creation of the knights in Ireland and what effects those creations would have on English society and politics. That, of course, was a time of war. Here we are dealing with a period of peace, and one in which we can see the first blushes of an issue that would come to prominence in England in the 1620s and Ireland in the 1630s: the perceived need to deal harshly with possible threats to the honour of the state or sovereign coming as a result of challenges to the honour of its/his chosen representatives.

A complaint brought by the Lord Chancellor, Dudley Loftus, over a scandal perpetrated against him offers a preliminary example through which we can view two important factors driving the perceived need to defend the honour of high officials: first, how contemporaries viewed the mixing of a man's personal honour and the honour accruing to his office; and second, how seemingly 'personal' affairs could have very public consequences. The case in question involved one Paul Sherlock, who evidently attempted to secure some land by fraudulent means and later, when the case about this was to be heard in Chancery, attempted to bribe the Chancellor.[35] The details of Sherlock's next series of moves are not entirely clear, but it appears that he eventually brought a complaint to the English Privy Council against the Chancellor, alleging that the latter had conducted himself dishonestly and against the complainant's interests in the Chancery proceedings. In April of 1614 the Irish House of Commons considered how best to deal with Sherlock. From these discussions we can glean some information on commonplace views of the role of the defence of honour and politics. One Mr Lutterell, for example, abstracted the offence to be one against nobility and gentry as well. For as he said, 'Nobility began in the Second age of the World, about Ninus Time, and here is a Wrong to Nobility, and so to him that should be Moderator of the Law'.[36] Oliver St John, later to be Buckingham's right-hand man in Ireland, drew a more immediately damning genealogy of offence when he proclaimed Sherlock's actions to be an 'Offence double, ad personam et ad sellam' since he had come to his place as

---

[35] The following discussion is based upon material taken from *CJ*, I, pp. 52–4.
[36] Ibid., p. 54.

Archbishop and Chancellor 'not by Reversion, but by desert' and because if Loftus were corrupted then there could be no justice in the realm since he was its head.[37] But it was left to a certain Mr Crewe to draw out what would prove the most damning link for Sherlock. Crewe noted that by perverting justice, Sherlock had done offence to the King, since the monarch is 'sworn at his coronation to do Justice, which he cannot do himself, and therefore intrusteth the Lord Chancellor therewith, whom Mr. Sherlock sought to corrupt'.[38] Thus, Sherlock had scandalized not only the Lord Chancellor, in his person and his office, but the King and his government too. This elaboration of his offence into an indirect attack upon the honour of the King served to seal the case against Sherlock. He was censured, made his submission, and removed from his seat in the lower house.[39]

Perceived assaults upon the honour of the Lord Deputy drew from the Crown and privy council their most passionate calls to act in the defence of monarchical honour. They also threatened to drive a wedge between sovereign and aristocratic interests in Ireland. The honour of the Lord Deputy, both as person and office, was not to be questioned. In spite of its rhetorical excesses, Sir John Davies' opening remarks as Speaker of the House well demonstrate the near-sacred quality of the viceroy's honour. To the assembled luminaries Davies posed the following rhetorical question:

Hath he [Chichester] not acted his part so well upon the theatre of honour, as no man is ambitious to come upon the stage after him, knowing it is more easy to succeed him in his place, than to follow him in painful and prudent courses of government; and that he must be as strong as Hercules to undergo the burthern, that such as an Atlas hath borne before him?[40]

To Davies, honour was not giving way to an internalized sense of virtue but remained something glorious to be displayed on a public stage. Moreover, he went on to praise Chichester's virtue and worth as also being public qualities, declaring that 'You had need be a virtuous and most worthy deputy, since you sit in the throne, and represent the person of the most virtuous and excellent king in the world'.[41]

That exalted sense of vice-regal honour was threatened, however, by the grievances of the native peers and gentry who, as we saw above, were embittered by the government's packing of Parliament with Protestants and by their own exclusion from certain aspects of parliamentary business.

---

[37] Ibid. [38] Ibid., p. 53. [39] Ibid., p. 54. [40] Farmer, 'A chronicle', p. 192.
[41] Ibid., p. 193.

In a list of eighteen grievances presented to the King, the aggrieved signers closed with this final, defining complaint:

neither is it to be passed over in silence, that the ancient nobility of the kingdom are, for the most part, not only debarred from publick employments, but also are vile, pended, and set at nought, disgraced by those that are newly raised to honour, place and means, who might very well content themselves with the greatness of your highness's bounty, and not derogate from others, whose ancestors and themselves have long deserved, with the price of their blood, those titles and estates, which are descended to them of antiquity.[42]

Here was a compelling case for the defence of ancient nobility, and the notions of honour upon which it was built, against the incursions of newly made men. It was also a crystalline bit of commentary on the sorts of disruptions to a society of orders caused by the creation of a new Irish peerage to be filled by English, Scots and Irish alike. Yet it went too far because there had only been three noble creations since 1603: Rory O'Donnell, who had died in exile following the Flight of the Earls; Theobald Butler, Viscount Tulleophelim; and Chichester, the current Lord Deputy. As prescient a commentary as it may have been on the social dangers posed by an inflation of the Irish peerage, it was indefensible as a commentary on the current state of relative noble status and esteem because the finger pointed, if not intentionally, directly at Chichester himself.

This the Deputy was quick to point out. Chichester's response to the charges, contained in a letter to the King, began with a counter to the charge that men of ancient breeding were left out of positions of office. We allow them to be justices of the peace, he declared. That was not only the greatest office 'we can give them in the commonwealth', he added, but their holding it was a matter of favour anyhow since the Catholic nobility, by refusing to take the oath of supremacy, were not legally permitted this honour.[43] Their ingratitude was to the Deputy simply galling. But it was upon the matter of public esteem that matters turned personal and devolved to a question of the defence of honour, as his further comments make plain:

Their lordships have their due respects given them by us all; but we cannot value those that complain, as they value themselves, capable to govern and sway the whole kingdom, unless your majesty do so appoint it; and therefore we give them their due honours at all times, and at no time vilipend them, as they term it. Sure we are, that their complaints are vilely penned to traduce the ground and honesty of such as his majesty hath appointed chief ministers under him here. Whom they mean by those newly raised honours, I cannot conceive, unless it be the lord

---

[42] Ibid., pp. 250–1.   [43] Farmer, 'A chronicle', p. 275.

deputy; for his majesty hath given the honour of baron to no other person here. And being so meant, I may in my honest defence say, and that without vain boasting, or the thought of an ambitious man, I hope, that as I acknowledge to have received my honour out of meer grace and favour from my master; so, if desert might challenge it, I have spent more days, and lost more blood in honourable service done to the crown, than they that framed these articles, or any other their ancestors, from whom their honours are descended.[44]

Here Chichester provided a damning critique of his detractors' honesty and claims to honour. His comments also offer a clear declaration of the importance of merit over lineage. His intervention would not, however, end matters, for there remained a contingent of Irish peers at court complaining of Chichester's conduct. The Deputy expressed his wish not to come in person to England to respond to the charges on the grounds that doing so would 'in common construction be interpreted to your disgrace, contrary to our princely meaning, who intend the same highly for your grace and honour'.[45] Fortunately for him the matter would for the time being go no further since James came to his defence: regarding the various complaints against his Deputy, James affirmed that he had 'found nothing done by him but what is fit for an honourable gentleman'.[46] Nevertheless, the precedent would prove a dangerous one.

As the history of this Parliament makes clear, it did not require an inflation of titles for questions of honour to disturb Irish society and politics. Debates and squabbles over honour not only threatened to derail the proper functioning of government, but also appeared as a possible point upon which distrust and anger between king and Irish subject could crystallize – and all this in a period when a mere three men, and one of them of Gaelic stock (O'Donnell), had been promoted to the Irish peerage. Nevertheless, as the grievances of the Irish barons reveal, an appeal to honour principles could provide a strategy by which exclusions based upon religion could be challenged from a more advantageous position. And looking ahead, those complaints presaged the sorts of stresses and fault lines that were opening up in a rigidly hierarchical society once that hierarchy was reconfigured and filled with new men of varying nationalities.

That last concern would prove more troublesome in England. For once the inflation of honours began in the late 1610s, two of the major issues contributing to the crisis of authority occasioned by the sale of titles were the nationality of the new peers and the realm in which they held their titles. In the wake of the Nine Years' War, Ireland was intended to cease being a

---

[44] Ibid., pp. 275–6.   [45] Ibid., p. 296.   [46] Ibid., p. 311.

thorn in England's side. And true, the threat of armed rebellion was greatly reduced. But the often cynical creation of an Irish peerage would serve to destabilize the society that was supposed to serve as the model of civility for the sister realm. Ireland pacified was thus perhaps more of a threat to British socio-political order than it was when in rebellion. It is to these matters – of Ireland, honour, high politics and the breakdown of English civic harmony – that we must turn next.

ENGLISH PRECEDENCE AND POLITICS AND THE THREAT FROM THE PROVINCES

One of the problems facing a multiple monarchy like that ruled over by the Stuarts was the management of different national nobilities. Bacon identified this potential fly in the imperial ointment when commenting on James' union of the English and Scottish crowns. He worried about potential contests over place and precedence between the English and Scottish nobility and, further, about their relationships to the Irish nobility. To grant the English precedency in all cases would undoubtedly be an affront. Nor would a reference to antiquity work since, as he wrote, 'I hear their [the Scottish] nobility is generally more ancient'.[47] And so he floated a compromise: 'And therefore the question will be, whether the indifferentest way were not to take them interchangeably; as for example, first, the ancient Earl of England, and then the ancient Earl of Scotland, and so *alternix vicibus*'.[48] It was a ludicrous suggestion since the very idea of precedence and hierarchy was based upon the unmistakable certainty of relative status. Were it not so, then precedence disputes would not occur in the first place. That so brilliant a mind as Bacon's could see no way out of these problems of 'noble integration' signalled trouble for the new 'British' polity.

The working out of the particulars of that integration would fall initially upon Parliament in April 1604. According to the Venetian ambassador Nicolo Molin, the very first issue to spring up was the Scottish claim to all the honours and dignities enjoyed by the English. To this the English were amenable, he reported, but on two conditions: that the 'four great offices' of Lord High Constable, Lord Chancellor, Lord Keeper and Lord Chamberlain were reserved for Englishmen; and that no Scotsman would be raised to office for the next twelve years.[49] The second point of contention was over precedence, the English denying their noble counterparts

---

[47] *The works of Francis Bacon*, 10 vols (London, 1824), 3, p. 280.   [48] Ibid.
[49] *CSP Venetian 1603–07*, p. 148.

from Scotland equivalent place and the latter, as Bacon foresaw, claiming the same and favouring that 'seniority of patent alone shall count'.[50] This was a matter of the utmost importance; only after these matters of the relative rank of the respective 'national' peerages were considered did discussion move on to questions of how the Scots and the English were to be taxed in the new system. We are familiar with taxes being a heated political issue, but here they ranked second to matters of honour.

In spite of that inauspicious beginning, the issues over the integration of Scottish and English honour systems – what Salisbury termed the 'union of nobility'[51] – lay largely dormant for the first eighteen years of James I's reign. There were, of course, the odd cases of incompatibilities of honour codes and precedence. Differences over what was required in the defence of honour famously led to the execution of the Scottish Earl of Sanquire for killing a fencing master in London who had done him the dishonour of taking out his eye while 'playing at Rapier and Dagger'.[52] Sanquire had the swordsman killed – an act perhaps honourable in Scotland but which did not play well in London where less martial notions of honour prevailed. In terms of precedence, the clash of the Scottish Earl of Argyll and the English Earl of Pembroke led the former to use exactly the argument the Venetian ambassador had claimed was favoured by the Scots: place should be determined by seniority alone, argued Argyll, 'as becoming all Britains'.[53] Yet these were passing incidents, dealt with as they arose, and not yet indicative of a trend. All the same, concern over the strife arising from honour squabbles between peers of the different kingdoms seems to have been increasing throughout the early years of the reign. Commenting on this development, John Nichols, the eighteenth-century historian of Elizabethan and Jacobean progresses, noted contemporary opinion that the 'English now begin to startle at it now it touches their freehold'.[54]

Although Nichols was right in identifying the English nobility's growing concern over the threat posed to their standing by the integration of Scottish and Irish peers into the Stuart multiple monarchy, his financial explanation for it is insufficient. It was not so much the 'real' economic concern that Scotsmen would gobble up English estates that worried these men, but rather quite the opposite, that lesser-born Englishmen would purchase

---

[50] Ibid.

[51] Quoted in Keith Brown, 'The Scottish aristocracy, anglicization and the court, 1603–38', *The Historical Journal* 36 (1993), p. 565.

[52] *A compleate collection of state-tryals* …, 4 vols (London, 1719), I, p. 86. Electronic resource accessed through www.galenet.galegroup.com/servlet/ECCO. I owe this reference to Dr Alastair Bellany.

[53] Quoted in Brown, 'The Scottish aristocracy', p. 565. [54] Ibid.

Scottish and/or Irish titles. This rankled for three main reasons. First, it was something of a scandal amongst the established gentry and nobility that men of questionable character were being raised to the peerage. Second, and more importantly, was the effect this might have on political authority at home. There was fear that this class of new peers could constitute a voting block in Lords with interests in competition to those of their English title-holding counterparts. Third, and perhaps of greatest importance, was the simple question of relative status. The making of Irish and Scottish peers created opportunities for men to race up the status ladder and perhaps leapfrog their erstwhile social superiors. For who was to say which enjoyed higher place, an English, an Irish or a Scottish earl? Or did an Irish or a Scottish earl outrank an English viscount? And what place would the sons of the English nobility enjoy relative to these provincial peers?

Honour politics and the 1621 English Parliament

These questions would come to trouble the British political nation in the 1620s.[55] As in Ireland, it would take a Parliament to bring out the true potential of these stresses on the three newly integrated kingdoms. The assembly of 1621, tense enough over matters of the Spanish Match and possible entry into war on the continent, also saw the beginning of what would prove a troubled decade of honour disputes. As with Chichester's Parliament of 1613–15, the English Parliament of 1621 got its first taste of disruption over precedence matters during the ceremonial opening. James named three Scottish peers – the Earls of March, Cambridge and Holderness – to head up the processional. Led by members of Southampton's circle, a full twenty-six English barons, angry at this unprecedented ordering of precedency, subscribed to a complaint in which they declared that 'Our humble desire is that with your gracious allowance we may challenge, and preserve our Birth-rights, And that we may take no more notice of these Titulars to our prejudice than the Law of this doth, but that we may be excused, if in civil courtesie, we give them not our respect and place'.[56] James was furious and called the principals before him, individually, to explain themselves. Although the King's intervention ended this movement towards debate on the precedency of Scottish and Irish peers,[57] the assembly would continue to be troubled by questions of honour.

---

[55] Debates over the creation of baronets initially brought these issues to the fore. On the controversies raised by the baronetage, see Stone, *Crisis of the aristocracy*, pp. 82–97.
[56] Snow, *Essex the rebel*, p. 105.   [57] Ibid.

Plaguing both houses was the question of which, if any, house the 'foreign' nobility should sit in. In February the lower house took up the case of Sir John Vaughan, controller to Prince Charles and recently made a baron in Ireland.[58] Vaughan had served in the lower house previously but failed to respond to Commons' summons in 1621. By way of explanation he referred to his creation as baron in the Kingdom of Ireland.[59] The question before the Commons was whether given his new barony – received since he had last sat in the lower house – Vaughan was to sit in the Irish House of Lords and no longer in the English Commons. The House unanimously rejected the baron's defence, arguing that Ireland, though 'held' of England, was its own kingdom with its own laws. Thus, his promotion there had no bearing on his parliamentary responsibilities in England.[60] Sir Edward Coke's acquiescence in this opinion was, however, contingent upon the provenance of the letters patent. If the letters patent were issued under the seal of England, argued Coke, then Vaughan was a baron of England as well, and so excused from the lower house. But if they were under the seal of Ireland, Coke concluded, then Vaughan 'cannot be sewe hear but by name of a Knight and is a Comoner in England, and as good men as he sitt hear, being nom[ina]tive Lords, and he is no more' and thus could not to be excused from attendance.[61] At least one other MP, however, thought Vaughan should be excluded from Commons on account of his barony. John Carvile made the case that since Vaughan was eligible to sit in the Parliament of Ireland, it would not be right to admit him to the English assembly as well. The patent was called for, revealed to be under the seal of Ireland, and thus it was resolved that Vaughan should sit in the lower house. A baron of Ireland, he was but a knight in England.[62]

The second case, that involving Sir Henry Cary, was slightly more complicated, but touched on many of the same issues raised in the Vaughan case. Cary had been returned as one of the knights from Hertfordshire. In the time between the election and the sitting of Parliament, however, he had been created Viscount Falkland in the Scottish peerage. As in the Vaughan case, the question was whether Falkland was to sit in Commons as one of the knights from Hertfordshire. Coke again brought his considerable learning to bear upon the case and declared that Cary should be admitted to the lower house since his title was a foreign one, of which English law took no notice.[63] But

---

[58] As Baron Vaughan of Mullingar.   [59] BL Add MS 36856, fols 28–29v.   [60] Ibid.

[61] W. Notestein, F. H. Relf and H. Simpson (eds.), *Commons' debates in 1621*, 7 vols (New Haven, 1935), 3, pp. 412–13 (hereafter *Commons' debates*).

[62] BL Add MS 36856, fols 28–29v.   [63] *Commons' debates*, 2, p. 36.

others feared the precedent of admitting Scots nobility to the legislative body of England. Most strident on this point was Sir Edward Montagu, who claimed it was 'dangerous and an evil precedent to admit any Scottish viscount of our House, for that may be a mean to bring in all the noblemen of Scotland that are naturalized'.[64] Mallot drew upon the ancient division of the two houses as a means to back up Montagu's scepticism, noting that the lower house had been created so that knights and burgesses could discuss their business freely without the pressure of 'great men'.[65] Thus, he argued, it would be dangerous to allow a peer into their ranks for fear of the top-heavy pressure a viscount's presence could exert. Montagu's request to postpone judgment on the matter pending further deliberation was accepted, and the matter seems not to have been resolved by the time of Parliament's dissolution.

The precedency disputes of 1621 were relatively gentle affairs, small enough in number not to cause a crisis, and discussed fairly amicably in largely constitutional terms. However, the intervening seven years would witness a series of social and political changes that would darken the tenor of these disputes and raise their stakes. For one, the numbers of creations shot up sharply, peaking in 1628. However, it was not only the numbers but also the increasingly cynical manner in which these creations were peddled, and the descending quality of the men who purchased them, that disturbed the established nobility. And anger over this inflation of honours grew more virulent as men became bolder in attacking its engineer, the Duke of Buckingham. The real opening of hostilities over matters of precedence came, perhaps unsurprisingly, in 1628 – the year of the unsuccessful impeachment of the Duke and, later, of his assassination.

Honour politics and the 1628–9 English Parliament

The opening salvo was fired in February of 1628. Certain members of Lords felt aggrieved by those of their countrymen who had procured Scottish or Irish titles and 'thereby do pretend to have Place and Precedency, in all Commissions and Meetings, above the Nobility of this Kingdom'.[66] They looked around for means of redress. Three options were discussed: an Act of Parliament to be passed by both Houses, a petition to the King, or a joint protestation of the house.[67] It was decided to pen a petition to the King which would deliver the following fundamental grievance:

---

[64] Ibid., p. 37.   [65] Ibid.
[66] *Journals of the House of Lords of England*, vol. 4 (London, 1767), pp. 25–6 (hereafter *LJ*).
[67] Ibid.

Touching Precedency. We conceive that no Foreign Nobility hath any Right of Precedency within the Realm of England, before any Peer of this Kingdom: Yet notwithstanding, of Courtesy, a Precedency hath been allowed to Noblemen of Foreign Kingdoms, according to their Ranks, which it is no ways our Intentions to alter: But, in regard of late many Englishmen, both by Birth, Estate, and Abode, and the more considerable because of their great Number, have had several Honours, in the Kingdoms of Scotland and Ireland conceived to be very disservicable to His Majesty, and prejudicial to the Peers; that which the Committee do in Humility offer unto the House is, To consider what Way and Course is the fittest, to be taken, for addressing ourselves to His Majesty, for the remedying and redressing of that Inconvenience.[68]

Conspicuous on the committee charged with drafting the petition were such devotees of 'Old English Honour' as Essex, Montague and Dorset – all veterans of the precedence wrangles of seven years prior. Within two days these men had drafted a document for the King's eye, to which they appended six 'reasons' explaining their complaints. The entire collection was presented to Charles on 17 February.

The petition summed up what the peers felt to be incursions upon their privileges and honour as aristocrats. Men recently ennobled in Ireland or Scotland were using those titles to 'claime the right to take place and have precedency before the peeres and nobillity of England and their children within this realm'.[69] Although chiefly a problem of their own, their lordships played on the national character of this situation by decrying the fact that those who were 'natural born' to the kingdom and held their principal estates there should be demoted in status below those who were 'of late but comoners'. This, they claimed, was not only disparaging to them personally, but also to the King and to nobility itself, and that it was in the King's 'tender care to preserve the ancyent honors and dignity of your nobillity'. In spite of the gravity of their concerns, the petitioners were eager not to come across as too aggressive. Thus, they did not threaten any insubordination on their own part should matters not be resolved, but rather raised the spectre of social chaos should respect for the nobility be weakened by the King's failure to 'maintain [his] Nobillity in their ancyent lustre'. Should this example of social inversion continue, they argued, it would only serve to breed 'ill effecte to the service of your Majestie and the publique and disvallue and contempt [?] betwixt your Majestie and your people'.[70]

---

[68] Ibid.
[69] Bodl., North MS b. 1, fols. 65–6: 017/5: petition of Lords; a shorter copy of the petition is also to be found in the Drury Halstead MS in Maidstone, Kent County Record Office.
[70] Ibid.

Appended to the petition, as mentioned above, were six 'reasons' that spelled out the specific points behind their concerns. The first stated that men should only hold titles where they reside. The second built on this criticism of aristocratic absenteeism by arguing that those who held non-residential titles in foreign kingdoms were consequently unconcerned about the defence of those kingdoms and thus should not be allowed voice in their parliaments. The third claimed, furthermore, that these men then used their noble status to dodge duties and services in the places were they did reside – that is, England – and thus left the burden of their fulfilment to fall on the 'native' English peers and gentry.[71] The fourth argued that it was in fact contrary to England's 'Institutions' to grant men heritable titles in areas where they had no duty to defend or do service. Moreover, here the petitioners took on the issue of precedence, complaining that such foreign elevations served to place those of 'meaner quality in whom little cause appeareth but ambition' above those of merit and antiquity. The fifth moved the discussion from the practical to the theoretical, to a discussion of questions of relative status and concerns for the purity of honour itself as challenged by these precedency cases: 'we hold it [that is, these creations] in no small degree derogatory to the very foundation of Nobility it self (which is the step and circle which compasseth your Royal Throne)'. The sixth summarized the preceding points, repeated the concern over social inversion and beseeched Charles to 'maintain your nobility in their ancient lustre'.[72]

A number of the above 'reasons' closely mirror the arguments put forward by the Old English nobility during the honour disputes of the 1613–15 Irish Parliament. The attention to nationality of title, the argument against absenteeism, the raising of the spectre of social inversion and chaos, and the attempt to subtly implicate the King's own honour in the defence of the nobility's collective honour. One further argumentative similarity, however, was of a far greater significance in England of 1628 than it could possibly be in Ireland at any point, namely the appeal to custom and tradition in the face of potential executive innovation. The entire colonial project in Ireland was one of innovation, of socio-cultural revolution, and one to which counter-claims based upon antiquity of blood and custom could expect to secure only limited purchase. England, however, was supposed to be the stable anchor of the triple-monarchy experiment, and change there, if it was perceived to encroach upon ancient rights and liberties, would elicit a flurry of protest from those who did actually wield political power. Thus the understated, but inescapably

---

[71] The Vaughan case, for instance, was driven by such concerns.
[72] Bodl., North MS b. 1, fols 55–6. This particular copy was in the possession of the Earl of Downe.

threatening, criticism by these lords of Charles (and, implicitly, of his father) for his cheapening of the august ranks of the peerage through the unrestrained granting of 'foreign' titles to non-resident, English unworthies, and for the concomitant derogation of the monarchical duty to 'maintain your nobility in their ancient lustre', fed into the growing controversy over royal prerogative and subjects' rights. This precedence struggle was not a retrograde squabble over medieval titles, but a potentially destabilizing quarrel central to the main political debates of the day.

The King's initial response was guarded as he tried to buy time in responding to a potential rift between himself and those who were 'intermediate between him and his people'. Do not expect an immediate answer, he cautioned the lords, for it will take a 'great many days Consideration, And I must say there is a greater difficultie to reverse a thing that is done, then to prevent it'.[73] A working copy of a draft order from the council upon these issues highlighted two issues of executive concern. The first was precedence. Here the author, whose identity is uncertain, stated perfunctorily that lesser titles could in no way enjoy precedence over greater ones. Thus, despite the complaints of the English peers, a landed English viscount could not rank above an absentee Irish earl. This being but a working out of the executive opinion, the author submitted this opinion to 'judgement'. The draft's second concern regarded the fees paid by the foreign nobility. Only hinted at in the petition, this question was debated throughout the spring. The author's opinion was that the Irish barons should pay some fee, the issue being how much. Admitting that this was still being worked out, the author requested the help of 'learned counsell' in penning the final declaration.[74]

Although it is unclear how Charles decided upon the question of fees, it is evident that he generally supported his English landed peers in their quest to maintain supremacy of precedence. In a speech delivered to Lords, he announced that those bearing Irish and Scottish titles were to be placed behind their titular English counterparts. In delivering this edict, Charles' intentions were twofold. First, to allay the fears of the English nobility he declared that he had no wish to 'clogg and fill with number the House of the Lords of the Parliament here in England'. Second, to avoid insulting the Scottish and Irish peers, he reassured them that they were in no way 'uncapable' of serving. At his command, this was to be passed under the great seal immediately.[75]

---

[73] *LJ*, 4, pp. 25–6. [74] Bodl., North MS b. 1, fol. 64. [75] Ibid.

The matter did not die with Parliament's dissolution in June, however, for the Scottish and Irish peers were still to have their say. This came in the form of a general petition to which was appended a rebuttal of each of the English peers' six 'reasons'. The petition laid out the general framework of their counterclaims. Initially they played to their own antiquity of blood, writing how

> Your Majesty having done but the same things for your own Royall designs and considerations as his Majesty did unto Gentlemen in their Blood and Fortunes now wayes incomparable unto those then complayned of or to many of their Lordships now complayning; most of us either anciently Barons of this Realme or Gentlemen of ye Best Rancke even from the Conquest; and therefore we doe most humbly beseech your Majesty, in case you will admitt of any dispute of your prerogative and Royall Acts done by your selfe.[76]

This was followed by an appeal to the privileges of nobility itself, for they argued that they could not be legally deprived of their places but for 'capitall offences'. The petitioners also reminded the King that this matter had also arisen during James' reign, and had been laid to rest then. Here they not only used precedent to answer this question of precedence, but also attempted to place the blame for the renewed debate on the shoulders of those who had gained their titles after 1621 rather than on those 'more ancient'. According to this spin the whole dispute was not the product of the wounding of the honour of the ancient nobility, but merely the sour grapes of new-made men.

Their main defence, however, as the end of the above quote suggests, rested upon an appeal to royal prerogative. Only Charles was fit to decide on these issues; the words of Parliament or learned council were useless here for Charles alone, as king, was the 'fountain of honour'. Their argument for the primacy of royal prerogative, while on the face of it very traditional, was at the same time stunningly innovative. For they did not leave the matter there, as one to be decided by royal will, but rather pushed forward this logic so as to define honour in such a way that it came to appear a disembodied category unconnected to much of anything other *than* the royal will. The English lords, by contrast, had mobilized a sort of organic, bottom-up notion of nobility and honour grounded in military feats, landed property, good lordship and service to the Crown over the ages. Honour and nobility, then, were things to be determined by negotiation between noble privilege and royal will. By contrast, these concepts as defined in the petition of the

[76] Ibid., fol. 53.

Scottish and Irish peers were entirely top-down and disassociated from the traditional criteria of landed estate and good lordship. For they wrote

That should it be held for a good argument where the person hath not an estate he cannot keep his rank; it may trench into some of their Lordships' liberties not only in this Kingdom but others where they bear titles though they have no lands there and it being allowed universally through the world that he that hath a title from his sovereign hath place by his title in what civil kingdom soever he cometh without question [of?] whether he have Lands in the Country of his title or not. And if it be so with us in parts remote; it can be no less unto us in the limits of those your Majesty's own Kingdoms where you are the only sovereign.[77]

The petitioners thus not only accused their accusers of holding landless titles too, but also, and more importantly, employed something of a foreign relations comparison to argue their domestic rights – namely once an earl, always an earl, and one should be treated as such wherever one went. But in doing so they imagined a new sort of nobility, something of a cosmopolitan nobility, which existed only at court and was connected to no 'country', and which sprang fully formed from the mind of the prince. Thus they divorced their nobility from the commonly held notion that such status was the outgrowth of local lordship. This was something new, and must have seemed dangerously so in the eyes of the landed English nobility to whom it must have smacked of endorsement of absolutist political theory.

The responses of the Scottish and Irish peers to the English lords' 'reasons' further elaborated the positions set out in the petition. In doing so they charted a rather complex and innovative position on conceptions of honour and constitutional relations within the three Stuart kingdoms. To the charge that their absenteeism bred a lack of concern over matters of defence and thus the possibility of losing Ireland to rebellion or foreign invasion, they responded that it was curious that no one in Ireland seemed concerned about this, only members of the English peerage. More substantively, they argued that it was a good thing to place men of 'Honor and office' in Ireland who were not beholden to the 'devotion of the Natyves', adding that concern over legislative gaps or gaffs was alarmist given the constraints of Poynings' Law. They continued with an interesting take on the relationship between landed estate and honour: to the complaint that holding land was necessary if one were to 'love' the place in which the title was held, they retorted that 'if he have any thing of a man in him he cannot have a greater obligation by any Land or estate then by his Honor, and the place of his Tytle'. On matters of precedence they even appealed to

---

[77] Ibid., fol. 67.

law – civil, common and natural – claiming that 'to place superior Tytles under inferior, Earles under Viscounts, Viscounts under Barons etc (as was endeavoured) were monstrous and would cause quarrells & confusion'.[78]

Of particular interest was their meeting head-on the 'foreign' argument used against them by the English peers, for the way in which they did so entailed a curious element of theorizing about the constitutional make-up of the Stuart multiple monarchy. They began by stating that they had come by their titles in the same way as any English peer and thus those titles were valid 'in all places where Civillity is knowne, not as Strangers but as to the Essential Ranke and precedence due [?] to the Tytles'. From here they spun out further this 'international' defence, arguing that the nobility of Scotland and 'much lesse Irelande' could not be termed 'Strangers' for all were under 'one absolute Soveraigne' and their citizens 'naturalized heere as absolute as the Englishe soe soone as borne'. Moreover, they pointed out that no other nation termed its far-flung or provincial nobility foreigners – not France, not Germany, not Spain. Spain's subjects of Naples or Milan, for instance, though '1000 myles distant from Spayne' were not so designated; nor should the Irish lords when in England, they argued, since Ireland was 'a p[ar]te of the Ile of great Brittaine and soe established'.

Their position ultimately rested upon a very muscular notion of the royal prerogative. They claimed, for instance, that the English nobility's demand for the abolition of absenteeism was tantamount to a direct challenge to monarchical prerogative. Here they argued that aristocratic titles were valid throughout the Stuart dominions because they were all under the same sovereign and that, therefore, 'honor cannot be lymmytted to this or to that man or within this or that Dominion'.[79] Who were these men, the petitioners asked, to call into question the King's grace, which was the fountain of their reward? And who were they to attempt to curtail the King's powers and privileges, and so weaken them beyond what his predecessors had

---

[78] This paragraph summarizes and quotes from a copy found in Bodl., North MS b. 1, fols 69–73.

[79] This line of argument is similar to the victorious argument in Calvin's Case (1608). Calvin was a postnatus Scot (that is, born in Scotland after 1603); the case revolved around the issue of whether he could, in the words of D. Alan Orr, 'inherent land in England and enjoy the benefit of English law' (D. Alan Orr, 'England, Ireland, Magna Carta, and the common law: the case of Connor Lord Maguire, Second Baron of Enniskillen', *JBS* 39 (2000), pp. 389–421, quotation p. 400). The winning side in the case argued that loyalty was to the person of the monarch, not the abstract state. Whereas both petitioning sides must have been aware of this decision, they did not expressly reference it. The Irish and Scottish peers did, however, point to civil law as supporting their position. This suggests their engagement with the thorny matter of the relationship between aristocratic rights and the common and civil law traditions; see North MS b. 1. On Calvin's Case and its relevance to Ireland, see Orr, ibid., and more generally, Orr, *Treason and the state: law, politics and ideology in the English Civil War* (Cambridge, 2002).

enjoyed? Thus, in addition to meeting the challenges of the English nobility head-on, these responses raised important constitutional questions: Was nobility really no more than the gift of the monarch? Was Ireland in fact nothing more than a part of a greater Britain? These ostensibly personal squabbles over matters of honour thus had great potential to influence the course of state formation in the three kingdoms.

In typical Caroline style, the King tried to appease both parties when deciding on this dispute. Charles held up the existing orders of precedence – something that benefited the 'foreign' lords at the expense of the sons of English nobility – yet he also favoured the English lords in his declaration that non-English peers could not serve on royal commissions without special royal direction.[80] This was an ineffectual response for it essentially dodged the issue of precedence by declaiming that the King reserved the right to make 'further determinacon thereof to such tyme & place as may best suite with a business of so great weight & most make for the honour and satisfaction of the parties being of such eminent note and quality'. This was almost exactly like the non-committal move made by James I when dealing with the potentially disruptive precedence disputes in the Irish Parliament of 1613–15. But unlike in the Irish case, here there could be no defence that pressing business required the tabling of disputes over relative place because there was no assembly sitting at the time of the declaration. Rather, it seems more an attempt to diffuse a potentially troubling situation in which his nobility – those who should be his natural allies in the face of growing Puritan and gentry insolence – threatened to turn on each other and on the Crown. This view is reinforced when we consider that the closing lines of the declaration promised severe consequences should such disputes continue: 'His Majesty will hold and esteem those persons not worthy of his favour that hereafter shall any way either in words or actions raise debate and quarrels for precedency considering this his Majestie's order & pleasure herein signified'.

Early Caroline society was already careening toward constitutional impasse and conflict between king and subject. The injection of a contentious strain of honour politics only increased the threat to British social and political stability. This was largely a product of the repercussions of Ireland's pacification, and was exacerbated in turn by the release of pent-up frustration over the powers enjoyed by the now-dead upstart, the Duke of Buckingham. Ireland, free of rebellion, was thus a problem for the Crown. But at least it was an indirect one,

---

[80] The discussion and quotations in this paragraph are drawn from BL Add MS 64898, fols 41–2. I wish to thank Dr Richard Cust for providing me with a transcription of this important document.

since precedency disputes were, again, but local manifestations of the Caroline effort to reform Ireland and create a British ruling elite. Attacks on Crown officers, such as those against Lord Deputy Chichester by various Irish peers, represented a much more direct assault on the royal honour. Were such assaults to become more numerous and/or virulent, they would demand a more robust response than did precedency squabbles. And this they did at the end of the 1620s – a development that elicited a predictably stern call for the restoration of true honour in the pacified, yet still most troublesome, of the Stuart kingdoms, and so to Britain as a whole.

CHAPTER 7

Wentworth, the Irish Lord Deputyship and the Caroline politics of honour

In 1631, the former Lord Deputy of Ireland, Henry Cary, Viscount Falkland, initiated a cause in the English Star Chamber against a group of influential figures in Irish politics. The primary defendants were Sir Francis Annesley, Lord Mountnorris, and Vice Treasurer of Ireland; and Sir Arthur Savage, an ex-military commander in Ireland.[1] The suit arose from allegations made by Mountnorris and Savage that Falkland had been party to judicial murder in Kildare. Proclaiming his innocence, Falkland brought them to court for spreading the rumour throughout London. And he won; Mountnorris and Savage were found guilty of having 'joyned and combined together to lay a scandall' upon him.[2] During sentencing, it was made clear that at stake in the case was not merely the personal honour of Falkland, but also that of his office, his administration and the King. 'The whole matter', declared the Attorney General, 'was a grievous scandal layd upon the Lord Viscount Falkland, and his Government, and to impoyson his credit and reputation with the Duke, and with the King, and the rest of the Nobles here, and tended also to the King's dishonour'.[3] To repair the rent fabric of honour in Ireland, the sentence was to be read aloud at the Irish council table, the court of Castle Chamber and the Kildare assizes. Driving the effort to publicly repair Falkland's honour was, in part, the concern that Ireland remained an honour-free zone – and a continual security threat as a result – and thus in need of state intervention to enforce proper behaviour in all of its inhabitants. According to the Lord Keeper, the land itself bore some responsibility. 'The Country of Ireland is full of boggs on the ground and mists in the aire', the Lord

---

[1] The ensuing discussion is derived from material provided in S. R. Gardiner (ed.), 'Reports of cases in the courts of star chamber and high commissions', *Transactions of the Royal Historical Society*, vol. 39 (1886).

[2] Ibid., p. 2.   [3] Ibid., p. 4.

Keeper observed, adding that these helped to foment 'great mischiefes'.[4] The Bishop of Winchester dissented on the source of Ireland's 'mischiefes', holding that 'I thinke the poyson of the creatures in Ireland is all in the men'. And thus in Ireland, even more so than in England, '… it concerneth the justice and wisdome of the state to keepe men's affections in due place'.[5]

This chapter considers efforts made during the 'personal rule' to 'keepe men's affections in due place' in Ireland, and so protect the honour of office, state and monarch. As a number of scholars have argued recently, Charles was concerned about the erosion in England of true honour, and the complex of behaviour patterns, rights and duties that it entailed.[6] As the previous chapter of this study has suggested, the King and his potentially schismatic English peers were increasingly aware that the defence of honour would also have to be fought out in Ireland. For in the way that the precedence disputes occasioned by the emergence of an Irish peerage had destabilized the hierarchical structure of England's society of orders, so the increasingly virulent attacks by Irish peers and gentry upon the hand-picked representatives of the Crown in Ireland, most spectacularly Falkland, threatened not only political stability in the recently pacified kingdom, but also touched the honour of the monarch. And a man like Charles, as sensitive as a medieval aristocrat to honour slights, and confident in the belief that a respect for honour and its codes of conduct was one sure way to restore order and harmony to his kingdoms, would be keen to see these honour issues resolved permanently. Ireland, then, would prove a necessary and very important theatre in Charles' defence of honour. His choice of Sir Thomas Wentworth as point man in that defence would prove a fateful one.

The management of honour in an Anglo–Irish context would, however, differ in important ways from that in England alone. The colonial nature of the realm, the background of the 'civilizing' mission, the enormous opportunities Ireland offered for self-enrichment and social climbing, and the tremendous authority vested in the vice-regal Lord Deputy all combined to make Anglo–Irish honour culture complex and highly charged, and its accompanying politics of frighteningly high stakes. The numerous, and notorious, clashes with various Irish elites in which Wentworth became

---

[4] Ibid., p. 34.   [5] Ibid., p. 26.
[6] This is most comprehensively discussed in Cust, *Charles I*. See, also, Mark Kishlansky, 'Charles I: a case of mistaken identity', *P&P* 189 (2005), pp. 41–80.

embroiled offer a sharp lens on to these high stakes honour politics. Historians have typically understood these encounters as the products of an absolutist political agenda – the inevitable outgrowths of 'Thorough' – exacerbated by Wentworth's domineering and aggressive personality.[7] It has recently been suggested that his conduct was fed by a desire to act the King in Ireland.[8] Others have depicted Wentworth as representative of an older social code that was destined to clash with the corruption of New English opportunists.[9]

The Deputy's words and actions, however, reveal the importance honour played in these clashes, and thus complicate our understanding of his tenure in Ireland, specifically, and of Caroline honour culture and politics, generally. Regarding the standard high politics explanation for these clashes, it was frequently the case that matters of honour soured Wentworth's relations with Irish elites before political competition did. Wentworth was certainly interested in constructing an administration to his liking, but he was also interested in effecting something of a reformation of manners. The latter project, while it was concerned with political legitimacy not political authority, could lead to falls from political grace. This is most dramatically seen in Wentworth's conflict with the Irish Lord Chancellor, Adam Loftus, Viscount Ely. Not only does the Loftus affair demonstrate how cultural matters could have political ramifications, but it also shows the importance of family honour, heavily gendered, in Anglo-Irish society and politics.

Arguments that posit Wentworth as representative of an older social code overlook the fact that Wentworth's 'ancient' honour was an arriviste's creation and, furthermore, that his obsession with honour in politics was very much a contemporary, even avant-garde, Caroline one.[10] This becomes clear by considering the English back story to his Irish career, in particular his attention to matters of honour as Lord President of the Council of the North. His understanding of honour and politics during the deputyship was not the importation of old 'English' honour to an Irish setting; rather, Ireland simply provided one more theatre in the construction of a larger

---

[7] See Hugh Kearney's evocatively titled *Strafford in Ireland 1633–41: a study in absolutism* (Manchester, 1961); also, C. V. Wedgwood, *Wentworth: a revaluation*.

[8] Dougal Shaw, 'Thomas Wentworth and monarchical ritual in early modern Ireland', *The Historical Journal* 49 (2006), pp. 331–55.

[9] C. V. Wedgwood, *Strafford* (London, 1935).

[10] And here I should stress again that I am not arguing that he was in fact honourable, but rather that he thought himself to act honourably and that he found the language of honour a useful legitimizing one for his actions. His 'true' nature is, thus, immaterial to the argument and not of my concern. On the pitfalls of portraying a virtuous Strafford, see Terence Ranger, 'Strafford in Ireland: a revaluation', in *P&P* 19 (1961), pp. 26–45.

'British' culture and politics of honour. Consequently, the idea of
Wentworth acting as alter Rex misses the fundamental point that he understood his power to derive not from physical distance from the king – thus
allowing him free rein to act in his own interest – but rather from his
intimacy with Charles, which would allow him to push aggressively the
interests of an absolutist monarch. Wentworth was a difficult man with an
autocratic bent, but he was not treasonous; his efforts to revive monarchical
ritual in Ireland were not intended to parade himself as king, but instead to
overawe onlookers with the power of the majesty he represented. As
Wentworth fawned before his liege, so those below him in Ireland –
which, given his capacity of viceroy, meant everyone – were expected to
comport themselves with comparable humility. His clash with the one man
in Ireland who outranked him socially – Richard Burke, Earl of Clanricard
and St Albans – demonstrates most clearly his deployment of the honour of
the office-holder to counter that of the overmighty noble. In turn, it
demonstrates that his sense of his own authority derived fundamentally
from two things: he was Viceroy of Ireland and, as such, he was the personal
representative of the King.

By looking at these three aspects of Wentworth's political career, this
chapter argues that honour politics were important in the Wentworth
deputyship, and that the Irish theatre was an important one in the wider
context of the Caroline politics of honour. If Charles was busy defending his
and the Crown's honour in England, Wentworth was busy defending it in
Ireland; the two, however, were connected since both King and Deputy had
a larger 'British' context in mind while doing so.

WENTWORTH AND THE HONOUR POLITICS
OF STUART ENGLAND

A study of the honour politics of Wentworth's deputyship must begin in
England. Without a sense for the development of his own sense of honour
in Jacobean and Caroline perspective, it is too easy to see his actions in
Ireland as personal, autocratic excess enabled by Ireland's 'colonial' status
and abetted by his distance from direct monarchical supervision.
Wentworth, however, came to Ireland highly attuned to the honour imperatives of office and imbued with the Caroline desire to strengthen vertical
honour bonds throughout the three realms.

From the outset of his public career, Wentworth pursued membership in
England's highest honour circles. On at least two occasions during James I's

reign he sought to purchase a title.[11] Although unsuccessful, he did inherit his father's baronetcy in 1614. As debased a title as 'baronet' had become by the 1620s, it was still one he was keen to defend even as he took a principled stand against Charles' forced loan.[12] Informed by the clerk of the council of his impending confinement in the Marshalsea as a loan refuser, Wentworth reacted angrily not to his impending incarceration but to the clerk's not addressing him by his full titular honours:

for he will still commit me, warn me to prepare and confine me too by another man's name, not my own. For if he look upon my appearance, he will find me appear as knight and Barronet and not knight which other men are styled and not I. Neither will he mend it for anything I can say. Such warrants as these I must indeed stick upon, lest I might seem voluntary to embrace that which of all other I would avoid, to be thus made a stranger to my own country and estate.[13]

Wentworth's interest in titles of honour was matched by a desire for high office. In 1614 he was returned as an MP for Yorkshire; the following year he was appointed *custos rotulorum* (keeper of the rolls) in Yorkshire. These positions he would fight tenaciously to retain, in part because he saw them as elements of his personal honour. Facing the prospect of losing the keeper's position in 1617 to a rival, Sir Thomas Savile, Wentworth fretted to his father-in-law, the Earl of Cumberland, that losing the post 'would be a great disgrace unto [me] in the country'.[14] When his efforts to retain an office failed, as when the Crown blocked his return to Parliament in 1625 by 'pricking' him to be sheriff of Yorkshire, he felt keenly the shame of this pointed demotion.[15]

Loss of reputation stemming from loss of office was not, however, a matter of simply personal import but a threat to the well-being of the entire family. It has recently been argued that family honour, as an example of collective honour, was one of the means by which honour could promote social stability and did not simply serve as the grounds for individualistic violence. Wentworth understood clearly the importance of family honour, but felt it was something worth fighting over; slights to the collective could

[11] Wedgwood, *Wentworth: a revaluation*, p. 32.
[12] The shameless selling of it to the highest bidder helped, in Lawrence Stone's argument, to diminish public respect for titles of honour and so in turn provoke a crisis in authority. Stone, *Crisis of the aristocracy*, pp. 65–128.
[13] Wentworth to Mr Chancelour of the Dutchy (25 July 1627). *WP*, p. 261.
[14] 'Copy of a letter to be hereafter writt to his majestie by my lord of Cumberland if need be, 1617'. This letter was never sent. Ibid., p. 54.
[15] Ronald G. Asch, 'Wentworth, Thomas, first earl of Strafford (1593–1641)', *Oxford Dictionary of National Biography*, Oxford University Press, Sept 2004; online edn, Jan 2008, www.oxforddnb. com/view/article/29056, accessed 19 Aug 2008.

require as vigorous a defence as those to the individual. Thus he exhorted Lord Clifford that failure to defend his family's good name would 'not only blemish you in reputation … but in good faith threatens your house with a fearful ruin'.[16] The honour stakes of political tussles were of the gravest importance to Wentworth because to him they were not purely 'political' but could determine the life or death of a noble house as much as that of a public career.

This situation he would experience first-hand after 1628, the *annus mirabilis* of his official and titular ambitions. This would have seemed unlikely early in the year. In 1627 he had gone to the Marshalsea rather than pay the forced loan; in Spring 1628 he not only lost the post of *custos rotulorum* in Yorkshire but was also instrumental in pressuring Charles to accept the Petition of Right (7 June). Prospects of royal favour must have looked slim indeed. Yet the following month he accepted the titles Baron Wentworth of Wentworth Woodhouse and Baron of Newmarch and Oversley (22 July). In December he traded up for a Viscountcy, being created Viscount Wentworth on 13 December, and accepted two comple-mentary positions of high office: Lord President of the Council of the North and Lord Lieutenant of Yorkshire. Although the authority he would wield in the north derived ostensibly from the offices themselves, it would be expressed through and mediated by a developing concept of honour that combined his intense interest in personal and family honour with the arriviste's zealous defence of the traditional rights and privileges afforded peers.

We can see, then, why the elevations of the second half of 1628 were so transformative for Wentworth. Obsessed with titles, he was now a viscount; eager for office, he was now governor north of the Trent; highly attuned to the responsibilities of service, he was now the direct representative of the King. This confluence of awesome privileges and duties upon so touchy a man as Wentworth would be a risky proposition in any setting; in England of the late 1620s it would prove explosive. He had always felt that the honour imperatives of office, service, family and person were mutually dependent and reinforcing and that they required diligent defence. For example, he was concerned in the latter years of James I's reign that royal service had fallen into some disrepute, and that those of high birth were increasingly shying away from assuming the responsibilities of office.[17] Yet at the same time, he felt only men of worth, regardless of birth, should hold

---

[16] Wentworth to Lord Clifford (8 Oct 1622). *WP*, p. 177.
[17] Wentworth to Sir George Calvert (16 June 1623). Ibid., p. 188.

office lest the reputation of government service dip lower. Thus he wrote in 1617 to Lord Keeper Bacon encouraging him to reconsider the appointment of one William Vessy to the High Constable's place in the West Riding of Yorkshire, on the grounds that 'the man himself [is] of a proud conceit scorning to serve the country in so mean a place'.[18] Thus it was not that he experienced a change of sides in 1628 and suddenly became a co-opted defender of royalty and its aristocratic servants, but rather that only then were those responsibilities his.[19] The slippage since Elizabeth's reign in the powers and authority of the office of Lord President,[20] combined with his long-held concern with the reputation of royal service generally, made Wentworth eager to answer any and all challenges to it and so restore it to its former glory, the reflected glow of which would fall on its holder. Moreover, a hair-trigger touchiness to personal slights became more sensitive still once his personal honour was integrated with the need to protect the honour of office. On this count, we must bear in mind the larger context of the increasingly acrimonious relationship between Crown and opposition which was damaging public respect for the King's servants. In November, the month before his appointment as Lord President, Wentworth had expressed concern over the profusion of libels against Buckingham and Charles.[21] Once a Crown representative himself, he would brook no such trespasses.

In the wake of his appointment, challenges to all of these honour precepts – of person, of title, of office, and of king – came quickly and in number. The first came from a certain William Ellis who upon entering the council chambers at York had refused to doff his hat to the new Lord President. Wentworth was determined to see this breach of protocol punished. Ellis consented to apologizing to Wentworth in his capacity as Lord President, but not to his person.[22] Only months later, Harry Bellasis, eldest son of Lord Fauconberg, made a similar 'statement'. Despite being brought before the council in London to answer for not having removed his hat in

---

[18] Wentworth to Lord Keeper Bacon (13 July 1617). Ibid., p. 94.
[19] Cust suggests that the 'change of sides' question is a red herring based upon a problematic notion of a static self that suggests one can know the 'true' Wentworth and thus when he violated his own principles. Cust argues persuasively that Wentworth was able, and willing, to deploy a number of discourses to his own ends and that his actions, in turn, were constrained in ways determined by the limiting factors of those very discourses. Cust, 'Wentworth's "change of sides" in the 1620s', in Julia Merritt (ed.), *The political world of Thomas Wentworth, earl of Strafford, 1621–1641* (Cambridge, 1996), pp. 63–80.
[20] Fiona Pogson, 'Wentworth as President of the Council of the North, 1628–41', in John C. Appleby and Paul Dalton (eds.), *Government, religion and society in northern England 1000–1700* (Thrupp, Gloucestershire, 1997), p. 189.
[21] From Clare; 15 Nov 1628: *WP*, pp. 308–9.   [22] To Ed. Stanhope; 19 Feb 1629. Ibid., p. 315.

Wentworth's presence, Bellasis insisted that he would only apologize to Wentworth the office-holder, not Wentworth the man.[23] Disrespect for the king's servants was alive and well in the north.

Wentworth's quarrel with Sir David Foulis was the defining one of his tenure as Lord President. In it we see most clearly the defence of the full panoply of honour imperatives. Foulis was a Scotsman who had come south seeking preferment in the wake of James' accession. He was knighted in 1605, naturalized by Act of Parliament in 1606, and the next year granted a patent for making alum in Yorkshire. In 1609 he bought the manor of Ingleby in Yorkshire from Ralph, Lord Eure. His rise was capped in 1620 with the purchase of an English baronetcy. At the end of the decade, however, he ran afoul of the Crown, most likely the result of suspicion that his personal fortune came from embezzlement committed during his time in the royal household.[24] He also burned his bridges with Wentworth by circulating the rumour that the Lord President himself had misappropriated funds, specifically that he had not paid into the Treasury money he had gathered as collector of fines.[25]

Wentworth sought satisfaction against Foulis through the courts, not through personal challenge. In this the apple had not fallen far from the tree, for his father had famously avoided responding to a challenge from a fellow gentry landowner in York, Sir Thomas Reresby.[26] Wentworth, however, had about as much stomach for lawyers as he did for duelling and was suspicious of their ability, or desire, to defend matters of honour. Writing to Cottington in 1633 he groused that he did not wish any 'Gownemen' playing 'some trick on him'. 'They hate me damnably already', he declared, and went on to complain of their blindness to matters of honour:

I confesset I disdaine to see them in this Sort hange their Noses over the flowers of the Crowne; Blowe and snuffle upon them till they take both sent and beauty off them; Or to have them put such a prejudice upon all other sorts of Men, as if none were able or worthy to be entrusted with Honoure, And Administration of Justice but themselves.[27]

Nevertheless, he understood that the pursuit of extra-legal vengeance would only further weaken the office's prestige. And since Charles, like James

---

[23] Wedgwood, *Wentworth: a revaluation*, pp. 106–7.   [24] Ibid., p. 107.
[25] Wedgwood writes that this was very likely done in an effort to deflect attention from himself. Ibid.
[26] The dispute was over land in the manor of Hooten Roberts. Following Sir William's refusal to meet him in combat, Reresby physically assaulted the elder Wentworth on the bench of the Rotherham Quarter Sessions. Gilbert, Earl of Shrewsbury's letters to William Wentworth. *WP*, pp. 42–3.
[27] Wentworth to Cottington (22 Oct 1633). Str P 3/23 (consulted on microfilm at Firestone Library, Princeton University).

before him, wished to see duelling disappear from aristocratic circles, such gallantry would only offend the master (he whom the combatant was ostensibly seeking to defend). Moreover, the defence of honour through the law was increasingly acceptable in Caroline aristocratic circles: Charles had revived the High Court of Chivalry in the 1630s to deal with honour disputes, and the Star Chamber continued to hear matters of libel and slander against the great and powerful.[28]

Foulis was brought before the Star Chamber in February 1633, charged with the attempt to 'to draw a scandal upon the said Lord Viscount Wentworth, and to bring him into disesteem in the Hearts and Minds of the Gentlemen of that Country'. This was an important case for the Crown and Lord President because Foulis was not some disaffected noble in the north. He was a principal officer in his own right: a member of the council, a deputy lieutenant, and a justice of the peace in the North Riding where he lived. That such a creature of Crown patronage would have so spectacularly broken ranks and impugned the name of the Crown's offices and officers must have struck the government as a fiasco not to be repeated. Foulis was duly convicted for having, 'breathed out so much Faction and Disobedience' and trying to 'draw disesteem and scandal' upon the court and the Lord President ('a Noble Person of singular worth and merit'). Foulis was to be removed from all offices, committed to the Fleet at the King's pleasure, and made to pay a £5,000 fine. He was also to make public acknowledgement of his offence toward the King and Wentworth in the Star Chamber and at the Court of York. The decree itself was to be read aloud at the York Assizes. Finally, he was to pay £3,000 damages to Wentworth himself, 'Relator in this Court, whom this Court highly commended for vindicating his Majesty's Honour.'[29]

The Foulis case marked a new turn in Wentworth's honour politics. Earlier sparrings with the likes of Savile over the office of custos rotulorum were about personal reputation, place and patronage. The confrontation with Foulis reflected far greater concerns: the legitimacy of political office; respect for the King's appointees; and the maintenance of the sanctity of aristocratic and official honour – those things that mediated authority in a society with no police force or standing army and limited access to the courts. It may also have introduced issues of nation and ethnicity, Foulis being a naturalized Scot, but

---

[28] On the Court of Chivalry generally, see G. D. Squibb, *The high court of chivalry: a study of the civil law in England* (Oxford, 1959). See also the excellent website constructed by Steve Rea and Richard Cust: www.court-of-chivalry.bham.ac.uk/index.htm.

[29] Rushworth, *Collections*, 1, pp. 215–20. His son Henry was fined £500 and committed to the Fleet.

there is not hard evidence of this. Crucially, however, the Foulis case involved the fate of the President's newly ennobled house. The near-simultaneous titular elevations and political promotions visited upon him in 1628 gave the honour-obsessed Wentworth much to crow, but also to worry, about. His promotion to the Lord Deputyship of Ireland in 1632 would raise those concerns yet further; the cross-border, cross-cultural context of Ireland would make negotiating them more difficult.

WENTWORTH AS VICEROY

Raised to the Irish deputyship, Wentworth would continue to mix honour imperatives with governance. Although he had moved no higher in the peerage, his status had been significantly boosted by the promotion. Whereas the active power of the Council of the North was subject to close scrutiny by the centre, the Irish Deputy had far more autonomy. As G. E. Aylmer observes, the Irish deputyship was more like a scaled-down monarchy than an enhanced – Scaled-up – Council of the North or of Wales.[30] The holder of the office, as Viceroy, was the embodiment of the King's honour, and he presided over his own court. The honour stakes of Wentworth's public career had thus been increased.

Certain peculiarities about the Irish experience further sharpened Wentworth's attention to honour imperatives. The autonomy of the position meant that he became more squarely positioned as defender of the church – be it from Catholics, non-conforming Protestants, or simply laymen who had appropriated Church property – and as guarantor of Crown finances. Along with the deputyship, he was at the same time named General of the King's Army in Ireland. To this point, Wentworth had largely eschewed militaristic honour principles; after it, he would zealously tout and protect his martial honour.[31] Most importantly, perhaps, he became part of a metropolitan civilizing mission intent upon anglicizing the Gaelic Irish and bringing the Old English and New English in line with Caroline social norms and the interests of the Crown. Indeed, for all his posing with armour, Wentworth was no Essex. He was more a new St Leger: a man who sought the political integration of Ireland into a multiple monarchy based in London through a process of making Irish

---

[30] G. E. Aylmer, *The king's servants: the civil service of Charles I, 1625–42* (London, 1974), p. 24.
[31] One need look no further for demonstration of this fact than his sitting for portraits in armour – a common practice among the early seventeenth-century English elite – until after taking up the deputyship. See Shaw, 'Thomas Wentworth and monarchical ritual', pp. 340–7.

elites proper 'British' nobles and who, in doing so, fully understood that his power for such cultural-political engineering was based on royal favour, not vice-regal autonomy. Consequently, Wentworth's greatest trials would not be in the field but in the courts, and in the court of public opinion, as he sparred with Ireland's peers.

Wentworth's initial interactions with Ireland's ruling elites, however, showed a calculated effort not to offend or overawe. He did not arrive until July 1633, not wishing to take up his new duties until the Foulis case had been settled. In hindsight, this decision did not bode well for his relationship with the realm's power brokers. Nevertheless, he showed a remarkable public deference toward the Lord Justices he was displacing – Richard Boyle, Earl of Cork, and Adam Loftus, Viscount Ely and Lord Chancellor – and, more generally, a brilliant ability to manipulate public ceremony to his own ends. Viceroy or not, he took pains not to create animosity between himself and the Justices through ostentatious display at his entrance. Instead he began his entrance to the city on foot, having landed 'ere the Lord Justices had any notice of his arrival'.[32] This was in marked contrast to the arrival of the Lords Essex and Cromwell the previous Saturday who were, according to one eyewitness

> brought in with great state by the Lord Justices, Lord Primate, and all the people of quality that were about this town and highewaies, and streets especially thronged with people to see him, that hardly could the coaches pass.[33]

And although the ever-attentive Cork did catch wind of his arrival and rode out to meet him, the fact that Wentworth made his entry in a private coach (Cork's) ensured there was 'not so much as one piece of Ordinance shot off'.[34]

This public humility was in marked contrast to the unseemly precedence wrangles that had plagued the 1613–15 Parliament and that had set the 'foreign' (that is, Irish and Scottish) and English nobilities against one another at the end of the 1620s. Yet it was not humility for humility's sake, but rather a performance with pedagogic intent. Later he would make personal visits to the Justices' houses – a thing, he assured the King's Secretary Sir John Coke, never seen before in the realm but 'which albeit not formerly done by other Deputies, yet I conceived it was a duty I owed them, being as then but a private person, and also to show an example to others what would always become them to the supreme governor, whom it

---

[32] BL, Add MS 29587, Hatton-Finch papers, fol. 19.   [33] Ibid., fol. 17v.   [34] Ibid., fol. 19r.

should please his Majesty to set over them'.[35] Wentworth, by personal example, was educating Ireland's elites in the rights and responsibilities of an anglicized society of orders.

In spite of these humble beginnings, Wentworth well-understood the symbolic power and social currency of public display. There was an official element to this in that he directed official ceremonies and was given the authority to determine matters of precedence.[36] Given that Wentworth was instructed to preside over a Parliament – the first since the troubled session of 1613–15 – both he and the Crown were eager to avoid the sorts of disruptions over precedence that had dogged Chichester's only Parliament. In this they seem to have been rather successful, for no such contests disrupted the legislative proceedings. Moreover, they seemed to have reached some conclusion on at least one of the points at issue between the Irish and English peers in their conflict during and immediately after the 1628–9 parliamentary sessions in England. In July 1634 Charles wrote to his Deputy that those who enjoyed Irish titles, and thus who 'enjoy[ed] Place and Precedency, according to those Titles respectively', but lived in England, would be required to 'contribute to all Publick Charges and Payment taxed by Parliament in that Kingdom'.[37] This was followed the next month by a move to require non-resident peers to purchase within two years lands in Ireland commensurate with their rank or else forfeit their titles.[38]

There was a less official, more personal, aspect to this manipulation of symbolic power. Once installed as chief executive, Wentworth's inferiors would be expected to treat him as he had them when he was but a 'private person'. To that end, he cultivated a certain grandeur in both his official and personal lives to match his vice-regal status. The most immediate manifestation of this came through his desire to renovate Dublin Castle, which he found to be in a shameful state of disrepair. His personal lodgings would be no less grand. At Jigginstown in Kildare he undertook the construction of the greatest house Ireland had ever seen. He claimed its extravagant size was intended to ensure its appropriateness for the King's entertainment, were he ever to visit the realm. This may have been true, but no English monarch had set foot in Ireland since 1399 (Richard II) and it was hardly likely that the embattled Charles I would

[35] Wentworth to Coke (3 August 1633, Dublin). *Strafford letters*, 1, pp. 97–100. This diversion from custom, however, was soon to cause consternation. The new Lord Deputy clearly intended to put his stamp on the ceremonies of power, and if his entrance showed a certain humility, his novel means of receiving the sword of the deputyship smacked of a potentially divisive hubris. Rather than accept the sword in the church, he did so in the Council Chamber, an action that was not received with unanimous approval for it was noted that 'common woyrd murmurs that their antient customes are by him sleighted'. Hatton-Finch papers, fol. 19r.
[36] *Strafford letters*, 2, p. 407.   [37] Journals of the House of Lords, Gale Group, p. 10.   [38] Ibid., p. 20.

break the pattern.[39] Rather, the audience for this spectacle was to be found not above Wentworth – in the person of his master, the King – but below him. In such a visually attuned culture, Jigginstown was meant to overawe the locals as a physical embodiment of the Deputy's official and social pre-eminence.

The Deputy also fashioned his personal life as a model of honourable conduct. His court was a centre of hospitality and he set the standards of public entertainment, notably overseeing the opening of the first theatre in Dublin and luring the popular London dramatist James Shirley to town to write for it.[40] He dictated sartorial standards, declaring that no Irish 'wearing Trouses or not appelled after the English habit, [were] to be admitted to come within the [Castle] gates'; nor were secretaries to accept petitions from the same unless they first 'conform themselves in their appell'.[41] His own personal dress was understated, perhaps in an effort to avoid the suspicion that excessive finery signalled the parvenu. This was a tack pursued by the Earl of Northampton in England, who, early in James I's reign, took to wearing plain black clothing. Amongst the colours of the court, this was an aggressive and conspicuous flaunting of true, ancient lineage.[42] Caught in a similar situation in Ireland – one in which his 'ancient' lineage stood alone amongst the arrivistes of the vice-regal court – Wentworth adopted a similar approach to that taken by Northampton when surrounded by James' Scottish hangers-on. Writing to his brother in November 1634, he asked for shirts from London and was very particular to demand that they should have no lace or trimming.[43]

The Deputy's preference for understatement in dress was amusingly contradicted by his evident joy at cutting an imposing figure about town on horseback. In September 1633 he thanked Newcastle for the gift of a horse, one of the noblest ever sent to Ireland, he declared. Among the horse's peerless qualities was a keen nose for status distinction, for Wentworth wrote how one of Cork's men had rubbed the animal only to be kicked hard by it. This clearly pleased its owner: '… now that they find he is not to be rubbed upon by such Course Staffe, he and I on his back, a'warrant you passe as quietly as may

---

[39] Wedgwood, *Stafford: a revaluation*, p. 225.

[40] Tallis to Rawdon (20 Jan 1636, Dublin). *CSPI*, 17, p. 127.

[41] BL, Add MS 29587, Hatton-Finch papers, fol. 19r.

[42] It was remarked upon by William Wentworth, Sir William's son, to Sir William Wentworth. *WP*, p. 58.

[43] Wentworth to George Wentworth (18 Nov 1634, Dublin). Str P 8/159–61. See also: Wentworth to George Wentworth (25 March 1635, Dublin Castle), *Strafford letters*, 1, p. 391, in which the Lord Deputy mentions items that a certain Captain Russell is to buy for him in the Low Countries. For an excellent recent discussion of sartorial matters, see Amanda Bailey, *Flaunting: style and the subversive male body in Renaissance England* (Toronto, 2007).

be, Every man very willingly giving us as much way as we have need of, I assure you my Lord Chancellor and my Lord of Corke will neither of them come within ten yards of his heels.'[44] The Deputy may have forsworn frills on his shirt, but it was not out of any desire to pass unnoticed through the city.

This public 'show' was matched by a very personal, and often intrusive, 'tell'. For Wentworth saw fit on occasion to explicitly educate Irish elites on the sorts of lifestyles, behaviours and attitudes he considered befitting holders of high office and/or social status. Perhaps the most curious example of this was his tutoring Loftus on the eight points of female friendship and Platonic love. Some physicians, Wentworth claimed, advocated that the mixing of sexes with wine and dancing 'comforts the naturall vigor, and is a Cure for melancholy, or at least an alleviation thereof. As likewise it may be observed that Love doeth allay Anger, as a bagge of wooll deads a cannon bullet shot into it.' But female friendship could be more than a refreshing diversion from matters of state; women could be useful for intelligence-gathering. For, as the Deputy declared, 'women are more inquisitive into sundry particulars then most men are: and weake persons both men and women are apt to tell women such secrets, as they will not reveale to men of ordinary acquaintance. Subtle men know how to make great advantages of such engines; and others have been ruined thereby.'[45] In Loftus, Wentworth clearly believed he was dealing with not just a status or 'official' inferior, but a social and cultural inferior as well. Moreover, the document suggests a concerted effort to live classical ideals of 'honour and Prudence', incorporate them into his governing style and self-presentation, and to educate the New English in their finer points.

Wentworth's attention to honour in his dealings with Ireland's elites was not merely a pedagogical diversion. Rather it was constitutive of his governing style and, as with the Foulis case in England, a driving force shaping ostensibly 'political' relationships. Given Wentworth's gentry origins, this may seem something of an odd obsession. Who was he to hold forth on matters of aristocratic conduct? He was his master's loyal servant, and his concerns testify to his internalization of Charles' effort to restore the bonds of vertical honour across the realms.[46] And Wentworth approached this reformation of Irish manners with characteristic zealousness. Which of the available languages of honour he chose to deploy in dealing with Ireland's elites, however, depended on factors unique to each contest and reveals different characteristics of both his political style and his attempted

---

[44] Wentworth to Newcastle (30 September 1633). Str P 8/22.
[45] Wentworth to Loftus. Str P 34/2.   [46] Cust, *Charles I*, pp. 197–210.

reformation of Anglo-Irish manners. The remainder of this chapter explores two quite different instances of Wentworth's honour politics: the play to the honour of office and the civilizing mission when dealing with the Earl of Clanricard, and the deployment of a heavily gendered sense of family honour in his dispute with Lord Chancellor Loftus.

The dispute with Clanricard

Although not the first of his tenure, the conflict with Richard Burke, Earl of Clanricard and St Albans, most clearly demonstrates the 'British' aspects of the honour politics of Wentworth's deputyship. As noted in Chapter 5, above, Clanricard was a truly amphibious character, able to pass back and forth with ease between the English court and the decidedly less refined setting of East Galway. Although he was an exemplar of the period's socio-cultural fluidity and the possibilities it offered, it is not exactly right to see him as a model of early-Stuart social climbing or inversion. For while he did manage to enter the English peerage – the only Irishman in the age to do so – he was nevertheless of ancient lineage: he crossed national and cultural boundaries, not ones of class. As such, his clash with Wentworth would look different to those between the Deputy and other grandees like Cork, Loftus and Mountnorris, all of whom were peers but, relative to Clanricard, upstarts. These men owed their titles and fortunes to their own manoeu-vrings and opportunism within a fast-changing colonial setting, and, despite attempts at creative heraldic research, could claim no pedigree even remotely paralleling that of the Burkes. Nor could Wentworth. This, then, was Wentworth's only contest in Ireland that was with a family as much as an individual, and it would pass unabated from one generation to the next: at his father's death, Ulicke, the 5th Earl of Clanricard, took up the standard against the Lord Deputy.

At issue was the Deputy's effort to plant Connaught, which would naturally impinge upon Clanricard's landholdings and authority. This dispute involved very high economic and political stakes, yet the protago-nists couched their arguments in terms of honour and status. Clanricard argued against the scheme on the grounds that his local authority was essential to ensuring that Crown authority prevailed in the Gaelic west, but added that to enact such a scheme would be an affront to his privileges as a great officeholder and nobleman. Wentworth turned that position on its head, arguing that Clanricard's immense power challenged, rather than augmented, Charles' authority in the far-flung western reaches of the monarch's kingdom. He proposed reform by plantation. To support this position, Wentworth depicted the Earl as a combination of three negative ideal types: the 'over-mighty noble', the rebellious Irish lord, and the Catholic conspirator.

All three stereotypes he deployed in the wake of a Galway jury's refusal in 1635 to confirm the King's title to disputed lands in the county. By strong-arming hastily called and intimidated juries, the Lord Deputy had previously established the King's title for one quarter of the lands of Mayo, Sligo and Roscommon.[47] This 'legal' express stalled at Galway, however, and Wentworth was livid. In a letter to Coke, he gave three reasons for the troubles in Galway.[48] The first two blamed religious difference: there were no local Protestant freeholders, and thus the jurors were all recusants. The third faulted Clanricard himself and introduced the need to counter his 'over-mighty' authority as a basis for plantation:

Thirdly and lastly (which in the duty we owe his majesty we may not forebear to declare, though we honour much the nobleman's person and acknowledge his merits) the dependence, which all this County in general have of the Earl of St. Albans and Clanrickard, whose great estate in this country together with his far spread kindred, the great relations both priests and lawyers have to this lordship, and all this fortified with his majesty's power now in the said earl's hands, as Governor of the town and county of Galway, in nature little less than a County Palatine, renders him a person so potent in this County, as nothing which is carried in an ordinary course of proceeding can move here without him.

Though resident in England, Clanricard was accused of having master-minded the successful resistance of the Galway jury by means of secret correspondence. Wentworth then invoked the Crown's ongoing 'civilizing mission' by which the colonial presence would bring law and order locally and release the natives from the grip of tyrannical chiefs. This last and greatest of 'all Irish Dependences', he wrote, '… hath been in the Ages before us a strong and forcible means of many great Disservices to the Crown of England, and of many grievous Oppressions upon this People'.[49] Finally, he raised the possibility of Irish complicity in international Catholic conspiracy, suggesting that the Earl and his Galway underlings were besotted with Spain and that the region's good harbours made their seeking Spanish aid a real possibility. The only rational solution to the threats posed

[47] Wedgwood, *Thomas Wentworth*, p. 172.
[48] Wentworth and Commissioners of Plantation to Mr Secretary Coke (25 August 1635, Portumna). *Strafforde letters*, I, pp. 450–4. The commissioners, whose signatures were attached to the document, were R. Ranelagh, R. Dillon, Gerrard Lowther, Chr. Wandesford, Ph. Manwaring, Ad. Loftus and Geo. Radcliffe.
[49] Wentworth to Charles (24 July 1635, Portumna). Ibid., pp. 442–4.

by the Earl lay in greatly reducing his authority, which Wentworth claimed was 'little less than that of a Count Palatine', by seeing 'the county reduced back as it formerly was, under the provincial government of the President of Connaught'.[50] By mobilizing these three discourses of the over-mighty noble, the oppressive Irish lord, and the Catholic conspirator – all immediately recognizable to English audiences – Wentworth attempted to undercut his adversary's ability to play to his status as courtier and ancient, loyal peer, and thereby short-circuit the Earl's efforts to lobby on his own behalf against the plantation.

To contrast Clanricard's overweening autonomy, Wentworth paraded himself as the idealization of the so-called 'service nobility': the lower-ranking, if still high-born, officer who surrendered personal ambition to the greater good of the monarchy and used the law to rein in a 'medieval' magnate and his sprawling affinity. An early example of this rhetoric, from October 1634, came as Wentworth complained to Coke over the absentee Clanricard's retaining a company of foot. The Earl, he wrote, must either be present to oversee the company or relinquish control of it. Knowing he was challenging a well-connected peer, Wentworth played the long-suffering servant:

I have a hard Part to play, when I must on the one Side displease the greatest by calling for the Performance of their Duties, and have not left me, any Place free, whereby to encourage others to assist me in the Service, and so am like to be shortly in the case of Ishmael, every man's hand be against me and mine against every Man, a Condition the most against my nature possible.[51]

His complaints brought results; Coke responded that St Albans was to get the necessary licence if he were to be absent.[52] He could hope the strategy would bring similar success with the planting of Connaught.

---

[50] Wentworth and Commissioners of Plantation to Mr Secretary Coke (25 August 1635, Portumna). Ibid., p. 454. The Earl's Gaelic enemies could also play the same game of depicting the Earl as too powerful. Clanricard wrote to Donelan (1618–19) with concern over one Sir Roger O'Shaughnessy who was challenging his right to some lands in the barony of Kiltartas, 'alleging in pride and tomfoolery to my Lord Deputy and council that neither myself nor any my ancestors had any jurisdiction there, meaning be like that to be a country palatine by itself, how false that is everyone there knoweth very well, and that he is a foul liar. … Those kind of people insult upon my long continuance from thence, and think of other advantages, but in the end I hope in God they will to their shame and grief find the contrary, when it will be too late'. Cunningham, 'Clanricard letters', p. 198.

[51] Wentworth to Coke (6 October 1634, Dublin Castle). *Strafforde letters*, 1, pp. 304–10. Wentworth may also have been looking to benefit by comments made by Lord Deputy Falkland that Clanricard was one of those chiefly responsible for scuttling any agreement on army support. On this we have Clanricard's comments to Henry Lynch: 'The deputy hath not dealt well with me, for I hear in a public assembly he said that the people there if <they> found the proposition made for maintaining of an army hard, they might thank my [Lord] of Westmeath and Sir John Bath and I for it.' Cunningham, 'Clanricard letters', p. 200.

[52] Coke to Wentworth (6 October 1634, Dublin Castle). *Strafforde letters*, 1, pp. 304–10.

Yet Wentworth's positioning himself as the model of self-effacing, loyal rectitude, in opposition to the Earl's aristocratic freedom of action, had its limits. On his tour through Connaught, during which he oversaw the legal proceedings that would clear the way for plantation, he abruptly changed tack in his sparring with Clanricard and aggressively attempted to wound the Earl in his honour. Lodged at the Earl's house in Portumna, Wentworth treated the estate with contempt, most famously by tossing himself on the Earl's bed clad in his riding boots. This was hardly the sort of behaviour expected of a man who had embraced the service nobility's abandonment of aggressive honour displays for the 'modern' quietism of internalized virtue. Rather, this was a symbolic throwing down of the gauntlet against the Earl in absentia, the sort of aggressively disrespectful action natural for a man like Wentworth who believed honour was something actuated through public display. There are any number of things that may have provoked Wentworth's conduct: the intransigence of the Galway jury and the Earl's perceived role therein, Clanricard's relative (if not total) success in getting Charles to exempt his territories from the plantation scheme, a sense that the Earl was in fact not Wentworth's superior at all but merely an Irishman grown too big for his britches, simple personal animosity, a fit of pique, and so on. Whatever the reason, it is possible that a sense of impotence on Wentworth's part (brought on by his failure to counteract the Earl's lobbying at court) was a key factor; an idea made even more plausible by the fact that in no other dispute pitting Wentworth against Ireland's elites did he lose control so blatantly as he did at Portumna.

If Wentworth's conduct at Portumna was meant to wound the Earl in his honour, it was successful. The pamphlet from which we derive our knowledge of the affair's details makes that abundantly clear. Entitled 'A Discourse between Two Councillors of State, the One of England, and the Other of Ireland', it dwells on issues of relative status and acceptable comportment amongst English and Irish elites. Most likely penned in the 1640s by a Connaught lawyer with ties to the Burkes and to the Confederate Catholics during the War of the Three Kingdoms, this anonymous tract seems to have been a piece of Confederate counter-propaganda.[53] It also provides an exquisite exposition of the importance placed by one Old English observer on the need for great office-holders to follow the precepts of honour.

The text is structured as a dialogue between an English councillor, seeking explanations for the insurrection of 1641, and an Irish councillor,

---

[53] Clarke (ed.), 'A discourse'. The speculation as to authorship and purpose is Clarke's.

attempting to provide them. It plays on the notion, shared by many, that the rising had shattered a long-standing peace, Wentworth here serving as catalyst for the breakdown. Unlike Wentworth's own account of himself as the lesser man than Clanricard in terms of rank, yet the greater by virtue of loyalty and service, the text faults the Lord Deputy for playing the role of petty king, peerless in the backwaters of the third kingdom. If Wentworth accused the Earl of being an over-mighty noble, this pamphlet accused the Deputy of being an over-mighty Crown officer whose 'insolent pride' put him at odds with a benevolent king and led him to trample upon local interests. Details of his conduct at Portumna, the locus classicus of a tyrannical egotism, provided the text's climactic scenes.

The details of Wentworth's alleged behaviour were explosive, but they were just part and parcel of the pamphlet's overarching aim to tar the then-deceased Lord Deputy as a man who acted well outside the norms of an honour code seen as common to the nobility of all three kingdoms. Curiously, both dialogists are English, one living in Ireland where he served as a privy councillor, the other resident in England and of equivalent office there. The text, therefore, does not offer an 'English' view versus an 'Irish' one but rather those of two Englishmen experienced in the culture and politics of two of the Stuarts' three realms. The use of the English privy councillor suggests that one intended audience was members of the English political nation. But why an English-born Irish councillor rather than a native-born one? Presumably this allowed the author to air expertise on Irish affairs without his readers dismissing the arguments as Irish special pleading. It is also important to bear in mind that the best guess at authorship suggests an Irishman. Thus, the reader confronts the viewpoints of two Englishmen, but as constructed by an Irishman who was fluent in the language of the cross-cultural mixing of honour codes articulated so well by Clanricard himself.

The text sets out immediately to portray the Irish as law-abiding and Wentworth as an absolutist loose cannon unable to rein in his passions. The Irish councillor opens by describing how he himself had come to live in harmony with the locals:

and having some competent fortune of my own (which truly I resolved not to augment by any sinister or unlawful means, although it was a thing much in fashion, and that consuetudo et peccantium claritas nobilitanerit culpam) I lived peaceably and friendly with the natives, thereby gaining the goodwill of all about me, and being familiar with some principal persons I discerned in them (and indeed generally in the common people) a great desire to live in peace, under the protection of the laws.[54]

The statement succinctly delineates the major outlines of what will emerge as the author's case against Wentworth: his milking of the deputyship for his own enrichment (in spite of both an ample pre-existing fortune and his own statements that he wished no personal profit from the deputyship); his disregard for the interests of native and new nobility alike; his sinister character; his flouting of law and precedent; and his unwillingness to socialize with the locals. The Irish councillor was not blind to the various corruptions and power struggles that had occasionally marred the governments of the last three decades – for, he admitted, such had existed – yet he argued that, combined, they were 'but a peccadillo compared with the huge mass of oppressions and personal indignities laid upon the nobility, gentry and people by that (vizier, bashaw) the Earl of Strafford who after the first year governed them with a rod of steel'.[55] To his counterpart's astute question, 'He pleased you well then the first year?', the Irish councillor replied:

He was always very high, and kept too much distance with the officers of state and nobility, by which he lost ground in the affections of men, but generally gave hopes that he would prove a just though an austere governor, being often heard to protest against profit, as a thing he looked not after, and being known to have a great estate at home which might have kept him from those shifts to have enriched himself, which necessity constrained in some of his predecessors.[56]

Wentworth's breaking his promise over the Graces, however, proved the watershed moment in the Deputy's descent into tyranny. These were a series of concessions granted to Old English Catholic elites by Charles I in return for subsidies. Although these concessions were typically respected in the wake of their negotiation, they were not legislatively formalized.[57] Of paramount interest to the Old English was to ensure their ratification in the Parliament of 1634. Wentworth, however, managed to push through further subsidies – the most pressing business of the session – with the promise that ratification of the Graces would follow. He did not, however, follow through on his side of the bargain. This, according to the dialogue's author, did not bode well for the new administration: profiteering and haughtiness may have been distasteful, but the Deputy's not keeping his word showed

---

[54] Clarke (ed.), 'A discourse', p. 162. It is probably no coincidence that he describes himself as having arrived in 1607, the year of the Flight of the Earls, and thus the end to the threat posed by the Ulster earls to Crown authority.
[55] Ibid., p. 166.   [56] Ibid., p. 167.   [57] On the Graces generally, see Clarke, *Old English*.

him to be a man of no honour, and so not to be trusted to act in any socially or politically responsible way. By the councillor's reckoning, then, it was no surprise that once the subsidies were passed the Lord Deputy turned his back on the native nobility's call to pass the Graces into law and 'began to play at Rex'.[58]

The English councillor, however, was curious as to why the attentions of Dublin's *alter Rex* fell so heavily upon 'my noble and ancient friend the Earl of St. Albans, than whom I never knew braver man or more loyal subject to the crown of England ... that man whom all that knew him loved and honoured'.[59] The reason proffered is surprising for its simplicity: Clanricard had offered advice to Wentworth on the latter becoming Lord Deputy, an act that greatly offended Wentworth, in spite of its having been 'delivered with such civility, courtesy and modesty (it being impossible to his sweet nature to do otherwise) as might become a man of much inferior quality and parts'.[60] As portrayed here, the animosity between the men was not born of conflicting self-interest and governmental vision in the face of a massive transfer of land and authority in the proposed plantation of Connaught. Rather the poison was personal, and grew out of Wentworth's outrage that Clanricard would think himself fit to advise the new Deputy in the art of governance. While it is unfortunate there is not more detail given as to the content of that advice, it nevertheless seems reasonable to venture that Wentworth took the offer as an affront to his honour. As his conflict with Foulis while Lord President of the Council of the North in England had already demonstrated, Wentworth was keenly attuned to the honour of office; the audacity of one of the King's Irish subjects to offer him political advice most likely offended that sensibility. It seems equally reasonable to view his carrying-on at Portumna as, in part, a response to that perceived insult.

To the dialogue's author, the stay at Portumna was both emblematic of Wentworth's insensitivity to honour imperatives and the high-water mark of the Lord Deputy's provocation of Clanricard. Wentworth came, so the Irish councillor was made to explain, to the Earl's Galway seat '... there to remain at his pleasure (a style the king doth not use, but when his majesty progresses ends at some of his own houses)'. Once settled, he tossed himself on the Earl's bed in his riding boots, killed most of his deer, browbeat the servants, placed a guard to stand menacingly in the hall, and generally raised 'such havoc ... of everything as if the house had no master'. This gross assault took the English councillor by surprise, for he declared 'I daresay there was not any nobleman or gentleman in England (that man excepted)

---

[58] Clarke (ed.), 'A discourse', p. 167.   [59] Ibid., p. 168.   [60] Ibid., p. 170.

what would not have been careful to yield the Earl of St Albans great respect and honour.'[61]

Even the King was expected to respect the Earl's honour. Charles, the author protested, should have been more active in curbing his viceroy's actions. In fact, the pamphlet went so far as to charge Charles too with dishonouring Clanricard. After Wentworth's execution, the King passed the titles and fortune intact to the deceased's son, William. '... what kind of justice is it', queried the exasperated Irish councillor, 'that he being raised from a private gentleman, his son should succeed to his earldom and a vast estate acquired, or at least augmented, by his oppressions, whilst the sons of noble servitors (through his exorbitant power) of the fair patrimony their ancestors bled for, are exposed to neglect and contempt, the inseparable concomitants of want?'[62] In the mind of the Irish councillor, Wentworth's playing at Rex was merely that, playing, and the squire from Yorkshire but a parvenu beside the pedigreed Clanricard, a true exemplar of a noble honour code based both in blood and virtue. That being the case, it was incumbent upon the King – the 'fountain of honour' – not to legitimate the former Lord Deputy's over-reaching by allowing his ill-gotten honours and wealth to remain with his descendants. That Charles had not reversed his decision on Wentworth's estate provoked unflattering historical comparisons with the noble actions of even non-Christian kings. As the English councillor remarked:

I was much grieved at that passage, and thereupon calling to mind the notable sentence pronounced by Abbas, the late king of Persia, against his favourite the governor of Casbine (convicted of the like extortions and oppressions) was very sensible that an infidel should so far transcend the best of our Christian princes in so exact and necessary a point of princely virtue, justice being the greatest ornament and glory, as it is the sure foundation of monarchy.[63]

Charles I, as we have seen through the Chichester and Falkland cases, perceived assaults upon the honour of his viceroys as affronts to his own. Yet here we see the inverse of that interconnection: dishonourable conduct on the part of the Deputy, if unchecked by the Crown, could diminish the King's reputation. This dialogue's author was sensitive to the role of honour in politics – or at least aware that, if nothing else, an

---

[61] Ibid., p. 170.

[62] Ibid., p. 167. Wentworth's titles were forfeited on account of the attainder. Charles however issued a fresh grant of the titles to the son, William, on 1 December 1641.

[63] Ibid., p. 167.

appeal to royal honour and virtue offered a last-ditch strategy to move the King.[64]

But if Wentworth's attempts to wound Clanricard in his honour were successful, they were perhaps too successful. His actions at Portumna certainly raised the stakes in his sparring with Clanricard, but they also caused unwanted attention about court. Coke, however, assured Wentworth in October that Clanricard's own son, Richard Lord Tunbridge, saw no truth in the gossip.[65] The issue may very well have died there were it not for the fact that the Earl himself died the following month. This event was greeted with 'much grief' in England,[66] and the Deputy's conduct toward the aged Earl suddenly appeared in a more sinister light. Rumours swirled that Wentworth's conduct toward the Earl, particularly his conduct at Portumna, had played a central role in his death. As the author of the dialogue would later describe the situation, 'These things, when they came to the hearing of that brave lord, took such impression that he fell into a deep melancholy and in a few days his memory decayed, and soon after he fell sick and died.'[67] The Earl of Danby, having attended Clanricard's funeral, wrote to Wentworth that although the Earl had 'dyed in the 72 yeare of his Age, full of Honour and Dayes according to David' yet 'his People report that the apprehention of your Lordship's Discourteyes and Misrespect hastened his End'. Moreover, he warned how the son Ulicke seemed 'very Sensible' of the charge and 'also possest with many other Causes of Complaint under your Government wherein as I presume hee meanes in person to Crave Redress from your Lordship's owne hand, soe soone as the Season and some English occasions will permitt his Journey into Ireland'. In addition to a warning of the growing clamour over Wentworth's role in the old Earl's death, the letter was one of recommendation for the heir. Danby urged the Lord Deputy to 'remember the Extraordinary Meritts of that Noble man deceased farre above any of his Nation in our tymes', and pressed that the son was imbued with the same

---

[64] Aidan Clarke has portrayed the 1635 mission of a group of Galway men to court to protest plantation schemes for Connaught as 'largely an appeal to royal honour', albeit one 'shrewdly supplemented by an offer to double crown rents in the county'. Aidan Clarke, 'The government of Wentworth', *New History of Ireland* 3 (Oxford, 1991), p. 254. On Wentworth's attempts to get the Irish Parliament to 'trust' its sovereign, and on Old English fury at Wentworth, and thus the King, for failing to 'honour' their word, see Anthony Milton, 'Thomas Wentworth and the political thought of personal rule', in Julia F. Merritt (ed.), *Political world of Thomas Wentworth*, pp. 146–8, and Canny, *Making Ireland British*, pp. 405, 457, 459.

[65] Coke to Wentworth (26 Oct 1635, Hampton Court). *Strafforde letters*, 1, pp. 475–7.

[66] Mr Howell to Wentworth (28 November 1635, Westminster). Ibid., pp. 488–9. It is worth noting that Howell describes this news as an example of 'home matters'.

[67] Clarke (ed.), 'A discourse', p. 170.

qualities and so deserving of the Deputy's favour.[68] Thus, it was a situation of 'The Earl is dead; long live the Earl!' – and the Deputy could not have welcomed the prospect of having to continue his struggle with a new generation of Galway Burkes.

Wentworth's response to the controversy was measured and confident at first, almost nonchalant, but would quickly turn angry, even panicky. In a letter to the King dated December 5th he offered only a brief statement of his innocence against the rumour that his 'harsh usage broke his [Clanricard/St Alban's] heart', concentrating instead on how the new situation in Galway should be exploited.[69] Just over a week later, in a letter to Coke, he expanded further on his innocence, saying how he had given proper notice of his coming and had brought ample provisions for himself and his entourage. Should there be a next time, he swore he would be content in 'a lesser house and worse lodging'.[70] By the end of the month his growing concern was abundantly evident. Responding to Danby, he acknowledged that the 'noyse hath gon very loude upon me indeed concerning the Earle of St Albans death'. This he attributed to the 'Course of Fortune that I have run in this world', regarding it as yet another 'calumny' against him. He protested he 'neither in Publicke nor in private mentioned the Noble Gentleman, but with all the Honour and Estimation of him possible'. Wentworth conceded that they had been at odds over the proposed plantation, yet 'personal Disrespect never past from me towards him in all my life'. As to Sir Ulicke's growing braggadocio, he chalked it up to a combination of the young man's concern for his father and inheritance, but also as 'incident to younger years, where the imotions are many tymes soe precipitate as gives men noe leisure to be rightly informed, before they proceed to judgment'.[71]

The rhetorical calm of this letter, penned to a man ill-disposed toward Wentworth, was just that, rhetorical, for Wentworth's tone was positively shrill in a letter to the Reverend George Garrard. Here he lamented how his foes insisted upon 'blasting my faithfall Round proceedings in the Services of my Master, Colouring all I doe over with the Attributes of severity …'.[72] In response, Garrard downplayed the rumours by saying that he 'knew since last summer he had a much wasted body, and drank an extraordinary quantity of hot waters daily, which would quickly bring him

---

[68] Earl of Danby to Wentworth (27 November 1635, St James'). Str P 8/333.
[69] Wentworth to King Charles (5 December 1635, Dublin Castle). *Strafforde letters*, 1, pp. 491–3.
[70] Wentworth to Coke (14 December 1635, Dublin Castle). Ibid., p. 495.
[71] Wentworth to Danby (31 December 1635, Dublin Castle). Str P 8/334.
[72] Wentworth to Garrard. Str P 8/331–2.

to his grave'.[73] Wentworth, however, was right to be concerned; an earlier letter from Laud mentioned that the Earl of Holland was furious with Wentworth's having supposedly hounded the Earl to his death.[74]

Wentworth's actions toward Clanricard, therefore, while they constituted no actual wrongdoing in point of law, demonstrated how the hectoring of a great man, regardless of 'ethnic' or religious background, could lead to trouble. Just prior to Clanricard's death, Laud had written to Wentworth cautioning him to be less sensitive to 'the barking of discontented persons', such as Clanricard, and urging him to find a way to do his master's service 'and decline these storms'. Such a change in approach, Laud assured him, 'would be excellent well thought on'.[75] The Earl's death, however, would put an abrupt end to any such hopes. The controversy would continue to grow: not only did it pass *intactus* to the son Ulicke, but, more generally, it also transformed into a rather large stick with which his enemies could beat him. Holland's anger at the Lord Deputy was but one example of the outrage circulating in England over Wentworth's 'moral responsibility' for the death of a man who was both an English earl and the greatest Catholic peer of Ireland.[76] It would not take long before that outrage would synchronize with complaints arising from other questionable actions on the Deputy's part towards other Irish grandees, most spectacularly in the case of Adam Loftus, the Lord Chancellor.

The dispute with Loftus

If Wentworth played the part of the honest councillor in his dispute with his social superior Clanricard, he played the messenger of reformed Caroline honour in that with Loftus. True to historians' general approaches to the history of Strafford in Ireland, this episode is seen as either a clash of wills or one more power play in the continuing drama of 'Thorough'.[77] The gravity of the dispute is not in question; as Wentworth wrote to Laud in May of 1638, his asking for news of the quarrel was tantamount to asking 'in plain truth, whether we shall have a government or no …'.[78] The Deputy's

---

[73] Garrard to Wentworth (25 Jan 1636, no place given). *Strafforde letters*, pp. 509–11.

[74] Laud to Wentworth (2 Jan 1635/36). William Laud, *The works of the most reverend father in God, William Laud, D. D.* 7 vols (New York, 1975), 7, pp. 216–22. (Hereafter abbreviated to *LW*).

[75] Laud to Wentworth (16 November 1635, no place given). *Strafforde letters*, 1, p. 480.

[76] Clarke, *NHI*, 3, p. 255.

[77] For the first interpretation, see Lady Burghclere, *Strafford*, 2 vols (London, 1931); for the second, see Kearney, *Strafford in Ireland*; and especially Wedgwood, *Wentworth: a revaluation*.

[78] Wentworth to Laud (23 May 1638, Coshaw). *Strafforde letters*, 2, pp. 172–3.

handling of the affair would in turn provide the basis for article 8 during his impeachment trial.[79] But historians disregard the seriousness of the matter that brought on the contest: the alleged failure, or refusal, of Loftus to honour a marriage promise made to his son Robert and his daughter-in-law Eleanor Rush. Wedgwood remarks that the 'affair itself was domestic and even trivial'; Kearney that it was an 'apparently minor incident over a dowry'.[80] But to contemporaries dowry questions were not trivial, and marriage as a path to political, social and material advancement was a very high-stakes game (of which the most notable example was the Spanish Match between England's Prince Charles and Spain's Infanta, Isabella). And this match included the passing of a viscountcy. Nor should we misunderstand the importance of living like nobility. Perhaps even more so than in England, it was of vital importance for the nobility of Ireland to live to standards that would set an example for Old English and Gaelic pretenders. To call the dowry dispute of the Lord Chancellor's son trivial is to be insensitive to contemporary concerns. Moreover, the affair came to a head not merely over the disputed dowry, but because the Lord Chancellor was believed to have cut Robert and Eleanor out of the line of inheritance in favour of the younger son Edward and the daughter Anne. This flouting of normative practices of primogeniture was a significant breach of domestic order, and without understanding the importance of a well-ordered domestic sphere to the right to office and honour, one is left with little option but to see this episode in terms of a personality clash or as a cheap excuse by which to dispose of a political rival. However, to contemporaries, such a breach of household and patriarchal honour was deemed quite serious indeed.[81] In Ireland it was a double offence: against English aristocratic expectations, and against the efforts to introduce primogeniture into Ireland after 1541 as a means to civilize the nobility.

I wish to suggest that Wentworth's pursuit of Loftus was not a weak case pursued in order to effect a desired political/administrative change. This is the position taken by C. V. Wedgwood who writes that 'During the whole of the year 1637 Wentworth had been preparing for the last trial of strength with one of the "great ones" of Ireland.'[82] Hugh Kearney presents the

[79] And yet none of the authors in the collection edited by Merritt focuses on the affair; Merritt (ed.), *Political world of Thomas Wentworth*; nor does Canny in his magisterial sweep of early modern Ireland, *Making Ireland British*.

[80] Wedgwood, *Wentworth: a revaluation*, p. 242; Kearney, *Strafford in Ireland*, p. 72.

[81] Cynthia Herrup, *A house in gross disorder: sex, law, and the 2nd earl of Castlehaven* (New York, 1999); and Alastair Bellany, *The politics of court scandal in early modern England: news culture and the Overbury affair, 1603–1660* (Cambridge, 2002).

[82] Wedgwood, *Wentworth: a revaluation*, p. 239.

initiation of the proceedings as a means by which the Deputy could complete his control over the Court of Castle Chamber.[83] Ronald Asch's recent *Dictionary of National Biography* entry for Wentworth makes no mention of the particulars behind the 'long-standing judicial feud' between the two officers.[84] Even W. N. Osborough, who acknowledges the domestic nature of that 'long-standing feud', seems to dismiss the importance of the dowry dispute.[85] By contrast, I hope to demonstrate that the familial basis of the dispute was influential in determining its later development. The connection between proper household and the right to serve was quite real, and the Chancellor ran afoul of those contemporary concerns. That, in turn, helped to create his political problems. This, then, was not an instance of political rivalry having been displaced into a trumped-up domestic flap. As much as Wentworth may have desired political control and social eminence over Ireland's elites, this episode reveals his parallel desire to civilize them. That it ended so poorly for both parties highlights the difficulty in managing the politics of honour in the three Stuart kingdoms.

Adam Loftus was a model of New English ascendancy. Born in Yorkshire, he had come to Ireland in the 1590s lured by the promise of political and social advancement. It was a promise quickly fulfilled, and by 1619 he had risen to Lord Chancellor – the second most powerful office in Ireland. Eleven years later he would take yet a half-step higher: upon the recall of Lord Deputy Falkland in 1629 he was named a Lord Justice (Cork being the other), charged with overseeing the Dublin government until a new Deputy could be installed. This hold on supreme executive power would only be relinquished with Wentworth's arrival in 1633. Political success was mirrored by social advancement, and he entered the Irish peerage in 1622 as Viscount Loftus of Ely.

His fall was dramatic, and overseen by Wentworth. But it was not quick, nor premeditated. One would not think this from reading the historiography. Historians have ignored the long gestation of the conflict between

---

[83] Kearney, *Strafford in Ireland*, pp. 72–3.

[84] Ronald G. Asch, 'Wentworth, Thomas, first earl of Strafford (1593–1641)', *Oxford Dictionary of National Biography*, Oxford University Press, Sept 2004; online edn, Jan 2008, www.oxforddnb.com/view/article/29056, accessed 25 March 2008.

[85] W. N. Osborough, 'Loftus, Adam, first Viscount Loftus of Ely (1568–1643)', *Oxford Dictionary of National Biography*, Oxford University Press, 2004, www.oxforddnb.com/view/article/16935, accessed 25 March 2008. Osborough revives the contemporary rumour that Wentworth may have been romantically involved with Eleanor Loftus, bride of the Chancellor's son. He also notes that Eleanor's sister Anne was married to George and that there was only one witness to the alleged promises. As a result, he writes that 'suspicion necessarily attaches to Gifford's bona fides and, indeed, to Wentworth's role in the entire affair'.

the two men, preferring to see its start as a matter of unexpected opportunity – a family scandal – quickly seized upon by a calculating Wentworth
to crush his last great rival in the Irish administration.[86] The scandal came to
the Deputy's attention in the form of a petition by one John Gifford, half-
brother of Eleanor Loftus, wife of the Chancellor's eldest son Robert. The
petition accused the Chancellor of having reneged on promises of financial
support made to Eleanor and Robert and of having disinherited Robert in
favour of the younger son, Edward.[87] This domestic spat, so the standard
argument goes, offered Wentworth the chance to bring about Loftus'
downfall, and so remove the last obstacle in his drive to construct an
administration of hand-picked appointees and allies.[88]

However, and quite to the contrary, knowledge of the Loftus family
dysfunction would colour the relationship between Deputy and Chancellor
in the years leading up to Gifford's petition. Indeed, by the time the petition
was filed Wentworth had worked for years to bring resolution to the Loftus'
domestic strife. That he was unsuccessful, and the Chancellor unappreciative
of his efforts, would poison their political relationship. Historiographical
orthodoxy has it that Wentworth's conduct here was duplicitous, in that he
contrived to inflate the importance of a relatively insignificant dispute in
order to mask his true intention, which was to initiate a purge of the existing
Irish elites. I would suggest, however, that the episode was instead an
extraordinary case of executive efforts to manage family honour leading to
political chaos.

At issue initially were the marriage negotiations themselves. Eleanor
Rush was the daughter of Sir Francis Rush, one of Essex's knights and
long an intimate of Loftus, the two having served as privy councillors under
Chichester and as members for King's County in the 1613 Parliament.[89]
When the office of Lord Chancellor became open in 1619 it was Rush who

---

[86] By far the best account of the pre-history of the affair is provided by Lady Burghclere; see her
Strafford, 2, pp. 116–31. Her 'human-interest' approach to the subject allows her to focus on less
overtly political aspects of Wentworth's career. With that said, it is an idiosyncratic account. For
example, she is the only historian to write at any length on the marriage negotiations conducted by
Wentworth on behalf of his brother George; and yet she gets the name of the bride-to-be wrong,
calling her Frances instead of Anne. Ibid., *Strafford*, 2, p. 116.

[87] *HMC Report IX, appendix II*, pp. 158–9.

[88] See DNB entry and Wedgwood, *Wentworth: a revaluation*, p. 239. The new DNB article by Asch
reports nothing in depth about the affair.

[89] The electoral return from King's was the pair's first brush with controversy. Neither was a resident of
the county and it was only by virtue of the sheriff's disregard of the overwhelming local support of two
Gaelic Irish candidates that they were returned, although the commission appointed to investigate
electoral irregularities in the calling of the Parliament found no evidence of wrongdoing. *CSPI*, 14,
pp. 102, 359–64, 384–5, 439–40.

lent Loftus the £800 needed to secure the place. The marriage proposal, Rush's wife Mary would later claim, was made by way of thanks for that loan. For all the apparent intimacy between them, however, Rush seemed 'very unwilling to condescend' to the match and expressed a desire to instead find a partner for his daughter in England.[90] Loftus persisted and, after nearly a year, convinced Rush, in part by impressing upon him the size of the estate he would leave to the couple.

The exact details of the prenuptial agreement between the parents are uncertain. Later accounts agree that Sir Francis paid £1750 sterling as his daughter's portion. Gifford's petition of 1636 claimed the following in addition: the Lord Chancellor was to estate £1500 worth of lands in England and Ireland upon his son, including the family estate at Monasterevan, in Kildare, with the understanding that the gift would amount to much more depending on the Chancellor's future fortunes; he was to allow the couple to reside at Monsaterevan, or provide them with comparable living conditions; furnish Robert with £200 in rents for maintenance; and supply Eleanor with a jointure worth £300 per annum. Other witnesses added that Rush was 'to procure the King's letter for settlement of his foot company on Robert Loftus'.[91]

The real issue was not the details themselves, but whether the Chancellor would sign his name to them. At the time of the wedding (held in Monasterevan), with the Rushes pressing him, Loftus pleaded the need to consult certain 'writings' in Dublin before he would sign the marriage contract. To allay the mother-of-the-bride's concerns that what was promised might not be delivered, Loftus reportedly assured her that 'the day that I break with you or prove false to you or yours God confound me'.[92] The ceremony, thus, went off as planned. The Rushes would spend much of the next decade seeking the formalization they failed to get from Loftus on that first day of the families' union.

In his frequent refusals to sign his name to any document formalizing the prenuptial promises, the Lord Chancellor appealed to his honour and rank. To Sir William Cooley, the go-between who had brokered the match, Loftus reportedly complained that the Lady Rush had heard his words and that committing them to paper was fit only for 'mechanical men and tradesmen and not between men of their quality'.[93] In response to her

---

[90] Essex County Record Office, D/DL L56/13, bundle 19 (hereafter, *ERO*).

[91] Ibid.   [92] Ibid., bundle 5.

[93] Ibid., bundle 4. Also appears in bundle 1 as 'fit to be done by mechanical men and not between persons of their quality'.

requests to have matters in writing, he reportedly 'in a disdainful manner answered her and said "you need not be so importunate for a jointure for your daughter, for any great portion she did bring to her husband, there is not a Clerk in Dublin that marries a wife but he will look to have as great a portion as your daughter's was"'.[94] He was not merely stonewalling, but attempting to best the Rushes at their own game by volleying the onus of honour back to them. He focused not on the signature but on the regrettable fact that they were so 'ordinary' as to require such a thing in the first place. Thus, he questioned their honour by implying that they were impugning his. Moreover, the Chancellor sought to make them suffer for their by-the-letter exactitude by portraying himself as one who not only would perform what he promised – that is, prosecute the original contract – but who would provide more to his son 'than in strictness he was tied to' – an offer that was off the table should they formalize the original details.[95]

All this manoeuvring may not have moved the Lord Chancellor to sign the papers, but it did destabilize the Rushes' marriage. Sir Francis apparently said he would no longer be advised by his wife, Mary, in matching any of his daughters, having just 'thrown one away'.[96] Mary acknowledged she had negotiated and agreed to the match, but defended herself on the grounds that she had worked assiduously to get the particulars in writing. Embittered and despairing, Sir Francis on his deathbed is reported to have replied that 'If the oaths and imprecations of a Christian were not as great a bond as any writing he knew not how to trust any man.'[97] Nor was his anguish restricted to the fate of his daughter; he was dreadfully concerned about his own reputation to posterity. Having been duped and abused in Eleanor's match to Robert Loftus, he 'feared he should dye branded a foole'.[98] Fool or not, Rush died in 1629 with his daughter Anne unwed.

The matching of Anne would bring the Deputy into the story, for she would eventually marry his younger brother George. The experience of the protracted and contentious wrangle with the Lord Chancellor would shape Mary Rush's negotiations with the Wentworths. Refusing to be 'branded a foole' in her own right by settling for a less than airtight agreement, she took a hard line with the Deputy. Wentworth – responsible for the negotiations as he was the eldest brother, and their father deceased – worked diligently to present himself as the honourable counter to Loftus' dishonourable handling of affairs. In doing so he not only sought to secure the match, but to

---

[94] Ibid., bundle 20.   [95] Ibid., bundle 4.   [96] Ibid., bundle 20.   [97] Ibid.   [98] Ibid.

actively instruct Ireland's elite, particularly the Lord Chancellor, in proper aristocratic comportment.

For each complaint that Mary Rush (now Mary Jephson, as she had subsequently remarried Sir John Jephson, an English military officer) had lodged against the Chancellor over the years, there was a corresponding prenuptial wrangle with the Deputy. But whereas Loftus shirked responsibility for promises made, and impugned the honour of those who enquired after them, Wentworth presented himself in his letters to the Jephsons and Anne Rush as a model of patriarchal norms and gentlemanly honour. Loftus, for instance, had been accused of not having estated upon Robert and Eleanor the lands he had pledged. When Wentworth promised Sir George and Anne £500 lands in Ireland, Mary demanded that it be executed prior to the ceremony. Wentworth pleaded that there was not enough time to do so, and therefore arranged for them to enjoy the rents of his lands at Maynooth and Naas, lands of value well in excess of £500.[99] Mary had long complained that Robert and Eleanor were denied maintenance money while living with the Chancellor at Monasterevan, and that they were constrained to contribute to their own room and board costs and those of their servants and horses.[100] Wentworth, by contrast, assured the parents that the couple would be 'most wellcome to live with me soe long as I stay in Ireland, and their diet and house cost them never a penny'.[101] The conflict with Loftus centred, of course, on his not formalizing promises made to bring about the marriage. Wentworth sought to effect prior to the union as many of the provisions to which he agreed with Mary as he could. On the military preferment promised George, the Deputy wrote to Mary's husband Sir John Jephson in September 1634 that he had already made George a captain in Army, 'which will be a meanes in the Conclusion to free you from any concearned feare or doubt in the ambiguity or uncertainty of the observance'.[102] Above all Mary was determined to see any outstanding promises formalized: 'I hould it not fitting that my daughter should upon thes last proposicions mad unto her be drawne to a finiall conclution afore the estat and joynture wer fully perfected and assured'.[103] For his part, Wentworth too was at pains to bind himself to the perfection of what he had pledged. Unlike the Lord Chancellor, he willingly committed the details to writing and attached his name to them. To Anne Rush herself he wrote that

---

[99] Wentworth to Anne Rush (20 Feb 1634/35, Dublin). Str P 8/192–3.   [100] *ERO*, bundle 20.
[101] Wentworth to Sir John Jephson (24 Sept 1634, Dublin). Str P 8/153–4. For an almost verbatim sentiment, see Wentworth to Anne Rush (last of April 1634, Dublin). Str P 21/115.
[102] Wentworth to John Jephson (24 Sept 1634, Dublin). Str P 8/153–4.
[103] Mary Jephson to George Wentworth (3 Dec 1634, Froyle). Str P 14/222.

should he not respect these promises, 'this paper might recorde me a person neither of faith, nor honour among men'.[104] This point he made even more emphatically two months later, declaring that were he to 'faile [her] in one Tittle, or to performe every point of that which you have under my hand concerning his Estate, let this handwriting rise up in judgement againt me, and expresse me to the whole world the unworthyest Creature that lives'.[105] Both sides, then, worked to ensure there would be no repeat of the Rush–Loftus saga.

Wentworth also played heavily upon his own family's honour as a means to secure the match. Here again was a clear counter to the troubled Loftus household. The strategy was also due, in part, to the fact that George was neither the lone nor the wealthiest of Anne's suitors. Rumour suggested that Sir George would not be able to win her hand as he was a younger son and she sought greater 'preferment' in England.[106] The promise of a well-ordered and honourable household was meant to offset more materially substantial offers. 'You may find a better fortune elsewhere', Wentworth cautioned Anne directly, 'but nowhere else more affection than in this family; where you are desired too, I assure you, much more for the Confidence wee have in your vertue, than for the fairnesse of your por-tion'.[107] His own personal honour stood behind the claim: 'I take my self in honour and common honesty bound to endeavour all that ever I can [to make you happy] which here I vow in the faith of a gentleman I will most intentively apply myself unto with all the witt and power I have.'[108] Moreover, he further gave his word as security for his brother's future conduct as her husband: should George treat her unkindly, he pledged to 'hold him ever after, for the unworthiest man livinge, and should never esteem him'.[109]

What surely gave this promise, and its attendant threat, substance was the fact that Sir Robert Loftus, Anne's brother-in-law, was experiencing that very fate at the hands of his father the Lord Chancellor. Wentworth's

---

[104] Wentworth to Anne Rush (last of April 1634, Dublin). Str P 21/115.
[105] Wentworth to Anne Rush (18 Nov 1634, Dublin). Str P 8/162.
[106] Robert Smyth to Secretary Nicholas (3 Sept 1634, Dublin). *CSPI*, 17, p. 76.
[107] Wentworth to Anne Rush (23 Aug 1634, Dublin). Str P 8/146–7.
[108] Wentworth to Anne Rush (20 Feb 1634/35, Dublin). Str P 8/192–3.
[109] See, also, Str P 8/150–2: Wentworth to Anne Rush (24 Sept 1634, Dublin), in which Wentworth contrasts George's love for Anne with the young Jephson's covetousness. Wentworth was quite concerned about Jephson's advances, since they both were at Froyle. He wrote to George how he would not be sure of business with Anne, 'till I see Mrs Ruishe on this side for till then shee will be still open to their practises on that side. I have therefore intreated my Lady Loftus to be instant with her to hold her resolution, of comeing over the next spring'. Wentworth to George Wentworth (18 Feb 1634/35, Dublin). Str P 8/188.

contemporaneous knowledge of that fact suggests that the parallels between his words and actions and those of Loftus were more than just coincidence or the rhetorical norms of matchmaking. That Wentworth was cognizant of the problems between the Lord Chancellor and his eldest son is made explicit through a series of letters concerning disputed rentals in the Ulster plantation. These were held by Trinity College, Dublin, and leased to Sir Francis Rush in his lifetime. At his death his widow Mary held them. They came up for renewal in 1634, at which point there emerged a three-way contest for them involving Mary and her new husband Sir John Jephson, Sir Robert and Eleanor Loftus, and a third party, Sir Henry Tichborne. Wentworth used his influence to secure the lucrative lease for the young couple on the grounds that the Lord Chancellor was unlikely to leave them any of what he had promised before their marriage or anything befitting their social rank. The only potential problem here, however, was whether the Deputy's actions would anger Mary Jephson and so negatively affect George's courting of Anne. Mary indeed was angry, but Wentworth simply attributed that to her husband's wanting the lands, confident that 'in private she probable understands that no ill's been done her in the matter'. Still, he was concerned how Anne might react, suspecting that her mother had complained to her about the matter. In a letter to George, he detailed the fundamental reason why he believed Anne would understand and forgive his decision on the Ulster rentals:

… she will heare upon her Coming hither [that is, from England], that considering how my Lord Chancellor is wrought upon, in favour to Sir Edward Loftus, and my Lady More, in prejudice of Sir Robert, and especially of his little daughter; shee will I say (her quality considered) find little Nan Loftus, will well stand in need of as much help in her future preferment as an other for I doe not find the Chancellor like to leave a plentifull fortune either in present to his Sonne, or in the future to his grandchild. I have and shall doe all I can to stay the old man, and to decline him as much as I can from an act so unjust and dishonourable, But so strongly doth the old Lady, and those her younger Children, worke upon his affections, as I know not what good I shall be able to effect for my Lady Loftus and her Children, But all I can doe I will doe.[110]

By neglecting the responsibilities of aristocratic and family honour, the Chancellor and his wife had left Robert and Eleanor at the mercy of the state. Wentworth, as self-proclaimed champion of Caroline honour, stepped into the breach to serve as proper father figure to a couple unjustly disinherited. Not all contemporaries shared this view, and the Deputy had

---

[110] Wentworth to George Wentworth (18 Feb 1634/35, Dublin). Str P 8/189.

to counter rumours that he had secured the lease for the pair merely to boost George's chances of winning Anne's hand and had no intention of carrying through with it once the match was completed.[111] Worse yet, he had to counter whispers that his favouritism was due to improper affections toward Eleanor.[112] Whatever the 'real' motivation behind his actions, Wentworth was aggressively presenting himself as a model of gentlemanly behaviour in contradistinction to the dishonourable comportment of Loftus.

Nor was that modelling for Anne's eyes alone; Wentworth was at the same time trying to broker a rapprochement between the Chancellor and his eldest son. By early 1636, things between the two had degenerated to the point where Robert was intending to leave Ireland to pursue his fortune abroad. Of this the Deputy had not been informed; when notified he was not pleased, it being the law to seek executive permission before leaving the realm.[113] In February Sir Robert wrote to apologize for this breach of law and etiquette and to explain his surreptitious planning. He begged Wentworth to understand that his leaving was necessary on account of his father's declining favour, and that to have gone through the process of securing permission would merely have made this family tragedy a greater public scandal than it already was. He had tried, he assured Wentworth, to last out what he hoped would prove but a temporary lapse in paternal favour, yet the Lord Chancellor's decision to pass his estate and title on to the younger brother, Edward, escalated the situation beyond hope of repair. He despaired that his father was also intending to favour Edward with 'our land in Yorkshire, the Ancient seat of our Family, And with it gives from mee that am his heire, the Bones of my Ancestors'. Nor could he fathom why his brother – single and childless – should be so favoured while 'I and mine must ever expect howbeit the heires both of the house and honour'. As for the Chancellor's decision that in the event of Robert's and Eleanor's deaths, all their property should go to Robert's sister, the Lady Moore, and none to his own daughters, this was not only a transgression of honour but also a clear violation of 'Common Law'. Yet for all his father's alleged mistreatment, Sir Robert would speak no ill of him and blamed matters

---

[111] Wedgwood, *Wentworth: a revaluation*, p. 242.

[112] Wedgwood notes the rumours, but dispenses with the idea that there may have been an affair. Ibid.

[113] This relates to the decree that people may not leave Ireland without official approval. Sir Robert Loftus to Wentworth (21 March 1636, Youghal), Str P 8/379. This decree of the King's of 17 September 1635 is referred to in a letter from the Lord Deputy and council to Coke (8 May 1638), *HMC various*, 3, p. 175: 'whereby all the nobility and undertakers and others who hold estates or offices in this Kingdom (such persons only excepted as are employed in his Majesty's service in England, or attend there by his special command) should reside here and not depart hence for England or any other place without the privity or licence of me, the Deputy'.

on unnamed confidants of his father's. He therefore wished to leave Ireland not merely to support his family financially, but also to avoid becoming the object of public derision or finding himself pitched into battle against his father. 'Nor is it only to avoyd to be a looker on upon my owne sad tragedy,' he wrote, 'but much more to avoyd being an actor in my owne Ruin by signing or doeing any thing tending to the prejudice of my Children, or by the refuseing of what my lord may require at my hands, seeme to be guilty of the least disobedience of a Father, having hitherto preserved my self from any such foule stayne'.

Nor would the father cast aspersions on his son. Wentworth sent the Chancellor a copy of his son Robert's letter – a clear sign that he was still deemed a friend, or at least a man to be reasoned with – and asked after its charges. The Chancellor responded with the fantastic claim that the letter could not have been the work of his son and must be a forgery. This he explained by stating that 'the Laws of God, of Nature, & Man, have ordained the Father to be the aptest the most fitt & equall Judge betwixt his owne children, And to that end requires a strickt obedience from them to their father's Command & layes a malediction upon them that despiseth the same'. The work was surely that of evil plotters, he wrote, and he suspected the notorious Dr Atherton to be behind them.[114]

Wentworth took the elder Loftus' response to be a dodge, chided him for not discussing the actual charges levelled, and urged him to settle matters while damage limitation was still an option. Professing a reluctance to get involved, he urged the reparation of the circle of honour about this family: 'it becomes me not to meddle betwixt friends soe neare, and in businesse of soe tender a nature. Only I shall wish there may be that right understanding betwixt you, as may be for the future peace and Honour of your House.'[115] But, of course, Wentworth *was* willing to meddle, and did so in very explicit language. He criticized at length Loftus' conduct over the marriage settlement of Sir Robert and Eleanor:

… I beseech you, albeit you can, and yet being justly and respectively moved to manifest this intention by Sir Francis Ruishee in his life tyme, Sir John Jephson and his Lady, and lately by my brother and Sir John Gifford, authorised unto by their mother, you have ever ridgidly refused to doe it, as if persons too meane for your

[114] Adam Loftus to Wentworth (2 April 1636, no place given). Str P 8/382. Atherton's appointment to an ecclesiastical post had been held up by the Lord Chancellor; see *LW*, 7, p. 302. On Atherton generally, see Aidan Clarke, 'A woeful sinner: John Atherton', in V. P. Carey and U. Lotz-Huemann (eds.), *Talking sides? colonial and confessional mentalités in early modern Ireland: essays in honour of Karl S. Bottigheimer* (Dublin, 2003), pp. 61–77.
[115] Wentworth to Adam Loftus (28 March 1636). Str P 8/367.

Lordship to vouchsafe the smallest satisfaction unto. How can this comply with those promises they pretend you, upon soe great and valewable Considerations, made unto them before marriage of lands to be estated, of present Maintenance, and Jointure to be provided, And if all that your eldest sonne must trust to, are Intentions that were, not expressing what they now are, Secret ones, only known to yourselfe, whilest you doe in soe lardge a measure upon all occassions declare your love in publick professions and authentike Acts to the advantage of your younger sonne, your Daughter the Lady Moore and their Children, out of the Course of all indifferent affection or Nature, for any thing that you are pleased to make appeare, How can it be said that noe cause of your sonns departure or discontentm[en]t can be in the least degree whatsoever ascribed to your Lo[rd]ship? Certainly if it be to be granted that Sir Robert Loftus hath the ordinary emotions of either sonne, father or husband it can not Choose but infinitely, in all these respects greeve and discomfort him, to see himselfe Wife and Children, thus neglected and postposed contrary to all ground of Desert, Justice or Nature.[116]

From specific criticisms of the Chancellor's conduct toward Sir Robert, Wentworth then employed a more abstract rhetoric, hoping to move the elder Loftus by reminding him that the duties of a father weighed on Sir Robert as well, he being the father of two girls:

My Lord I acknowledge the parentall power and Authority is very Great and Justly given by all Law and reason; yet as many of the Casuists as I have heard of, how strickly soever they restraine a Child to a passive Suffering yet doe they not bind him in an active Concurrence to his owne Disinherison, And it is to be Considered That as hee is a Sonne to you, soe is hee alsoe a Father to his Children, And I Have good authority to say that if hee had not an equall and provident regard towards them hee were worse than an Infidell, which goes very farre, if not in a Justification, yet in Certaine Greatly to Excuse and attenuate what misconstruction soever can be put upon him.[117]

Sensitive to the authority and power invested in a male head of household – both theoretically and practically – Wentworth knew he was pushing the boundaries of propriety himself by intruding in the matter. To his mind, however, the situation demanded just such a breach of familial autonomy.

This correspondence was but one episode in an extended effort on Wentworth's part to bring the dispute to arbitration and so keep it from the courts and further public consumption. Eventually the Chancellor agreed to have the Deputy arbitrate the settlement of his estate.[118] The timing was bad, however, for Wentworth was on the point of travelling to England. Upon his return he again found the Chancellor unco-operative, the latter declaring that in regards to the settlement 'he always meant to

---

[116] Wentworth to Adam Loftus (4 April 1636). Str P 8/383–6.   [117] Ibid.   [118] Ibid.

keep a power of revocation in his hand, and that rather than part with that power he would be torn in pieces by wild horses'.[119] Things were now turning personal for Wentworth and he believed his own honour was getting bruised in the affair. Following this rebuke by the until recently conciliatory Lord Chancellor, the Deputy was 'with shame enough inforced to excuse myself to Lady Jephson, to crave pardon for Rashly assuming more power then I found was measured out for me by his lordship' and he swore he would no longer serve personally as an arbitrator in the dispute.[120]

It must have been apparent to contemporaries that resolution was doubtful. Wentworth certainly thought so, and thus redoubled his efforts to make sure that the leases in Ulster he had secured for Sir Robert and Eleanor were finalized. The assistance of Bishop Bramhall of Derry was essential in securing these leases. In a letter to him, Wentworth discarded the veneer of civility he had hitherto adopted in his dealings with the Lord Chancellor and gave vent to his true feelings. There were, he wrote, some rents due at Clones and the Trinity College lands and he desired Bramhall to gather and send them with all speed since Eleanor Loftus 'had no money left by her husband [Sir Robert having gone abroad], and must of necessity provide for paying the College rent, for returning money over to her husband, and furnishing herself and children; for, poor Lady, there will be no living for her with the Chancelour, and that fury his Lady; so as you see it is as well a Christian charity to help so noble and so abominably a misused creature'.[121] The way forward, then, would lead through the courts, and in full public view.

It was Gifford's petition, presented to the Lord Deputy in February of 1637, that precipitated the move of the Loftus–Loftus–Wentworth dispute into the courts. The petitioner, the half-brother of Eleanor, was spurred to act by the couple's formal disinheritance. With Robert abroad, Gifford took it upon himself to steer the matter through the official channels of restitution. The case would usually have gone through Chancery – but a Chancery case against the Lord Chancellor offered little prospect of success. Thus the matter landed at the Deputy's feet in the Court of Castle Chamber. Three times between 14 March and 25 April 1637 the Chancellor, at the behest of the Deputy and Council, answered the petition; not once did he meet its charges head on. An angry Wentworth reported to Coke that Loftus'

---

[119] Ibid.; see also Wentworth to Lord Keeper (23 April 1638). Str P 10 (A)/116–18.
[120] Wentworth to Lord Keeper (23 April 1638). Str P 10 (A)/116–18. The letter is a reflection on the evolution of the case, thus the later date.
[121] *The Rawdon Papers*, ed. E. Berwick (London, 1819); Wentworth to Bramhall (23 April 1636), pp. 24–6.

answers were 'soe frivolouse that it seemed rather a scorne to the table than otherwise'.[122]

This was a conflict of the greatest gravity – involving as it did Ireland's two chief officers – and reports of it to court had to be handled delicately. Wentworth assured Coke of his continued concern for Loftus' well-being and described the escalation of the proceedings as a necessary, if unfortunate, means towards the ultimate goal of defending the King's honour: 'I confess I wish well to his Lordship's person, but such is the zeale I have to my master's Honoure and Justice, that I would rather his Lordship then they should suffer.'[123] Coke forwarded the King's permission to take the seal from the Chancellor if he would not conform to the administration's orders.[124] Not only did Loftus refuse to conform, but he fled Dublin to Monasterevan 'in Contempt of the order of the board'. Nor would his son Edward, transferred from England by messenger to help resolve the matter, co-operate. Come December, Wentworth decided the only way forward was to formally call witnesses. With third-party depositions in hand, the Deputy and Council ruled in the petitioner, Gifford's, favour in February 1638.

In a long, passionate speech before the Council Board, Wentworth introduced the Board's decree on the matter and explained the reasoning behind it.[125] The existence of overwhelming evidence suggesting that the Chancellor never intended to honour the promises made to the Rushes was, Wentworth declared, crucial to an understanding of the Council's judgment. Summing up the Council's findings, the Deputy declared that when the families were collected at Monasterevan for the wedding, Loftus had pretended 'that his writings were at Dublin; so yt no performance was then, nor as yet is. And heer, I pray you, see my Lo: Chancellor's covert carriage, and cunning dealing, that never intended anie thing lesse, when as yt only he would conferre upon this without anie witnesses whatsoever, and still by fayre and smooth words keepe them off'.[126] Such conduct, he went on, was unconscionable in 'him, that is the Chief in the High-Court of Chancerie, where Conscience only ought to be manifest, and to be expected'.[127]

Defending the decree in the court of public opinion was a more difficult, though no less necessary, task. To silence whispers about the impropriety of a son prosecuting his father, Wentworth declared that Robert had always

---

[122] Wentworth to Coke (3 April 1637). Str P 9/218.
[123] Ibid.   [124] Coke to Wentworth (25 April 1637, Whitehall). *Strafforde letters*, 2, p. 69.
[125] SP 63 256/56.   [126] Ibid., p. 5.
[127] Ibid., p. 7. Wentworth went on to illustrate the point with the story of Solomon, but unfortunately the manuscript is torn and so cuts it off.

been a dutiful son who trusted to his father's love.[128] Responding to that question's inverse – namely should Robert unconditionally defend his father? – the Deputy gave assurance that

the dutie of the sonne bindeth him not to the father for the ruin of him and his. True it is, that in case the parent were in danger, or wanted, ye sonne is to afforde all helpes and assistance to provide for the father, but not to suffer his owne ruine; wch plainly may appeare in the strange, and un-Christianlike carriage of my Lord, yt preferreth the Lady Moore and her offspring, and Sir Edward and his children … before his naturall sonne, the oldest.[129]

As for the seeming oddity of the daughter-in-law being the one, through her half-brother Gifford, seeking redress, Wentworth stated that her request 'in all conscience and equitie cannot be denied. Ffor who shuld seeke for the daughters help more than she! Or who can be more wronged in this, then the noble Ladie? Or what restitution can be sufficiently made unto her in this case, that hath lost her virginitie and years, and being brought to that exigent, readie to starve!'[130] He added that she, like her husband, had had no interest in going public with the dispute but had instead repeatedly begged her father-in-law to settle matters. Just recently, with the aged Chancellor in poor health, she had managed to get his promise for the jointure.[131] But having given his word to his daughter-in-law, to her face, he then gave the agreed lands to his other children. Turning to the defendant, Wentworth said, 'my Lord, you are like a cunning fencer, that smiles and laughes at his fellow to his face, and gives him a sore blow unexpected; and that without word'.[132] Wentworth further charged the Chancellor with having been as niggardly in his maintenance as he had been dishonest in his provision of lands. He was to have supported the couple at Monasterevan to a standard commensurate to their status, yet 'the noble Ladie upon her oath hath declared, that she never had so much as a smock, or a new gowne, to herself or her children, to this howre' but had to ask her mother for money for clothes.[133]

It was a delicate matter when the authorities of home and state entered into conflict, especially when a noble house was in question, but here the derogations of patriarchal duty and honour were so blatant that the state had no choice but to intervene. As Wentworth described it, however, state intervention should not only protect sons and daughters, but should also serve to return erring lords to the path of virtue:

[128] Ibid., p. 8. [129] Ibid., p. 9. [130] Ibid., p. 10. [131] Ibid., p. 11.
[132] Ibid., p. 12. [133] Ibid., p. 13.

ffor as he [the King] hath power to give honour; so is it no lesse in his power to preserve it. And this may we know by all the lawes of good policie and nature whith have their power, to preferre one before another, and to preserve the houses of great men, and their original luster, and not to suffer their ruine and destruction, for the honour of the crowne; which courses have alwaies been taken, not only heer, but in other nations. Witnes in Spayne a great Grandee, being debaist, by the State confined, his debts to be payde, and his portion allowed, and became afterwards a vertuous and good man …[134]

At stake in this family honour squabble was not only the honour and lustre of a noble house, but that of the King and state also.

Whatever its effects on the Lord Chancellor's character, the Board's decree hit him hard in the wallet.[135] Monasterevan and the viscountcy were to pass to Sir Robert, and Edward's inheritance was reduced to a £200 annuity. Was this a grossly disproportionate award, Sir Robert getting so much, his brother so little? Certainly not, the Board had reckoned, for 'it was esteemed a sufficient competencie for a Viscounts younger sonne; comparing with the Case with the Earl of Northumberland, who left his youngest sonne but £600 a yeare, and his eldest sonne above £30,000 to my knowledge'.[136] This was an explosive judgment against a great officer of state and peer, a thorough dismantling of his honour and reputation combined with a heavy material imposition. Nevertheless, there was hope that an amicable outcome could still be negotiated. Observers as diverse as Robert Loftus (happy with the outcome) to the Lord Keeper (less pleased), encouraged Wentworth to proceed gently with the Chancellor and find a resolution that would heal the wounds of the scandal for all parties involved – including the state.

A happy ending would prove elusive. In part this was because the personal bitterness between Deputy and Chancellor continued to deepen. In May, Wentworth complained to the Keeper of Loftus' 'haughty disdainfull looks and carriage, [which] soe scandalized all his fellow councellors, despiseing them as person over meane in ranke and understanding to be admitted his judges'.[137] A veteran of many honour battles, the Deputy nonetheless declared himself to have been in this affair 'all along so damnably abused, as is almost above patience to be born, and hath, to speak truth, more vexed me, than anything that ever befel me in all my life'.[138] In part the inability to reach settlement was the product of a wave of new complaints against the Chancellor. These included charges of irreligion (for

---

[134] Ibid., pp. 13–14.   [135] The decree is printed in *HMC Report IX*, Part ii, pp. 303–6.
[136] SP 63 256/56, p. 17.   [137] Wentworth to Lord Keeper (7 May 1638). Str P 10 (A)/120–2.
[138] Wentworth to King Charles (6 August 1639, Naas). *Strafforde letters*, 2, pp. 375–7.

non-attendance at church), a general inability to respect the honour of great men (he was accused of having insulted and dishonoured the Earl of Kildare), and, most damningly, of tyranny in office. The most spectacular allegation was that he had imprisoned a Chancery suitor, one Fitzgerald, without cause and against his will. This general disrespect for the offices of government and the men who held them was then made manifest in Loftus' refusal to kneel before the Council Board when the decree in the marriage case was read. Here Loftus literally made his stand against the Deputy and the Dublin administration. On 20 April 1638 the Deputy and Council unanimously voted to sequester the Chancellor, and he was arrested the following day.

Loftus' subsequent imprisonment attracted just the sort of public attention to the case Wentworth had hoped to avoid. His intense fear of court intervention in his governance of Ireland had driven him all along to try to settle the matter quickly and quietly. From the time of the original petition he had begged correspondents to keep quiet about the matter.[139] This was difficult since Loftus was busy publicizing the case at home and abroad: he appealed directly to the King to effect his release so that he could come to England to petition his case,[140] and he wrote to powerful court figures asking for their intervention on his behalf. In the wake of Loftus' arrest in April, the affair was the talk of London. Garrard reported, 'this late commitment of the Lord Chancellor there makes a great noise here'.[141] Richard Hutton's comments echo Garrard's, for he found it 'loudly and frequently spoken of, being a matter very rare, and of great consequence, and full of expectation' – just what Wentworth feared.[142] There was one dissenting voice on this issue, Newcastle's. As for the business 'with the Chanselor', he comforted Wentworth, 'I heer little of Itt, so little as Mee thinkes heer they doe nott Care Iff you hange him … There was a bit at first but it died off. I thinke it is no great matter'.[143] Yet Newcastle seems to have been as wrong as he was singular in his judgment. Even Laud confessed how troubled he was over the affair's reception in England, but 'only for the public and not in regard of your

---

[139] See, for example, his letter to Coke of 3 April 1637. Str P 9/218.
[140] This, incidentally, Wentworth took as a further affront. The first appeal by Loftus to the Deputy and Council did not come until August 7, which Wentworth took as a sign of the former Chancellor's lack of respect for the Irish administration and the men who filled it. *HMC various*, 3, p. 191.
[141] Garrard to Wentworth (10 May 1638, Charter-house). *Strafforde letters*, 2, pp. 164–8.
[142] Richard Hutton to Wentworth (13 June 1638, Serjeants Inn, Chancery Lane), ibid., pp. 177–8. See Str P 10 (A)/120–2: Wentworth to Lord Keeper (7 May 1638) for Wentworth's fear that the commitment of Loftus would spark an outcry in England.
[143] Newcastle to Wentworth (25 June 1638, St James). Str P 18/57.

private at all.'[144] Finding himself once again having to defend from afar his actions, Wentworth began a damage-limitation exercise.[145]

Of prime concern was the Queen's opinion. Loftus had an ally in the Earl of Holland, who Wentworth suspected was using the affair to further poison his already low reputation with Henrietta Maria. As such, Wentworth was eager to give the impression that formal proceedings against the Chancellor had been pursued with great reluctance and, when they were, with the purest of intentions. On the first count, he wrote to her secretary Sir John Wintour that

> … the Lord Chancellor by himself and agents hath so wantonly slighted and unduly calumniated the proceedings of this council therein, that less than a public hearing will not by this whole state be pressed and sued for from his Majesty, as the only fit way to vindicate the honour of the proceedings, and their own good name to the world, every of us taking himself to be concerned equally, one as deep as the other.[146]

On the second, he sought to convince the Queen and her party that this was, plain and simple, a matter of honour and household order, not of politics. Having assured Wintour that the Council's decision was just, and that it was the Lord Chancellor's side that was wanting in 'honour, conscience, nature, or common honesty', Wentworth went on to explain the case in a way that excised the elements of derogation of duty and official irregularity and tyranny. All the additional charges introduced in the wake of the 1638 decree disappeared in this return to first principles. The case, he argued, was about the natural deserts of a young noble woman and bride, and the responsibilities invested in a matchmaking father: 'the question there in effect being no more than, whether a lady nobly descended, that brought her husband an estate better than fifteen thousand Pounds, should be provided … according to the Lord Chancellor's own clear agreement with Sir Francis Rush Father to the Lady.'[147] Yet justice was in danger from that 'unclean-mouthed daughter of his, the Lord Moore's wife, [who] busieth herself up and down the court, affirming with her accustomed truth, that the Chancellor hath done all appointed for him, yet cannot procure his liberty; which is very false'.[148] Here he portrayed Anne as the

---

[144] Laud to Wentworth (8 Oct 1638). *LW*, 7, p. 488.
[145] Julia Merritt, 'Power and communication: Thomas Wentworth and government at a distance during the Personal Rule, 1629–35', in Merritt (ed.), *Political world of Thomas Wentworth* (Cambridge, 1996), pp. 109–32.
[146] Wentworth to Sir John Wintour (20 Oct 1638, Dublin). *Strafforde letters*, 2, pp. 227–8.
[147] Wentworth to Wintour (20 Oct 1638, Dublin). Ibid., p. 227.
[148] Wentworth to Wintour (10 Dec 1638, Dublin). Ibid., p. 257.

perverse product of a disordered household. It was the moral duty of the
Crown and its more honourable servants to aright the wrongs brought by
her and her father's unnatural actions.

Unfortunately for the Deputy, court intrigue was not the sole threat
awoken by this public scandal: there were the inhabitants of Dublin to
contend with as well. Wentworth feared the immediate, larger Irish public
and the effects the case would have on its conduct and deference toward the
government. English historians are just now probing the public sphere of
the metropole; we know next to nothing of its shapes, behaviours and
demography in Ireland. Yet there clearly was such a beast, and the Loftus
affair – not to mention the whole Wentworth deputyship itself – was the
sort of occasion on which it could open wide and threaten to disrupt the
functioning of politics as envisioned by the Crown and its appointees. As
early as April 1638, immediately following the decree, he was 'unable without amazement to hear myself reported, nay cried out aloud in the Streets,
to be Outrageous, where verily I take myself to be the Patient; and that
intirely for the Service of my Master'.[149] Over the remainder of the year the
Council would call additional witnesses to look into the marriage settlement
and other charges, and attempt to secure the Chancellor's co-operation.
Onlookers in Dublin closely followed all the developments. As the following comments to Laud make clear, Wentworth grew increasingly fearful of
the Irish populace and its clamour over the Chancellor's fate:

… this state is soe generally scandalized by his Neglect, Pride, and foule Language,
and concerning [?] the Honour thereof soe ingaged, as they could not be persuaded
to leave out that which they judged materiall to manifest the truth to his Majesty.
The offence he gives here unto them is not to be credited allmost, such [in/is?] good
saddnesse as I am become the most moderate of all the Company, yet are we not
transported beyond reason neither, and very rightly judge the issue of it as the
Approaching Settlement or Disturbance of this Government. & in the sorrie sense
and expectance every day shews us the whole Kingdom lookes after it allsoe, for
when any part of the cause comes to be questioned you would wonder to see what a
presse of people are still gott into the Chamber, and how there are a company of ill
and mutinous affected persons runn presently up and down the Towne, magnify-
ing all his Lordship's unmannerly language and carriage as Acts of great Bravery and
Courage, which occassions them here to sett their harts and rests [?] upon it
exceedingly and not without cause, for whither this tends you know as well as I
can tell you.[150]

---

[149] Wentworth to Charles I (22 April 1638). Ibid., p. 161.
[150] Wentworth to Laud (12 Feb 1638/39). Str P 7/162v.

To this he added thoughts on what constituted a proper trial of a great officer's conduct:

my Catholike Rule is thus. If you be not satisfyed in your Deputy doe not prophane soe high an Authority as is lodged in him, in the sight of this people, but send for him home in the name of God; there let all be fairely and clearly heard. If the Deputy be in fault, punish him as deeply as you can, But on the other side, if acquitt before your justice, let him have Honour, Publick Justification, and his Accusers lege talionis suffer the same Shame for their false as he have done for their true information. And this I thinke you a great Bishop will say is Orthodox.[151]

Agitation against the administration, then, was not restricted to the great and to the rooms and corridors of the Castle, but spilled out into the streets and most likely travelled quite far down the social ladder.[152]

The Loftus affair, in the end, exemplifies the role of honour in the politics of the Wentworth deputyship. Wentworth clearly thought his role in Ireland was one of socio-cultural, as well as administrative, reform. The protracted debate with Loftus over the latter's conduct toward his son and daughter-in-law pays eloquent tribute to his desire to make Irish elites British. Yet to his dismay, and eventual undoing, that definition was more vigorously contested than he had envisaged. London's court intrigue and Dublin's popular unrest, both of which having been awakened by his conflict with the Chancellor, brought home quite clearly that the future shape of that multi-national polity would be determined as much by the words and actions of those operating on the geographical margins of the three kingdoms as by those emerging from the metropolitan centre. The issue of kneeling before the Council – a seemingly inconsequential act of deference that proved so instrumental in exacerbating the Wentworth–Loftus feud – beautifully encapsulates the extent to which, or so Wentworth feared, people would go to counter the authority of the state once they lost their respect for and fear of it. When the Lord Chancellor was ordered to kneel before the Board, 'he answered that it was more than ever he saw done by a person of his quality, and it again being urged him, he said

---

[151] Ibid., p. 163r–v.

[152] See Thomas Cogswell on the political effects of popular displeasure with state policy, 'England and the Spanish match', in Richard Cust and Anne Hughes (eds.), *Conflict in early Stuart England* (London, 1989), pp. 283–303. See also Bellany, *The politics of court scandal*, on the circulation of news and rumour and their role in undermining governmental legitimacy. For the role of news and rumour in Irish society and politics, see Raymond Gillespie, *Reading Ireland: print, reading and social change in early modern Ireland* (Manchester, 2005), and Mícheál Ó Siochrú, 'Propaganda, rumour and myth: Oliver Cromwell and the massacre at Drogheda', in Edwards, et al. (eds.), *Age of atrocity*, pp. 266–82.

he would not kneel, he would die first'.[153] Such melodramatic posturing Wentworth saw as symptomatic of the loss of Crown authority in those troubled times, and it worried him desperately. Newcastle wrote to Wentworth that June, assuring him that people were not so concerned about the Loftus affair as the Deputy feared. The reason Newcastle gave for this – that English eyes were focused on Scotland – brought Wentworth no comfort.[154] He saw Loftus' dishonour and disloyalty, and that of the Scots, as complementary parts of one unsavoury whole: 'I do very much fear', he wrote to the King concerning the Chancellor's intransigence, 'if the honour and justice of this state be not in this particular vigorously born forth against his untruths and incivilities, the regal authority will perchance be shortly as much invaded, as roughly dealt with in this kingdom as in other places'.[155] The reference to Scotland is clear, as is the fear that many others were willing to 'die first' before they would bow to the authority of the Crown and its appointed representatives.

Historians and literary scholars have identified honour culture as fundamental to understanding English politics of the 1620s and 30s. This chapter has detailed three aspects of Wentworth's political career in order to explore the larger 'British' dimensions of that culture. It has argued that the defence of honour, so important to Charles' rule in England, was deemed equally important in the governance of Ireland. Moreover, it has suggested that the serial offences against monarchical honour coming out of Ireland made the island a priority in that defence. Wentworth certainly made the restoration of proper vertical honour bonds – based in the person of the King and mediated through himself, the King's personal representative in the realm – a priority in his deputyship. This is not to argue that he was indeed honourable, merely that he presented himself as such and that he judged people and read events through the frame of honour. Recognition of that fact forces us to consider the cultural aspects of 'Thorough'. Not simply concerned with absolutist power politics or self-aggrandizement – the focus of the prevailing historiography – Wentworth attempted a reformation of manners through which New and Old English grandees would abide by the principles of true honour. In doing so, he followed a pattern that marked his political career in England; a concern for honour imperatives defined his

---

[153] Proceedings of the Lord Deputy and Council concerning the Lord Chancellor (19–26 April 1638), *HMC Report IX*, appendix 2, pp. 170–3.
[154] Newcastle to Wentworth (25 June 1638, St James). Str P 18/57.
[155] Wentworth to Charles I (9 September 1639, Dublin). *Strafforde letters*, 2, p. 387.

tenure as Lord President of the Council of the North as much as it did his spell as Lord Deputy of Ireland.

Yet there were important differences. Wentworth had numerous enemies in England, but against none of them could he have so fundamentally challenged the natural rights of an aristocrat as he did when quarrelling with Clanricard. The colonial nature of Stuart Ireland, with its attendant civilizing language, allowed him to aggressively contrast the honour of office against that of title and family in a way that would have been unimaginable in England. His ability to tar Clanricard with stereotypes of the tyrannical Irish chieftain undercut what would otherwise have been a virtually unassailable position as peer of the realm. The fact that Clanricard was a peer of two realms left him more vulnerable to Wentworth's attacks than had he held the earldom of St Albans alone. There was a Caroline fascination with the restoration of true nobility, and Wentworth's actions reveal its hold on the official mind beyond English borders.

Turning to the Loftus affair, Wentworth's protracted dispute with the Lord Chancellor illustrates perfectly the importance of cultural matters to Anglo–Irish politics. This was not a clash of cultures pitting Irish against English, however, but one between two Englishmen holding high office in Ireland over gendered codes of family honour. In a way, what Wentworth was attempting with Loftus was little different to what he had attempted with those men who challenged his honour in the north of England: Ellis, Bellasis and Foulis. Ireland once again was yet another theatre in the Caroline politics of honour. But as with the Clanricard case, Ireland's colonial status allowed for aggressive persecution of a peer. It seems unlikely that Wentworth could have so fundamentally intruded in the business of an aristocratic household had Loftus been an English peer. The Deputy's intrusive and patronizing efforts to school Loftus in the particulars of right conduct only seem possible in an Irish context; only there, where the nobility were already suspect in honour, civility and loyalty, could he so systematically tutor a peer and chancellor. Moreover, the case suggests limits to recent suggestions of the peacekeeping aspects of family honour, and of women's roles in such peacekeeping, once we extend our gaze outside England.[156] Here it was Loftus' wife and daughter, as much as the Chancellor himself, who were tearing the family apart. Differing notions of family honour, and of the state's role in their governance, led to this clash that Laud considered the greatest of Wentworth's deputyship.

---

[156] Pollock, 'Honor, gender, and reconciliation'.

Wentworth's quarrels with Clanricard and Loftus highlight the need to see Caroline honour culture within a 'British' perspective. Without the Nine Years' War, Clanricard would never have entered the English peerage. But without the colonial project in Ireland, he would not have crossed swords with the Lord Deputy over the plantation of Connaught. In his conflict with Clanricard, Wentworth was fighting a very odd battle: Burke was an Irish-born, Old English Catholic, who was nevertheless his social superior and based at court while Wentworth fought his side from Dublin. Burke was also a paragon of neo-chivalric honour, a fixture in England's culture of heraldic performance, and seemingly a model of the Caroline restoration of nobility. And yet Wentworth could attack him for blocking the spread of civility to the darker corners of Charles' realms. With Loftus, too, Wentworth was waging a curious little war. Unlike Clanricard, Loftus was English-born and not of noble parentage. Nevertheless, he used the opportunities offered in colonial Ireland to rise socially and politically. Here, then, Wentworth was engaged in a struggle with a fellow country-man, but one who had gone native in the provinces and seemingly refused to bow to the commands of the governor he was sworn to obey. The origins of these quarrels must be seen in their 'British' contexts, and so must their implications. Charles and Wentworth's inability to restore true honour to Ireland would play a role in bringing on the deluge that would claim them both.

Conclusion

In 1641 Rory O'More and Phelim O'Neill, two gentlemen planters of Gaelic stock, plotted and carried out an uprising against the government. Their plan was simultaneously to occupy strongholds in Ulster and Dublin Castle; their goal was to set themselves up in a position of strength from which to wrench from the Crown the privileges and authorities they felt were their due. The Ulster Rebellion, or 1641 Rising as it is variously known, thus began as something of a variation on baronial revolt.[1] O'More and O'Neill did not seek the overthrow of English authority or the restoration of an exclusively Catholic Church, but rather they aimed to re-insert themselves into the ruling oligarchy by seizing the machinery of government.[2] These men were not holy warriors or the vanguard of an assertive ethnic or nationalist identity, but rather subjects who had received lands in the plantation and wielded state-sanctioned local authority. What provoked them to rise was their falling status and power within the system to which they had pledged themselves, the crushing debt they had assumed in their planting schemes, and the petty insults of those who had risen above them. By forcing the Dublin administration to surrender, they hoped to make it regrant them the status and authority they believed befitted them in the British province of Ulster. Honour politics still mattered one hundred years after Henry VIII was made King of Ireland. At this time, however, it was a dangerous game to play: the uprising of limited ends envisioned by O'More and O'Neill was quickly drowned in the deluge first of religious, then of nationalistic, forces as general insurrection swept the island.[3]

[1] See Jane Ohlmeyer, 'The baronial context of the Irish civil wars', in J. S. A. Adamson (ed.), *The English Civil War: conflict and contexts, 1640–49* (New York, 2009), pp. 106–24. I wish to thank Prof. Ohlmeyer for allowing me to read this paper pre-publication.
[2] Clarke, *Old English in Ireland*, pp. 161–2.
[3] On the violence of the early months of the rising, see Nicholas Canny, 'What really happened in Ireland in 1641?', in Jane Ohlmeyer (ed.), *Ireland from independence to occupation, 1641–1660* (Cambridge, 1995), pp. 24–43.

One of the first victims of this re-emergence of rebellious honour politics had been none other than the Lord Lieutenant himself, Sir Thomas Wentworth (recently made Earl of Strafford), attainted by the English Parliament and executed the previous May. Ostensibly he was sentenced for treason, that is, for allegedly conspiring to raise an army in Ireland to use against the King's opponents in England. But damning as well, in both its volume and its details, was the testimony of those on the receiving end of his (Wentworth's) failed reformation of manners in Ireland. Clanricard and Loftus were but two of the Irish elites who regaled Parliament with tales of 'Black Tom Tyrant's' oppressive rule of the King's subjects and his complete disregard for the nobility's rights and privileges. In addition to their concerns over property, constitutional rights and good government, they were enraged by Wentworth's aggressive rejection of the claim to honour made by Irish elites of all stripes.[4] The politics of honour had produced strange bedfellows under St Leger's plan of surrender and regrant in the 1540s, pairing together as it did Gaelic and English nobles to form a new 'British' aristocracy. To Wentworth's undoubted dismay, matters of honour continued to bring about odd political matches a century later, when he was faced with Catholic, Protestant, Old English and New English enemies. Like the rebels O'More and O'Neill, Wentworth found this a dangerous time to play the politics of honour, for the stakes were now life and death.

The larger casualty of the wars of the 1640s was the politics of honour itself – at least as it had been conducted over the previous century. A British culture of honour was built upon a foundation of bridgeable social/cultural difference: the notion that English and Irish elites inhabited the same wider orbit of European aristocracy. The horrors of the Protestant massacre at Portadown and other atrocities of 1641 (real and invented), however, would go a long way towards justifying and spreading the harshest anti-Irish views propagated by England's theorists of the civilizing mission. The Irish became not just enemies, but inherently dangerous and irredeemable ones.[5] Yet they were not simply pawns in an emergent politics of difference dictated from London. The setting up of a Confederate parliament in Kilkenny by the Irish 'rebels', and that body's declaration of legislative independence, put the seal on this sense of divergence and unbridgeable division.[6] Moreover, the arrival

---

[4] For a recent overview of motivating factors behind Irish attacks on the Deputy, see Canny, *Making Ireland British*, especially chapters 6 and 7.

[5] Keith J. Lindley, 'The impact of the 1641 rebellion upon England and Wales, 1641–5', *IHS* 70 (1972), pp. 143–76.

[6] On independent Ireland, 1641–9, see Jane Ohlmeyer, 'Introduction. A failed revolution?', in Ohlmeyer (ed.), *Ireland from independence to occupation*, pp. 1–23.

of a Papal nuncio at Kilkenny would extinguish the prospect of Irish Catholics as a loyal segment of the population and would further raise the temperature of religious conflict in Anglo–Irish relations. From that point on it would prove significantly more difficult to cross the confessional divide in pursuit of status and place than it had at any time since Henry VIII's reign.[7] What began in Ulster as an attempt to shuffle political personnel – very much a species of honour rebellion – ended with Cromwell's call of forced migration of the Irish to reservations in the west, a plan enshrined in the famous phrase 'To hell or Connaught'. Honour politics were perforce a changed factor in Anglo–Irish relations: after 1641, matters of honour, nation and religion – always present on the same stage, yet frequently able to act independently – would intersect and overlap much more intimately.

Looking back over the hundred years covered in this study, it appears that the revolutionary changes of 1541 opened up all three of these forking paths in the Anglo–Irish theatre of British state formation: confessional difference/conformity, national determination/union, and neo-feudal assimilation/aristocratic resistance. The creation of the Church of Ireland, with Henry VIII as its head, pointed the way towards either religious unification or separation; the government's making Ireland a kingdom helped establish it as a corporate entity, as a political, social and cultural unit commanding its own political recognition.[8] But matters of faith and *patria*, so fundamental to determining the character of Anglo–Irish relations (and British relations more generally) from 1641 on, did not drive the initial stages of British state formation in the mid sixteenth century. Instead, it was the attempts at a concordance among the realms' nobles, capitalizing on significant points of socio-cultural contact, that did so.

It is no surprise that assimilation was the first tactic pursued in making both Ireland and England part of a multiple monarchy. From the English perspective it was inexpensive (the bribes St Leger offered his surrendering subjects were a mere fraction of the cost of waging a war), structurally uncomplicated (it mapped onto existing power structures), and had great potential to stabilize relations by creating a single ruling caste centred on the monarch. It was an approach welcomed by many Irish elites, too, both

---

[7] Tadhg Ó hAnnracháin, *Catholic Reformation in Ireland: the mission of Rinuccini, 1645–49* (Oxford, 2002). But see John Morrill on Cromwell's attitude to Catholics, and the origins of his conduct at Drogheda. Morrill, 'The Drogheda massacre in Cromwellian context', in Edwards, et al. (eds.), *Age of atrocity*, pp. 242–65.

[8] For the argument that Irish national imaginings were largely a result of the Tudor state's 1541 designation of Ireland as a constitutionally defined political unit, see Steven Ellis, *Ireland in the age of the Tudors*, pp. 259–64.

Gaelic and 'English-Irish'. For those wishing to see their status rise (or at least not fall) in the new dispensation, it provided a clever and very useful strategy. Especially as the sixteenth century wore on, one could not maintain status by making a stand on religion or national consciousness. These were inherently divisive issues, appeals to which best served those, like James Fitzmaurice, interested in resistance. And even after the Nine Years' War and the emergence of a mature discourse of faith and fatherland, there were many Irish elites (Gaelic and Old English alike) who believed they could live and prosper within the new British dispensation.[9] The language of honour provided perhaps the best means for them to succeed in that effort.

This is understandable once it is remembered why honour served, as stated in the introduction to this study, as the social glue of early modern societies. On the one hand, power was intensely personal in this period, and thus the 'individual/personal' and the 'collective/public' were inseparably intertwined. Honour, inasmuch as it involved both spheres, held great political importance. On the other hand, the social hierarchy, connected as it was by the rights and responsibilities of vertical honour, was deemed divine and one of the chief guards against social and political chaos. An appeal to honour, then, played into concerns for the defence of hierarchy shared by people across Europe, regardless of nation, faith or ethnicity. Socially, there could be no equivalent to Western Europe's political and religious model of *cuius regio, eius religio* ('whose the region, his the religion'). Whereas people had come by the end of the sixteenth century to accept that there would be numerous sovereign polities, and that some would be governed by heretics, others by minions of the Antichrist, no one accepted the view that executive authority should be wielded by the base-born and socially illegitimate. That was unthinkable. Consider the fate of the Anabaptists. Their theology may have offended, but it was their social practices that positively scandalized. It was the threat of social chaos seen as inherent in their theology, rather than its unorthodox precepts in their own right, that drew the wrath of Europe's Catholic and Protestant leaders down upon them.[10] Seen in this context, the anxieties over social levelling and/or inversion voiced by Gaelic lords like Hugh O'Neill and poets like Muiris Mac Gearailt were not simply expressions of pre-modern Gaelic conservatism. Instead, they were expressions of a concern more fundamental than

---

[9] Ó Buachalla, 'James our true king'; Clarke, *Old English in Ireland.*
[10] See H. P. Hsia, 'Munster and the Anabaptists', in Hsia (ed.), *The German people and the Reformation* (Ithaca, 1988), pp. 51–69.

that produced by religious or proto-national difference, and one shared by all of Europe's ruling classes: fear of a world turned permanently upside down.

One of this book's chief aims has been to give concerns over status and secular hierarchy a more prominent place in the study of Anglo–Irish relations. Recent scholarship has delineated the roles played by ideologies of civility, faith and fatherland in those relations; this has transformed, and continues to transform, our understanding of the period. It does not explain, however, the very real efforts at cultural convergence – at least on the elite level – in the mid sixteenth century, or the efforts of Gael and Gall alike to make a space for themselves in late Tudor and early Stuart Britain. To take a few examples from the previous chapters Connor O'Brien could have bardic poets at his installation as 3rd Earl of Thomond; Hugh O'Neill, architect of a 'faith and fatherland' ideology of resistance to the Tudor state, could live with a Protestant monarch; and Tadhg Ó Cianáin, narrator of Counter-Reformation Gaelic honour, could reveal an interest in the Swiss confederation of 'heretics' and Catholics. Not one of these men, however, would countenance having an underling lord it over him. Gaelic Irish and Old English elites would spend much of the period under consideration here (and later) attempting to argue the compatibility of loyalty to both Rome and London; they would also adapt to new cultural forms and adopt the trappings of the new civility. By contrast, they would not, and did not, accept the elevation above them of their social inferiors. That the Crown was willing to allow upstarts and 'mechanical' men to wield power over those of noble blood was scandalous to Gaelic and Old English elites alike, and diminished their respect for the government. Did the state itself not respect hierarchy? If not, its power would lack legitimacy and the honour claims of its servants would be difficult to affirm.

If the Irish grew suspect of the honour of Crown and Castle, the English came to the point of simply rejecting that of the Irish. The reasons for this are numerous. Most frequently cited are Gaelic Irish refusal to follow anglicized patterns of civility, and Gaelic and Old English rejection of religious reform.[11] But as argued above, native rejection of innovative cultural and religious forms was not pre-ordained. Indeed, the state-building tool of surrender and regrant was based on perceived cultural compatibility and the possibility of assimilation. Why then did English actors go from accepting Irish honour claims to rejecting them? In part this rejection came about because it benefited the interests of officials, soldiers

[11] Braddick, *State formation*, pp. 380, 394.

and planters. Denying the claims to honour of Irish elites, and thereby weakening their ability to hold office and high status, meant more opportunities for the newcomers. The English, like the Irish, also had recourse to the charge of their opponents' perfidy. Stung repeatedly by what they felt to be Irish double-dealing, many New English simply discounted the Irish as inherently untrustworthy, and so dishonourable. This was not, however, simply an English–Irish, or Protestant–Catholic, dynamic. Wentworth's clashes are evidence of one of the more curious aspects of British intervention in Ireland: the repeating phenomenon of one generation of English officials distrusting that which came before. It is not the case, therefore, that there were set 'honour codes' in England and Ireland and that these proved incompatible, or that one modernized while the other remained mired in the medieval. Rather, there was progressive unwillingness on the part of people in both polities to accept claims to honour made across religious, ethnic, national and – vitally in the 1630s – political lines.

Whatever the specific reasons or interests behind that unwillingness, Ireland's status as colony provided the framework through which native Irish claims to honour could be rejected. As the freshly minted realm took on the character of a colony, its people became less subjects than subject peoples, and its elites no longer members of a pan-European nobility but unwanted charges of a conquered nation. In turn, the discourse of English civility and Irish savagery provided the intellectual grounds for the denial of Irish honour claims. Once deemed savages, ancient elites could be cast from the bonds of both horizontal honour (by denying them status as British nobles) and vertical honour (by discounting their loyalty as subjects). The early days of conflict in 1641 demonstrate the differences in how Irish and English combatants saw their opponents' suitability for honourable treatment. In the chaos that followed the outbreak of rebellion in Ulster, the Gaelic Irish demonstrated their respect (or fear) of social hierarchy and attacked only those deemed their equivalents and left their superiors alone.[12] The New English, however, showed no such restraint. Able as they were to deploy the language of savagery, and so to dismiss Irish claims to honourable status, the English saw no meaning in native hierarchies. Once cast 'outside the protection of honour and humanity', everyone became a potential victim.[13]

---

[12] Kenneth Nicholls, 'The other massacre: English killings of Irish, 1641–3', in Edwards, et al. (eds.), *Age of atrocity*, pp. 178–9.
[13] Barbara Donagan, 'The web of honour: soldiers, Christians, and gentlemen in the English Civil War', *The Historical Journal* 44 (2001), p. 389. See, too, Mícheál Ó Siochrú, 'Atrocity, codes of conduct and the Irish in the British civil wars 1641–1653', *P&P* 195 (2007), pp. 55–86.

The influence that colonialism had on the British culture and politics of honour was not purely of the constitutional and ideological varieties, however. It had a complementary structural element, too, produced by the disruption that Tudor expansion brought to kinship bonds. How this affected Gaelic notions of honour is self-evident: the move to primogeniture and the cutting off of claims to lordship from the extended family (*deirbhfine*), fraught as it may have been, transformed traditionally horizontal honour bonds (those linking potential claimants to a lordship) into vertical ones (those between the dynastic line and its cadet branches).[14] Of similar importance, though perhaps less obvious, is the case of the New English. Honour in England was intimately linked to local reputation and the maintenance of the collective honour of the extended family.[15] Removed to cities and settlements in Ireland, English men and women were cut loose from those bonds and forced to construct new ones. Given the newness and instability of the Irish urban experience and of plantation life, these were always going to be pale reflections of the original.[16] It is little surprise, then, that English planters and officials played up loyalty to the state and the power of the law when using a language of honour to claim status, compete for place, and resolve disputes. Nor is it surprising that they acted individualistically and in favour of the interests of the nuclear family: they simply had little other choice, cut off as they were from long-standing lineage networks that had helped to organize society and regulate behaviour.[17] The seeming modernity of English honour claims in Ireland may be less intentional, and more structural, in origin than has generally been supposed.[18]

Honour as operative throughout 'British' England and Ireland, therefore, was an oddly and awkwardly syncretic entity. Its character is only partly

---

[14] Canny, 'Hugh O'Neill, earl of Tyrone'.

[15] Cust, 'Catholicism, antiquarianism and gentry honour'; Pollock, 'Honor, gender, and reconciliation'.

[16] Movement to English cities also disrupted kinship structures. See Bryson, *From courtesy to civility*, for the relationship between urban migration and the adoption of new patterns of civility. The contention here, however, is that Irish urban society offered the more disorienting experience on account of its distance from England and the novelty of New English ascendancy.

[17] A parallel may perhaps be seen in the Normans' need for centralized justice when establishing their rule in England and Scotland, kinless as they were in their new territories. Jenny Wormald, 'Bloodfeud, kindred and government in early modern Scotland', *P&P*, 87 (May, 1980), pp. 54–97.

[18] Steven Ellis has argued that the appearance of northern English and Irish societies as lineage societies is actually a product of Tudor governmental mismanagement of those areas and not a sign of their backwardness (that is, they were not mired in pre-modern social forms but had actually regressed due to misgovernment). My contention here is that the supposed modernity of those who came to govern in those regions was not purely a factor of their having been bearers of advanced, metropolitan sensibilities. Rather their seemingly modern appeals to the law and the state were largely a result of their not having any local connections through which they could work to resolve disputes, advance interests, and so on. See Ellis, *Tudor frontiers*.

explainable by attempts to describe it in national isolation. Irish bards may have been more aggressive in making the connection between Gaelic cultural forms and noble honour, but they also plied their trade for New English masters; Gaelic nobles may have looked to defend faith and fatherland, but typically this was done as a last resort when other arrangements seemed lost. Many aspects of 'English honour' also look different when viewed from a British perspective. The much vaunted diminution of violence among English elites, and the correlative preference for internalized virtue over chivalric display as the nobleman's defining trait, evidently disappeared once those men made the short trip across the Irish Sea. Complicated, too, is the notion that honour was a prerequisite for office: those captains and soldiers who terrorized the Irish provinces, martial law commissions in hand, hardly seem to fit any scholar's definition of early modern English concepts of honour. In short, attempts to essentialize Irish or English honour, or to periodize their developments, are deeply problematized by expanding our field of focus to encompass a broader British context.

If the British context is important to understanding Anglo–Irish honour culture, surely that cultural factor is no less vital to making sense of British state formation. Consideration of matters of honour suggests three ways in which the development of the Tudor–Stuart dynastic state may have differed from continental trends.

First, the British experience may diverge from what seems the accepted trajectory of European state formation. Recent historical work has lain to rest the hoary theory that early modern states consolidated their strength by taming their nobilities. The rise of the state is now seen as more of a process of mutually beneficial negotiation between monarchs and traditional elites.[19] This appears to have been the case in England; but less so in Ireland. Not all Tudor and Stuart provincial elites were English, and not all English-born nobles held their titles at 'home'. How the centralizing state interacted with these men also needs to be borne in mind when looking at British state formation in a European context. And if the relations between central government and Irish provincial nobles were defined by negotiation throughout the period 1541–1641, after that date they certainly were not.

Second, it appears that the 'British' aristocracy may have been less resilient than other European nobilities. Scholars agree that definitions of honour changed dramatically in the period covered by this book. England

---

[19] See William Beik, 'The absolutism of Louis XIV as social collaboration', *P&P* 188 (2005), pp. 195–224. For overviews of prevailing views on the relationship between states and nobilities, see Asch, *Nobilities in transition*, and Dewald, *The European nobility*.

and Ireland were no exceptions. Importantly, however, the literature also tells us that this did not mean that ancient elites were replaced wholesale by modern ones who had adopted the new honour's trappings. Instead, members of the traditional ruling class simply used their place and power to ensure that they were the arbiters of the new honour too. As numerous comparative studies of Europe's nobilities argue, this may have been the case in England. In Ireland, however, it was not. Definitions of honour underwent great change there as well, but so too did the ranks of the nobility. The great families of Ireland circa 1641 were not the great families of Ireland one hundred years earlier. Demographic change, as much as continuity, marks the early modern experience of British aristocracy.

Third, Ireland may have been unique in that it fits neither of the two prevailing models of state formation: state-driven taming of the nobility, or state–noble interaction. We have already noted the unsuitability for Ireland of the latter model. As for the former, Ireland's traditional nobles were certainly humbled, but not in the way theorists of the rise of civil society postulate. This was not a case of an independent-minded aristocracy browbeaten into submissive loyalty by an aggrandizing bureaucratic state, or of a warrior class forced to adapt to novel codes of civility in order to compete with a rising noblesse de robe for monarchical favour.[20] (Indeed, the Crown itself was frequently the Irish nobility's greatest ally and advocate against the predations of 'mechanical men' and religious bigots.) Nor were these traditional Irish elites replaced by a well-educated bureaucratic class, loyal to the state that created them, but by a wholly new nobility. Curiously, however, these new Irish nobles were typically upstarts of English or Scottish birth – planters, officials and non-resident peers-for-pay who had used the novel opportunities presented in colonial Ireland to rise to very traditional-looking positions of status and authority. That wholesale change in the ranks of the nobility was driven less by state pressure from above than by the incessant undercutting and provocation of social inferiors. Who was the major power broker in early Stuart Ireland and the wealthiest man in Britain? Richard Boyle, commoner of Kent and colonial land speculator extraordinaire. Who was the bane of the Gaelic lords who accepted earldoms through surrender and regrant? Less the Crown than the petty captains and provincial officials like the Bagenals and Binghams who found martial law commissions much more to their liking than honour principles. Although

---

[20] There is evidence, however, for the government having favoured the lesser nobility over the aristocracy by the late sixteenth century. See Canny, *Elizabethan conquest*, p. 98. More broadly, see Hans Pawlisch, *Sir John Davies and the conquest of Ireland: a study in legal imperialism* (Cambridge, 2002: new edition).

conservative English observers would decry the low-lives who inhabited the Cromwellian regime of the 1650s, the Irish had seen this phenomenon long before. But to say that Irish complaints over change were mere conservatism misses the point. S. J. Connolly has argued that eighteenth-century Ireland displayed many of the characteristics of a typical European *ancien régime* society, most notably a hereditary elite lording it over a disenfranchised majority. But the social origins of that class suggest that there was very little about that *régime* that was *ancien*. Indeed, Anglo–Irish high politics in the period 1541–1641 presented not a textbook case of the taming of the nobility, but rather a realization of that European-wide nightmare of the power elite: a world turned upside down in which the low-born governed the high.

Perhaps the great irony in the story of the politics and culture of honour in Britain and Ireland, 1541–1641, is that as Anglo–Irish culture came to look more uniform, so the divisions between its elites became more marked. Chiefly this occurred after 1641 when national and confessional differences came to dominate in a way they could not have in 1541. Appeals to ancient lineage, loyalty or virtue as a means to trump those divisions became less successful. English and Gaelic sources alike attest that in the 1640s honour claims would have to accommodate the sterner stuff of faith and fatherland. The religious face of honour in England is well-described in the literature, and so the last word here will be given to the Gaelic Irish. On completing the great historical synthesis of Irish annals, *Annala Ríoghachta Éireann*, Mícheál Ó Cléirigh declared the project to have been undertaken 'for the glory of God and the honour of Ireland' (*dochum glóire Dé agus onóra na hÉireann*).[21] Likewise, the changed fortunes of the politics of honour were reflected in a bardic composition addressed to Hugh O'Reilly in which *eineach* and *uaisle* were described as wandering the land in search of a home.[22] This was not a motif without precedent, but appearing in the middle-to-later seventeenth century imbued it with a certain pathos and almost self-conscious archaism.[23] 'Where will honour (*eineach*) and nobility (*uaisle*) find a home?' the first stanza asks rhetorically. The answer, naturally, is with Hugh, son of Toirdhealbhach O'Reilly, the subject of the composition. But it is significant that this Hugh was no latter-day Gaelic lord, but rather a priest. Even in the supposedly backward Gaelic Ireland (or at least its remnants), honour may have remained important, but it nevertheless had difficulty finding a home, or even a protector, outside of religion.

---

[21] Quoted in Ó Buachalla, 'James our true king', p. 21.
[22] Carney (ed.), *Poems on the O'Reillys*, poem 27, pp. 135–9.
[23] Carney notes that the poem marks an attempt to write in an outmoded style and thus has an 'antiquarian' feel to it. Ibid., p. 231.

The culture of honour operative across England and Ireland did not disappear in 1641. This book has not attempted to chart a 'rise and fall' of British honour politics so much as explore its transformation over time. The fact that division and difference (religious, national and ethnic) have dominated Anglo–Irish relations for centuries has served, however, to obscure the very existence of a cross-realm culture of honour and its place in the story of British state formation. In reconstructing some of the main aspects of that culture, and describing elements of its attendant politics, this book has argued that Anglo–Irish cultural difference, while very real and often tragically so, is not solely constitutive of the two polities' relationship. In recent years, historians have been chastised for forgetting the violence of sixteenth-century English–Irish interaction. Doing so, it is argued, whitewashes that history of its tragic element. This is a salutary reminder. But nor should we forget the long history of cultural affinity and interplay between the two societies. In light of this history, we can better understand both the efforts at harmonizing the realms after 1541, and the very personal character that resistance to state centralization frequently took in Ireland. In both cases, appeals to noble honour played a crucial role.

Bibliography

MANUSCRIPT SOURCES

BRITISH LIBRARY

Add MS 4821, 'commonplace book of James Ware'
Add MS 36856
Add MS 64,898
Add MS 29587, Hatton-Finch papers
Cotton Titus B XI
Harleian MS 38 and 983
Lansdowne MS 323

ESSEX COUNTY RECORD OFFICE, CHELMSFORD

D/DL L56/9, L56/13

KENT COUNTY RECORD OFFICE, MAIDSTONE

Drury Halstead MSS

LAMBETH LIBRARY

Carew MSS

LINCOLN'S INN

Hale MS 83

OXFORD UNIVERSITY, BODLEIAN LIBRARY

MS Selden Supra 125
North, MS b. 1
North MS c. 7

PUBLIC RECORD OFFICE: KEW, LONDON

PRO SP 63: State Papers, Ireland
PRO STAC 18/84/18, 18/84/19: Burke v. Clark, et al.

SHEFFIELD CITY LIBRARIES

Wentworth Woodhouse Muniments (consulted on microfilm)

NATIONAL LIBRARY, IRELAND

G. O. MS 158

TRINITY COLLEGE DUBLIN

TCD MS 842: Rothe's biography of Ormond

PRINTED PRIMARY SOURCES

Acts of the Privy Council of England, 1532–1631, 46 vols (London, 1890–1964), 1613–14.
Aithdioghluim dána, 2 vols, ed. and trans. Lambert McKenna (Dublin, 1935 and 1939).
The Annals of the Four Masters, vols I–VI, ed. and trans. John O'Donovan (Dublin, 1856).
The Annals of Loch Cé: a chronicle of Irish affairs from A.D. 1014 to A.D. 1590, 2 vols, ed. and trans. William M. Hennessy (London, 1871).
Bacon, Francis. *The works of Francis Bacon,* 10 vols (London, 1824).
Bergin, Osborn. *Irish bardic poetry* (Dublin, 1974).
Calendar of the Carew manuscripts preserved in the archiepiscopal library at Lambeth, 6 vols (London, 1867–73).
Calendar of state papers relating to Ireland, 24 vols (London, 1860–1911).
Calendar of state papers and manuscripts relating to English affairs, existing in the archives and collections of Venice … (London, 1864–1947).
Calendar of state papers preserved in the Public Record Office, domestic series, 81 vols (London, 1856–1972).
The letters of John Chamberlain, 2 vols, ed. Norman McClure (Philadelphia, 1939).
'Chichester letterbook', ed. R. D. Edwards, *Analecta Hibernica* 8 (1938), pp. 3–177.
'Clanricard letters: letters and papers, 1605–1673, preserved in the National Library of Ireland manuscript 3111', ed. Bernadette Cunningham, *Journal of the Galway Archaeological and Historical Society* 48 (1996), pp. 162–208.
Curtis, Edmund and R. B. McDowell (eds.). *Irish historical documents, 1172–1922* (London, 1943).

Davies, Sir John. *A discovery of the true causes why Ireland was never truly subdued and brought under obedience of the crown of England ...* (Washington, DC, c1988).

de Brun, Pádraig., Breandán Ó Buachalla and Tomás Ó Concheanainn (eds.). *Nua-Dhuanaire* I (Baile Atha Cliath, 1971).

'A discourse between two councillors of state, the one of England, and the other of Ireland' – Egerton MS 917, ed. Aidan Clarke, *Analecta Hibernica* 25 (1970).

Farmer, William. 'A chronicle of Lord Chichester's government of Ireland ...', in *Desiderata curiosa Hibernica or a collection of state papers* (Dublin, 1772), pp. 151–326.

Gerald of Wales. *The history and topography of Ireland*, trans. with intro. John J. O'Meara (London, 1982).

Greville, Fulke. *The life of the Renowned Sir Philip Sidney* (1652): a facsimile reproduction with an introduction by Warren W. Wooden (New York, 1984).

Hadfield, Andrew and Willy Maley (eds.). *A view of the present state of Ireland: from the first printed edition (1633) / Edmund Spenser* (Oxford, 1997).

McLaughlin, Joseph. 'New light on Richard Hadsor, II: select documents XLVII: Richard Hadsor's "Discourse" on the Irish state, 1604', *Irish Historical Studies* xxx (1997), p. 349.

Ó Donnchadha, Tadhg (ed.). 'in Lae Ó Mealláin', *Analecta Hibernica* 3 (1931), pp. 1–61.

Ó Raghallaigh, Thomas. *Duanta Eoghain Ruaidh Mhic an Bhaird* (Galway, 1930).

Quinn, D. B. *The Elizabethans and the Irish* (Ithaca, 1966).

'The bills and statutes of the Irish Parliaments of Henry VII and Henry VIII', *Analecta Hibernica* 10 (1941), pp. 71–170.

Sorlien, Robert Parker (ed.). *The diary of John Manningham of the Middle Temple 1602–03* (Hanover, NH, 1976).

Vossen, A. F. (ed.). *Edmund Campion's two bokes of the histories of Ireland* (Assen, 1963).

Historical Manuscripts Commissions
  - D'Lisle and Dudley MS
  - Report IX, appendix 2
  - Salisbury MS
  - Various Collections III

Iomarbhaidh na bhfileadh; the contention of the bards, ed. and trans. Rev. L. McKenna (London, 1918).

Journals of the House of Commons of the Kingdom of Ireland, 1613–1791, 25 vols (Dublin, 1753–91).

Journals of the House of Lords of England (London, 1767).

Keating, Geoffrey. *Foras feasa ar Eirinn: the history of Ireland*, 4 vols, ed. and trans. David Comyn and P. S. Dinneen (London, 1902–14).

Trí biorghaoithe an bháis, ed. Osborn Bergin (Dublin, 1931).

Kinsella, Thomas (ed. and trans.). *The new Oxford book of Irish verse* (New York, 1989).

Laud, William. *The works of the most reverend father in God, William Laud D.D.* 7 vols (Oxford, 1857).

Lebor gabála Érenn: the book of the taking of Ireland., ed. and trans. R. A. Stewart Macalister (Dublin, 1938–56).

Letters and papers, foreign and domestic of the reign of Henry VIII, eds. J. S. Brewer, J. Gairdner, R. H. Brodie, et al. 21 vols in 32 parts, and addenda (London, 1862–1932).

Macalister, R. A. Stewart (ed. and trans.). *The story of the crop-eared dog and the story of eagle-boy: two Arthurian legends* (Dublin, 1908).

Duanta Eoghain Ruaidh Mhic an Bhaírd ed. and trans. Thomas, Ó Raghallaigh (Gaillimh, 1930).

Mac an Bháird, Maolmuire Mac Con Uladh. 'Address to Red Hugh O'Donnell in 1590', in Pádraig Breathnach, 'Select documents XL: an address to Aodh Ruadh Ó Domhnaill in captivity, 1590', *Irish Historical Studies* xxv, no. 98.

Dánta Mhuiris Mhic Dháibhí Dhuibh Mhic Gearailt, ed. Nicholas Williams (Baile Atha Cliath, 1979).

Duanaire Mhéig Uidhir: The poembook of Cú Chonnacht Mág Uidhir, Lord of Fermanagh 1566–1589, ed. and trans. David Greene (Dublin, 1991).

Notestein, W., F. H. Relf, and H. Simpson (eds.). *Commons' debates in 1621*, 7 vols (New Haven, 1935).

'Tadhg Ó Cianáin's Flight of the Earls', ed. and trans. Paul Walsh, *Archivium Hibernicum*, appendix to vols 2–4 (1913–15).

Ó Cléirigh, Lughaidh. *Beatha Aodha Ruaidh Uí Dhomhnaill*, 2 vols, ed. and trans. Paul Walsh (Dublin, 1948, 1957).

O'Donnell, Red Hugh. 'The last will of Red Hugh O'Donnell', ed. J. J. Silke, *Studia Hibernica* 14 (1984–88), pp. 51–60.

O'Sullivan-Beare, Philip. *Ireland under Elizabeth: chapters towards a history of Ireland in the reign of Elizabeth*, ed. and trans. Matthew J. Byrne (Port Washington, NY, 1970).

Knott, Eleanor (ed. and trans.). *The bardic poems of Tadhg Dall Ó hUiginn*, 2 vols (Dublin, 1922).

Pairlement Chloinne Tomáis, ed. and trans. N. J. A. Williams (Dublin, 1981).

Poems on the O'Reillys, ed. James Carney (Dublin, 1997).

The Rawdon Papers, ed. E. Berwick (London, 1819).

'Reports of cases in the courts of star chamber and high commissions', ed. S. R. Gardiner, *Transactions of the Royal Historical Society*, vol. 39 (1886).

Rushworth, John. *Historical collections*, I, II, III (London, 1680).

Spenser, Edmund. *A view of the present state of Ireland*, ed. W. L. Renwick (Oxford, 1970).

'An unspeakable Parliamentary fracas: The Irish House of Commons, 1613', ed. John McCavitt, *Analecta Hibernica* 37 (1998).

Wentwozth, Sir Thomas. *The letters and dispatches of the Earl of Strafforde*, 2 vols, ed. W. Knowler (London, 1739).

Wentworth Papers 1597–1628, ed. J. P. Cooper (London, 1973).

SECONDARY WORKS

Adams, Simon. 'Favourites and factions at the Elizabethan court', in Ronald Asch and Adolph Birke (eds.), *Princes, patronage and the nobility: the court at the beginning of the modern age c.1450–1650* (Oxford, 1991), pp. 265–87.

Andrews K. R., N. P. Canny and P. E. H. Hair (eds.), *The westward enterprise: English activities in Ireland, the Atlantic, and America 1480–1650* (Detroit, 1979).

Asch, Ronald. *Nobilities in transition 1550–1700: courtiers and rebels in Britain and Europe* (London, 2003).

'Wentworth, Thomas, first earl of Strafford (1593–1641)', *Oxford Dictionary of National Biography*, Oxford University Press, Sept 2004; online edn, Jan 2008, www.oxforddnb.com/view/article/29056, accessed 25 March 2008.

Aylmer, G. E. *The king's servants: the civil service of Charles I* (London, 1974).

Bailey, Amanda. *Flaunting: style and the subversive male body in Renaissance England* (Toronto, 2007).

Barber, Charles. *The idea of honour in the English drama, 1591–1700* (Göteborg, 1957).

The theme of honour's tongue: a study of social attitudes in the English drama from Shakespeare to Dryden (Göteborg, 1985).

Barry, John. 'Guide to records of the genealogical office, Dublin, with a commentary on heraldry in Ireland and on the history of the office', *Analecta Hibernica* 26 (1970), pp. 3–43.

Beik, William. *Absolutism and society in seventeenth-century France: state power and provincial aristocracy in Languedoc* (Cambridge, 1985).

'The absolutism of Louis XIV as social collaboration', *P&P* 188 (2005), pp. 195–224.

Bellany, Alastair. *The politics of court scandal in early modern England: news culture and the Overbury affair, 1603–1660* (Cambridge, 2002).

Bernard, G. W. 'The Tudor nobility in perspective' in Bernard (ed.), *The Tudor nobility* (New York, 1992).

Braddick, Michael. *State formation in early modern England, c. 1550–1700* (Cambridge, 2000).

Bradshaw, Brendan. 'Cromwellian reform and the origins of the Kildare Rebellion, 1533–34', *Transactions of the Royal Historical Society* 27 (1977), pp. 69–93.

The Irish constitutional revolution of the sixteenth century (Cambridge, 1979).

'Native reactions to the westward enterprise: a case-study in Gaelic ideology', in K. R. Andrews, et al. (eds.), *The Westward enterprise*, pp. 65–80.

'Manus "the Magnificent": O'Donnell as Renaissance prince', in Art Cosgrove and D. McCartney (eds.), *Studies in Irish history, presented to R. Dudley Edwards* (Dublin, 1986), pp. 15–36.

'Nationalism and historical scholarship in Ireland', *IHS* 28 (1993), pp. 227–55.

'Geoffrey Keating: apologist of Irish Ireland', in B. Bradshaw, A. Hadfield and W. Maley (eds.), *Representing Ireland* (Cambridge, 1993) pp. 166–90.

The British problem c. 1534–1707: state formation in the Atlantic archipelago (New York, 1996).

Brady, Ciaran. 'The O'Reillys of East Breifne and the problem of "surrender and regrant"', *Breifne: Journal of Cumann Seanchais Bhréifne* 6 (1985).

The chief governors: the rise and fall of reform government in Tudor Ireland, 1536–1588 (Cambridge, 1994).

Shane O'Neill (Dundalk, 1996).

Breatnach, Pádraig. 'The chief's poet', *Proceedings of the Royal Irish Academy* 83c (1983), pp. 37–79.

'Irish records of the Nine Years' War: a brief survey, with particular notice of the relationship between *Beatha* and the *Annals of the Four Masters*', in Ó Riain (ed.), *Beatha … historical and literary contexts* (Dublin, 2003).

Brigden, Susan. *New worlds, lost worlds: the rule of the Tudors, 1485–1603* (New York, 2000).

Brooks, James. *Captives & cousins: slavery, kinship, and community in the southwest borderlands* (Chapel Hill, 2002).

Brown, E. A. R. 'The tyranny of a construct: feudalism and historians of medieval Europe', in L. K. Little and B. H. Rosenwein (eds.), *Debating the Middle Ages: issues and reading* (Oxford, 1998), pp. 148–69.

Brown, Keith. 'The Scottish aristocracy, anglicization and the court, 1603–38', *The Historical Journal* 36 (1993), pp. 543–76.

Bryson, Anna. *From courtesy to civility: changing codes of conduct in early modern England* (Oxford, 1998).

Bryson, Frederick R. *The point of honor in sixteenth-century Italy: an aspect of the life of the gentleman* (New York, 1935).

The sixteenth-century Italian duel: a study in Renaissance social history (Chicago, 1938).

Burghclere, Lady. *Strafford*, 2 vols (London, 1931).

Caball, Marc. *Poets and politics: reaction and continuity in Irish poetry, 1558–1625* (Notre Dame, 1998).

'Pairlement Chloinne Tomáis I: a reassessment', *Éigse* 27 (1993), pp. 47–57.

'Providence and exile in early modern Ireland', *Irish Historical Studies* 114 (1994), pp. 174–88.

Canny, Nicholas. 'The flight of the earls 1607', Historical Revision XVI, *Irish Historical Studies* xvii (1970–71), pp. 380–99.

The Elizabethan conquest of Ireland: a pattern established (London, 1976).

The upstart earl: a study of the social and mental world of Richard Boyle, first earl of Cork, 1566–1643 (Cambridge, 1982).

'The formation of the Irish mind: religion, politics and Gaelic Irish literature 1580–1750', *P&P* 95 (1982), pp. 91–116.

'Hugh O'Neill, earl of Tyrone, and the changing face of Gaelic Ulster', *Studia Hibernica* 10 (1970), pp. 1–35.

'The permissive frontier: social control in English settlements in Ireland and Virginia, 1550–1650', in Andrews, et al., *The Westward enterprise*, pp. 17–44.

'Taking sides in early modern Ireland: the case of Hugh O'Neill, earl of Tyrone', in Vincent Carey and Uta Lotz-Huemann (eds.), *Taking sides? Colonial and confessional mentalités in early modern Ireland* (Dublin, 2003), pp. 94–105.

'What really happened in Ireland in 1641?', in Jane Ohlmeyer (ed.), *Ireland from independence to occupation, 1641–1660* (Cambridge, 1995), pp. 24–43.

'The attempted anglicisation of Ireland in the seventeenth century: an exemplar of "British History"', in Merritt (ed.), *The political world of Thomas Wentworth*, pp. 157–86.

Making Ireland British (Oxford, 2001).

Carey, Vincent P. 'John Derricke's *Image of Irelande*, Sir Henry Sidney, and the massacre at Mullaghmast', *Irish Historical Studies* 31 (1999), pp. 305–27.

'Atrocity and history: Grey, Spenser and the slaughter at Smerwick (1580)', in Edwards, Lenihan and Tait (eds.), *Age of atrocity*, pp. 79–94.

Carney, James. *The Irish bardic poet; a study in the relationship of poet and patron as exemplified in the persons of the poet, Eochaidh Ó hEoghusa (O'Hussey) and his various patrons, mainly members of the Maguire family of Fermanagh* (Chester Springs, PA, 1967).

Carpenter, Christine. *The Wars of the Roses: politics and the constitution in England, c. 1437–1509* (Cambridge, 1997).

Clarke, Aidan. 'The government of Wentworth, 1632–40', in Moody et al., (eds.), *New history of Ireland* 3 (Oxford, 1976) pp. 243–69.

'Sir Piers Crosby, 1590–1646: Wentworth's "tawney ribbon"', *Irish Historical Studies* 26, no. 102 (1988), pp. 142–60.

The Old English in Ireland, 1625–42 (London, 1966; Dublin, reprint 2000).

'A woeful sinner: John Atherton', in Vincent P. Carey and Uta Lotz-Huemann, *Taking sides? Colonial and confessional mentalités in early modern Ireland: essays in honour of Karl S. Bottigheimer* (Dublin, 2003), pp. 61–77.

Cliffe, J. T. *The Yorkshire Gentry: From the Reformation to the Civil War* (London, 1969).

Cogswell, Thomas. 'England and the Spanish Match', in Cust and Hughes (eds.), *Conflict in early Stuart England*, pp. 283–303.

Connolly, S. J. *Contested island: Ireland 1460–1630* (Oxford, 2007).

Cooper, J. P. 'Ideals of gentility in early modern England', in Cooper (ed.), *Land, men and beliefs: studies in early modern history* (London, 1983), pp. 43–77.

Cunningham, Bernadette. 'Native culture and political change in Ireland, 1580–1640', in Ciaran Brady and Raymond Gillespie (eds.), *Natives and newcomers: essays on the making of Irish colonial society 1534–1641* (Dublin, 1986), pp. 148–70.

'The anglicisation of East Breifne: the O'Reillys and the emergence of County Cavan', in Raymond Gillespie (ed.), *Cavan: essays on the history of an Irish county* (Irish Academic Press, 1995), pp. 51–72.

'From warlords to landlords: political and social change in Galway, 1540–1640', in Gerard Moran (ed.) and Raymond Gillespie (assoc. ed.), *Galway – history and society: interdisciplinary essays on the history of an Irish county* (Dublin, 1996), pp. 97–129.

Cust, Richard. 'Honour and politics in early Stuart England: the case of Beaumont v. Hastings', *P&P* 149 (1995), pp. 57–94.

'Catholicism, antiquarianism and gentry honour: the writings of Sir Thomas Shirley', *Midland History* 23 (1998), pp. 40–70.

'Wentworth's "change of sides" in the 1620s', in Merritt (ed.), *The political world of Thomas Wentworth*, pp. 63–80.

Charles I: a political life (London, 2005).

Cust, R. and A. Hughes (eds.). *Conflict in early Stuart England: studies in religion and politics, 1603–1642* (London, 1989).

Dewald, Jonathan. *The European nobility, 1400–1800* (Cambridge, 1996).

Donagan, Barbara. 'The web of honour: soldiers, Christians, and gentlemen in the English Civil War', *HJ* 44 (2001), pp. 365–89.

Downey, Declan M. 'Irish-European integration: the legacy of Charles V', in Judith Devlin and Howard B. Clarke (eds.), *European encounters: essays in memory of Albert Lovett* (Dublin, 2003), pp. 97–117.

'Purity of blood and purity of faith in early modern Ireland', in Alan Ford and John MacCafferty (eds.), *The origins of sectarianism in early modern Ireland* (Cambridge, 2005), pp. 216–28.

Duffy, Eamon. *The stripping of the altars: traditional religion in England, c. 1400–c. 1580* (New Haven, 1992).

Duffy, Patrick J., David Edwards and Liz FitzPatrick (eds.). *Gaelic Ireland c. 1250–c. 1650* (Dublin, 2001).

Dunlop, Robert. 'The plantation of Leix and Offaly', *English Historical Review* 6 (1891), pp. 61–96.

Dunne, Tom. 'The Gaelic response to conquest and colonization: the evidence of the poetry', *Studia Hibernica* 20 (1980), pp. 7–30.

'Ireland, Irish and colonialism', *Irish Review* 30 (2003), pp. 95–104.

Edwards, David. *The Ormond lordship in County Kilkenny, 1515–1642: the rise and fall of Butler feudal power* (Dublin, 2003).

'Collaboration without anglicisation: the MacGiollapadraig lordship and Tudor reform', in Patrick J. Duffy, David Edwards and Elizabeth FitzPatrick (eds.), *Gaelic Ireland c. 1250–1650: land, lordship and settlement* (Dublin, 2001), pp. 77–96.

'The escalation of violence in sixteenth-century Ireland', in Edwards, Lenihan and Tait (eds.), *Age of atrocity*, pp. 34–78.

Edwards, David, Pádraig Lenihan and Clodagh Tait (eds.). *Age of atrocity: violence and political conflict in early modern Ireland* (Dublin, 2007).

Elliott, John. *Imperial Spain 1469–1716* (New York, 1973).

Ellis, Steven. *Ireland in the age of the Tudors: English expansion and the end of Gaelic Ireland* (New York, 1998).

Tudor frontiers and noble power: the making of the British state (Oxford, 1995).

'More Irish than the Irish themselves? The "Anglo-Irish" in Tudor Ireland', *History Ireland* (Spring, 1999), pp. 22–6.

'Civilizing Northumberland: representations of Englishness the Tudor state', *Journal of Historical Sociology* 12 (1999), pp. 103–27.

Ellis, Steven and Christopher Maginn. *The making of the British Isles: the state of Britain and Ireland, 1450–1660* (New York, 2007).

Falls, Cyril. *Elizabeth's Irish wars* (London, 1950).

Flower, Robin. *The Irish tradition* (Oxford, 1947).

Ford, Alan. *The Protestant reformation in Ireland, 1590–1641* (Frankfurt, 1985).

Foyster, Elizabeth. 'Male honour, social control and wife beating in later Stuart England', *Transactions of the Royal Historical Society* 6 (1996).

'Parenting was for life, not just for childhood: the role of parents in the married lives of their children in early modern England', *History* 86 (2001), pp. 313–27.

Gillespie, Raymond. 'Negotiating order in early seventeenth-century Ireland', in Michael Braddick and John Walter (eds.), *Negotiating power in early modern society: order, hierarchy and subordination in Britain and Ireland* (Cambridge, 2001), pp. 188–205.

Reading Ireland: print, reading and social change in early modern Ireland (Manchester, 2005).

Gowing, Laura. 'Women, status and the popular culture of dishonour', *Transactions of the Royal Historical Society* 6(1996), pp. 225–34.

Haigh, Christopher. *English reformations: religion, politics, and society under the Tudors* (New York, 1993).

Hammer, Paul. *The polarization of Elizabethan politics: the political career of Robert Devereux, 2nd earl of Essex, 1585–1597* (Cambridge, 1999).

Herrup, Cynthia. *A house in gross disorder: sex, law, and the 2nd earl of Castlehaven* (New York, 1999).

Hexter, J. H. 'The education of the aristocracy in the Renaissance', *The Journal of Modern History* 22 (1950), pp. 1–20.

Hicks, Michael. *English political culture in the fifteenth century* (New York, 2002).

Hsia, H. P. 'Munster and the Anabaptists', in Hsia (ed.), *The German people and the Reformation* (Ithaca, 1988), pp. 51–69.

Hunter, R. J. 'The end of O'Donnell power', in William Nolan, Liam Ronayne and Máiréad Dunleavy (eds.), *Donegal: history and society* (Dublin, 1995), pp. 229–66.

James, Mervyn. 'English politics and the concept of honour, 1485–1642', in Mervyn James (ed.), *Society, politics and culture: studies in early modern England* (Cambridge, 1986), pp. 308–415.

'At a crossroads of the political culture: the Essex Revolt, 1601', in James (ed.), *Society, politics and culture*, pp. 416–65.

'The concept of order and the Northern Rising of 1569', *P&P* 60 (1973), pp. 49–83.

Kearney, Hugh. *Strafford in Ireland 1633–41: a study in absolutism* (Manchester, 1961).

Kerney Walsh, Micheline. *An exile of Ireland: Hugh O'Neill, Prince of Ulster* (Dublin, 1986).

Kishlansky, Mark. 'Charles I: a case of mistaken identity', *P&P* 189 (2005), pp. 41–80.

Lake, Peter and Michael Questier (eds.). *Conformity and orthodoxy in the English church, c. 1560–1660* (Rochester, NY, 2000).

Lander, J. R. 'The crown and the aristocracy in England, 1450–1509', *Albion* 8 (1976), pp. 203–18.

Leerssen, Joep. *Mere Irish and Fior-Ghael: studies in the idea of Irish nationality, its development and literary expression prior to the nineteenth century* (Dublin, 1990).

   The contention of the bards (Iomarbhagh na bhFileadh) and its place in Irish political and literary history (London, 1994).

Lennon, Colm. *Sixteenth-century Ireland: the incomplete conquest* (New York, 1995).

Lindley, Keith J. 'The impact of the 1641 rebellion upon England and Wales, 1641–5', *IHS* 70 (1972), pp. 143–76.

Little, L. K. and B. H. Rosenwein, *Debating the Middle Ages: issues and readings* (Oxford, 1998), pp. 148–69.

Lyons, Mary Ann. *Franco-Irish relations, 1500–1610: politics, migration and trade* (Woodbridge, 2003).

Lyttleton, James and Tadhg O'Keeffe (eds.). *The manor in medieval and early modern Ireland* (Dublin, 2004).

McCabe, Richard. *Spenser's monstrous regiment: Elizabethan Ireland and the poetics of difference* (New York, 2002).

McCavitt, John. *Sir Arthur Chichester: lord deputy of Ireland 1605–16* (Antrim, 1998).

McCormack, Anthony. *The earldom of Desmond 1463–1583: the decline and crisis of a feudal lordship* (Dublin, 2005).

Mac Craith, Mícheál. *Lorg na hIasachta ar na Dánta Grá* (Dublin, 1989).

   'Beatha Aodha Ruaidh Uí Dhomhnaill in the context of the literature of the Renaissance', in Ó Riain (ed.), *Beatha … historical and literary contexts*, pp. 36–53.

   'Gaelic Ireland and the Renaissance', in Glanmor Williams and Robert O. Jones, *The Celts and the Renaissance* (Cardiff, 1990), pp. 57–89.

   'Literature in Irish, *c.* 1550–1690: from the Elizabethan settlement to the Battle of the Boyne', in Margaret Kelleher and Philip O'Leary (eds.), *The Cambridge history of Irish literature*, 2 vols (Cambridge, 2006), I, pp. 191–231.

Mac Eiteagáin (McGettigan), Darren. 'The Renaissance and the late medieval lordship of Tír Chonaill 1461–1555', in William Nolan, Liam Ronayne and Mairead Dunlevy (eds.), *Donegal history and society: interdisciplinary essays on the history of an Irish county* (Dublin, 1995), pp. 203–28.

   Red Hugh O'Donnell and the Nine Years War (Dublin, 2005).

MacFarlane, K. B. *The nobility of later medieval England* (Oxford, 1973).

McGurk, J. J. N. 'O'Brien, Donough, fourth earl of Thomond (d. 1624)', *Oxford Dictionary of National Biography*, Oxford University Press, 2004 (www.oxforddnb.com/view/article/20453, accessed 22 Feb 2007).

McKibben, Sarah. 'Bardic poetry and the postcolonial politics of close reading', *Proceedings of the Harvard Celtic Colloquium* 21–22 (2000–1).

McLaughlin, Roisin. 'A threat of satire by Tadhg (Mac Dáire) Mac Bruaideadha', *Ériu* 55 (2005), pp. 37–57.

McManus, Damian. 'The language of the *Beatha*', in Ó Riain (ed.), *Beatha … historical and literary contexts*, pp. 54–73.

Maginn, Christopher. *'Civilizing' Gaelic Leinster: the extension of Tudor rule in the O'Byrne and O'Toole lordships* (Dublin, 2005).

''Surrender and regrant'' in the historiography of sixteenth-century Ireland', *Sixteenth Century Journal* 38 (2007), pp. 956–61.

'The limitations of Tudor reform: the policy of "surrender and regrant" and the O'Rourkes', *Breifne: Journal of Cumann Seanchais Bhréifne* xi (2007), pp. 429–60.

Maley, Willy. 'Nationalism and revisionism: ambiviolences and dissensus', in Scott Brewster, Virginia Crossman, Fiona Becket and David Alderson (eds.), *Ireland in proximity: history, gender and space* (London, 1999), pp. 12–25.

' "The name of the country I have forgotten": remembering and dismembering in Sir Henry Sidney's Irish *Memoir* (1583)', in Thomas Herron and Michael Potterton (eds.), *Ireland in the Renaissance c. 1540–1660* (Dublin, 2007), pp. 52–73.

Mayer, Thomas. 'On the road to 1534: the occupation of Tournai and Henry VIII's theory of sovereignty', in Dale Hoak (ed.), *Tudor political culture* (Cambridge, 1995).

Mayes, Charles R. 'The early Stuarts and the Irish peerage', *English Historical Review* 73 (1958), pp. 227–51.

'The sale of peerages in early Stuart England', *Journal of Modern History* 29 (1959), pp. 21–37.

Mears, Natalie. *Queenship and political discourse in the Elizabethan realms* (Cambridge, 2005).

Merritt, Julia (ed.). *The political world of Thomas Wentworth, earl of Strafford, 1621–1641* (Cambridge, 1996).

'Power and communication: Thomas Wentworth and government at a distance during the Personal Rule, 1629–35', in Merritt (ed.), *The political world of Thomas Wentworth*, pp. 109–32.

Midelfort, Erik H. C. 'Curious Georgics: the German nobility and their crisis of legitimacy in the late sixteenth century', in Andrew C. Fix and Susan C. Karant-Nunn (eds.), *Germania illustrata: essays on early modern Germany presented to Gerald Strauss* (Kirksville, MO, 1992), pp. 217–42.

Mignolo, Walter. *The darker side of the Renaissance: literacy, territoriality, and colonization* (Ann Arbor, 1995).

Miller, Helen. *Henry VIII and the English nobility* (New York, 1986).

Milton, Anthony. 'Thomas Wentworth and the political thought of personal rule', in Merritt (ed.), *The political world of Thomas Wentworth*, pp. 133–56.

Moody, T. W., F. X. Martin and F. J. Byrne (eds.), *A new history of Ireland* 3 (Oxford, 1984; Dublin, reprint 1991).

Morgan, Hiram. *Tyrone's rebellion: the outbreak of the Nine Years War in Tudor Ireland* (Dublin, 1993).

'Mid-Atlantic Blues', *The Irish Review* II (1991–92), pp. 50–5.

'Hugh O'Neill and the Nine Years War in Ireland', *The Historical Journal* 36 (1993), pp. 21–37.

'Tom Lee: the posing peacemaker', in Brendan Bradshaw, Andrew Hadfield and Willy Maley (eds.), *Representing Ireland*.

'British policies before the British state', in B. Bradshaw and J. Morrill (eds.), *The British problem*, pp. 66–88.

(ed.). *Political ideology in Ireland, 1541–1641* (Dublin, 1999).

'"Slán Dé fút go hoíche": Hugh O'Neill's murders', in Edwards, Lenihan and Tait (eds.), *Age of atrocity*, pp. 95–118.

'The real Red Hugh', in Ó Riain (ed.), *Beatha … historical and literary contexts*, pp. 1–35.

Morrill, John. 'The British problem, c. 1534–1707', in Brendan Bradshaw and John Morrill (eds.), *The British problem, c. 1534–1707: state formation in the Atlantic archipelago* (New York, 1996).

'The Drogheda massacre in Cromwellian context', in Edwards, Lenihan and Tait (eds.), *Age of atrocity*, pp. 242–65.

Moryson. Fynes *An history of Ireland from the year 1599 to 1603*, 2 vols (Dublin, 1735).

The Irish sections of Fynes Moryson's unpublished itinerary (Dublin, 1998).

Moss, Rachel, Colmán Ó Clabaigh and Salvador Ryan (eds.). *Art and devotion in late medieval Ireland* (Dublin, 2006).

Neuschel, Kristen. *Word of honor: interpreting noble culture in sixteenth-century France* (Ithaca, 1989).

Nicholls, Kenneth. *Gaelic and gaelicized Ireland in the middle ages* (Dublin, 1972).

'Worlds apart? The Ellis two-nation theory on late medieval Ireland', *History Ireland* (Summer, 1999), pp. 22–6.

'The other massacre: English killings of Irish, 1641–3', in Edwards, Lenihan and Tait (eds.), *Age of atrocity*, pp. 176–91.

Ó hAnnracháin, Tadhg. *Catholic Reformation in Ireland: the mission of Rinuccini, 1645–49* (Oxford, 2002).

Ó Buachalla, Breandán. 'James our true king: the ideology of Irish royalism in the seventeenth century', in D. G. Boyce (ed.), *Political thought in Ireland since the seventeenth century* (London, 1988).

'*Annala Ríoghachta Éireann* is *Foras Feasa ar Éireann*: an comhthéacs comhaimseartha', *Studia Hibernica* 22–3 (1985), pp. 59–105.

Aisling ghéar: na Stíobhartaigh agus an taos léinn, 1603–1788 (Dublin, 1996).

The crown of Ireland (Galway, 2006).

Ó Cuív, Brian. *The Irish bardic duanaire or poem-book* (Dublin, 1973).

Ó Dúshláine, Tadhg. *An Eoraip agus litríocht na Gaeilge 1600–1650: gnéithe den bharócachas Eorpach i litríocht na Gaeilge* (Dublin, 1987).

Ó Fearghail, Feargus. 'The tomb of Hugh O'Neill in San Pietro in Montorio in Rome', *Seanchas Ard Mhacha* 21 (2007–08), pp. 69–85.

O'Grady, Hugh. *Strafford and Ireland* (Dublin, 1923).

Ó Háinle, Cathal. 'D'fhior chogaidh comhailtear síothcháin', *Léachtaí Cholm Cille* 2 (1971), pp. 51–73.

Ohlmeyer, Jane. *Civil war and restoration in the three Stuart kingdoms: the career of Randal MacDonnell, marquis of Antrim* (reprint: Dublin, 2001).

(ed.). *Ireland from independence to occupation, 1641–1660* (Cambridge, 1995).

'Introduction. A failed revolution?', in Ohlmeyer (ed.), *Ireland from independence to occupation*, pp. 1–23.

'The baronial context of the Irish civil wars', in J. S. A. Adamson (ed.), *The English Civil War: conflict and contexts, 1640–49* (New York, 2009), pp. 106–24.

O'Leary, Philip. 'Verbal deceit in the Ulster Cycle', *Éigse* 21 (1986), pp. 16–26.

'*Fír fer*: an internalized ethical concept in early Irish literature?', *Éigse* 22 (1987), pp. 1–14.

'Magnanimous conduct in Irish heroic literature', *Éigse* 25 (1991), pp. 28–44.

Ó Muraíle, Nollaig. 'Cuntas Thaidhg Uí Chianáin ar Thuras Deoraíochta na dTaoiseach Ultach, 1607–09', *History Ireland* 15 (2007), pp. 52–5.

Ó Riain, Pádraig (ed.). *Beatha Aodha Ruaidh: The life of Red Hugh O'Donnell: historical and literary contexts* (Dublin, 2003).

O Riordain, Michelle. *The Gaelic mind and the collapse of the Gaelic world* (Cork, 1990).

Orr, D. Alan. 'England, Ireland, Magna Carta, and the common law: the case of Connor Lord Magurie, Second Baron of Enniskillen', JBS 39 (2000), pp. 389–421. Treason and the state: law, politics and ideology in the English Civil War (Cambridge, 2002).

Osborough, W. N. 'Loftus, Adam, first Viscount Loftus of Ely (1568–1643)', *Oxford Dictionary of National Biography*, Oxford University Press, 2004, www.oxforddnb.com/view/article/16935, accessed 25 March 2008.

O'Scea, Ciaran. 'The significance and legacy of Spanish intervention in west Munster during the battle of Kinsale', in Thomas O'Connor and Mary Ann Lyons (eds.), *Irish migrants in Europe after Kinsale, 1602–1820* (Dublin, 2003), pp. 32–63.

Ó Siochrú, Mícheál. 'Atrocity, codes of conduct and the Irish in the British civil wars 1641–1653', *P&P* 195 (2007), pp. 55–86.

'Propaganda, rumour and myth: Oliver Cromwell and the massacre at Drogheda', in Edwards, Lenihan and Tait (eds.), *Age of atrocity*, pp. 266–82.

O'Sullivan, Catherine Marie. *Hospitality in medieval Ireland, 900–1500* (Dublin, 2004).

Palmer, Patricia. ' "An headlesse ladie" and "a horses loade of heades": writing the beheading', *Renaissance Quarterly* 60 (2007), pp. 25–57.

Language and conquest in early modern Ireland (Cambridge, 2001).

Palmer, William. *The problem of Ireland in Tudor foreign policy, 1485–1603* (Woodbridge, NY, 1994).

'That "Insolent Liberty": honor, rites of power, and persuasion in sixteenth-century Ireland', *Renaissance Quarterly* 46 (1993), pp. 308–27.

'Scenes from provincial life: history, honor and meaning in the Tudor north', *Renaissance Quarterly* 53 (2000), pp. 425–48.

Parker, Geoffrey. *The military revolution: military innovation and the rise of the west, 1500–1800* (Cambridge, 2002: new edition).

Pawlisch, Hans. *Sir John Davies and the conquest of Ireland: a study in legal imperialism* (Cambridge, 1985).

Peltonen, Markku. *The duel in early modern England: civility, politeness and honour* (Cambridge, 2003).

Peristiany, J. G. (ed.). *Honour and shame: the values of Mediterranean society* (London, 1966).

Pitt-Rivers, Julian. 'Honour and social status', in Peristiany (ed.), *Honour and shame* (Chicago, 1966).

Pogson, Fiona. 'Wentworth as President of the Council of the North, 1628–41', in John C. Appleby and Paul Dalton (eds.), *Government, religion and society in northern England 1000–1700* (Thrupp, Gloucestershire, 1997), pp. 185–98.

Pollock, Linda. 'Honor, gender, and reconciliation in elite culture, 1570–1700', *JBS* 46 (2007), pp. 3–29.

Power, Gerald. 'The viceroy and his critics: Leonard Grey's journey through the west of Ireland, June–July 1538', *Journal of the Galway Archaeological and Historical Society* 60 (2008), pp. 78–87.

Questier, Michael. *Catholicism and community in early modern England: politics, aristocratic patronage and religion, c. 1550–1640* (Cambridge, 2006).

Ranger, Terence. 'Strafford in Ireland: a revaluation', *P&P* 19 (1961), pp. 26–45.

Rea, Steve and Richard Cust. 'The court of chivalry website': www.court-of-chivalry.bham.ac.uk/index.htm.

Reddy, William M. *The invisible code: honor and sentiment in postrevolutionary France, 1814–1848* (Berkeley, 1997).

Schalk, Ellery. *From valor to pedigree: ideas of nobility in France in the sixteenth and seventeenth centuries* (Princeton, 1986).

Shagan, Ethan (ed.). *Catholics and the 'Protestant nation': religious politics and identity in early modern England* (Manchester, 2005).

Sharpe, Kevin. *The personal rule of Charles I* (New Haven, 1992).

Shaw, Dougal. 'Thomas Wentworth and monarchical ritual in early modern Ireland', *HJ* 49 (2006), pp. 331–55.

Shuger, Debora. 'Irishmen, aristocrats, and other white barbarians', *Renaissance Quarterly* 50 (1997), pp. 494–525.

Simms, Katherine. 'Guesting and feasting in Gaelic Ireland', *Journal of the Royal Society of Antiquaries of Ireland* 108 (1978), pp. 67–100.

'Bardic poetry as a historical source', in Tom Dunne (ed.), *The writer as witness: literature as historical evidence* (Cork, 1987), pp. 58–75.

From kings to warlords: the changing political structure of Gaelic Ireland in the later middle ages (Dublin, 1987).

'Bards and barons: the Anglo-Irish aristocracy and the native culture', in Robert Bartlett and Angus MacKay (eds.), *Medieval frontier societies* (Oxford, 1989), pp. 177–97.

Smuts, Malcolm. *Culture and power in England, 1585–1685* (Cambridge, 1998).

Snow, Vernon F. *Essex the rebel: the life of Robert Devereux, the third earl of Essex 1591–1646* (Lincoln, NE, 1970).

Squibb, G. D. *The high court of chivalry: a study of the civil law in England* (Oxford, 1959).

Stewart, Frank Henderson. *Honor* (Chicago, 1994).

Stone, Lawrence. *The crisis of the aristocracy, 1580–1641* (Oxford, 1965).

Tait, Clodagh. *Death, burial and commemoration in Ireland, 1550–1650* (Basingstoke and New York, 2002).

Takaki, Ronald. 'The "Tempest" in the wilderness: the racialization of savagery', *Journal of American History* 79 (1992), pp. 892–912.

Treadwell, Victor. 'The house of lords in the Irish Parliament of 1613–15', *English Historical Review* 80 (1965), pp. 92–107.

Buckingham and Ireland 1616–1628: a study in Anglo-Irish politics (Dublin, 1998).

Verstraten, Freya. 'Images of Gaelic lordship in Ireland, c. 1200–1400', in Linda Doran and James Lyttleton (eds.), *Lordship in medieval Ireland: image and reality* (Dublin, 2007), pp. 47–74.

Walsh, Helen Coburn. 'The rebellion of William Nugent, 1581', in R. V. Comerford, Mary Cullen and J. R. Hill (eds.), *Religion, conflict and coexistence in Ireland: essays presented to Monsignor Patrick J. Corish* (Dublin, 1990).

Watts, John. *Henry VI and the politics of kingship* (Cambridge, 1996).

Wedgwood, C. V. *Strafford* (London, 1935).

Thomas Wentworth first earl of Strafford 1593–1641: a revaluation (London, 1961).

Williams, Nicholas. *Armas: sracfhéacaint ar araltas na hÉireann* (Dublin, 2001), pp. 4–15.

Wormald, Jenny. 'Bloodfeud, kindred and government in early modern Scotland', *P&P* 87 (May, 1980), pp. 54–97.

THESES AND UNPUBLISHED WORKS

Ball, John. 'Popular violence in the Irish uprising of 1641: the 1641 depositions, Irish resistance to English colonialism, and its representation in English sources' (unpublished PhD dissertation, The Johns Hopkins University, 2006).

Cunningham, Bernadette. 'Political and social change in the lordships of Clanricard and Thomond, 1569–1641' (unpublished MA thesis, U.C.G., 1979).

McKibben, Sarah. 'Endangered masculinities: gender, colonialism, and sexuality in early modern literature in Irish, 1540–1780' (unpublished book manuscript).

Index

Act of Absentees
  effects on Irish and English peers 34
Aguila, Don John de
  view of Irish honour 102, 120
Anabaptists 271
anglicization 7, 26
Anglo-Norman 1
annals 16
  as historical source 52
Annala Ríoghachta Éireann (*Annals of the Four
    Masters*) 119, 277
Annals of Loch Cé 17, 46, 50
  as source for Gaelic views of honour 52–66
  compared with *Beatha Aodha Ruaidh Uí
    Dhomhnaill* 140
Annesley, Sir Francis, Lord Mountnorris
    221, 235
aristocracy
  'British' 21, 269, 275–6
  necessary role in legitimate government 41
  of Europe 6, 18, 269
Asch, Ronald 11, 247
Atherton, John 255
Aylmer, G. E. 230

Bacon, Sir Francis 208
Bagenal family 276
  Henry 33, 110
  Mabel 33
bardic poetry
  as historical source 47–51, 66–7
bards 16, 22
  as arbiters of honour 7–8, 23, 47
  as arbiters of political legitimacy 23, 45,
    80, 118
  as members of Irish court 7–8
  chief's poet 23–4, 80
  ollamh (*ollúna*) described 47
  satire of 7, 24
  status level of 47
baronial revolt 268
Barry, John 165

Beatha Aodha Ruaidh Uí Dhomhnaill (*Life of Red
    Hugh O'Donnell*) 18, 135–44
  audience for 143–4
  compared with Fulke Greville's *The Life of the
    Renowned Sir Philip Sidney* 143–4
  compared with Ó Cianáin's *Flight of
    the Earls* 136
  generic uniqueness of 135–6
  language of 135, 136
Bingham, Richard 55, 57, 60, 63–4, 276
blood
  as basis for precedence 216
  as basis of honour 55, 136, 157, 159–60
  difference between aristocratic and royal 29
Blount, Charles, Lord Mountjoy 115–16
Boru, Brian 22, 149, 164, 171
Boyle, Richard, 1st Earl of Cork 9, 159, 160, 231,
    233–4, 247
  as new nobility 169, 179, 235, 276
Bramhall, Bishop 257
Brehon law 22, 23, 47
Brehons 22
Braddick, Michael 28
Bradshaw, Brendan 3, 49, 50, 56
Brady, Ciaran 38, 42
Brian, son of Maelrunaidh 61
Brigden, Susan 93
British
  as historical category 12–13, 16
  state 15
  (see also *honour*)
Brooks, James 14
Bryson, Anna 8–9
Burgh, Lord 101
Burke family 180, 182, 238
  and surrender and regrant 32, 38
  Honora 188
  Richard (Sassanach), 2nd Earl of Clanricard 38,
    44, 182
  Richard, 4th Earl of Clanricard and Earl of
    St Albans 18, 19, 38, 94, 120, 121, 146–7,
    181–93, 269

accused as member of international Catholic conspiracy 236–7
accused as 'over-mighty noble' 223, 239
and anglicization 189
as 'British' noble 235
as Crown loyalist 118
at English court 182–3
attitude to noble titles 190–1
conflict with Earls of Thomond 172
conflict with Lord Deputy Wentworth 224, 235–45, 266, 267
desire to live in Ireland 186–7
English peerage 184–5, 235
financial problems of 186
legal cases in England 183–4
offence towards Lord Deputy Wentworth 241
patronage of 188
social management of lands 187–8
Richard, Lord Tunbridge 242, 243
Richard Og 55
Ulick, 1st Earl of Clanricard 182
Ulick, 3rd Earl of Clanricard 38
Ulick, 5th Earl of Clanricard 235, 243–4
conflict with Lord Deputy Wentworth 244, 245
Butler
Theobald, Viscount Tulleophelim 205–7
Thomas, 10th Earl of Ormond 97, 113

Caball, Marc 7, 9, 49–50, 51, 68, 83
on *Pairlement Chloinne Tomáis* 153–4
Campion, Edmund 8
Canny, Nicholas 9, 36, 41, 91, 197
Carew, Sir George 99, 102–3, 106, 119, 159, 168
Carney, James 68
Cary, Sir Henry, Viscount Falkland
seating in English Parliament of 211–12
Star Chamber case of 221–2
Castle Chamber, Court of 144, 196
Cavendish
William, Earl of Newcastle 233, 261, 265
Cecil family 96
Robert, Earl of Salisbury 99, 104, 106, 108, 116, 117, 209
William, Lord Burghley 167, 168
Chamberlain, John 182, 183, 185
Chancery, Irish Court of 257, 261
Charles I 3, 19, 144, 211, 213, 215, 221, 227, 232, 244, 267
alleged insensitivity to subjects' honour 242
anti-duelling campaign of 228
arbitrates precedence disputes 215–19
defence of honour in Ireland vs. England 222–3, 265, 266, 267

his defence of honour 18–19, 194, 195, 222, 234, 242, 243
role in dispute between Loftus and Wentworth 258, 261
Charles V 1, 25
Chichester, Arthur, Lord Deputy of Ireland 196, 200, 205–7, 232, 248
honour of defended 205–7
management of precedence disputes 200–2
chivalry 144, 189, 267
and Henry VIII 29
Court of Chivalry 144, 229
themes of in Gaelic writing 24
Church of Ireland 151, 270
cing 58
civility (vs. savagery) 41, 95, 222, 235, 272
as Gaelic critique of Tudor state 41–2, 81
as justifying discourse of state expansion 39, 40, 273
civilizing mission 224, 246, 247, 266, 267, 269
Clarke, Aidan
Old English in Ireland 181
clú 51
in *Flight of the Earls* 129
in Maguire poembook 70–2
in poems of Tadhg Dall Ó hUiginn 76–7
'Cnoc Samhradh' (poem) 185–6
Coke
Sir Edward 211, 237, 242, 243, 244, 257–8
Sir John 231
Commons, English House of 211
Confederate Catholics 238, 269
confession
as socio-political division between English and Irish 277
(see also *faith and fatherland*)
Connolly, S. J. 26, 277
Cooley, Sir William 249
Cork, Earl of
(see *Boyle, Richard*)
Cottington, Francis 236
Croft, Sir James 40, 41
Cromwell, Oliver 270
regime of 277
Crown
of Ireland 29
cultural contact 17
as challenge to honour politics 13–14
compared with British North America 27
culture
compatibility of English and Gaelic 21–43
difference as explanation for English–Irish conflict 42, 266
differences between English and Gaelic 20–1, 22–3, 277

Cumberland, Earl of 225
Cunningham, Bernadette 32
Cust, Richard 6, 15, 169

Dal Cais 44
  (see also *O'Brien family*)
Danby, Earl of 242, 243, 244
Daniels, Jane and John (servants of 2nd Earl of
    Essex) 184
daonnacht
  as used in *Annals of Loch Cé* 55–6
Davies, Sir John 195–6
  views of the honour of office 205
degeneration
  as Gaelic critique of state collaborators 42
deirbhfhine 23, 35, 39, 274
Desmond, Earls of
  and surrender and regrant 54
  Crown efforts to manage earldom 104–7
  Gearóid Fitzgerald, 15th Earl 44
  Gearóid Íarla, 3rd Earl 27
  James, 6th Earl 53
Desmond Rebellion 41, 64, 92
Devereux
  Robert, 2nd Earl of Essex 17, 94, 120, 183,
    230, 248
    honour concerns of 99
    negotiations with Hugh O'Neill 112–14
    rebellion of 116
  Robert, 3rd Earl of Essex 183, 213, 231
Dewald, Jonathan 12
'Discourse between two councillors of
    state …' (anti-Wentworth
    pamphlet) 238
  audience for 239
domestic order 252
  and political legitimacy 246, 247
Donelan, John 186, 187
Dorset, Earl of 213
dowry, politics of 246
Duanaire Mhéig Uidhir (Poembook of the
    Maguires) 46, 50
Dublin
  political demonstrations by residents 263–4
Dublin Castle 232, 264, 268
Dudley, Edmund 29
Duffy, Eamon 6, 18
duine maith
  applied to Gael and Gall 56
duine uasal
  applied to Gael and Gall 56–7
Dunne, T. J. 48, 50, 66

Edward VI, King of England 38
Edwards, David 32

eineach 277
  as generosity 53–4
  compared with *féile* 69
  compared with *uasal* 54–5
  defined 51, 90
  in *Annals of Loch Cé* 52–4
  in *Beatha Aodha Ruaidh Uí Dhomhnaill* 136
  in *Flight of the Earls* 129
  in Maguire poembook 68–9, 73
  in poems of Tadhg Dall Ó hUiginn 75–6, 86, 87
eiric 88
elite formation 12
Elizabeth I 94, 96, 120, 153
  and military honour 100–1
  as *prinnsa* 59
  as *rí* 58, 110
  concerns over social elevation 101–2, 116
  honour challenged by servants 99–102, 112–16
  honour concerns of 9, 17, 97
  honour protected by servants 98–9
  view of Irish honour culture 104–5
Elliott, John 143
Empson, Richard 29
English–Irish
  and surrender and regrant 32, 271
  as 'Gaelicized' 23
  relations with Gaelic Irish culture 26–7
ethnography
  of Irish by English 167
Europe, Gaelic discussions of 65

'Faghaim ceart a chlann Eibhir' (poem by Tadhg
    McDáire) 185
'Faisean Chlair Eibhir' (poem) 134, 147, 151, 165
faith and fatherland
  as political ideology 41, 42, 64–5, 91, 93, 117,
    120, 139, 145, 270, 271, 272, 277
Farmer, William 200
féile 51
Fenton, Sir Geoffrey 114, 115, 118
file (poet)
  defined 47
Fitzgeralds 1
  James Fitzgerald 105–7
  James Fitzmaurice 92–3, 121, 271
  James FitzThomas (*sugán* earl) 105–7
  Joan Fitzgerald 106
Fitzpatrick, Barnaby 26
flaith 128, 136, 138
flaitheas 59
'Flight of the Earls' 18, 195
Flight of the Earls (Tadhg Ó Cianáin) 18, 122
  audience for 143–4
  generic uniqueness of 130–1
  history of text 125

Flower, Robin 47
'forced loan' (of Charles I) 226
fosterage 32, 42
Foulis, Sir David 228–9
French Crown 29
'Fúbún fúibh, a shluagh Gaoidheal' (bardic
        poem) 41
Fuentes, Duke of 126

Gaelic Ireland
    as composite society 82–4
    court culture in 23–4
    'order' described 22–3
Gaelic Irish 270, 271, 272, 273, 276, 277
    and English law 86–7
    as naturally peace loving 81–2
    clothes and habits of 23
    continental influences on culture of 24–6
    English interests in origins of 167–8
    English legal efforts to suppress 26
    Greek origins of 164, 168, 170
    not to take 'English' titles or offices 88–9
    placed outside English honour circle 98
'Gaelicization' 26
Garrard, Rev. George 244–5, 261
genealogy (see also *pedigrees*)
    as sign of status 158
    English Catholics' use of 169–71
    of Gaelic families 80
Geraldine League 1, 25
Gifford, John 248, 249, 255
    petition for Eleanor Loftus 257, 258, 259
Giraldus Cambrensis (Gerald of Wales) 130, 131
glóir 51
    in *Flight of the Earls* 129
    in the poems of Tadhg Dall Ó hUiginn 77
glory 11
    military 5
'Graces' 240–1
Greene, David 68
Greville, Fulke 143–4
Grey, Lord Leonard 2

Hadsor, Richard 34, 190, 192
Haigh, Christopher 6
Hayes-McCoy, G. A. 106
Henrietta Maria, Queen of England
    role in dispute between Wentworth and Adam
        Loftus 262
Henry II, King of England 28
Henry VIII, King of England 1, 15, 19, 268, 270
    as honour-obsessed 29
    as *rí* 58
    concerns for honour relating to surrender and
        regrant 28–32

relationship with English nobility 29
threats if dishonoured 33–4, 91
heraldry 267
    amongst Gaelic Irish 24
high-kings of Ireland 163
Holland, Earl of 245, 262
honour
    and cultural contact 9–10, 16
    and Gaelic culture 7, 61–2
    and hospitality 63
    and imperial visions 29
    and landholding 150
    and masculinity 19, 100
    and providence 142
    and 'reformation of manners' 18, 19
    and religion 10, 133, 136, 139–40, 151, 207, 277
    and service 99
    and Spanish colonialism 14
    and subjecthood 30
    and violence 5–6, 7, 13, 14, 81–5, 275
    as language of resistance 17, 120
    as nationally bounded 8–9, 10
    'British' culture of 7, 11, 14, 19, 120, 146, 224,
        235, 269
        and Nine Years' War 92, 94, 97, 117
    collective of Ireland 54
    defined in *Beatha Aodha Ruaidh Uí Dhomhnaill*
        136–7
    defined in 'Mór idir na haimsearaibh' 149–52
    defined in poems of Ó hUiginn 79–89
    definitions of 5, 14–15, 136, 216, 242, 243, 276
    difficulty in defining 11, 119, 196
    English views of Irish military 102–3
    family honour 19, 141, 248, 253, 255, 260, 266
        women's role in maintaining 266
    gendered notions of 266
    horizontal 10, 15, 27, 274
    in England 4–7, 12
    in Ireland 7–8, 11
    in wartime 100–2
    monarch as fount of 13, 54, 65, 111, 242, 243–5
    monarchical 3–4, 9, 18, 205, 265
    monarchical vs. noble/aristocratic 93, 100–1,
        112–16
    monarchs honour-bound to Irish 22
    need for lexical study of terms for 51
    not restricted by national boundaries 11–13, 18,
        273, 275
    of Crown officials 204–5, 229
    of English Crown 18
    of Gaelic lords on continent 127–8
    of Irish chief governors 205–7, 221
    of Spanish 143
    patriarchal 246
    sartorial markers of 148, 151

honour (cont.)
  Scottish notions of 209
  vertical 10, 15, 27, 224, 234, 265, 271, 274
  vs. virtue 205
  vs. wealth 80
honours (titles), inflation of 194–5, 206,
    207, 212
hospitality 7–8
Hunter, R. J. 120
Hutton, Richard 261

inauguration of kings 59
  rituals of Gaelic lords 44–5
Indians, New World 167
inheritance, politics of 246
intermarriage
  Gaelic and English 33
  Gaelic and Old English 27
Ireland
  as colony 15, 16, 22, 27, 222, 224, 236, 266, 267,
    273–4, 276
  as lordship 2–3, 28
  comparison with Wales and north of
    England 28
  kingdom, making of 2–3, 13, 15
  national consciousness in 7
Israelites 85–6

James, Mervyn 4–6, 14, 190, 191
James I, King of England 154, 173, 197, 202, 208,
    224, 228
  anti-duelling campaign 203, 228
  arbitrates precedence disputes 203, 207, 210,
    216, 219
  Scottish courtiers of 233
Jephsons 251
  John, Sir 251, 253, 255
  Mary (see also *Rush family*)
Jigginstown 232–3

Kearney, Hugh 246
Kerney Walsh, Micheline 124
Kildare, Earls of
  rebellion of 2, 34
kingship (see also *lordship*)
  Gaelic distinctions between local and crowned
    kings 25
  highkingship in Ireland 22
Kinsale, Battle of 95, 141–2

Lake, Peter 6
Laud, Archbishop William 245, 261, 263
law
  English disrespect for 63–4
  Gaelic critiques of English law 152, 155

Lebor gabala 83
Lee, Thomas 97, 108
Leerssen, Joep 7, 9, 49, 50, 51, 108
lineage (see also *blood*)
  as basis of status 158
London 120, 261, 264, 269, 272
Loftus
  Adam, Viscount Ely 4, 231, 234, 235, 269
    biographical details 247
    clash with Lord Deputy Wentworth 223,
      245–65, 266–7
    clash with son Robert 252–60
    controversy surrounding marriage of son
      Robert to Eleanor Rush 248–50
    historiography of 245
    imprisonment of 261
  Anne (Lady Moore, daughter of Lord
    Chancellor) 246, 253, 254, 256, 259, 262
  Dudley 247–8
    scandal case concerning 204–5
  Edward (younger son of Lord Chancellor) 246,
    248, 253, 256, 258, 259, 260
  Eleanor (*née* Rush, wife of Robert) 246, 248,
    249, 250, 251
  Nan (daughter of Robert and Eleanor) 253
  Robert (eldest son of Lord Chancellor) 246,
    248, 249, 250, 251
    clash with father 252–60
  Sarah, wife of Adam 257
Lords, English House of 215
Lords, Irish House of 211
'lords of the Pale'
  petition of to James I 197
lordship 1
  as political unit in Gaelic Ireland 22
  Gaelic notions of 84–7, 132, 172
  in *Beatha Aodha Ruaidh Uí Dhomhnaill* 138,
    142–3
Lorraine, Duke of 126
Lynch, Henry 187, 188, 189, 190, 191, 192–3

Mac an Bhaird
  Eoghan Ruadh 117–18, 123–4, 133, 135
    'Sorrows of Éire' (poem) 126
  Ferghal 69
    'Three crowns in James' charter' (poem) 132,
      172, 173
  Laoiseach
    A fhir a ghlacas Galldacht 41
mac an iarla dispute (Clanricard Burkes) 182
Mac Bruaideadha, Domhnaill
  and poem at installation of 3rd Earl of
    Thomond 44–5
McCavitt, John 159
Mac Craith, Mícheál 143

MacDiarmada
    Aedh 56
    Ruadhri 54
MacDonnell, Randal, Viscount Dunluce 172, 173
Mac Gearailt, Muiris mac Dáibhí Dubh 147, 155,
        172, 271
    (see also '*Mór idir na haimsearaibh*')
Mac Giolla Phádraig (MacGillapatrick)
    Brian, first baron of Upper Ossory 31, 42
    Brian (poet) 148
McManus, Damian 142
Madrid 120
Maguires 22
    as case study of surrender and regrant 37
    Cú Connacht Maguire 37
        honour of 72–4
    poems to chief of 17, 67–75
    Seaán Maguire 37
maithibh 128–9, 133
Malby, Sir Nicholas 42, 57
Maley, Willy 43
'mandates' 196
marriage, politics of 246
Mary I, Queen of England
    as *cing* 58
Mayes, Charles 194
Mears, Natalie 97
modernity 5, 7, 144, 145, 274
    modern code of honour 190, 191, 273
Molyneux, Daniel, Ulster King of Arms 164–5,
        166, 168
    attacked over precedence dispute 202–3
Monasterevan (Loftus estate) 249, 251, 258, 259, 260
Montagu, Sir Edward 212, 213
'Mór idir na haimsearaibh' (poem) 147,
        149–52, 155
    critique of professional classes 152
Morgan, Hiram 9, 93, 97
Moryson, Fynes 130, 131
Mountnorris (see *Annesley, Sir Francis*)

naisiún (nation) 133, 201
    as 'dynastic' 145
national consciousness 133, 268, 277
    and ethnicity 173–9
    (see also *faith and fatherland*)
New English 19, 134, 170, 265, 269, 273, 275
    conflict with Old English 196
    kinship networks of 274
Nichols, John (historian) 209
Nine Years' War (1594–1603) 17, 154, 182, 267, 271
    as religious conflict 120
        (see also *faith and fatherland*)
    historiography of 95
Noah 85–6

nobility
    and state formation 276–7
    'British' 231
    Catholic barred from office 206
    designation of 24
    European 21, 273, 275–6
    expectations of political role of 205–7
    Gaelic 19
    living as 246, 259
    of England 208–19
        concerns of Scottish competition post-1603
            209–10
    of Europe 11
        precedence norms 218
    of Ireland 18, 208–19
        and state formation 276–7
        precedence of 210, 232
        right to seating in English
            Parliament 211
    of Scotland 18, 208–19
        precedence of 209
    service 5, 10, 167
    warrior 5, 6
noble titles 260
    personal wealth needed to support 30
North, Sir John 184
Northampton, Earl of 233

O'Briens 30, 148, 157
    as case study of surrender and regrant 38
    Connor, 3rd Earl of Thomond 38, 44–5, 272
    Domhnall 45
    Donough, 2nd Earl of Thomond 38, 45
    Donough, 4th Earl of Thomond 18, 38, 94, 120,
            121, 146, 147, 158–80
        anglicized character of 118, 159
        attitude toward House of Commons 160
        Lord President of Munster 169, 171
        patronage of bards 172
        pedigrees of 161–79
    Henry, 5th Earl of Thomond 147
    Murrough, 1st Earl of Thomond 38, 45
Ó Buachalla, Breandán 48–9, 50
O'Byrne, Phelim McFeaghe 113
Ó Cianáin, Tadhg 122, 272
    historians' inattention to 124
    political theory of 132–3
Ó Cléirigh, Lughaidh 122, 135–45
Ó Cléirigh, Mícheál 277
O'Connor Don 55
O'Connor Sligo 54, 59, 61–2, 75
    tensions with Red Hugh O'Donnell 108–9, 138
O'Donnell family 1, 117
    and surrender and regrant 42
    Manus O'Donnell 25–6, 56

O'Donnell family (cont.)
    Niall Garv O'Donnell 134
    Red Hugh O'Donnell 94, 95, 105–6, 110, 120, 142
        in *Flight of the Earls*
        views of honour 107–9, 111
    Rory O'Donnell, Earl of Tyrconnell 117–18,
        119, 134–5, 162, 206
Ó Fearghail, Feargus 131
Ó Fiaich, Tomás 124, 135
Ó Gnímh, Fear Flatha 123–4, 133, 135
    'After the Flight of the Earls' (poem) 126, 172
    pedigree of Randal MacDonnell 172, 173
Ó hUiginn, Tadhg Dall 17, 46, 50
    poems of 75–91
O'Kelly, Ferdorogh 188
Old English 214, 238, 240, 265, 269, 271, 272
    concerns for privilege 197–8
    conflicts with New English 196
    critiques of Lord Deputy Wentworth 239–43
    (see also *English–Irish*)
O'Mores 40
    Rory 268, 269
O'Neill family 1, 24
    Aedh Buidhe 53
    as case study of surrender and regrant 36–7
    Conn Bacach, 1st Earl of Tyrone 31, 36
    Hugh, 2nd Earl of Tyrone 33, 37, 60, 94, 95, 117,
        141–2, 196, 271, 272
        connections to 1st Earl of Essex 33
        in *Flight of the Earls* 131, 134–5
        sense of self as European nobleman 112–14
        views on honour 109–12
    Matthew (Baron of Dungannon) 36–7
    pedigree of 164, 171–2
    Phelim 268, 269
    Shane 36, 37, 38
    Toirdhealbhach Luineach 37
onóir 51
    changing definitions of 130
    in *Annals of Loch Cé* 54
    in *Beatha Aodha Ruaidh Uí Dhomhnaill* 136
    in *Flight of the Earls* 129–30, 134
    in Maguire poembook 69–70
    in poems of Tadhg Dall Ó hUiginn 76
O'Reilly, Hugh 277
O Riordain, Michelle 48, 50
Ormond, Earls of 40, 54
    and earldom of Wiltshire 35
    (see also *Butler*)
Osborough, W. N. 247
O'Sullivan, Catherine 7
O'Sullivan Beare, Philip 95–6, 120

Pairlement Chloinne Tomáis (The Parliament of
    Clan Thomas) 134, 148, 152–7, 165

Pale, the English 26
Palmer, William 9–10
Parliament of England 269
    1621 210–12
    1628–9 212–19
    and Scottish nobility 208–9
    Gaelic lords attending 30
Parliament of Ireland
    1585–6 203
    1613–15 195–207, 210, 214, 219, 248
        honour issues debated 198–9
        'packing' of 196–7
        penal legislation of 196–7
    1634 240
pedigrees
    as signs of status 156–7, 158
    English passion for 166
    fraudulent uses of 166
peerage
    English 12, 21, 267
    Irish 12, 206, 247
        creation of and effects on England 34–5,
            208–20
        precedence of 210, 212–20
    Scottish
        precedence of 210, 212–20
        right to seats in English Parliament 211–12
Peltonen, Markku 8–9
Perrot, Sir John 92–3
'personal rule' (of Charles I) 222
Philip III of Spain 95, 120, 138
Pilgrimage of Grace 33
plantation
    Gaelic proprietors in 40
    Leix-Offaly 40–1
    Munster 41
    relationship to surrender and regrant 40–1
Pollock, Linda 6
Pope, Paul V 127
Portadown (massacre of) 269
Portumna Castle, Galway 183, 186–7
    (see also *Wentworth*)
Poynings' Law 217
precedence
    and law 217–18
    granted Gaelic lords on continent 127
    royal prerogative to determine 216–17, 218–19
    (see also *Wentworth*)
precedence disputes 18, 190, 192–3, 194–220
    barons of Delvin and Killeen 200
    barons of Lixnaw and Delvin 201, 203
    barons of Trimblestown and Dunsany 201
    Clanricard vs. Thomond 190–1, 192–3
    during 1613–15 Irish Parliament 199–203, 231, 232
    involving Sir William Stewart 202–3

of English commissioners in Ireland 201–2
Viscounts Gormanston and Buttevant 200–1
primogeniture 23, 35–6, 58, 274
politics of 246
prinnsa 58, 128
public sphere 263

Questier, Michael 6

race
as explanation for English–Irish conflict 39
English views of Irish 167, 168
reform
Tudor efforts in Ireland 21
Renaissance
influences in Ireland 24–6
rí 25
applied to non-Irish 58, 118, 128
ard-rí 22, 59
dropped as referent to Gaelic Irish 128, 129
in *Annals of Loch Cé* 57–8
in *Beatha Aodha Ruaidh Uí Dhomhnaill* 136
in poems of Tadhg Dall Ó hUiginn 77–8
vs. 'crowned kings' 59
vs. *tiarna* 49
Richard II, King of England 28, 31, 232, 233
Rinuccini, Cardinal and Papal nuncio 270
ríocht 59
Rome 25–6, 69, 73, 120, 124, 125, 126, 127, 135, 151, 272
Henry VIII's break with 6
Rush family 249, 250, 258
Anne (sister of Eleanor) 250, 251, 252, 253–4
Eleanor (see *Loftus*)
Francis, Sir 248–9, 253, 255, 262
marriage difficulties of 250
Mary 249, 255, 257
negotiates daughter Anne's match to George Wentworth 250–3
negotiates daughter Eleanor's troubles with Adam Loftus 253
Russell, Sir William, Lord Deputy of Ireland 98, 102

St Anthony's College (Louvain) 125, 127, 131
St John, Sir Oliver 188, 190, 191, 204
St Leger, Sir Anthony 15, 16, 19, 21, 22, 23, 24, 230, 269, 270
role in creation of the Kingdom of Ireland 2–4, 27
views of Gaelic Irish 27
St Patrick 153, 154
Sanquire, Earl of 209
saor 137
Savage, Sir Arthur 221
Savile, Sir Thomas 225
Saxey, William, Chief Justice of Munster 113

Scythians 167, 168
Shagan, Ethan 6
Sherlock, Paul (defendant in scandal case) 204–5
Shirley family, genealogical research of 169–70
Shirley, James 232, 233
Shrewsbury, Earls of
and earldom of Waterford 35
Sidney, Sir Henry, Lord Deputy of Ireland 37, 182
Sidney, Sir Philip 183
(see also *Beatha*)
Simms, Katherine 7, 48, 49, 50, 51, 52, 89, 91, 133
From kings to warlords 57
Smerwick, massacre of (1580) 104
Smuts, Malcolm 10
social hierarchy 272
English views of that amongst Irish 106
fears of inversion of 17, 18, 147–80, 271–2
in *Flight of the Earls* 128–9, 133
Southampton, Earl of 100
Spain 236
Spenser, Edmund 95, 167, 168, 173
A view of the present state of Ireland 167
Spinola, Marquis 127
Star Chamber, Court of 144, 229
case against Sir David Foulis 229, 231, 234
case of Henry Cary, Viscount Falkland 221
state formation
British and continental examples compared 275–7
Statutes of Kilkenny 26, 41
Stone, Lawrence 166, 194
The crisis of the aristocracy 181
Summerhill Manor, Maidstone, Kent 183
(see also 'Cnoc Samhradh')
surrender and regrant 17, 21, 56, 117, 120, 190–1, 269, 272, 276
and culture of honour 28, 30–1
and elite formation 27–8
and redefinition of Irish violence 33
compatibility with Gaelic social order 32–3
destabilizing effects in Ireland 36–7
effects on Gaelic succession 35–6
end as policy 39–40
reasons for success of 32–3
state's role in failures 38–9
successes of 31–2
viability over course of the sixteenth century 39–42
Surrey, Earl of 1
Sussex, Earl of 38, 44
Swiss 132–3, 272

'Thorough' (description of governance of Sir Thomas Wentworth) 223, 245–7, 265
tiarna 133
applied to Gael and Gall 57

tiarnas 59
Tichborne, Sir Henry 253
titles, heraldic
  in *Annals of the Four Masters* 128
  in *Flight of the Earls* 128, 133
  in Gaelic writings 59–60
titles, of office
  as requisite for status 160
  in Gaelic writings 60
  (see also *Wentworth*)
treachery
  as theme in Gaelic writings 62–4, 65, 82
Treadwell, Victor 194, 198
Trinity College Dublin 253

uasal 51, 277
  as used in *Annals of Loch Cé* 54–5
  as used in *Flight of the Earls* 133, 134
Ulster, earldom of 31
Ulster King of Arms 166
  (see also *Molyneux, Daniel*)
Ulster plantation 253, 257, 268
Ulster Rising of 1641 238, 268, 269, 270, 273

Vaughan, Sir John 211
Vessy, William 227
Villiers, Sir George, 1st Duke of Buckingham 184,
    185, 212, 219, 221, 227
  role in creating Irish peers 194
violence
  English towards Irish 20
  legitimate vs. illegitimate 83–4
virtue 5, 10

Walsh, Rev. Paul 125, 131, 135
Walsingham, Frances 183
Walsingham, Sir Francis 183
War of the Three Kingdoms 4, 238
Ware, Sir James 167–8
Warren, William 112
Wars of the Roses 6
Wedgwood, C. V. 246
Wentworth
  George
    marriage negotiations of 250–4
  Thomas 3, 18–19, 222
    accused of role in death of Earl of Clanricard
      242, 243–5
    and crown finances 230
    and personal combat 228
    and precedence 232
    and public architecture 232–3

arbitrates dispute between Adam and Robert
  Loftus 252–60
as member of 'service nobility' 237, 238, 239
'change of sides' of 227
conduct at Portumna Castle 238, 239,
  241–2, 243
conflict with Adam Loftus, Lord Chancellor
  of Ireland 245–65, 266–7
conflict with Earl of Clanricard 190, 192,
  224, 235–45, 266, 267
conflict with Henry Bellasis 227–8, 266
conflict with Sir David Foulis 228–30, 231,
  241, 266
conflict with William Ellis 227, 266
defender of Church 230
defender of King's honour 234, 258
dislike of lawyers 228
educates Irish peers in points of honour 234,
  264, 266
ennoblement of 226
family honour of 225–6, 235, 252
gentry origins of 234
governing style and honour 234–5, 267
historiographical views of conflicts with Irish
  elites 223–4
honour of office 225, 226–9, 235
impeachment and attainder of 246, 269
Lord Deputyship of Ireland and honour
  230–1, 266
Lord President of the Council of the North
  223, 226, 241, 266
martial honour of 230
negotiates marriage for brother, George
  250–4
notions of honour 223–4
on 'female friendship' 234
patriarchal notions of honour of 256,
  258–9, 262
personal honour of 252, 257
plantation of Connacht 235, 241, 244, 267
public comportment of 231–4
'reformation of manners' as policy 223,
  234–5, 265
relationship with Charles I of England 224
sartorial concerns of 233
social ambitions of 223, 224–7
views on female agency 259
William, father of Sir Thomas 225, 228
William, son of Sir Thomas 242, 243
Williams, N. J. A. 152, 153
Wintour, Sir John 262
Wolsey, Cardinal Thomas 29